Women Online: Research in Women's Studies Using Online Databases

Haworth Series on Library and Information Science

Series Editor: Peter Gellatly

Volume 1. *The In-House Option: Professional Issues of Library Automation*, by Webb

Volume 2. *British University Libraries*, by Burrows

Volume 3. *Women Online: Research in Women's Studies Using Online Databases*, by Atkinson and Hudson

Women Online: Research in Women's Studies Using Online Databases

Steven D. Atkinson
Judith Hudson
Editors

The Haworth Press
New York • London

Women Online: Research in Women's Studies Using Online Databases is Volume Number 3 in the Haworth Series in Library and Information Science.

The Haworth Press, Inc. 10 Alice Street, Binghamton, NY 13904-1580
EUROSPAN/Haworth, 3 Henrietta Street, London WC2E 8LU England

Library of Congress Cataloging-in-Publication Data

Women online : research in women's studies using online databases / Steven D. Atkinson, Judith Hudson, editors.
    p. cm — (Haworth series on library and information science ; 3)
    Includes bibliographical references.
    ISBN 1-56024-037-7 (alk. paper) ISBN 1-56024-053-9 (pbk.)
    1. Women — Research — Data bases. 2. Women's studies — Data bases. I. Atkinson, Steven D., 1953- . II. Hudson, Judith. III. Series: Haworth series on library and information science ;
3.
HQ1180.W675   1990b
305.4'072 – dc20   90-4430
                                                                     CIP

This collection is dedicated to our mothers, grandmothers, and daughter, who instill in us a sense of caring: ASB, EAA, SRH, JFS, JFP, LJO, and WOA.

CONTENTS

ABOUT THE EDITORS

Steve Atkinson, MLS, is Assistant Coordinator Computer Search Service at the University Libraries of the University at Albany. He recently received a joint Faculty/Librarian grant from the Council on Library Resources to study "Online Databases in the Humanities: Implications for Researchers in the Humanities." He also co-authored *Hypertext/Hypermedia: An Annotated Bibliography* from Greenwood Press. Mr. Atkinson received a BS from Mississippi State University and an MLS from Peabody College.

Judith Hudson, MLS, is Head of the Cataloging Department at the University Libraries of the University at Albany, and a Faculty Associate of the University's Women's Studies Department and its Institute for Research on Women. She holds BS and MLS degrees from Syracuse University and an MS in Human Development from Pennsylvania State University.

Introduction

Steven D. Atkinson
Judith Hudson

In 1980 there were more than 300 women's studies programs in colleges and universities across the United States (Howe and Lauter 1980). Ten years later there are more than 600 programs offering courses and supporting research in women's studies. Catharine R. Stimpson (1989), Dean of the Graduate School at Rutgers University, suggests that the intellectual agendas of such courses and research must include the following questions:

Steven D. Atkinson is Assistant Coordinator, Computer Search Service, University at Albany, State University of New York 12222. Judith Hudson is Head, Cataloging Department, University at Albany, State University of New York, 12222.

The University at Albany, State University of New York, provided seed money for this project through a Faculty Development Grant awarded to the editors.

The database vendors – BRS, DIALOG, Wilsonline, VU-TEXT, Mead Data Central, and Westlaw – all made substantial contributions through complimentary passwords and/or designated dollar support for the authors of the sixteen articles.

ABC-Clio provided Dr. Joyce Duncan Falk with facilities and additional search support for her research on *America: History and Life, Historical Abstracts*, and *ARTbibliographies Modern*.

The institutions and libraries with which the authors are affiliated provided inkind contributions that facilitated the completion of their work.

Jeffrey W. Merrick made many editorial suggestions that improved the style .and clarity of the articles.

The idea for this collection originated with Judith Hudson's investigation of online databases in women's studies and Steven Atkinson's suggestion that we transform this investigation into a collective project by soliciting essays from librarians and information professionals working in women's studies. Now that this book has materialized, we would like to thank our collaborators across the country for their contributions and also thank each other for all we learned from working together.

1

1. Why do we seek to dominate each other? Some women, of course, have exercised power over other women and some men. What are the structures, psychologies and language of domination? How do we maintain them?
2. How have women mobilized on their own behalf? How have they named their own interests? Have the discourses of motherhood empowered women? Imprisoned them? Both?
3. How do we end the sexual division of labor and the pauperization of women?
4. What are the new reproductive technologies? Who controls them? In what terms?
5. How diverse and varied are family forms?
6. What are the relationships among education, literacy and gender equity?
7. How have gender identities and sexual identities been produced and reproduced?
8. What have been the connections between general historical changes, e.g., the development of capitalism or state communism and gender changes? Who accepts which changes? Who resists which?
9. How do we imagine a different and better future?

In order to investigate these kinds of interdisciplinary questions, students, scholars, and librarians who work with them must be able to locate relevant sources from many fields dispersed throughout the mass of information currently available in published and electronic form.

Technology has expanded along with information, and online databases have taken on a significant role in providing access to research materials in most traditional areas of study. Online searching for sources is more complicated in newer and more interdisciplinary fields. The *Catalyst* database (which focused on career issues of concern to women) was discontinued on BRS in June 1988, and no single database currently available covers the field of women's studies comprehensively. The Research Libraries Group's Program for Research Information Management (Gould 1988) underlined the limitations of *Women's Studies Abstracts* and emphasized the need for an online bibliography for women's studies. Standard guides to research in this field (Searing 1985 and Ariel 1987) identify some of the general and disciplinary databases which include material on women and women's issues.

Several innovative articles analyzing the coverage and content of online databases applicable to women's studies research were published in the 1980s. In her pioneering article on European women's history (1983), Joyce Duncan Falk introduced bibliographic and non-bibliographic databases to women's studies scholars. Helen Rippier Wheeler (1983) compiled a reference list of seventy-five periodical indexes, abstracting services, citation indexes, and online databases. Sarah M. Pritchard (1984) formulated "Guidelines for Evaluating Databases in Women's Studies." Ellen Gay Detlefsen (1986) analyzed features of databases that complicate access to materials about women, especially materials written from a feminist perspective. Suzanne Hildenbrand (1986b) focused on indexing problems that complicate online searches for information about women. Capek (1987) and her collaborators confronted these problems in *The Women's Thesaurus* by providing a hierarchical list of terms to assist in free-text or full-text searching in online databases.

This collection addresses many of the issues of coverage and content in online research defined by Falk, Pritchard, Detlefsen, and Hildrenbrand. The sixteen articles support the RLG findings about the lack of retrospective coverage of both serial and monographic literature in databases and the omission of feminist journals, newsletters and conference reports, small press publications, visual and graphic materials, machine-readable data files, and older printed documents (Gould 1988). The articles discuss the problems of investigating interdisciplinary topics in women's studies, working with controlled vocabularies and inconsistent indexing, and locating feminist scholarship. They not only analyze these problems in general terms but also suggest practical strategies for making online research more effective and productive.

Women Online is intended to be useful not only to students, scholars, and librarians who search databases but also to producers who design and market them. Database producers should expand their coverage of materials and promote access to resources in interdisciplinary fields like women's studies. They should consider the development of a women's studies database to be distributed in CD-ROM and/or online format.

The articles which follow are organized into three groups covering broad disciplinary categories such as humanities and social sciences, particular types of files such as non-bibliographic and cited reference databases, and specific topics such as lesbian studies and women of color. The authors employ a variety of methods to analyze issues of coverage and content. They compare the results of controlled vocabulary and free-text or full-text searching, and use search examples, cited reference and multi-file searching, and bibliometric techniques, including analysis of recall, precision, overlap, relevancy, uniqueness, and trends in file growth. The Database Matrix provides an alphabetical listing of files discussed in the articles and serves as a directory for online research in women's studies.

BIBLIOGRAPHY

Ariel, Joan, ed. *Building Women's Collections: A Resource Guide*. (CHOICE Bibliographic Essay Series, No. 8). Middletown, CT: CHOICE, 1987.

Beck, Evelyn Torton. "Asking for the Future: Women's Studies at Twenty." *The Women's Review of Books* 6 (February 1989): 21-22.

Butler, Johnnella. "Difficult Dialogues: Women's Studies at Twenty." *The Women's Review of Books* 6 (February 1989): 16.

Capek, Mary Ellen S., ed. *A Women's Thesaurus: An Index of Language Used to Describe and Locate Information By and About Women*. NY: Harper & Row, 1987.

Detlefsen, Ellen Gay. "Issues of Access to Information about Women." *Special Collections* 3 (Spring-Summer 1986): 163-171. (Also appears in *Women's Collections: Libraries, Archives, and Consciousness*. pp. 163-171. NY: The Haworth Press, 1986.)

Dickstein, Ruth, Victoria A. Mills, and Ellen J. Waite. *Women in LC's Terms: A Thesaurus of Library of Congress Headings Relating to Women*. Phoenix: Oryx Press, 1988.

Dinnerstein, Myra. "Questions for the Nineties: Women's Studies at Twenty." *The Women's Review of Books* 6 (February 1989): 13.

Falk, Joyce Duncan. "The New Technology for Research in European Women's History." *Signs* 9 (Fall 1983): 120-133.

Garber, Linda. "Still Coming Out: Women's Studies at Twenty." *The Women's Review of Books* 6 (February 1989): 17-18.

Gould, Constance C. *Information Needs in the Humanities: An Assessment*. Research Information Management of The Research Libraries Group, Inc. Stanford, CA: Research Libraries Group, 1988.

Hildenbrand, Suzanne. "End User Satisfaction with Computerized Bibliographic Searches in Women's Studies: Preliminary Report of an Investigation." In

Proceedings of the National Online Meeting. pp. 215-219. Medford, NJ: Learned Information, 1985.

Hildenbrand, Suzanne. "Researching Women's History on Bibliographic Databases." In *Databases in the Humanities and Social Sciences.* pp. 218-224. Osprey, FL: Paradigm Press, 1985.

Hildenbrand, Suzanne, ed. *Women's Collections: Libraries, Archives, and Consciousness.* NY: The Haworth Press, 1986.

Hildenbrand, Suzanne. "Women's Studies Online: Promoting Visability." *RQ* 26 (Fall 1986): 63-74.

Hoffman, Nancy Jo. "Feminist Scholarship and Women's Studies." *Harvard Educational Review* 56 (November 1986): 511-519.

Howe, Florence. "A Symbolic Relationship: Women's Studies at Twenty." *The Women's Review of Books* 6 (February 1989): 15-16.

Howe, Florence and Paul Lauter. *The Impact of Women's Studies on the Campus and the Disciplines.* Washington, DC: National Institute of Education of the Department of Health, Education, and Welfare, 1980.

Josephine, Helen B. and Deborah K. Blouin. "New Reference Sources on Women: An Analysis and Proposal." *The Reference Librarian* 15 (1986): 109-122.

Lochhead, Ishbel. "Bibliographic Control of Feminist Literature. *Catalogue & Index* 76-77 (Spring/Summer 1985): 10-15.

Marzone, Jean and Sharon Strover. *Computer Searching: A Resource for Women's Educational Equity.* ED 195 238. 1980.

Pritchard, Sarah M. "Developing Criteria for Database Evaluation: The Example of Women's Studies," *The Reference Librarian* 11 (Fall-Winter 1984): 247-261.

Pritchard, Sarah M. "Linking Research, Policy, and Activism: Library Services in Women's Studies." In *Reference Service and Public Policy.* pp. 89-103. NY: The Haworth Press, 1988.

Searing, Susan. *Introduction to Library Research in Women's Studies.* Boulder, CO: Westview Press, 1985.

Searing, Susan. "A Quiet Revolution: Women's Studies at Twenty." *The Women's Review of Books* 6 (February 1989): 19-20.

Stimpson, Catharine R. "Setting Agendas, Defining Challenges: Women's Studies at Twenty." *The Women's Review of Books* 6 (February 1989): 14.

Watstein, Sarah Barbara. "Putting Words in Our Mouths." *The Women's Review of Books* 5 (January 1988): 15.

Wheeler, Helen Rippier. "A Feminist Researcher's Guide to Periodical Indexes, Abstracting Services, Citation Indexes, and Online Databases." *Collection Building* 5 (Fall 1983): 3-24.

Winkler, Karen J. "Women's Studies after Two Decades: Debates over Politics and New Directions for Research." *Chronicle of Higher Education* 35 (September 28, 1988): A4-A7.

Humanities

Joyce Duncan Falk

SUMMARY. Sixteen online databases that index material in the humanities, including art, architecture, history, literature, philosophy, religion and the performing arts, are analyzed for subject content and indexing vocabulary related to women. A comparison of retrieval on searches conducted across all the databases and analysis of additional searches in selected databases show the amount of material on women and feminism, the growth of the literature, the adequacy and accuracy of index descriptors, the relevancy of retrieval, and the overlap among databases. Given the great variations both among databases and within each one and the lack of consistent, reliable indexing, free-text searching of the basic index and the use of multiple databases are recommended for most searches on women's topics.

INTRODUCTION

Online searching for women-related topics in the humanities brings together two fields that have stuggled to make their place in the world of scholarly communication. Women's studies has now won its legitimacy as a field of study, and online searching in the humanities seems finally to have become part of the mainstream of information retrieval, as indicated by the inclusion of an extensive chapter on the humanities in an online searching manual[1] and the publication of several articles that review the characteristics of online searching in the humanities in general terms and in practice.[2]

It may be true that women's studies as a whole is more akin to the social sciences than to the arts and religion,[3] but reference librarians know that women-related studies are popular among teachers and

Joyce Duncan Falk is Historian, Librarian, 2726 Cuesta Road, Santa Barbara, CA 93105.

researchers in the humanities; furthermore, social science topics and current issues often have a historical, ethical, philosophical, or aesthetic component. Women's topics have been frequently used as examples in articles and presentations on humanities databases,[4] and at least the history databases and *MLA Bibliography* are well represented in a recent article on women's studies online.[5]

The humanities discussed here include the visual and performing arts, architecture, history, literature, philosophy, and religion. By women's topics and women's subjects I mean all kinds of information about women. Distinctions between feminist issues and viewpoints, women's studies, and more traditional queries concerning women, although important, are not part of the study in this chapter. The distinctions are not carefully made in the databases; beyond some general observations, treatment of them awaits a separate and more detailed analysis.

METHODOLOGY AND ORGANIZATION

This study of online searching for women's topics focuses on the subject content and the indexing vocabulary of 16 multidisciplinary and subject specific humanities databases (Table 1) and briefly describes additional ones. It discusses record content, retrieval features, and special problems of each database only briefly and only when they are particularly noteworthy. A working knowledge of online searching is assumed. For details about the databases and search systems, readers are referred to the documentation published by the information retrieval systems and the database producers and to the secondary literature cited in the notes. The extensive set of guidelines developed by Sarah Pritchard for evaluating databases in women's studies is a useful reminder of significant questions to address, but because this chapter selectively reviews a number of databases, those guidelines are not fully followed.[6]

The first section of this chapter is a general discussion of the amount of women's material represented in the databases, based on searches for some general words; the growth of the literature as represented by three sample terms, femini-, gender, and lesbian-; the relevancy of retrieval in a search on the interdisciplinary subject of romanticism; descriptors and vocabulary; and overlap among the

TABLE 1. DATABASES AND SYSTEMS WITH ABBREVIATIONS USED

Databases - General Humanities

Arts & Humanities Search	A&HUM
Humanities Index	HUM
Essay and General Literature Index	EGL
Eighteenth-century Short Title Catalogue	ESTC
Research in Progress Database	RIPD

Databases - Subject Specific, Core

America: History and Life	AHL
Historical Abstracts	HA
Modern Language Association International Bibliography	MLA
Philosopher's Index	PHIL
Religion Index	REL

Databases - Subject Specific, Arts

Art Index	ART
Artbibliographies Modern	ARTMOD
Art Literature International	RILA
Architecture Database	ARCH
Avery Index to Architectural Periodicals	AVERY

Online Retrieval Systems

BRS/Search Service	B
Dialog Information Retrieval Service	D
Research Libraries Information Network (RLIN)	R
Wilsonline Retrieval System	W

databases based on four searches and a selected list of journals indexed. The second section briefly describes the coverage and noteworthy characteristics of each database and discusses its particular performance on sample searches. To facilitate comparison of databases on similar topics, they are sorted into three groups in the discussion and some of the tables: (1) multidisciplinary, (2) subject specific, except the arts, and (3) subject specific, art, architecture, and music. Throughout the chapter comments on the databases are based on the searches performed specifically for this chapter, on my experiences in online searching in a university library, and on the searching done for two previous studies.[7]

The sample searches were designed to be run in several databases and are tailored to the individual databases in only a few instances.

The primary searches on sets of terms related to women and on romanticism are supplemented by three searches designed to illustrate databases or features not covered by the primary searches. Most of the databases are on the Dialog system, so the discussion usually uses the terminology and symbols of that system, assuming that readers can transfer the meaning into the terms of other search systems; for example, the question mark indicates truncation. Because of different practices among database producers, retrieval system conventions with regard to apostrophes cannot be relied upon; to be certain to retrieve women's, truncation is used: women?. The word descriptor is used generically to mean an assigned index term whether it is labeled descriptor, identifier, subject heading, or something else, and whether it is from a controlled vocabulary or not. Where there might be confusion with a field or index specifically titled Descriptor, the specific title is capitalized. In viewing the data in the tables, readers are cautioned to remember that the numbers are only approximate indicators. The number of records in a file changes frequently as a result of updates and work on the files by the vendor. Judgments about the databases should take into consideration all the variables of subject, source documents, record content, and indexing vocabulary. Differences among the databases in the numbers of entries retrieved are caused not only by the amount of material in the file but also by the number and type of descriptors used, by the presence of abstracts, and by the search strategy used.

COMPARISON OF DATABASES

Amount of Material on Women

To get a general idea of the amount of material related to women in each database, searches were conducted on a set of general women terms (wom?n? or female?), feminism terms, women's studies, and women's history (Table 2). Of the last two, women's history is by far the more prevalent concept in the literature of the humanities. Combining the two terms using the OR operator reveals that there is practically no overlap between the two concepts in the titles, abstracts, and descriptors of the bibliographic entries. Only in the history databases are the two terms used to any extent in the same entry, and then only for around five to six percent of the entries that have one or both terms.

When the databases are ranked by the number of records and the percent of records having a general women term, *America: History and Life* (AHL) remains in about the same position near the top (Table 3), reflecting its broad subject coverage as well as the presence of abstracts and descriptors for searching. *Arts & Humanities Search* (A&HUM) and *MLA Bibliography* (MLA), which have large numbers of records with a women term even though they do not include abstracts, fall into the lower half of the list when the number of women-term records is compared to the total records in the database. *Religion Index* (REL), *Historical Abstracts* (HA), and *Humanities Index* (HUM) exchange ranks but together hold the top of the second quarter of the rankings, followed by the art databases in the middle. There is no clear difference between the multidisciplinary databases A&HUM, HUM, and *Essay and General Literature Index* (EGL) and the subject specific ones in history, religion, and art. The most specialized databases, those in music and architecture, show the least evidence of women's issues in their literature. The poor showing of *Philosopher's Index* (PHIL) in both lists, at twelfth and thirteenth places, is something of a surprise since philosophy as a field is similar to history and religion in its concern with broad issues in humankind's study of itself, especially cultural and intellectual history. The percent of women-term records in the *Research in Progress Database* (RIPD) indicates the strength of women's topics in the most recent scholarly writing, albeit primarily in the field of literature. EGL, too, represents the strength of theory and research about women that is either (1) of sufficient interest to have its reports reprinted in collections or (2) on such new, specialized, or unusual areas that publication in collections is more feasible than in mainstream journals.

Another way of judging the increase in the attention to women in humanities literature is to sample the growth in the presence of a few selected terms, namely the broad concept feminism and two more specific concepts related to women's studies, gender and lesbianism, in nine databases, by year of publication of the source documents. Table 4 lists, in two five-year blocks of publication

TABLE 2. WOMEN-RELATED TERMS IN THE DATABASES

Database Name (& System used)	Total No. of Records 2/89	General Women Terms[1] No.	%	Feminism[2]	Women's Studies	Women's History	Women's Studies or History[3]
A&HUM (D)	1,000,480	12,542	1.3	2,950	49	321	367
HUM (W)	138,060	3,537	2.6	904	18	49	67
EGL (W)	16,840	1,149	6.8	378	20	8	28
ESTC (R)	216,267	1,601	.7	4	0	0*	0
RIPD (R)	944	43	4.6	27	1	1	2
AHL (D)	240,369	10,277	4.7	1,445	201	343	518
HA (D)	299,813	6,719	2.4	1,120	64	212	258
MLA (D)	897,910	9,734	1.	3,110	49	31	80
PHIL (D)	145,483	930	.6	666	12	7	19
REL (D)	330,174	7,261	2.2	1,754	53*	65	114
ART (W)	129,840	1,963	1.5	135	1	3	4
ARTMOD (D)	107,041	3,365	3.	1,050	22	30	51
RILA (D)	108,942	2,027	1.9	275	7	29	34
ARCH (D)	88,386	241	.3	6	0	0	0
AVERY (R)	66,747	114	.2	9	0	0*	0
RILM (D)	80,602	516	.6	30	24	6	29

1. General terms--D: wom?n? OR female? (A&HUM titles only). Terms in W and R similarly truncated. ESTC, tw only; RIPD, tw OR kw; AVERY, tw OR sw.

2. Feminism--D: femini? (A&HUM titles only); similarly truncated in W and R; ESTC, tw only; RIPD, tw OR kw; AVERY tw OR sw.

3. Women's studies or history--D: women?(ln)studies OR wom?n?(ln)history (A&HUM titles only). W: women: <lw> history OR phr women's history OR phr history of women OR wom#n: <lw> history (ti); limitation of the last phrase to titles avoids retrieval of the many subject headings that have the word women and some form of history. R: AVERY, tw wom#n studies OR sw wom#n studies OR tw wom#n history OR sw wom#n history; RIPD, tw OR kw; ESTC, tw only, but see note 4.

4. The ESTC search produced 34 records with the terms wom#n and history in the titles but this strategy does not locate the terms in close proximity and thus is not appropriate to the search for the phrases women's history or history of women.

5. In REL if the descriptor women(1)study is OR'd with the free-text search, the number increases to 72.

6. In AVERY two records were retrieved with the terms wom#n and history in the subject headings but, as in HUM and ESTC, they have the word woman and some variety of history, so the strategy is not appropriately restrictive.

TABLE 3.   DATABASES RANKED BY NUMBER AND PERCENT OF RECORDS
HAVING A GENERAL WOMEN TERM

Ranked by Number of Records		Ranked by Percent of Records	
Database	No. of Records	Database	% of Records
1. A&HUM	12,542	1. EGL	6.8
2. AHL	10,277	2. RIPD	4.6
3. MLA	9,734	3. AHL	4.3
4. REL	7,261	4. ARTMOD	3.
5. HA	6,719	5. HUM	2.6
6. HUM	3,537	6. HA	2.2
7. ARTMOD	3,365	6. REL	2.2
8. RILA	2,027	8. RILA	1.9
9. ART	1,963	9. ART	1.5
10. ESTC	1,601	10. A&HUM	1.3
11. EGL	1,149	11. MLA	1.
12. PHIL	930	12. ESTC	.7
13. RILM	516	13. PHIL	.6
14. ARCH	214	13. RILM	.6
15. AVERY	114	15. ARCH	.3
16. RIPD	43	16. AVERY	.2

TABLE 4.   GROWTH OF THE LITERATURE IN NINE DATABASES

Number of Records with Selected Terms, for 1970-75 and 1980-85 Documents

Database (& System Used)	Feminis?		Gender		Lesbian?	
	1970-75	1980-85	1970-75	1980-85	1970-75	1980-85
A&HUM (D)	na	1399	na	242	na	34
AHL (D)	175	657	12	230	0	30
HA (D)	83	515	1	131	0	14
MLA (D)	127	1197	52	367	1	55
PHIL (D)	44	295	1	60	0	5
REL (D)	61	838	3	197	2	34
ARTMOD (D)	240	354	4	30	0	4
RILA (D)	5	156	0	9	0	1
(only partial coverage for years 1970-75)						
RILM (D)	2	na	4	na	0	na
(file not updated since early 1983)						

na = not applicable

dates, 1970-75 and 1980-85, the number of records that contain
each of these terms. The increases from 1970-75 to 1980-85 are, as
expected, dramatic. Feminism appears in the records dated 1970-75
in all nine databases, especially in the history, literature, and *Artbibliographies Modern* (ARTMOD) databases. In looking at the individual years, feminism shows steady increases in A&HUM and

MLA during the 1980s, whereas in AHL the numbers level off after significant jumps in 1970, 1975, and 1980. Gender is present in 1970-75 records to a noticeable degree only in MLA, and lesbianism was virtually non-existent. By 1980-85, gender was well established in all but PHIL and the arts databases, though it did appear there a few times. It increased steadily during the 1980s in A&HUM and AHL; in MLA the increase was steady, then doubled in 1984 and doubled again in 1986. The figures for all three terms in MLA and REL indicate that the increase in interest is greatest in the fields of literature and religion and is significant in history. The high number in ARTMOD is a result of widespread use of the descriptor art and feminism.

Basic Index versus Descriptors

A comparison of the number of records having women and feminism terms in the descriptors with the number having the terms in the basic index (titles, abstracts, notes, descriptors) in each database shows the extent to which descriptors include the concepts expressed in the entries. Or, to put it another way, it indicates how much titles and abstracts contribute to retrieval. Table 5 lists the numbers of records found on each concept through searches of the basic index and the descriptors; it also lists the percent of basic index records that have the search term in the descriptors (i.e., the descriptor-term records as a percent of the basic-index-term records).

Databases that have a high degree of congruence between descriptors and terms in the basic index for both women and feminism are HUM (75% and 83%) and RILA (70% and 76%). This congruence supports observations that the indexing of HUM and RILA is accurate and fairly adequate, based on the analysis of the location of search terms (Table 7) and on examination of the entries themselves. On women terms the large databases A&HUM, AHL, HA, MLA, and REL, all have percentages of descriptors ranging from 60% to 69%. There is less congruence on the concept of feminism; the percentages of feminism descriptors range from 46% to 61%. ARTMOD presents the anomaly of having only 10% of the women terms in the descriptor field but 80% of the feminism ones. ART

TABLE 5. COMPARISON OF BASIC INDEX TERMS AND DESCRIPTORS

Database (& System Used)	Women Terms			Feminism		
	Basic Ind. / Desc.		Desc. as % of B. I.	Basic Ind. / Desc.		Desc. as % of B. I.
A&HUM (D)	20,154	12,542	62%	5,384	2,974	55%
HUM (W)	3,537	2,650	75	904	750	83
EGL (W)	1,149	608	53	378	251	66
ESTC (R)	1,601	na*	–	4	na*	–
AHL (D)	10,277	7,140	69	1,445	820	57
HA (D)	6,719	4,249	63	1,120	517	46
MLA (D)	9,734	5,792	60	3,110	1,890	61
PHIL (D)	930	462	50	666	514	77
REL (D)	7,261	4,529	62	1,754	852	49
ART (W)	1,963	384	20	135	90	67
ARTMOD (D)	3,365	350	10	1,050	843	80
RILA (D)	2,027	1,419	70	275	209	76
ARCH (D)	241	172	71	6	0	–
AVERY (R)	114	79	69	9	0	–
RILM (D)	516	197	38	30	1	3

Descriptors--D: de,id except A&HUM where titles serve as the descriptors.;
The combination of ti or cw= is used for the basic index in these two
searches in A&HUM. W: (sh). R: AVERY, sw; ESTC has no descriptors.

* na = not applicable.

also shows a sizable difference, 20% and 67% respectively. These data, together with that in Table 7, support the recommendation of not depending on descriptors for searches on women's topics. In fact, searching the combination of titles OR descriptors is not adequate except when a large number of records are retrieved and there are valid reasons for wanting to reduce that number.[8]

Relevancy

To compare the content, indexing, and relevancy of retrieval in the databases, a search was performed on the subject of women in romanticism, the historical, artistic, literary, and philosophical movement of the nineteenth century. To get the most comprehensive retrieval, free-text searching was used. Women terms were searched in the entire basic index; romanticism terms were searched in the descriptor fields and then in the basic index. The 1980-87 entries retrieved by the basic index search, or the first 50 of such entries, were analyzed for relevancy (Table 6). I judged the relevancy of the entries according to my knowledge of the subject as a student and teacher of intellectual history. In some cases a more informative entry for the same source document helped determine relevancy, and occasionally I used a reference work to verify an unfamiliar subject. Because of my own predilections about scholarship I was probably more generous in accepting an entry as relevant than some patrons would be (especially undergraduates), who inter-

TABLE 6.   SEARCH ON WOMEN IN ROMANTICISM[1]

Database (& System Used)	No. of Entries Retrieved			1980-87 Relevant Entries	
	R as Desc.	/ R Basic Index		No.	%
		Total /	1980-87		
A&HUM (D)[2]	75	176	156	33(of 1st 50)	66%
HUM (W)	15	19	17	14	82
EGL (W)	15	44	29	15	52
ESTC (R)	0	1	na[3]	-	-
AHL (D)	19	94	32	7	22
HA (D)	21	72	45	19	42
MLA (D)	90	92	73	43 31(of 1st 50	59 62)
PHIL (D)	5	9	5	2	40
REL (D)	3	16	14	3	21
ART (W)	4	4	2	2	100
ARTMOD (D)	20	104	44	13	30
RILA (D)	24	43	16	10	63
ARCH (D)	0	0	0	0	-
AVERY (R)	0	0	0	0	-
RILM (D)	4	122	36	15	42

1. Terms for the concept of women (W terms)--D: wom?n? OR female? OR femini? OR lady OR ladies OR wife OR wives OR girl? OR mother?. Terms for romanticism (R terms)--D: romantic?. Terms similarly truncated in W and R.

2. In A&HUM the search for W terms is limited to titles. The number listed for R as a descriptor actually represents R in the title. The number given for R in the Basic Index is the number of entries with a W term in the title and an R term in the title OR cw field.

3. na = not applicable.

pret their research topics rather narrowly or expect completely relevant retrieval.[9]

The word romanticism is ambiguous and even more so when it is truncated, as romantic love, scenes, moods, and stories abound. Limitation of the free-text search for romantic? to titles and descriptors, a strategy frequently recommended, misses a few relevant items but not usually ones that are centrally relevant. Another technique would be to search on specific terms instead of truncating, e.g., romanticism, romantics, romantic era, and romantic period. Descriptors for romanticism exist in some of the databases, but dependence on them would have seriously limited retrieval in this search. The usefulness of these techniques, the problems of the inadequacy and ambiguity of descriptors, and the issue of recall versus precision are discussed in the sections on the individual databases below. Generally speaking, comprehensive retrieval requires free-text searching on all data fields and toleration of a high degree of irrelevancy.

In the romanticism search there is little problem of the relevancy of the entries to the subject of women; they are almost all relevant to women in some way and, given the small number of hits in some of the databases, would be needed by a person researching the topic. The 1980-87 entries, both the relevant ones and the total number (or the first 50 of the total in the case of A&HUM and MLA), were analyzed to determine where in the record the women terms occur (Table 7). The databases with the most reliable descriptors are HUM, *Art Index* (ART), and PHIL, but the last two produced only two relevant entries each. Among the databases with the greatest retrieval, MLA scores the highest on relevancy and on having a women term in the descriptors, though it still has 15-20% of its entries with the term in the title only. RILA stands out among the databases with abstracts for having women descriptors on 70-75% of the entries, for the congruence between titles and descriptors, and for its lower percentage (25-30%) of entries with the women term only in the abstract. AHL, HA, REL, and ARTMOD all have considerable numbers of the search terms only in the abstracts. In judging whether to search the entire basic index or to restrict a search to titles and descriptors, one should compare the percentages in the last two sections of Table 7, the Title or Descriptor column and the Abstract Only column.

Vocabulary

Indexing vocabulary for women's material has been addressed from the point of view of cataloging, reference sources, and online databases,[10] and the sexist and stereotyped terminology of library cataloging schemes has received wide attention. This chapter does not include a discussion of that aspect of the indexing vocabulary in the humanities databases but concentrates on more general access problems. Studies of online databases point out the lack of specificity of the index terms, which fail to differentiate among varieties or subdivisions of a subject and fail to distinguish between women as actors or participants and women as objects, e.g., as the objects of attitudes or as depicted in literature and works of art. On the other hand, indexing schemes that index an entry at the most specific level—which may be a woman's personal name or an occupational name like actress—do not also index the same entry with a more general term like women or with a group term like women artists, so items about individual women are easily missed. (The lack of indexing both the specific thing and the category to which the thing belongs is not peculiar to the subject of women, of course, but it is a distinct problem.) Whereas the specificity of index descriptors like wives, widows, women landscape architects, and Jewish feminist filmmakers is necessary for relevant retrieval in many cases, the opposite problem of the multiplicity of descriptors and the lack of a broad, unifying term also exists. In searching the older volumes of abstracts databases (e.g., AHL, HA) and ones that depend on titles for search terms (the old MLA, A&HUM), one must use free-text methods and numerous synonyms to compensate both for the lack of standard, inclusive words like women and for the lack of thorough indexing. The terminology for many women's topics is relatively new, and either it does not appear in the indexing vocabulary or the descriptors, too, are of recent vintage and are not present throughout the entire database. Although a comparison of earlier volumes of abstracts (for example, AHL) with those of the last ten

TABLE 7. LOCATION OF WOMEN TERMS IN THE 1980-87 ROMANTICISM SEARCH ENTRIES, TOTAL ENTRIES AND RELEVANT ENTRIES PER DATABASE

Database (& System)	No. of Entries	Title No.	%	Title Only No.	%	Desc. No.	%	Desc. Only No.	%	Title or Desc. No.	%	Abstract or Notes Only No.	%
A&HUM (D) (Search limited to titles)													
Total	50	50	100%	50	100%	na	na	na	na	na	na	na	na
Relevant	33	33	100	33	100	na	na	na	na	na	na	na	na
HUM (W)													
Total	17	9	53	1	6	16	94%	7	41%	17	100%	0	0
Relevant	14	8	57	1	7	13	93	5	36	14	100	0	0
EGL (W)													
Total	29	14	48	6	21	12	41	4	14	19	66	10	34%
Relevant	15	7	47	3	20	7	47	3	20	10	67	5	33
AHL (D)													
Total	32	19	59	2	6	19	59	0	0	20	63	12	38
Relevant	7	4	57	2	29	4	57	0	0	5	71	2	29
HA (D)													
Total	45	15	33	1	2	25	56	2	4	26	58	19	42
Relevant	19	6	32	0	0	9	47	1	5	9	47	10	53
MLA (D)													
Total	50	32[1]	64	8	16	41	82	17	34	49	98	1	2
Relevant	31	23	74	6	19	24	77	7	23	30	97	1	3

PHIL (D)													
Total	5	3	60	1	20	3	60	0	0	4	80	1	20
Relevant	2	2	100	1	50	1	50	0	0	2	100	0	0
RFL (D)													
Total	14	3	21	0	0	6	43	1	7	6	43	8	57
Relevant	3	1	33	0	0	1	33	0	0	1	33	2	67
ART (W)													
Total	2	0	0	0	0	2[2]	100	2	100	2	100	0	0
Relevant	2	0	0	0	0	2	100	2	100	2	100	0	0
ARTMOD (D)													
Total	44	6	14	0	0	7	16	1	2	9	20	35	80
Relevant	13	2	15	0	0	5	38	1	8	5	38	8	62
RILA (D)													
Total	16	3	19	0	0	12	75	3	19	12	75	4	25
Relevant	10	3	30	0	0	7	70	2	20	7	70	3	30
RILM (D)													
Total	36	5	14	1	3	12	33	5	14	15	42	21	58
Relevant	15	4	27	0	0	9	60	3	20	11	73	4	27

na = not applicable. ESTC, ARCH, and AVERY omitted because of zero retrieval.
1. Three additional MLA entries have a non-English W term in the title.
2. The W terms are in the titles of works in the illustration field.

years shows a definite improvement in the identification of women through better indexing, there are still occasional instances of no assignment of descriptors, as all the sample searches here show. Worst of all is the lack of any identifying women term that can be retrieved by online searching without a lengthy list of related terms, for example, women named by reference to a man (Mrs. Smith or Smith's wife, mother, mistress, etc.) or referred to only by personal name and feminine pronouns (she, her). Other vocabulary problems, such as the ambiguity and changing meanings of terminology over time and among individuals, variations in terminology among disciplines, and difficulties of truncation, are not peculiar to women's topics and are no more problematical than for other topics in the humanities databases.

Overlap

Overlap among the databases can be measured by comparing the lists of source documents and by analyzing search results for duplicate entries. The first method, besides being very tedious — and directories that list the indexing services for periodicals are incomplete and inaccurate — is not particularly useful because some databases' coverage of periodicals is selective and inconsistent, and inclusion of types of source documents varies. There is considerable overlap between the journals indexed by A&HUM and MLA or HA, but because of selection policies and indexing schemes, a search will not necessarily retrieve duplicate entries. A test case of limited scope is a list of 27 periodicals in feminist and women's studies, including discipline-specific ones. Of the 13 databases checked (excluding EGL, ESTC, and RIPD), six index *Feminist Studies*; five databases index *Frontiers*, *Signs*, *Woman's Art Journal*, and *Women's Studies* (U.K.). Five of the titles are not indexed by any of the databases; the remainder are indexed by three, two, or one of the databases. Ten of the women's interest journals are selectively indexed by AHL and HA, the most of any database, eight by MLA, and seven by A&HUM. ARTMOD and RILA both index five of these titles, but RILA covers more specifically art publications while ARTMOD includes articles from general journals like *Feminist Studies* and *Signs*.

Analysis of the retrieval on the romanticism searches reveals a very low level of.overlap among databases. Only 20 of the 121 relevant documents dated 1984-87 appear in more than one database (Table 8); of those 20, six appear in three databases (six from MLA, five from A&HUM, four from HUM, two from HA, and one from EGL). The greatest overlap is between A&HUM and MLA and between A&HUM and HUM. For example, 16 A&HUM entries appear in one or more other databases, which total 21 occurrences of A&HUM entries in other databases. The nine HUM entries are also in A&HUM, four are also in MLA, and in all, HUM entries make 13 appearances in other databases.

The databases not represented in this analysis are absent partly because the search retrieved few entries on this topic and partly because the databases are not as current as A&HUM, Wilsonline databases, or even MLA. Except for one PHIL and one ARTMOD entry, all the PHIL, REL, ARTMOD, RILA, and RILM entries are pre-1984.

In a search on women in the theater in the 18th century performed in five databases, duplication among A&HUM, MLA, and HA was expected to be high, but in fact is not (Table 9). The obvious redundancy is the presence of entries for one particular book in HA and MLA and reviews of that same book in A&HUM and RILM. The low level of duplication is due primarily to the presence of abstract texts in AHL, HA, and RILM, which increases retrieval; to descriptors in the files other than A&HUM; to the difference in types of documents indexed (no books or dissertations in A&HUM, no book reviews in MLA); and to differences in the list of journals covered.

A search on a specifically art topic, the fallen woman theme, showed little overlap among the art databases and between them and A&HUM or HUM. There was more overlap between A&HUM and HUM, especially on book review entries (Table 10).

A search in ARTMOD, RILA, and the architecture databases also showed little overlap in coverage, or at least in retrieval (Table 11). Of a total of 212 entries retrieved in a search for women architects in four databases, 176 entries, or about 83% of the total, are unique. Thirteen are in both ARCH and AVERY, one is in ARCH and ARTMOD, and five are in ARTMOD and RILA. Again, the uniqueness is partially due to the greater currency of ARCH and

TABLE 8. OVERLAP AMONG DATABASES IN THE SEARCH ON
WOMEN AND ROMANTICISM

(Relevant 1984-87 entries analyzed = 121)

Database (& System Used)	No. of *Entries* in 1 or More *Additional* Databases	No. of Entries from Each Database That Also Appear in Each Other Database						No. of *Occurances* in *Additional* Databases
		A&HUM	AHL	EGL	HA	HUM	MLA	
A&HUM (D)	16	—	1	0	1	9	10	21
AHL (D)	2	1	—	0	0	0	1	2
EGL (W)	2	0	0	—	2	0	1	3
HA (D)	4	1	0	2	—	0	3	6
HUM (W)	9	9	0	0	0	0	4	13
MLA (D)	13	10	1	1	3	4	—	19
Total	46	(representing 20 original source documents)						

TABLE 9. OVERLAP AMONG FIVE DATABASES IN THE SEARCH ON
WOMEN IN THE THEATER IN THE 18TH CENTURY

Database	Number of Entries Total	Unique	Comments
A&HUM	19	14	15 entries are book reviews; 9 are reviews of one book.
AHL	10	10	2 entries are in MLA, 3 in RILM.
HA	39	35	4 entries are in MLA.
MLA	29	23	4 entries are in HA, 2 in A&HUM.
RILM	13	10	5 entries are reviews of 1 book, 3 of which are in A&HUM.
Total	110	92	18 of 110 entries are in more than one database.

TABLE 10. OVERLAP AMONG SIX DATABASES IN THE SEARCH ON THE
FALLEN WOMAN THEME

Database	Number of Entries "Found" /ti,de	Free-Text	Unique	Comments
A&HUM	na	37	30	Search expanded to include cr=nochlin 1, 1978 OR ca=rossetti OR cw=(found OR magdalen OR prostitute?). 5 entries also in HUM, 2 in RILA.
HUM	na	9	4	5 entries also in A&HUM.
ART	na	1	1	
ARTMOD	5	11	8	False drops on "found." 3 entries in RILA.
RILA	14	17	12	False drops on "found." 3 entries in ARTMOD, 2 in A&HUM.
REL	0	0	-	

TABLE 11. OVERLAP AMONG ART AND ARCHITECTURE DATABASES
IN THE SEARCH ON WOMEN ARCHITECTS

Database	No. of Entries Retrieved	Entries in an Additional Database No.	%	Unique Entries No.	%
ARTMOD*	27	6	22%	21	78%
RILA*	23	3	13	20	87
ARCH	103	14	14	89	86
AVERY	59	13	22	46	78
Total	212	39	17%	176	83%

* Three ARTMOD entries appear in one RILA collective entry. One
  RILA collective entry includes three items that are separate
  entries in ARTMOD.

AVERY compared to the considerable lag time in ARTMOD and RILA, but because the relevancy of retrieval was high in all four databases and they do index some of the same journals, a more detailed investigation of these databases is needed.

THE HUMANITIES DATABASES

Arts & Humanities Search

With over a million records, A&HUM is the largest humanities database and the most comprehensive in the subjects and types of material indexed. Its multidisciplinary coverage includes all the arts and humanities, even less mainstream ones like architecture, classics, folklore, film, television, dance, and theater. Women's topics are represented to the extent that women are discussed in the leading arts and humanities journals.

A&HUM is also unusually comprehensive in that it fully indexes some 1,400 periodicals and selectively includes items from almost 5,000 more journals in the sciences and social sciences. It indexes articles, editorials, letters, notes, poems, fiction, plays, musical scores, and reviews of books, recordings, and live performances (about 50% of the entries are reviews). Its breadth of coverage is counterbalanced, however, by its lack of depth in time (the online file begins in 1980) and in subject. It does not cover any one discipline in as much depth as the discipline databases do; for example, it covers about 200 history and general humanities journals, HA covers about 2,000. A&HUM differs markedly from most of the other databases in its currency and regular, frequent updating.

The most useful fields in A&HUM are the author, title (which includes title enhancements), source journal, and cited reference. Title words are changed to conform to a standard spelling, personal names are inverted, and titles of non-English-language articles are given only in English translation, all of which facilitates subject searching but plays havoc with bibliographic citation accuracy. (Titles of creative works referred to in article titles are not translated.) Additional information is given in fields for author's affiliation, language of the original, document type, and subject category of the journal. The last one is a feature of the online file not seen in the printed version. A&HUM records contain more information than other ISI databases, namely more title enhancements, titles of cited references, implicitly and indirectly cited references, and a cited author cross reference system. (Some improvements designed for A&HUM have since been added to *Social Scisearch*.) Certain characteristics of the records that make searching A&HUM cumbersome — conventions for personal names, abbreviations, truncation of names and titles in the cited reference field — are too complicated to detail here but are explained in the BRS and Dialog documentation and ISI's workshop materials.

Although some concessions have been made to accommodate the need for subject searching and the characteristics of humanities scholarship, it is important to remember that A&HUM was designed as a *citation* index and its greatest strength is its citation indexing. Citation searching can be done on the names of authors who have written on the subject; on names of artists, writers, or composers, etc.; on titles of books, journals, and creative works; and to find illustrations of works of art.

In A&HUM titles are the primary, though not the exclusive, field offering subject access. Terms for women are all the words that are used in the titles of articles about the myriad of subjects related to women. Today's humanists who write about women usually put some searchable term in their titles, except that articles about individual women often carry only the woman's name. Those searchers who use both BRS and Dialog will note that on Dialog the unqualified basic index search is of only the title field; on BRS, every word in the record is searched unless qualified to specific paragraphs. Additional subject access is sometimes afforded by the cited work field (part of the cited reference) and retrieval can be limited to journals in selected subject categories. The use of the cited work index for additional terms increases retrieval on women from about 12,500 to 20,000 hits and feminism from about 3,000 to 5,400 hits (Table 5). The romanticism search in A&HUM is for women terms in the title and romanticism terms in the titles or cited works (Table 6). This strategy keeps retrieval on women completely relevant and within a more manageable number while trying to maximize retrieval on the more elusive concept of romanticism. Examination of a sample of entries in which a romanticism term appears only in the cited works shows that half of them are relevant. In A&HUM more than any other database one must tolerate a low ratio of relevance to recall to achieve an acceptably comprehensive search. The usefulness of the cited work index for subject searching fails to reach its potential because the journal name, not the article title, is given for citations of articles, and abbreviations seriously limit the title words available for searching there.

A search on the fallen woman theme offers an opportunity to compare A&HUM and the art databases and to demonstrate the usefulness of the cited reference index to increase retrieval. A 1978 article by Nochlin studied Rossetti's painting of a prostitute, *Found*. The subject was searched in A&HUM as follows:

1. (fallen()wom?n OR cr=nochlin l, 1978?) [result 31]
2. (rossetti OR ca=rossetti?) AND (found OR cw=found OR magdalen OR cw=magdalen OR prostitute? OR cw-=prostitute?) [result 10]
3. 1 OR 2 [result 37]

The 37 entries retrieved include ones on the theme in both art and literature. The statements **fallen()wom?n, cr=nochlin,** and the Rossetti combination (set 2 above) all retrieve relevant hits. Only two entries are false drops, one citing a different Nochlin 1978 article and one on another artist's *Found*. A check of the journal subject categories of the entries citing Nochlin reveals that they are art, literature, general arts and humanities, and women's studies journals. Although a search like this one, but especially one that produced greater results, can be narrowed by selecting the art journal category, that technique is not necessarily advisable; in the case of this search, four quite relevant entries would be lost. Additional sample searches on women in the Vietnam War and women in the theater are discussed in comparison with other databases in the section on AHL and HA below.

The outstanding features of A&HUM are its currency, its multidisciplinary coverage, and citation indexing. The structure of the file makes it a difficult one to search on either BRS or Dialog, and the dependence on title words for subject searching makes it especially difficult to devise effective search strategies. It is best used to find very specific words or phrases that are likely to appear in titles, such as fallen woman, feminist theory, or midwives. Searches on more general topics like woman suffrage or working-class women are less satisfactory. Restricting a search by country or other geographic terms is highly unreliable and searching for historical periods is impossible. The high cost of connect time and prints adds to the problems of searching A&HUM efficiently and to the user's dissatisfaction with the retrieval of non-relevant entries.

Humanities Index and Essay and General Literature Index

HUM, like A&HUM, covers all the arts and humanities from archaeology to theology, history, literature, philosophy, and the performing and visual arts. *Essay and General Literature Index*'s (EGL) subject coverage is broader, emphasizing the humanities and social sciences. Women's topics are as numerous and diverse as writings in those disciplines, with British and American literature appearing to have an edge in HUM. EGL has the highest percent of women terms and the second highest percent of feminism terms of all the humanities databases (Tables 2 and 3).

For a database online only since 1984 and indexing only about 300 periodicals, HUM's size, nearly 140,000 records, is impressive. But, as with A&HUM, there is a lack of depth in any one discipline. Entries represent articles of all kinds, book reviews, performance reviews, and original works of fiction, drama, and poetry. EGL complements HUM by indexing articles in collections, including festschriften (called multiauthor works by other databases). With a beginning date of December 1985, it is the smallest of the files discussed here except RIPD. It covers approximately 3,800 articles in 300-325 collections per year for a total of about 17,000 entries in early 1989. Both HUM and EGL maintain the Wilson tradition of careful input and currency; the files are updated twice a week.

Records contain the usual fields for bibliographic data, document type, and language. Some unclear titles are enhanced; foreign titles are not translated. In the citation display format the subtitles are omitted for books reviewed in HUM and for collections in the analytic entries in EGL, although they are searched and are displayed in the title-subject-heading format and the full format. EGL records are of two kinds, both subject indexed: the main entry for a collection, which includes the titles of the articles in it, and analytic entries for each of the individual articles.

Descriptors are the familiar subject headings of the printed versions of Wilson indexes, based on Library of Congress Subject Headings supplemented as needed with additional terms. Online they appear as descriptor strings of headings and subheadings; they are both word and phrase indexed. Descriptors are generously assigned, up to six in HUM, up to eight on the main entries of EGL, and up to 4 on EGL analytic entries. The numerous subject headings and variety of forms used for women's subjects are sometimes redundant, especially for searches like the ones here on the broad concept of women, including feminism, but this characteristic is helpful in supplementing the subject content of titles and allows one to focus on specific aspects, such as mothers. In EGL the inclusion on the main entry record of the table of contents (titles of the individual articles) enhances retrieval; for example, in the search on romanticism a relevant main entry that has only a personal name for access in the title and the descriptor was retrieved because one individual title has a romanticism term and other titles have a women term. In fact, of the 15 relevant entries retrieved, four have a women term only in the table of contents list. On the other hand, of course, search terms scattered among individual titles also cause false drops.

Descriptors are more adequate in HUM than EGL and are better at predicting relevance of entries to women than to romanticism. In HUM, 13 of the 14 relevant entries have a women term in the descriptors; one has the term only in the title (Table 7). The presence and accuracy of descriptors for romanticism are fairly good. Ten of 14 entries have romanticism descriptors; and the overlap or match of titles and descriptors is high: 9 of the 10 entries have romanticism in both title and descriptor. There is still enough difference, however, for a search combining titles OR descriptors to be worthwhile. The three non-relevant entries also demonstrate the accuracy of the descriptors; the entries were relevant to women but had romanticism only in the title.

In EGL, of the 15 relevant entries, 10 have a women term in the title or descriptor and 5 have it only in the list of contents or series title (Table 7). The romanticism term, too, appears in the title or descriptor of only 10 of the 15 entries — but not the same 10 entries that have a women term in titles or descriptors (seven are the same). Thus there is not an exact match of the location of search terms in relevant entries. The romanticism descriptor is 100% accurate when it is assigned, but it is not assigned to all relevant entries. Significantly, the combination of titles or descriptors produces only 75% of the relevant entries, so a search in EGL should use unqualified free-text searching. As these Wilsonline files increase in size, dependence on the generally accurate, and in HUM ample, descriptors will become more important. These files, like their print counterparts, are excellent sources for references to widely available, mainstream periodicals and collections, mostly in English, for students and the general public who do not require exhaustive searches of the scholarly literature.

Eighteenth Century Short Title Catalogue

The ESTC is a bibliographic database of library holdings of 18th-century imprints on any subject, printed in English or in British territories. Arguments about woman's character, conduct (vices, virtues, follies), dress, education, and rights are typical entries, as are works of fiction about the loves and adventures of women. There are also petitions and observations on politics, religion, and legal matters by women. Being limited to 18th-century works, the database is of interest primarily for literary and historical studies of England and North America.

The some 216,000 records, expected to reach 400,000 by the mid-1990s, include books, House of Commons sessional papers, and ephemera like advertisements, political pamphlets, songs, lists, and timetables. The omission of playbills, though understandable, is lamentable. The record format is the MARC record, displayable on RLIN in shorter versions that include authors (called personal names); titles, including uniform titles, which are important for this material; and imprint data. Additional notes and holdings information are shown in the long display format. Entries for translated works have the uniform title in the original language but entries for non-English works do not have an English translation added. A genre index allows identification of some unusual materials such as advertisements, almanacs, and printing prospectuses.

There are no descriptors on ESTC entries, so subject access is limited to title words. If works by a certain author are the subject of one's search, of course, the personal name index can be used as well, and the library call numbers in the shelfmark index may be of use in some instances. For studies involving place of publication, publisher, or date, searches can be done in imprint place, imprint word, and imprint year indexes. Eighteenth-century titles are lengthy, which helps compensate for the lack of subject indexing, but title words are an uncontrolled vocabulary that produces many false drops and requires the imaginative use of search terms and spellings. In ESTC it is especially advisable to conduct a search and print 20 to 30 records, go offline and examine the results carefully, then expand the search using additional terms revealed by the initial results or exclude selected words.

The number and percent of entries with a general women term is low and the root femini- hardly exists (Tables 2 and 3). The latter does retrieve a French item that has no other women term in the title and a treatise on the feminine monarchy of bees. The search on romanticism turned up equally amusing titles but only one about women (Table 6). More appropriate searches in this database are ones on politics, education, reform, and France, all of which demonstrate the necessity to use the full list of women terms, perhaps adding fair sex. Female, lady, ladies, and wife appear as frequently in titles as woman or women; they also frequently cause false drops. Just as a relevant entry may be retrieved by the presence of an authorship phrase in the title ("letters from a lady," "by a woman"), so may a false drop result from a title phrase like "Lady Cowper's correct copy." A search for politic# OR government# AND the list of women terms retrieved 53 records. Of the 35 examined, 16 are for the same title in various editions; these also happen to be false drops. A search on all the women terms AND education OR school# resulted in 194 hits; of the 15 examined, eight titles are represented; there is one false drop on mother-tongue but that entry is still somewhat relevant in that it mentions "the youth of both sexes.'' The search for women and reform (**tw wom#n OR female# OR lady OR ladies AND tw reform#**) retrieved 35 entries; excluding religion OR church leaves 10 entries, including two serious pieces by or about women, a group of novels, and what appears to be a satire on a "parliament of women."

These searches illustrate the difficulties characteristic of searching ESTC: the limitations of the RLIN search system in manipulating sets and refining searches, the details of which are not fully explained in the documentation;[11] retrieval of a large number of duplicate titles; and the low relevance of search results. Despite these drawbacks, ESTC offers access to some fascinating primary source material for scholars of the 18th century.

Research-in-Progress Database

A small but promising addition to the humanities databases is RIPD, being developed by the Modern Language Association and the Research Libraries Group and now available on RLIN. At present its subject content is primarily literature and it has a strong women component. Among the databases discussed here it has the third highest percent of entries with a general woman term, after EGL and AHL, and it has the second highest percent of entries with a feminism term (Tables 2 and 3).

Entries represent articles accepted for publication in some 34 journals as of March 1989 (although 52 editors have agreed to contribute data) and grants by the Division of Research Programs of the National Endowment for the Humanities to support, for example, publications and conferences. Immediate expansion plans are for the National Council for Research on Women (NCRW) to add information on work in progress by and about women.

RIPD is partially menu driven and offers online instructions for the end-user searcher. Records for forthcoming articles include author; title; journal title, volume, date; number of pages if available; language; document type (e.g., bibliography); author's affiliation and address; subject indexing key words; and abstracts. Records for grants show author, title, funding agency, grant number, dates, amount, sponsoring institution (affiliation of author), address, keywords, and short descriptions in the abstract field. RIPD has an extensive list of indexes but the most important ones are the personal name index (i.e., author), title word index, keyword index, and journal title word index. The index and search terminology is confusing to the searcher unfamiliar with RLIN: a keyword search is not restricted to the assigned subject keywords but searches both the keywords and the abstract (or gloss); and the personal name index contains names of article and research project authors, not names of persons treated as subjects. Typical RLIN phrase indexing is available for title, journal, and subject. To see if a phrase search is more appropriate than a word search, one can browse the subject phrase index. There one finds more specific women terms such as women dramatists, women writers, and women's rights, female characters, feminism, and feminist approach. The assigned keywords, which comprise single words and phrases, are drawn from the *MLA Bibliography*. Most are single terms (words or two-word combinations) not a descriptor string of linked headings and subheadings. The only string or link so far is that of an author and title of a work, e.g., Wordsworth William: Prelude. The NCRW entries to be added in 1989 will be assigned terms from *A Women's Thesaurus*. As the file increases in size the subject phrase index will become more important but at this point a word search is usually effective.

This file is still in an experimental stage. The problems of using two different indexing schemes in one database are yet to be seen. Crucial to the success of the database, which is intended for direct access by scholars, is the addition of sources to extend the subject scope to more of the humanities, which in turn depends on the cooperation of many more journal editors and grants agencies administrators.

America: *History and Life* and *Historical Abstracts*

The history databases AHL and HA can be considered multidisciplinary files as they include related material on the arts, literature, and the social sciences. AHL covers the United States and Canada, pre-history to the present; HA covers the rest of the world 1450 to the present. AHL's subject coverage is broader than HA's in the areas of archaeology, folklore, popular culture, and contemporary social and political issues. Women's studies and women's history are well represented in both files (Table 2). AHL has the most entries specifically on women's studies and women's history of all the databases and has more material on current affairs than HA. AHL, with almost 10,300 entries having a general women term, is second only to A&HUM in total number of such entries (Table 3); it has the third highest percent of such entries after EGL and RIPD, both very small databases, and one of the highest percentages of occurrences of feminism. HA ranks sixth in percent of entries (tied with REL) and fifth in the total number of entries that have a general women term, well above the median in both cases.

Documents abstracted or annotated are articles from approximately 2,000 periodicals published worldwide and several hundred articles from collections. Coverage of additional types of source documents has been added at various times: books, book reviews, specialized journals, and dissertations in AHL beginning 1974; books and dissertations in HA in 1980. Book and dissertation entries do not have abstracts; about 60% of AHL entries and about 85% of HA entries have abstracts or annotations. AHL book entries include citation of one or more book reviews. Additional variations in coverage are given in the user manual for the files.[12] The collection, editing, and indexing of abstracts is a time-consuming operation that causes a one- to five-year time lag between publication of a source document and its appearance in AHL or HA.

The records themselves are mostly straightforward bibliographic citations with abstracts, annotations, or book review references; document type; and subject indexing, including historical period descriptors for *every* record that has descriptors — the only database to index all entries with historical dates. There are variations in the presence of descriptors: pre-1974 volumes of AHL and 1973-74 volumes of HA have no descriptors; standard format historical period descriptors (i.e., expressed as decades and centuries) are present since 1979. Book entries in AHL confusingly display the reviewer's name in the author field along with the book author's name. Combined entries, somewhat similar to analytic entries, are not always bibliographically complete; the entire group with complete data can be retrieved by selecting the AHL or HA accession number (not the Dialog number). Since 1980, too, data about an article's documentation, source material, and libraries and archives consulted are separated into a note field; the field displays but is not searchable. Non-English titles are given in their original language and an English translation (non-roman-alphabet titles are transliterated); all abstracts and annotations are in English. Language codes for languages other than English begin with 1980 records; otherwise retrieval may be limited to English or non-English.

Subject access is provided through free-text searching of titles, abstracts, and descriptors. Indexing is best thought of as natural-language keyword indexing. Some control is exercised through the use of a list of preferred subject headings, indexing rules, and authority lists, but a glance at the enormous variety of both lead terms and qualifiers in AHL and HA five-year indexes shows the limited nature of the control.[13] Expanding woman and women in AHL shows 19 multiword terms beginning with woman, from woman chief to woman voter, and 103 multiword terms beginning with women, from women achievements to women workers. There are actually more such descriptors; the online expand does not show ones that have the word woman or women followed by a comma.[14] Neither online nor in print is any distinction made between controlled and free vocabulary descriptors.

Besides the number of entries with women and feminism terms, AHL has nearly 650 entries with a descriptor beginning with sex role(s), or 12 descriptors in all, as well as 263 entries indexed sex discrimination. The search on romanticism produced a disappointing result of only seven of the 32 entries relevant to romanticism, although all are about women in some respect (Table 6). The ones less relevant to women are those about female characters in fiction, ballads, or art. Two of the seven relevant entries have a women term only in the abstract, illustrating the advisability of free-text searching for women terms unless a large number of hits is expected on the other concept(s). The problem terms were romanticized and romantic used in a general sense not specific to the romantic period. A more careful search could use separate, more specific terms: romanticism OR romantics OR romantic()(era OR period). In this case ambiguous phrases like romantic writer, romantic history, and romantic metaphor, that might or might not be relevant, would be missed. There is no sure way for a search to be both comprehensive and highly relevant on the concept of romanticism.

More successful searches in AHL are ones on women in the era of the American Revolution and women in the Vietnam War. The first search sought only the term wom?n? in titles OR descriptors and a combination of words and phrases for the historical period, further limited geographically:

1. **wom?n?/ti,de**
2. **american()revolution? OR 1760:1799 OR hp = (1760d OR 1770d OR 1780d OR 1790d)**
3. **1 AND 2 [result 331]**
4. **3 AND (massachusetts OR new()england) [result 39]**

The search retrieved entries that show the various activities of women of the latter half of the 18th century from lighthouse keepers, artisans, writers, criminals, and businesswomen to their roles in religion, benevolent organizations, divorce, the home, etc. This search illustrates the wealth of material on women in AHL and the capability of historical period searching (but see the user manual for full explanation).

Analysis of a search on a topic of fairly recent interest, women in the Vietnam War, compares the content of AHL and other humanities databases. The search strategy was:

1. **nurse? ? OR women/ti,de**
2. **(vietnam OR viet()nam)()(war OR conflict)**
3. **1 AND 2 [result 9]**

Two of the nine hits in AHL are about the anti-war movement and a peace organization, which are not really relevant. The same search in HA located only two entries, one a 1987 book and one about Vietnamese women. A similar search in A&HUM retrieved 12 hits, 9 of which are book reviews of four books and three of which are about Vietnamese history. In A&HUM the words war and conflict had to be omitted from the search statement in order to get more than one hit, and there is no way to search for the USA or American concept. A&HUM is much more current than AHL, so the results include more recent book reviews as well as more of them, whereas AHL entries are for two substantial articles and three dissertations about U.S. enlisted women, nurses, and women veterans. Only the HA book entry and one of the nine AHL entries are in the A&HUM

set because (1) titles do not contain all the search terms or (2) AHL entries are dissertations. Surprisingly, the search in PHIL and REL produced zero results.

HA and AHL share the same indexing scheme so, except that AHL has more material on women, the problems and possibilities are the same. In addition to entries with a general women term and the word stem femini-, HA has 44 entries indexed sex discrimination, 76 indexed sex roles, and a smattering of entries indexed sexism, sexuality, and other sex terms relevant to women. The romanticism search retrieved a moderate number of entries with moderate relevancy (42%) (Table 6). In view of the poor retrieval in PHIL, the search in HA is an important resource for material on romanticism in cultural and intellectual history, including philosophy. Nine of the 19 relevant hits have a women term in the title or descriptor, 10 have it only in the abstract (Table 7). Only two or three entries are of questionable relevance to women — ones with incidental references to women titled Lady and to an author's "delicacy toward women." Therefore, once again we see the necessity to use unqualified free-text searching to retrieve all, or at least most, entries relevant to women. As in AHL, the word romantic appears *only* in the abstract of both relevant and non-relevant entries; for example, the abstract of one relevant entry mentions German romantic philosophy, but because that is not the central focus of the article, neither the title nor the descriptors include a romanticism term.

A search for women in the theater during the 18th century in HA, AHL, A&HUM, MLA, and RILM affords an opportunity to compare the usefulness and problems of these files for theater history, which is related to both literary history and social history. The search strategy was rather complex in statement of the subject but simplified the historical period searching to free-text range searching and known words and descriptors:

1. **actress?/ti,ab OR (playwright? OR performer? OR entertainer?)(2n)(female OR wom?n)**
2. **(wom?n? OR female OR femini?) AND (performing()arts OR entertainment? OR spectacles OR theater? OR theatr? OR stage? ?/ti OR dancer?)**
3. **1 OR 2**

4. 1685:1699 OR 1700:1749 OR 1750:1775 OR 1776:1799 OR
   1800:1815 OR 18c OR hp = 1700h OR 18th()c OR (18th
   OR eighteenth)()cent?
5. 3 AND 4

In HA and AHL the term actress? was restricted to titles OR abstracts to avoid their ambiguous descriptor actors and actresses; in MLA and RILM it was searched in the basic index. In MLA the search on dates omitted the 1800:1815 set to avoid the descriptors 1800-1899 and 1800-1999, and included 1492-1799/de to retrieve the old MLA descriptor for American literature. Results:

	Total Entries	Relevant Entries
A&HUM	19	19
AHL	10	8
HA	39	33
MLA	29	29
RILM	13	8

Each of the five databases produced unique, relevant entries. Duplication among them was low (Table 9). The most satisfactory searches were in MLA and HA. Although all MLA entries are relevant, a few important articles from journals indexed by MLA are missed because search terms are not in the titles or descriptors. Likewise, all A&HUM entries are relevant but, of course, some entries are missed because dates are not in the titles of all relevant documents.

The advantages of HA demonstrated by this search are: presence of abstract text, subject descriptors, and adequate historical period descriptors; inclusion of entries for books and dissertations; coverage of journals in history and interdisciplinary fields. The disadvantages are that the abstract text does produce false drops. Searching databases with abstracts not only finds items missed by searching MLA and A&HUM but also contributes to the creativity of the research process by alerting the user to less obvious, related themes in source documents not directly identified as being about the original search topic, for example, transvestism among women in the 18th century or the influence of a particular actress on an important painter or composer. Because of differences in source documents covered, indexing, and database structure, it is worth searching on women in theater history or similarly interdisciplinary topics in both MLA and HA or AHL, depending on the geographical focus. A&HUM should be included if the most recent articles and a number of book reviews are desired.

In addition to their coverage of history and the other humanities, the history databases are important resources for material on many topics in political science, government, economics, anthropology, sociology, area studies, and policy studies, and sometimes even business and science if there is any historical dimension to the topic. AHL and HA cover numerous topics in the social sciences of concern to women, including, for example, abortion, education, professional and business women, social security, family organization, wage scales, sexual identity and roles, voting power, and stereotypes.

MLA Bibliography

MLA is the workhorse of the humanities databases.[15] It has the highest usage and in number of records is second only to A&HUM, far exceeding the next largest databases (Table 2). Although titled "modern language," its scope is medieval and all modern literatures, linguistics, and folklore, including the medieval or modern use of classical authors. MLA reflects the interest in women's themes exhibited in current literary scholarship. Women's topics include the creative and critical works of women authors of all countries, women as professional writers and artists, depiction of women, attitudes toward women, the education of women, and women's and feminist viewpoints.

MLA indexes an extensive list of journals and other serials (about 3,000) published around the world in practically all languages; dissertations from *Dissertation Abstracts International*; books; and collections of articles. Book reviews and creative works are *not* included. At present the file dates from 1964 and plans are to continue adding backfiles. Records are bibliographic citations, occasionally including a title enhancement or notes. About 50% of the original source documents are in English. Most non-English titles are not translated; therefore a searcher might want to consider including non-English words in a search statement. Significant changes in the database introduced in 1981 and unresolved problems with the 1970-1980 records are detailed in the Dialog documentation, which was updated in March 1987. Except for the 1970-1980 records, analytic entries for articles in collections, formerly called festschriften, include complete bibliographic information. The currency of MLA has improved; some 1988 records were online in early 1989 and the promises of monthly updates appear more likely to be fulfilled than in the past.

The most important fact about access is the use of two different indexing schemes, one for the pre-1981 volumes and a much improved one for the 1981 and later volumes of MLA. The pre-1981 descriptors are too few, too general, and are substantially, if not totally, controlled. In both the old and the new parts of the file the online descriptors correspond to the classification headings of the respective printed volumes; in 1981 and later volumes they also include headings from the subject index and natural language words and phrases selected from the source documents. Most entries on literature are indexed by nationality, time period, and genre or subject author, but the descriptors for national literatures, historical periods, and subject authors (personal names) vary between the old part of the file and the new part. Search terminology must be checked against both parts of the file and strategy devised that will work in both parts. The search on women in the theater in the 18th century conducted for this chapter had to be modified to include one old descriptor, 1492-1799; otherwise the searches here used free-text strategies and did not require attention to most of the problematical points in MLA.[16] In several instances the lack of a historical period descriptor on the record hindered determination of the subject of the document and hence of the relevancy of retrieval.

Descriptors for women in MLA include the titles of works that begin with female, woman, or women; groups of women, such as women directors, women dramatists, or actresses; and women, certain kinds of women (wife, prostitute), and female . . . as literary themes or as literary features. Feminism terms appear most frequently as the descriptors feminism, feminist approach (825 entries), feminist criticism, feminist literary theory, and feminist writers, but also as the literary themes of feminization and femininity. It is important to notice the specificity of the descriptors, e.g., besides feminist writers, there are descriptors for feminist critics, dramatists, novelists, poet, and poets, etc. Additional terms related to women also exist, for example 218 instances of sex roles or sex-role (notice the variation) and 75 occurrences of sex-differentiat- or sex differences (one of which is hyphenated). The new-style descriptors are coded to distinguish such types of descriptors as author and/or work, language, genre, group of people, theme, approach, and place and/or time. It could be useful in a search to distinguish between women as a group (women poets, critics, etc.) and women as a literary theme, but other distinctions, e.g., between feminism as a literary feature and feminism as a scholarly approach, are usually not needed. Besides the codes' not being present on pre-1981 records, there is the problem of matching a user's interpretation of the codes to the indexer's application of them. On the entries retrieved by searches for this chapter the distinction between the codes, especially between literary feature and literary theme, was not useful.

The searches on women's topics emphatically show the necessity to use free-text searching of the basic index: (1) The old descriptors do not contain words denoting women, so titles are the only source of search terms for them. (2) Despite the greatly enhanced information content of the new MLA records, they still do not have a descriptor indicating women on every record about women. In the romanticism search six relevant entries from the new part of the file have a women or feminism term only in the title; one has it only in the note (Table 7). The three entries with a non-English women or feminism term in the title do have appropriate descriptors, but that would not necessarily hold true and would not be true of the old part of the file. The search on women in the theater depended on title words for retrieval of all 13 of the pre-1981 entries and one of the later entries. (3) The numerous terms used in the descriptors for women make it advisable to use synonyms and related terms. For example, one descriptor reads literary theme — women readers and another one is literary theme — female reader; and entries indexed with the specific terms wife, actress, or prostitute do not usually also have a descriptor with a general term like women or female.

The MLA romanticism search is among the most successful in that retrieval is considerable and relevancy is about 60% (Table 6).

The problems are with ambiguous romanticism descriptors: seven relevant entries have no romanticism descriptor at all; entries indexed romantic fiction, romantic love, or romantic novel are sometimes relevant to romanticism, sometimes not; and the distinction between romanticism as a group, as a literary theme, and as a literary feature is unclear. Ideally the descriptor romantic period could be used but it appears on only a small number of the relevant entries. As in AHL, a search strategy using more specific free-text terms would increase relevancy: romanticism or romantic period or romantics. This would still miss a few relevant 1980-1987 entries (five of 31 analyzed) and a considerable number of the old records, which have no descriptor for romanticism, but it would eliminate virtually all the irrelevant ones.

The search on women in the theater was more satisfactory. It produced moderate retrieval (29 entries) and 100% relevancy. The MLA search results have the largest number of non-unique entries (Table 9) and the search missed some relevant entries (see the discussion under AHL and HA above), but the entries retrieved are for substantial articles with a central focus on the search topic.

Although the descriptors are not inaccurate, like several other databases (AHL, HA, REL), there are so many variations and so many fine distinctions among them that the accuracy and consistency of assignment, the user's ability to interpret the descriptors accurately, and the usefulness of such distinctions for the majority of searches is questionable.

Philosopher's Index

PHIL indexes the professional literature in philosophy. It serves, too, as a complement to other indexes for classics, ancient and medieval history and literature, and philosophical aspects of contemporary issues. The literature of philosophy, however, does not appear to be rich in considerations of women's issues. The percentage of general women terms in its entries is the lowest of the discipline databases examined here except for the music and two architecture ones (Tables 2 and 3).

PHIL's coverage begins in 1940, earlier than any other online index of secondary literature. It claims to index all major philosophy journals in English, French, German, Spanish, and Italian, plus selected journals in other languages, but the majority of the items are English-language ones. Documents include articles from about 300 journals currently (more than 400 including ones no longer indexed, an increase from about 50 in its earliest years and about 100 beginning 1967), and books that make original contributions to the field. The online file excludes the book review citations that are in the printed index. PHIL is reasonably current; it was last updated in November 1988 and searches retrieved a few 1988 items.

The bibliographic citations may include title enhancements and about 60% have abstracts. Non-English titles and abstracts occasionally occur; non-English titles are not translated. Analytic entries include the title of the collection along with the article title in the title field but do not contain complete bibliographic data. To find the main entry one searches the title field with proximity operators; retrieves a set that includes all related analytic entries and the main entry; then prints the last record of the set to get the main entry record. The named person index contains some subject descriptors and the descriptor index includes some names of philosophers, so both should be searched for comprehensive retrieval. Phrase indexing of the named person field and inconsistencies in the form of the name and in punctuation and spacing make the use of the Dialog expand command particularly necessary in PHIL.

Free-text searching of the Dialog basic index includes titles, abstracts, and descriptors; additional indexes are typical ones plus the named person index. Indexing of PHIL is done by professional philosophers from a controlled vocabulary, but in my experience the use of descriptors is not rigorously defined or controlled. Descriptors are double posted; most are single words, but since about 1980 some have been changed to pre-coordinated multiword terms. Sometimes philosophy is abbreviated and there are additional variations in format or punctuation of the descriptors. The *Philosopher's Index Thesaurus* does not show all the descriptors or the changes to them over time; it gives only the ones currently being used when it was published. Six historical period descriptors are used very selectively, and one of them, modern (meaning 17th-18th centuries) is misleading to the average user and to the historian.

The small number of descriptors for women's topics is appropriate to the number of entries on women in the database. Test searches revealed the use of the following descriptors: female, feminism, femininity, woman, women, and women's liberation. PHIL claims that indexers do not rely on title words and, with regard to plurals, they use the most appropriate form; but the indexing of Rousseau's views on citizenship, metaphysics, and the education of women sometimes as woman, sometimes as women, is either inaccurate or confusing. There is, of course, a difference between women and feminism, and of all the databases PHIL should be expected to make the distinction. The topic marxism and feminism stated as (**marx OR marxism**)/ti,de AND (**feminis? OR wom?n?/ ti,de**) retrieves 42 entries. The overwhelmingly favorite descriptor is feminism with 20 occurrences in the 33 entries examined, compared to five for woman, two for women, one for women's liberation, and one for femininity. Feminism is used for entries on the oppression of women; the women's movement; feminist theory, politics, analysis, etc.; reproduction; prostitution; and feminism. Woman is used for Marx's comments on women, a critique of feminist theory, and abortion—but another entry on abortion and a woman's right to decide has no descriptor at all for women; and in a search on women and abortion, two entries have no women or feminism descriptor. Femininity is used along with human nature as descriptors for an article on Marxist theory of women's nature, but another entry on Marxist social philosophy is indexed with the two separate descriptors women and nature.

A search on women's liberation shows that this term must be one of the new multiword descriptors that in earlier records is expressed by two descriptors, woman and liberation—but the problem is not that simple. Of the 44 entries retrieved by a free-text search (**women?(1w)liberation**), 17 have no descriptor in the form women's liberation. Of those 17, only two have the expected combination woman and liberation; one has female and liberation; one has feminism and liberation; three have no women or feminism descriptor at all. Although these three could be considered marginal, they are relevant, so the free-text search strategy is both necessary and efficient. If the results of a search on a women's topic were more numerous, one could eliminate the less centrally relevant entries by limiting the free-text search to titles OR descriptors OR the combination of that phrase AND a women OR feminism descriptor, e.g., **women?(1w)liberation/ti,de OR (women?(1w)liberation AND (wom?n OR feminism)/de)**.

PHIL makes a weak showing on general women terms and on romanticism, and is disappointing as a supplement to the history and literature databases for a broad search on eighteenth-century women; but it has three good entries on feminist critical theory. On the topic of the aesthetics of art, there are seven items related to women. PHIL is perhaps more promising as a supplement to REL; it has 52 entries on liberation theology which, when combined with women, produces four unique entries. A search on ethics shows 124 entries related to women or feminism of which 26 are about abortion. Thus PHIL is a resource for literature on the ethical, spiritual, aesthetic, and other philosophical aspects of women's issues.

The documentation for PHIL is woefully out of date: the Dialog chapter and the thesaurus are dated 1979; an article in *Database,* 1980; and a brief discussion published in 1983, was actually written in 1980.[17] On the other hand, the database producer has kept the cost of searching and printing down, which encourages use of the file.

Religion Index

REL's subject is religion worldwide, historical and contemporary, including theological and practical (ministral) studies and religion's manifestations in all the social sciences and humanities. It has considerable material on women, reflected in the presence of a general women term in more than 2% of its entries (Tables 2 and 3), a hefty 223 entries on women's liberation, and numerous descriptors for women, feminism-feminist, and sex. The database was moderately current when the first searches for this chapter were run; the latest update was June 1988 and the latest entries retrieved were dated 1987 (the file was updated again in February 1989).

Entries represent several kinds of documents beginning at various times, mostly in English but also in western European languages. Indexing of periodicals (currently about 400 regularly indexed) begins with 1949 but skips 1960-74; multiauthor books are indexed beginning 1960; book reviews, 1975; and doctor of ministry dissertations beginning 1981.

The record content also varies by time, document type, and other factors. Analytic entries for chapters in multiauthor works do not include the complete bibliographic data, so the main entry must be searched for separately using title words — unless the original search retrieved the main entry, which frequently happens. Titles in non-English languages are not translated. About one-third of the 1975-85 article entries have abstracts, occasionally in a foreign language. Article abstracts were dropped in 1986, but abstracts are included for dissertations, which begin 1981. Records for multiauthor works list the table of contents in the abstract field. Biblical citations, title enrichments, reprint information, and other notes may also be in the abstract field. Descriptors are not present on records for book reviews, records continued from a previous entry, reprints, or less substantial documents such as replies to articles. Historical period terms are used as subheadings in descriptors of some entries, but not even on all history entries! The dates may be traditional periods like 1789-1815, words like middle ages or enlightenment, or centuries in the form 1500-1599. Dates in the form of life dates are included in many personal name descriptors. Managing this variety of record types is not facilitated by any document type field or index. To distinguish document types one uses the entirely numeric accession number or, if appropriate, one of the form headings in the descriptor field: festschriften, festschriften in journals, obituaries, and conference proceedings.

Typical Dialog free-text searching of titles, abstracts, and descriptors and restricting the search to controlled-vocabulary descriptors are possible. Descriptors are single-word or multiword main subject headings and subheadings. They are indexed separately so may be searched individually without worrying about missing terms that occur as subheadings, although they may be searched more precisely using the Dialog L operator if desired. The indexing vocabulary is controlled, based on Library of Congress Subject Headings; the frequently used headings are published in the *Religion Indexes: Thesaurus*. The fine distinctions made by the numerous headings (for example, between women, buddhist and women in Buddhism; between women — Latin America and women, Latin American; and between women and religion and various other headings) may be too fine for most searches on women's topics.

Sample searches on women's studies and women and liberation theology raise questions about the accuracy with which they are assigned.

The search for women's studies in REL is frustrating because neither free-text nor descriptor searches are really satisfactory. ORing a statement that works well in other Dialog files (**women-?(1n)studies**) with the descriptor to which one is referred in the printed index (**women(l)study**) retrieves 72 entries, of which 41 (57%) have no women term descriptor; conversely, 19 have a women term only in the descriptor. The free-text search of the basic index retrieves too many false drops, for example, on a series title that includes the phrase studies in women and religion. But the descriptor women — study is also a very broad term and its application is either not consistent or not clear. For example, articles about the women's studies movement in Japan, women's studies programs in Catholic seminaries, and the analysis of women's studies in universities are found only by a free-text search of the abstracts. Instead of the free-text statement **women?(1n)studies**, a more restrictive statement is effective in producing 43 entries: **women's-()studies OR women(l)study**. (Note the inclusion of the apostrophe differs from standard Dialog practice.)

In a search on liberation theology and women OR feminis?, 29 of the 99 entries retrieved have both a women and a feminism term, 37 have only a women term, and 33 have only a feminism term. The descriptors include, along with liberation theology, a wide variety of women descriptors (women — third world; women in Christianity; women in the Bible; women(theology); theologians, women, etc.) and two feminism ones, most frequently feminist theology. A feminism descriptor rather than a women one tends to be used when the title of the work explicitly mentions feminism or feminist, but not always. One may wonder what distinction the indexing makes when a title states feminist theology but the descriptor is feminism, not feminist theology. In a few instances no women or feminism descriptor is present even when phrases like feminist liberation theology or feminist perspective are in the title.

For women's topics, therefore, searching the combination of titles or descriptors is the most effective strategy for comprehensive, relevant retrieval. Given the number of women and feminism descriptors and the question of the accuracy of the distinctions, one should probably use all of them, or at least weigh carefully the merits of selecting among them.

On other women's topics, too, REL is a valuable resource and a useful supplement to the history and literature databases. It covers ancient history — not covered by the history databases — as well as social history and contemporary social and political issues. It has 223 entries on women's liberation, both historical and contemporary aspects, compared to 199 in AHL, 52 in A&HUM, and 44 in PHIL. A search on eighteenth-century women complements a search in AHL or HA, although the majority of the REL entries are about the British scene. REL bears the worst earmarks of an index converted from a printed publication to an online database. The lack of full and consistent information in the records is an irritating impediment to its effective use.

Art Index

ART, like other Wilson indexes, is broad in subject coverage. It covers the fine arts, folk arts, crafts, industrial and interior design, architecture, city planning, film and photography, and related subjects. The majority of references to women are to women depicted in works of art, women artists and professionals in all the visual arts and crafts; also indexed are feminist art and feminism in relation to the arts.

The breadth of literature covered is somewhat less than the other art databases: about 240 periodicals, yearbooks, and museum bulletins, mostly in English but with more European-language journals than other Wilson indexes. Feature articles, book reviews, reproductions of works of art, and other items like conference reports, interviews, and exhibition announcements and reviews, are indexed. ART is further limited by the recency of the online file, which dates only from late 1984. On the other hand ART is kept current with twice-weekly updates. In early 1989, searches retrieved entries for documents published in the last quarter of 1988.

Records give the bibliographic data, including notes on physical description; document type and an additional contents tag for articles that indicates feature article or exhibit notice; subject headings;

and some identification numbers. Foreign-language titles are not translated. The database may be searched using free-text methods or field qualifiers. The controlled-vocabulary descriptors are Library of Congress Subject Headings and additions; fewer descriptors are assigned than in HUM and EGL.

ART is not very strong in material about women or feminism, ranking just below the median in both total number and percent of records having a general women term (Table 3). In the number and percent of feminism terms it ranks even lower, at eleventh and twelfth place respectively. The search on romanticism is disappointing in number of entries and, although they are relevant, the women terms appear only in titles of illustrations (Table 7). The search for the theme of the fallen woman was even less successful, locating only one entry (Table 10). To retrieve entries about works of art depicting women, it is necessary to use free-text methods as no descriptor is assigned to identify such works. ART would be more useful for general searches like feminist art or simply feminism.

Like HUM and other Wilson indexes, ART is useful for locating articles in readily available journals and for projects that do not require an exhaustive literature search.

Artbibliographies Modern

ARTMOD focuses on art in the 19th and 20th centuries, including movements and artists that bridge the 18th- to 19th-century. Within this period it has broad subject coverage and no geographical limits: all the fine arts, including film and photography, artists, art movements; folk art; applied arts; graphic and three-dimensional design, including dance and theatre; architecture; town planning; art museums, education, collecting, and the art market. Women's materials are predominantly on the iconography of women and on feminism, loosely defined.

About 80% of the documents represented in the database are articles from core journals, museum bulletins, and newsletters in English and all European languages, currently about 500 publications, plus selected articles from the periodicals indexed by AHL and HA. The remainder of the documents are books (11% of the file, currently about 1,000 per year), exhibition catalogs (9%), and dissertations (1%), although currently the latest dissertations are from 1983. The online database begins with volume 5 (1975) and includes items dating from 1972. As with most of the humanities databases, the number of sources surveyed and the number of records added have increased over the years. Production of ARTMOD is slow and subject to processing problems and delays; the file has not been updated since 1987. The latest entries retrieved in searches for this chapter are for documents published in 1987. Some retrospective work is being done, reflected in earlier publication dates for entries in the more recent updates.

The records provide bibliographic data, document type, abstracts, and descriptors. Non-English titles are translated and all abstracts are in English, but British spelling is used. Names of countries are in English in the country of publication index and the gallery index, but gallery names are in the original language and names of countries may vary. Descriptors are the controlled vocabulary of the 300 or so classification headings of the printed issues plus names of artists and groups of artists. New descriptors are added as needed, e.g., there is a descriptor feminist art workers that has been used only once so far. Because the descriptors are few and general in nature, free-text searching is almost always advisable; an exception would be a search on a well-known artist where incidental references in abstracts need to be avoided.[18] Descriptor leading terms and subheadings, which are used selectively, are both phrase and word indexed, but usually free-text methods are easier to use and produce more comprehensive results. The searcher should beware of assuming that there are historical period descriptors. Subheadings or qualifiers exist for 19th century and 20th century but are assigned very selectively and are rarely useful.

Entries on topics related to women appear abundant in ARTMOD. All three art databases include the same kinds of material about women but a higher percentage of records in ARTMOD have a general women or a feminism term than ART or RILA has (Tables 2 and 3). Since the literature covered by the three databases is similar, this difference appears to be caused by the indexing vocabularies and the presence of abstracts in ARTMOD and RILA, but a closer investigation is needed to pinpoint the exact reasons.

Entries in ARTMOD on women's topics are characterized by the use of the broad, inclusive descriptors iconography-themes-women and art-and-feminism. The first is the only descriptor containing the word women. There is no descriptor for women artists, so free-text searching is useful for finding entries not indexed with a women term or with feminism, such as entries that identify an artist as a woman, refer to problems of being a woman artist, discuss art of subjects that particularly touch women's interests, or give an artist's response to the accusation that her painting denigrates women.

The romanticism search emphasizes the problem of lack of identification of women in the titles and descriptors — and sometimes even in the abstracts (Table 7). In some entries about women artists the only clue is the use of the pronoun her or a feminine personal name. Such entries can be retrieved if the artist's name is already known and searched for or if the abstract mentions a women motif in the art discussed. Some, not all, entries on women artists can be found by a free-text search using proximity operators and generous spacing, e.g., **wom?n(2w)(artist? OR painter? OR sculptor? OR designer?)**. Likewise, female subjects are not consistently identified as women in titles or descriptors, e.g., an entry about the iconography of Sappho has a women or female term only in the abstract; the descriptors include the words sexuality, erotic, and Sappho (in the descriptor iconography-themes-sappho), but no term for women.

The catchall descriptor art-and-feminism, also not assigned to the entries mentioned above, is the only feminism descriptor. It is used for entries on a wide variety of subjects, such as particular feminist artists, an artist's discussion of feminism, works influenced by feminism, and problems of a woman artist. Despite being heavily used (842 instances), it is not consistently and comprehensively applied. Free-text searching for feminism retrieves mostly minor references but occasionally ones having to do with theory and criticism. The word feminist is useful as a free-text search term to locate references to a feminist perspective and particular feminist artists not indexed with women or feminism descriptors.

The romanticism search shows a disconcerting lack of reliability of titles and descriptors for expressing both the concepts of women and romanticism. Naturally the non-relevant entries have a high percentage of the search terms only in the abstract, but among the 13 *relevant* entries, eight have the women term and ten have the romanticism term only in the abstract; thus of the 13 relevant entries, only five have a women term in the title or descriptor (Table 7). False drops occur on the term mother (Motherwell, motherland) and non-relevant entries were retrieved through incidental references to men and women, to a wife of an artist, and to Lady as a personal title. Yet restricting a search to titles and descriptors would exclude retrieval of directly relevant items about the impact of muse portraits on the emerging French women romantics, the representation of women in painting of the romantic era, and a mid-19th-century sculptor's romanticism and celebration of feminine beauty.

The search on the fallen woman theme again poses the dilemma of free-text searching for comprehensive retrieval versus precision. The free-text search produced four false drops on the word found, which is the title of a painting, but when the search on that word was restricted to titles or descriptors, two relevant entries that had *Found* in the abstract were lost (Table 10 and the discussion of A&HUM above).

Whereas other databases require the use of free-text searching because descriptors are inadequate, inconsistent, or too numerous to be useful, it is the paucity and lack of specificity of descriptors in ARTMOD that make achieving an efficient search difficult.

Art Literature International

The third art database considered here, RILA, is the most sophisticated and information rich of the humanities databases. Its subject coverage is visual art in its broadest definition, including art history, theory, criticism; the fine arts, decorative arts, scenic art, and folk art; architecture and city planning; techniques, conservation, and museums; but it is limited to Western art since late antiquity, specifically European and related art since the 4th century, American art since the discoveries, and modern world art since 1945. Women's material is the same as in ART and ARTMOD: foremost is the iconography of women, followed by women artists and by feminism and art.

A wide variety of documents are represented. Almost 50% of the file is entries for articles in periodicals, collections, and proceedings, including interviews and obituaries; nearly 25% is for reviews of books, exhibition catalogs, and dissertations; 14% for exhibition catalogs; and about 15% for monographs. Although the file is described in documentation as beginning in 1973, at the time of this writing the years 1975-87 were listed as being online; a 1988 update was added shortly thereafter, which makes RILA more current than ARTMOD.

The records in RILA are long and organize the information in 26 searchable fields, an unusually high number for a humanities database. About 30% of the records are for non-English documents; titles are given in the original language and English translation. Abstracts, present on more than 50% of the records, vary from one sentence to 300 words. So far, they are in English but this may change with the merger of RILA and *Répertoire d'Art et d'Archéologie*. On main entry records for collections the abstract field contains a list of authors and titles with their respective RILA analytic entry numbers. Records for a work and reviews of it are connected by having the same main RILA number (AN) assigned to the entry for the work itself and all reviews of it. Reviews also have separate, unique numbers (RN) so that a particular review record may be selected; and, as in other files, all reviews can be excluded by selecting **NOT DT = review?**.

Indexing of RILA records, which is copious and often redundant, is provided in three forms, the most important of which is the Descriptor index. RILA Descriptors are the lengthiest and most specific of the index terms. They are from a controlled subject heading list, but like other initially controlled indexing schemes, new terms and natural language words and phrases are constantly added, especially at the last subheading level. At the other end of the spectrum, broad subject classification headings are used in the Section Heading index. They may be searched using code numbers, phrases, or individual words. Another kind of descriptor is the Identifier, used for three specific kinds of data: nationality, time period, and style, medium, and form. Terms in the Identifiers are often redundant with Descriptors but are fewer and more controlled, except the time period Identifiers. All three types of descriptors are both word and phrase indexed, so free-text searching of the basic index includes them along with titles and abstracts.

RILA accommodates historical period searching with a variety of index terms for dates, which is an example of its efforts to make access easy through thorough or even redundant indexing. The time period Identifier, labeled Subject Period on displayed records, includes both specific years expressed in four digits, such as 1975 or 1862-1899, and centuries expressed as in 1700-1800 or 1700-1900. Note that these sets of dates that begin and end with double zeros cause serious precision problems in free-text searches as a search on the second date (e.g., 1800) retrieves sets both ending and beginning with that date, or in other words, both the previous and following 100 years. The Identifier for a record may contain multiple dates; identifiers are missing from a few records, so free-text searching or combining with Descriptors should be used. Descriptors contain subheadings for time periods expressed in the form of centuries, e.g., 20th c. or 13th-19th cs.; the word medieval; and quasi period terms like Victorian and romanticism. Descriptors also include exhibition dates and life dates of indexed persons. The Section Headings express time periods in such broad categories as medieval or renaissance-baroque-and-rococo.

Descriptors for women are all in the Descriptor index, so further references in this chapter to descriptors are to ones in that index. They exist in almost as many forms as there are descriptors containing the word women, e.g., the descriptor women and art — 16th-20th cs. is on seven records, women architects on five, and women allegory on three. The majority of these descriptors appear on only one record. An important descriptor term, women artists, occurs on 560 records with numerous subheadings and as a subheading for other leading terms. Thus it is very important either to use free-text techniques, e.g., **women()artists/de** (result 560, including a few false drops), or to truncate the descriptor, as in women artists? (result 536). Remember, too, the term does not cover women architects, women photographers, etc., which must be searched for separately.

The same characteristics are true of the descriptor feminism, which is the term used to index entries about the women's movement. It occurs both as a single lead term and the first word in a phrase, with a wide array of subheadings, and as a subheading of other descriptors. The descriptor feminism and art is on 17 records, feminism and art by women 20th c. on one; feminism and art history is on nine records, feminism and art history marxist on one; and feminism and corsets is on five. One may wish to restrict a free-text search on women to the descriptor field, but before searching a descriptor as a bound phrase one would want to use the expand feature to see if it should be truncated.

Additional concepts related to women that might be useful are mothers, odalisques, priestesses, queens, and widows. The word feminist occurs in 120 records but not as a lead term in a descriptor (except in proper names).

In the romanticism search the phrase romantic love proved to be the false drop culprit, but irrelevant entries were also retrieved because of incidental references to women in the abstract (as in "men and women" or in titles of paintings in entries that have no focus on the women). At the same time, three of the ten relevant entries have the women term only in the abstract (Table 7). One of the non-relevant entries points up the problem of locating individual women artists and portraits of women. The entry about works of Vigée-Le Brun does not mention that the artist was a woman, and some of the portraits are identified only by a personal name without any indication that the subjects are women. The entry was retrieved through the presence of titles of paintings that include the words wife, woman, lady, and girl. Retrieval thus depended on the chance occurrence of words, not on deliberate identification.

The search on the fallen woman theme, quite successful with only three non-relevant entries out of 17 (Table 10), illustrates the random or inconsistent application of descriptor subheadings and the difficulties of searching for the concept of images of women.[19] The phrase images of women appears in a descriptor on one entry on the fallen woman theme but not on two other entries about Rossetti's *Found* and the femme fatale theme, although abstracts for both these entries use the phrase. Similarly the femme fatale entry is indexed femme fatale theme but the two entries on the fallen woman are not indexed fallen woman theme. Another variation is the use of the descriptor woman as subject and the descriptor phrase images of Victorian womanhood, rather than the descriptors images of women or woman as theme; the latter occurs on yet another entry. Femmes fatales is used here; elsewhere it is femme fatale theme. Most of these entries, as well as others in this search, could be retrieved by a free-text search for iconography in a combination of the descriptor, identifier, or section heading indexes, but to get the Rossetti-*Found* entry one would have to search for the word images.

RILA is a humanities database designed or redesigned as an online database. So far, it represents the most successful effort in the humanities of combining the information needs of scholars in a discipline, the characteristics of online information retrieval, and affordability. Its records are information rich with abstracts and numerous descriptors; its large number of access points allow sophisticated manipulation of the file. The variety, specificity, and mixture of controlled and uncontrolled indexing vocabulary is both a boon and a challenge that requires the searcher to choose between simple free-text searching or complex strategies that combine free-text and controlled vocabulary techniques. Its moderate price is a strong inducement to search RILA.

Architecture Database

ARCH covers technical and aesthetic aspects of architecture without geographic or period limits. General women terms occur in only about .3% of the records and feminist terms practically not at all, among the lowest percentages of the humanities databases (Tables 2 and 3). Women's topics represented are overwhelmingly the works and professional lives of women architects followed by the architecture of buildings for women and a few entries on issues such as employment, discrimination, career opportunities, and recognition. Because these documents are in specialty architectural sources not usually indexed by other databases, a search on these topics could profitably include ARCH. A search for women architects in four art and architecture files shows their relative strength (Table 11) and the characteristics of access to women's topics.

ARCH indexes articles in about 400 periodicals published 1978 and later, and books, pamphlets, catalogs, proceedings, and other publications cataloged by the British Architectural Library beginning 1984. It has about a fifty-fifty split between British and non-British source documents. The records are bibliographic citations with the usual language, country of publication, and document type indicators plus notes, descriptors, named architects, and identifiers. British spelling is used. An oddity is that book authors are duly listed in an author field but article authors are in a statement of responsibility index (SR, which also includes book authors) in the Identifier index, and sometimes in the note field.

Descriptors are the controlled vocabulary terms assigned from the *Architectural Keywords* thesaurus and are in a format similar to Library of Congress Subject Headings. Main headings and sub-headings are word and phrase indexed; they may be linked with the L operator. Names of architects appear in the descriptors, named person index, and identifiers. The named person index, coded NA and labeled architect(s) on the printed record, is intended to be the main field for names of architects who are the central focus of a document. In practice it seems to include names of architects or firms related to the specific project under discussion, whereas the identifier field contains the names of architects discussed in a more general context such as their body of work, life, or opinions, or who are not the main focus of the document; but this distinction is not always followed. Whatever the distinction, it is not a useful one for a search on women architects. The entries retrieved show no consistency and no clear rationale for putting names in one field rather than the other. Therefore, a search for a particular woman architect requires a strategy that works in the named person field, where names are inverted and phrase indexed, as well as in titles, notes, descriptors, and identifiers. For example, select **morgan(n)julia** to retrieve Morgan, Julia – 1872-1957 from the architect(s) field, Julia Morgan from titles and notes, and Morgan, Julia from descriptors.

In ARCH a combination of free-text and descriptor searching is advisable. A free-text strategy alone, using proximity operators, produces mostly relevant hits but does not retrieve descriptors consisting of the heading architects and subheading women. The following statement achieves high recall and relevancy: **(female? OR wom?n?)(2w)(architect? ? OR designer?) OR architects(l)wo-men**. Of the 103 entries retrieved, only 6 are not relevant; all six have a title in which a women's building is named followed by the indicator "architects:."

Although the descriptors are highly reliable (92 of the 103 entries have the descriptor architects – women), there are enough problems to make the free-text strategy necessary: an entry about women architects' experience in managing career and family has no women term in the descriptor; five entries about individual "great," "pioneer," or "first" women architects are not indexed with a women term; and in three instances the descriptor includes the subheading women architects instead of the usual heading, architects—women.

ARCH is a specialized database with some material on women architects and related topics. The mixture of types of data in the indexes and the lack of justification for such seemingly unplanned database design is annoying but not really problematical if index labels are ignored and free-text searching with proximity operators, including the L, is used.

AVERY

AVERY covers architectural design and history, including landscape architecture, historic preservation, city planning, and environmental topics. Women's issues represented are women architects, the architecture of buildings related to women (women's centers, colleges, hospitals), and architectural-environmental issues concerning women.

The database represents the cataloging by the Columbia University Fine Arts Library of articles published 1979 and later, thus beginning with the fourth supplement (1979-82) of its printed counterpart the *Avery Index to Architectural Periodicals*. It currently indexes about 700 architectural journals, an increase from 400 in earlier years. The record follows the MARC format and, like all RLIN records, can be displayed in full cataloging format, but the long display is the one usually preferred by searchers. It gives the bibliographic citation, notes, and subject headings.

Searches can be done on authors in the personal name index, corporate names, titles, journal titles, subject headings, and ISSNs. More precise searching is possible by using the exact personal name, title phrase, or subject phrase indexes if that exact data are known. The RLIN browse feature, similar to Dialog's EXPAND or BRS's ROOT, is available for the exact name index and the corporate name, title, journal, and subject phrase indexes. RLIN does not offer completely free-text searching, so one has to choose the indexes to search. Boolean OR, AND, and NOT operators can be used to make searches more specific, but search statements are limited to 240 characters.[20]

Because AVERY uses a well-controlled index vocabulary, modified and enhanced Library of Congress Subject Headings, and has a cross reference file available online, it is usually most efficient to determine the appropriate subject headings and use them. But for a search on women architects one should consider the potential of subject word searching (to retrieve women landscape architects and women as architects, for example, as well as women architects) compared to truncated subject phrase searching (**fin sp women architects#**) that retrieves the heading with all its subheadings, such as women architects — 20th century. A search of the title word index for architect OR architects OR designer# AND wom#n produces 20 entries of which 8 are not relevant. Two of the 20, however, have "woman architect" in the title — absolutely relevant entries — but no women term in the descriptors. Limitations on modifying searches by combining sets in the RLIN search system requires some toleration of non-relevant and duplicate entries if one wishes to achieve a truly comprehensive search.

RILM Abstracts

RILM attempts to cover international music literature of scholarly significance. This literature includes reference materials, theory, performance, instruments, pedagogy, history, and music in relation to other disciplines. The small amount of material related to women is on women composers, instrumentalists, vocalists, and teachers, and on music associated with women, especially songs.

The online file has approximately 80,600 records, which represent items published 1979 through 1983; a considerable number are non-English language items. Records represent articles in some 300 journals, books, dissertations, conference papers, catalogs, commentaries, and reviews of books, dissertations, and recordings. Selectivity of indexing periodicals varies so that items, especially reviews, may be omitted even from journals supposedly comprehensively indexed.[21] Source documents are selected by committees in countries around the world. RILM has had a serious time lag problem since its inception and is still five years behind. The last update is for the 1983 volume; the latest entries retrieved by searches here are from early 1983.

Records are in typical Dialog format for bibliographic citations and abstracts. Abstracts are present for most entries but not for records of translated books or reviews of books and dissertations. All non-English titles are translated and abstracts are in English. Both selection of a particular language of source documents and limiting of results to English or non-English are available. Five types of documents are indexed in the document type field and a special feature index may be used for the selection of bibliographies, catalogues, discographies, illustrations, portraits, and examples of music within the text of a document.

In addition to free-text searching of the basic index, subject access is provided in two indexes, subject headings and descriptors. Subject headings, which are the classification section headings of the table of contents of the print version, are eleven broad categories like historical musicology and performance, each with subcategories. The main subject headings are searched by individual words or bound phrases; subcategories are searched by words, bound phrases, or numeric codes. Descriptors are assigned from an authority list, called a thesaurus but really just a list of terms.[22] The descriptors are only moderately controlled, and only at the lead term. They are double posted so may be searched as bound phrases (hyphens and ANDs must be masked) or by using the L operator; free-text searching, however, is preferable. Personal names in descriptors occur in a variety of forms: the full name (inverted order) when a lead term; surname and initials when in second position in the descriptor string; surname alone when in third or later positions or in natural language phrases that are in the second position — unless initials are needed to avoid ambiguity.[23]

The descriptors related to women indicate that RILM indexing practice is more like that of AHL and HA than a controlled vocabulary. There are 10 descriptors beginning with female that have only one entry each (e.g., female blues singers). Words beginning with femini- are not used frequently; the descriptor feminist songs is on one entry. The majority of descriptors for entries related to women use women as the lead term, and most of these are women in music followed by subheadings for countries, named people, kinds of musicians (composers, organists, etc.), historical periods, and descriptive phrases. It appears that around 1982 the descriptor women in music was dropped and women's studies instituted. Subheadings following women's studies are the same kind as the ones for women in music. Other descriptors with the possessive form (women's bands, women's music, women's songs) are now used instead of the form women in music — songs.

The romanticism search points up the need to carefully select the search terms for women's topics, for example, to limit them to the basic words women and female or to the combination of terms in titles or descriptors, if high relevance is desired. This and other free-text searches of the basic index produced more entries only peripherally relevant to women in RILM than in other files. Abstracts of the less relevant entries frequently make incidental references to someone's wife, pretty girls, ladies, female characters or roles, or are about music for female voices.

A search for black women performers allows comparison of RILM, AHL, and A&HUM. The search for the concept black women stated as (black? ? OR negro? ?)(2w)(wom?n? OR female OR actress?) retrieved 10 entries in RILM and 427 in AHL. Because in A&HUM a search depends on title words, the strategy was modified to (black? ? OR negro? OR afro()american?) AND (wom?n? OR female? OR actress?), which retrieved 261 hits. Having retrieved only 10 entries, the search in RILM needed no further qualification, but to compare it to the other databases, the second concept was searched, too. The performance concept included a lengthy list of terms: performer? ?, performing()arts, stage/ti,de, theatr?, theater?, vaudeville, dance/ti,de, dancer?, singer?, music/ti,de, musician?, musical()theat?, jazz/ti,de, night()club?, nightclub?. Adding this concept, admittedly still incomplete, reduced retrieval in RILM to 7, AHL to 11, and A&HUM to 11 hits. All the entries were unique except that one book entry in RILM had a review cited in AHL and nine other reviews in A&HUM. Uniqueness is due to the different list of journals covered by each database; what overlap in journal coverage exists is obviated by the different dates of coverage and the time lag of RILM.

This search in RILM shows the use of the descriptor black

women (but not for all the entries about black women!) and the descriptor subheadings women—black and black—female blues singers. Beginning with 1982 publications the descriptor black studies appears along with the switch from women in music to women's studies.

Specific women concepts like black women are best searched in the full basic index whereas searches for the general concept of women should be restricted to the combination of titles OR descriptors, unless the other concept or concepts in the search are so specific or unusual that every possible reference to a woman is needed. Free-text searching of the descriptors can overcome their changes and inconsistencies.

RILM could be a useful resource for the field of music and for interdisciplinary studies in art, literature, and history if its producer could muster the resources to overcome its continual, excessive time lag. The Dialog file documentation is old; it is not easy to obtain reliable information about the file from Dialog or the producer; and there is little interest in discussing RILM in the literature of online searching or humanities information research.

Additional Databases

Not searched for women's material or discussed in this chapter are several more bibliographic, full text, and reference databases related to the humanities. Télésystèmes-Questel provides access to eight humanities databases produced by the French Institut de l'Information Scientifique et Technique and merged, along with 12 in the social sciences, into FRANCIS. The humanities databases are the online versions of seven parts of the *Bulletin Signalétique* plus *Répertoire d'Art et Archéologie*; they cover the fields of art and archeology, prehistory and protohistory, history of science and technology, literature, linguistics, religion, and philosophy. Their coverage of European and Latin American scholarly literature is generally stronger than U.S. databases.[24] The language of the databases is primarily French; original titles, sometimes with French translations are given. Abstracts and descriptors are in French for the most part. FRANCIS is not widely available in the U.S., but it is obviously a good resource for research on European, especially French, subjects.

Another bibliographic database that should be considered by humanists is the National Library of Medicine's HISTLINE, which corresponds to the printed *Bibliography of the History of Medicine*. Any search on women as individuals or as a group in relation to the medical profession, medical institutions, health, disease, or drugs, in a historical context, could profit from this specialized database.[25]

Full text online databases are rare in the humanities, but two should be noted: the *Bible (King James Version)* on Dialog and the *American and French Research on the Treasury of the French Language* (ARTFL) available from the University of Chicago. The latter has been available to subscribers for several years but only with the switch to a new computer system in 1988 can it be considered online. ARTFL is a collection of more than 1700 French texts in a variety of fields from the 17th to the 20th centuries, and a few earlier texts. Texts are classic works in French literature and nonfiction prose in literary criticism, biology, economics, history, and philosophy, including troubadour poetry, a selection of the 1789 cahiers, and 1848 revolutionary texts of newspaper articles, pamphlets, posters, and manifestos. Studies of women in literature, intellectual history, and political discourse could make use of ARTFL.[26]

A catalog of machine-readable texts in the humanities was begun at Rutgers University in 1982 and has now been added to the Machine-readable Data Files segment of RLIN, which includes entries for more than 600 of the ARTFL texts and some 1,300 records for files held by the Inter-University Consortium for Political and Social Research (ICPSR).[27] ICPSR files, although largely used by social scientists, do include collections of data of interest to researchers in history and interdisciplinary fields. Bibliographic control of machine-readable text and data files is an elusive goal but a national online catalog of them has begun on RLIN.

RLIN is also adding a non-bibliographic, numeric database itself, the *Medieval and Early Modern Data Bank* founded at Rutgers University.[28] In its present pilot version it contains more than 13,000 currency exchange quotations from the mid-12th century to 1500. Plans are to include all kinds of data that can be expressed in tabular form, such as wages, prices, household size, mortality, property-holding, taxes, imports, and exports; reference aids like gazetteers, calendars, and glossaries of weights and measures will also be added. How much information there will be about women is not known, but presumably wherever the original sources make any distinction between the sexes, the data will be appropriately coded.

Although these databases were not tested for their content on women or the effectiveness of their indexing for the discussion in this chapter, online search analysts, reference librarians, and researchers in the humanities should be aware of their potential usefulness.

CONCLUSION

The foregoing analysis of the extent of the material on women, the growth of that literature, and the retrieval capabilities of the databases confirms the widespread interest in women in recent humanities literature, especially in the fields of history, religion, art, and current scholarship in literature. The weaknesses of the databases and the problems of searching for women-related items are those of the humanities databases themselves and are not peculiar to the subject of women.

The online humanities databases date from the mid seventies and eighties, with some material dating back to the sixties in literature and history and back to the forties in philosophy and religion; thus much of the secondary literature needed by humanities scholars is not indexed online. Retrospective work has been done to fill in coverage and MLA is committed to converting earlier volumes to machine-readable form, but there are no plans to put earlier volumes of the Wilson indexes, *Arts & Humanities Citation Index*, or *Historical Abstracts* online. Ideally we need a number of serial bibliographies and specialized indexes to supplement the major indexes now online, but financing conversion appears unlikely given the difficulties of maintaining and improving the current bibliographies in the humanities. Humanists also typically need access to primary source material, which is not available online, although there are some developments in that direction. Both OCLC and RLIN have active programs to add records of archival and manuscript materials to their online catalogs and both include records for machine-readable data files. The primary source material itself is even scarcer, of course, but ARTFL in French studies is available online and the *Thesaurus Linguae Graecae* is available on CD-ROM. Other areas of weaknesses of the humanities databases are in the subjects of ancient history and literature, pre-19th-century non-Western art, dance, and theater; and books and collections are less well covered than periodicals.

The need for currency in humanities bibliography has not been as universally recognized as the need for retrospective coverage, but in my experience currency is frequently important to researchers in the humanities and is especially so in new and expanding fields like women's studies. The humanities databases, except for the Wilsonline ones and A&HUM, are plagued by problems of producing the databases and getting them online expeditiously.

To some extent currency is related to cost; at a higher price to the subscriber and the online user, the databases could be produced more quickly. Most of the database producers have chosen to keep the prices moderate, accepting the dictum that humanists do not have the resources to pay for significantly more expensive bibliographies. The higher cost of A&HUM is a factor to be weighed against its particular advantages when deciding which databases to search.

The online humanities databases, except for the Wilsonline ones, are characterized by the evidence of their derivation from databases developed to produce printed publications rather than being designed as databases for online retrieval. After some experience with their online versions, database producers have made piecemeal improvements to the files such as adding language codes, separating data into more individually labeled fields, standardizing historical period descriptors, and making analytic entries more bibliographically complete. The completely revamped indexing schemes of both AHL-HA and MLA improved the files for online retrieval as well as for manual use. Unfortunately it is not economically feasible for the back files to be re-indexed, so MLA has two different indexing schemes and AHL and HA lack indexing terms altogether on the earliest volumes online. (Indexing for an additional five volumes of AHL exists but the database producer has not bothered to provide new tapes for reloading.) PHIL and RILM exhibit less sweeping but still problematical modifications of their indexing. The Wilson indexes, A&HUM, and RILA, having debuted later, were designed with more attention to the needs of online retrieval and are more consistent files. Until files are reloaded on the host system certain newer system features are not available, e.g., on Dialog six of the humanities databases have no sorting capability.

Variation and change is also characteristic of the databases' coverage: types of documents are added and dropped at various times; the number of source documents surveyed increases over time and individual titles are added and dropped at various times; indexing of sources is usually selective; and the record content varies both by type of document (some types are abstracted, others not) and by selectivity or changes in policy (some articles are abstracted, some are not). Most of the databases (not A&HUM or Wilsonline ones) depend, in one way or another, on some volunteer assistance from scholars in the field, which introduces an element of inconsistent coverage of material as well as delays. Several database producers have undertaken major efforts of retrospective coverage and published additional separate volumes; some are filling in both gaps in years of coverage and missing issues of journals, seen online in the fact that the display of search results, which is in the order of last in first out, sometimes does not reflect roughly the publication order of most recently published, first out. A serious lapse in following through on the effort to make the coverage of journal literature consistent is ABC-Clio's failure to put the *AHL Supplement* online. Because of the policies of selective indexing of the list of journals covered, of including material from other databases by the same producer, and of allowing random additions of relevant items as they are noticed, it is difficult to determine the databases' coverage exactly.

Retrieval from the humanities databases, on women's topics as well as others, is hampered by the lack of certain features in certain databases. Foremost among these are the lack of descriptors in A&HUM—a database designed on such different premises that to expect indexing is unrealistic—and the lack of English translations of titles in MLA and REL—easy enough to remedy. One thing not handled well in any of the databases is diacritics. We have learned to do without them but their loss does lead to inaccurate citations. The lack of abstracts in MLA and for book and dissertation entries in other databases, and the dropping of abstracts for articles in REL leaves large numbers of records with less than adequate text for searching. The lack of book review entries in MLA and PHIL is thought to be a disadvantage until one considers the annoyance they cause in searches of A&HUM and AHL where books are not cited separately from their reviews.

Most important is the indexing: the number and type of indexes and the indexing vocabulary. As noted above, RILA has gone the farthest in dividing the record content into searchable fields, including three kinds of descriptors with one of those kinds having three distinctly specified types of data. Yet even RILA has no named person field. Theoretically a named person field in all the databases would be an advantage in searching in the humanities where people are a frequent subject of study. In practice the named person indexes that exist in PHIL and ARCH as well as MLA's supercodes for subject author and scholars, are not usually worth the trouble. The problems of searching for personal names in online databases — the choice of which name to use when more than one is possible; the form of entry for the name; the transliteration, spelling, and punctuation used; the variations among databases on all the foregoing points; inconsistencies within a database, both deliberate and unintentional — are not solved by having a named person index. Most problems with personal names can be solved by using free-text techniques, including the bidirectional proximity operator (N) on Dialog; searching for first names or initials or another concept for context; and, in certain cases, restricting the search to descriptors.[29]

A more significant need is for improved geographic and historical period indexing. Historical period descriptors exist in several databases but they are not applied to all entries. Problems stemming from the lack of period descriptors have been noted in searches in MLA, PHIL, and REL. It took Dialog and the database producer of AHL and HA — the first to use date descriptors — some time to realize and address the problems related to adapting the printed index descriptors to online searching. (It is surprising that, coming much later, RILA would make the mistake of beginning and ending date ranges with double zeros, e.g., 1700-1800.)

A serious need in the humanities databases is for hierarchical geographic indexing, that is, indexing that allows retrieval of all entries about a general geographic area and its subdivisions without having to search separately for all those smaller units that belong to it; e.g., one should be able to search for South America and retrieve entries on Venezuela, Peru, Buenos Aires, and all other countries and regions of South America as well as ones indexed with the general term South America. I know of no prospects of such indexing being adopted.

As for the indexing of women and feminist issues, there are four general approaches: (1) no indexing, namely in A&HUM and ESTC; (2) sparse and general indexing as in ARTMOD and PHIL; (3) Library of Congress Subject Headings, with additions, as in the Wilsonline databases, AVERY, and REL; and (4) schemes specific to the database with control on some terms but with natural language terms as desired, especially at the last subheading, as in AHL, HA, MLA, RILA, and RILM. The trend in indexing is clearly toward free vocabulary, so not too much time and effort should be spent on trying to control the present chaos. I agree with Hildenbrand in recommending free-text searching in most cases in most databases because of the inadequate indexing; the lack of accurate controlled vocabulary and guides to the vocabulary; and the fact that women's issues are not the focus of the particular database.[30] Even titles and (i.e., OR) descriptors are not sufficient in many cases, as the searches reviewed here demonstrate, and the passing reference in an abstract to women — expressed in a number of synonyms and related terms — may be crucial to optimum retrieval. Access to material with a feminist perspective[31] is explicitly offered in MLA (825 entries indexed feminist approach, 288 feminist criticism, and 145 feminist literary theory) and REL (23 entries indexed feminist interpretation, 409 feminist theology), but the best way to find it is to use free-text searching to locate the word feminist in close proximity to words like approach, perspective, criticism, theory, art, theater, politics, philosophy, etc.

The humanities and social sciences, whatever their academic and professional compartmentalization, are not clearly separable fields and research on women, whether traditionalist or feminist, is especially interdisciplinary. Some women's topics have little literature available on them so multiple database searching is needed to find whatever there is. Furthermore, viewpoints from different disciplines enrich research undertaken initially in the framework of one discipline. A search in one database can frequently find additional unique references in a second and third database. There is little overlap among the humanities databases despite their covering many of the same journals, and searches can be tailored to take advantage of each database's best features, e.g., currency, older material, reviews, abstracts, type of indexing, or particular subject strengths. The moderate cost of most of the humanities and social sciences databases encourages multiple database searching.

NOTES

1. Candy Schwartz, "Humanities," in *Manual of Online Search Strategies*, ed. C. J. Armstrong and J. A. Large (Boston, G. K. Hall, 1988), 623-78. Charles L. Gilreath, *Computerized Literature Searching: Research Strategies and Databases* (Boulder, CO: Westview Press, 1984), 140-152, makes some perceptive observations in a short chapter on the humanities and arts but omits *Religion Index* and unfortunately puts history in the social sciences chapter.

2. Anita Lowry, "A Consumer's Report on Humanities Databases," *Technicalities* 2 (August 1982): 1-3, 11-12; Peter Stern, "Online in the Humanities: Problems and Possibilities," *Journal of Academic Librarianship* 14 (1988): 161-164; Joyce Duncan Falk, "Database Characteristics and Search Problems in the Humanities," abstract, *Online '85 Conference Proceedings* (Weston, CT: Online, Inc., 1985), 102-106. A partial review of the literature on online databases in history, which omits important segments of it, Stuart F. Grinell, "Reference Service, Online Bibliographic Databases, and Historians," *RQ* 27 (Fall 1987): 106-111, with response by Joyce Duncan Falk, "Online Databases for History," *RQ* (Summer 1988): 594-595.

3. Elizabeth Futas, "Communication and Information Patterns in the Emerging Interdisciplinary Area of Women's Studies" (diss., Rutgers University, 1980), quoted by Ellen Gay Detlefsen, "Issues of Access to Information about Women," *Special Collections* 3 (Spring-Summer 1986): 164.

4. E.g., Joyce Duncan Falk, "The New Technology for Research in European Women's History: 'Online' Bibliographies," *Signs* 9 (Fall 1983): 120-33; idem, "In Search of History: The Bibliographic Databases," *The History Teacher* 15 (August 1982): 523-544; idem, "Researching Images of Women in Popular Culture and Art: Traditional and Computerized Tools," (paper delivered at the American Historical Association—Pacific Coast Branch Annual Meeting, San Francisco, CA, 12 August 1982): and others.

5. Suzanne Hildenbrand, "Women's Studies Online: Promoting Visibility," *RQ* 26 (Fall 1986): 63-74.

6. Sarah M. Pritchard, "Developing Criteria for Database Evaluation: The

Example of Women's Studies," *The Reference Librarian* 11 (Fall-Winter 1984): 247-61.

7. Falk, "Database Characteristics," and idem, "Researching Images of Women in Popular Culture."

8. Marcia J. Bates, "The Fallacy of the Perfect Thirty-Item Online Search," *RQ* 24 (Fall 1984): 43-50.

9. Bates, "Fallacy," discusses the reasons why patrons may mistakenly request inappropriate precision. A case in point is that patrons who do not understand the indexing and online searching of the history databases request historical period limits that are not appropriate to the research topic (Joyce Duncan Falk, "Searching by Historical Period in the History Databases," *National Online Meeting Proceedings, 1981* [Medford, NJ: Learned Information, 1981], 202-203). Connie Miller and Patricia Tegler, "Online Searching and the Research Process," *College & Research Libraries* 47 (July 1986): 370-373, point out the disadvantages of undue emphasis on precision and the often neglected contribution that online searching can make to the research process.

10. Detlefsen, "Issues of Access"; Ishbel Lochhead, "Bibliographic Control of Feminist Literature," *Catalogue & Index* 76-77 (Spring-Summer 1985): 10-15; Hildenbrand, "Women's Studies Online"; Falk, "The New Technology for Research"; Falk, "Researching Images of Women."

11. In addition to the manual *ESTC, The Eighteenth Century Short Title Catalogue,* 2d. ed. (Stanford: Research Libraries Group, 1986), see David Hunter, "Searching ESTC on RLIN," *Factotum* Occasional Paper 5 (March 1987): 3-22.

12. Joyce Duncan Falk and Susan K. Kinnell, *Searching America: History and Life (AHL) and Historical Abstracts (HA) on Dialog* (Santa Barbara, CA: ABC-Clio, 1987).

13. Joyce Duncan Falk, "Controlled and Free Vocabulary Indexing of the ABC-Clio Databases in History," *Data Bases in the Humanities and Social Sciences: Proceedings of the IFIP Working Conference . . .* (Amsterdam: North Holland, 1980): 309-313; idem, "America: History and Life Online: History and Much More," *Database* 6 (June 1983): 17. Schwartz, "Humanities," 634, mistakenly implies descriptors are a controlled vocabulary by stating that they are assigned from a thesaurus.

14. Falk, "America: History and Life Online," 17; Falk and Kinnell, *Searching,* 19.

15. Joyce Duncan Falk, "Survey of Online Searching in the Humanities in Four-year College and University Libraries" (ERIC document ED261687, 1986), 12-13.

16. See the Dialog documentation and Falk, "Database Characteristics."

17. Richard H. Lineback, *Philosopher's Index Thesaurus* (Bowling Green, OH: Philosophy Documentation Center, 1979); Mary Ellen Sievert, "The Philosopher's Index," *Database* 3 (March 1980): 50-61; Richard Lineback, "Philosopher's Index," *Urban Academic Librarian* 2 (1983): 86-91.

18. Additional quirks and advice are in Joyce Duncan Falk, "Artbibliographies Modern," *Urban Academic Librarian* 2 (1983): 92-95. The number of

classification heading (150) given in Schwartz, "Humanities," 650, is an error;
the 1979 Dialog documentation lists about 280 and that list was immediately out
of date as new terms are added each year. Also Schwartz's statement of an average of 10-12 descriptors per record is not borne out in my experience.

19. Falk, "Researching Images of Women in Popular Culture."

20. In addition to RLIN documentation, see Daniel Uchitelle, "RLIN and
Avery: The Online Index to Architectural Periodicals," *Database* 7 (December
1984): 66-69.

21. Michael Keller and Carol A. Lawrence, "Music Literature Indexes in
Review," *Notes: The Quarterly Journal of the Music Library Association*, 36
(March 1980): 595.

22. Ibid., 597.

23. Some information that supplements the Dialog documentation is in Naomi
Steinberger, "Selected Problems in Searching the RILM Database," *National
Online Meeting Proceedings, 1981* (Medford, NJ: Learned Information, 1981):
455-460.

24. Anita Lowry, "Searching the Humanities Online: An Analysis of the
FRANCIS Database," in *Data Bases in the Humanities and Social Sciences 1985*,
ed. Thomas F. Moberg (Osprey, FL: Paradigm Press, 1987): 261.

25. Robert E. Skinner, "Searching the History of Science Online," *Database*
6 (June 1983): 55-56. (But ignore the erroneous statement about historical period
searching in AHL and HA.)

26. *The ARTFL Project Newsletter* 3 (Winter 1987-88), 5. pp.; Alice Musick
McLean, Robert Morrissey, and Donald A. Ziff, "ARTFL: A New Tool for
French Studies," *Scholarly Communication* 8 (Spring 1987): 1, 6-9.

27. Marianne I. Gaunt, "Rutgers Inventory of Machine-Readable Texts in the
Humanities," in *The International Conference on Data Bases in the Humanities
and Social Sciences, 1983*, ed. Robert F. Allen (Osprey, FL: Paradigm Press,
1985), 283-288. "Records of Social Science Files Added to RLIN," *The Research Libraries Group News* 18 (Winter 1989): 18.

28. "The Medieval & Early Modern Data Bank," brochure ([Stanford, CA:
The Research Libraries Group], 1988).

29. David Everett and David M. Pilachowski, "What's in a Name? Looking
for People Online — Humanities," *Database* 9 (October 1986): 26-34. An example of context is the use of Turner thesis and the first name, Frederick(1w)Turner,
shown in James H. Sweetland, "America: History and Life — A Wide Ranging
Database," *Database* 6 (December 1983): 23-24. See also Falk and Kinnell,
Searching, 30-31.

30. Hildenbrand, "Women's Studies Online," 71.

31. Pritchard, "Developing Criteria," 256.

Social and Behavioral Sciences Databases

Ruth Dickstein
Karen Williams

SUMMARY. Women's Studies touches every aspect of the social sciences. Extricating specific sources on such an interdisciplinary topic from the vast network of social sciences information available online requires ingenuity. A comprehensive database for women's studies would simplify matters, but since no such service exists, searching often must be done in multiple files. This paper investigates selected topics in social sciences databases in order to determine which files offer the greatest precision, recall, and number of unique citations. It also examines the inclusion of articles from core women's studies journals in social sciences databases and the degree to which multiple file searching is necessary.

INTRODUCTION

Women's Studies scholarship is by definition interdisciplinary, with the disciplines of greatest interest to these scholars traditionally clustered in the social sciences. Suzanne Hildenbrand conducted a study at SUNY-Buffalo in 1985 offering free computer searches to anyone interested in literature relating to women. She found that most of the requesters were engaged in research involving one or more areas of the social sciences.[1] Elizabeth Futas' excellent dissertation about publishing in women's studies concluded that the discipline of women's studies belongs firmly in the social sciences.[2]

The social sciences themselves are equally interdisciplinary.

Ruth Dickstein and Karen Williams are Central Reference Librarians, University of Arizona Library, Tucson, AZ 85721.

Drinkwater points out that "It is frequently difficult to draw any kind of dividing line between subjects in the social sciences; an overlap of interests is probably more common than a clear distinction."[3] Similarly, Gardiner and Goodyear recognized that "subjects of research interest do not always come neatly divided into clear disciplinary categories."[4] Interdisciplinary inquiry requires doing research beyond the subject and methodological barriers of any one specialized field. Computer searching provides the mechanism to review a wide range of information sources quickly and easily across a broad array of subject areas. Given the varied interests of women's studies faculty and students, it is essential that the researcher understand how useful computer searching in the social science disciplines can be for scholarly work.

With the demise of the *Catalyst Resources for Women* database on BRS, due to a lack of staff and funding at the Catalyst library, women's studies researchers no longer have any resource devoted specifically to women's issues outside of the two print indexes, *Women Studies Abstracts* and *Studies on Women Abstracts*. To fill this gap it is important to identify the best databases for online searching on women and feminist issues in the social sciences.

OVERVIEW AND PURPOSE OF STUDY

Specific subject disciplines were targeted before reviewing the social sciences databases. The definition of social and behavioral sciences usually includes sociology, anthropology, psychology, economics, and political science.[5] Education, often considered a social science, is not included in this chapter, nor is political science, which is treated elsewhere. While anthropology is included and attempts were made to evaluate the selected databases from an anthropological viewpoint, Hildenbrand's conclusion that there is a "lack of significant anthropology coverage" remains valid.[6] There are no databases specific to anthropology, and other social science databases offer limited coverage. The current plan to convert the *Human Relations Area Files* microfiche to a full text CD-ROM database may lessen this problem.[7] However, this massive and expensive project still will not provide the same access to current periodical literature as do the standard periodical indexes.

The *Social Sciences Citation Index* challenged this study in the following statement from its "General Introduction":

> Because *SSCI* gives you in-depth, multidisciplinary coverage of the social sciences literature, there's no need to use several discipline-oriented indexes to achieve truly comprehensive searches. *SSCI* lets you start and finish a search with one reference tool.[8]

The idea of one database that will meet all needs is an attractive one but seems to experienced searchers too good to be true. This pilot study addresses the above claim as one of four study questions posed.

STUDY QUESTIONS

1. What are the most useful social science databases for finding women's studies materials?
2. Which database(s) offer the least duplication?
3. Is multiple file searching necessary and to what extent?
4. Which databases cover the core women's studies journals?

METHODOLOGY

Of the several commonly used methods for comparing and evaluating bibliographic databases,[9] the subject profile technique was selected because it is comparatively easy to implement and it provides information for answering the questions raised above. The subject methodology has been successfully used in several disciplines, including welfare and corrections, environmental sciences, criminal justice, and social work.[10] This type of study is divided into two parts. In the first part, a series of "hot topics" is run across a large number of databases as a screening mechanism to identify those with the best overall coverage. Part two of this technique entails developing general profile search strategies for several topics and running these strategies on the databases identified as most productive through the initial screening search. A third part was added to this study to determine coverage of the major women's studies journals in the selected databases.

PART I

Sixteen social science databases were selected for the screening search, but three had to be eliminated. *Work and Family Life* and *Population Bibliography* have been dropped by BRS and Dialog respectively. *Child Abuse and Neglect* was eliminated because it cannot be limited by year or update and does not contain citations to journal articles. *Agricola*, an agricultural database recommended by Hildenbrand as useful for searching women's economic role in the U.S., was added to the social science databases.[11]

The final phase of the screening search was then conducted on the thirteen databases listed below. The code used to identify these databases in subsequent charts is indicated in parentheses, preceded by the first year of coverage. Dialog was the vendor of choice; databases not available through Dialog were searched on BRS or WilsonLine.

> Abstracts of Working Papers in Economics 1972- (AWPE)
> Agricola 1970- (CAIN)
> Ageline 1978- (AARP)
> Economic Literature Index 1969- (ECON)
> ERIC 1966- (ERIC)
> Family Resources 1973- (NCFR)
> Mental Health Abstracts 1969- (MHAB)
> National Criminal Justice Research Service 1972- (NCJRS)
> PsycALERT (in-process file for PSYC) (PSAL)[12]
> PsycINFO 1967- (PSYC)
> Social SciSearch 1972- (SSCI)
> Social Sciences Index 1983- (SSI)
> Sociological Abstracts 1963- (SOCA)
> Social Work Abstracts 1977- (SWAB)

Searches were limited to the years 1983 through 1989 in order to compare data from the same range of years. Differences in backfile size do not figure in this study, although this factor would be important to those conducting comprehensive, retrospective searches.

Screening searches were done by entering one or more terms to represent a concept. Selection of terms for the screening search included at least one term to represent each of the specific social science disciplines selected for this study. "matriliny/matriarchy," for example, were chosen for anthropology, "dual careers" and "comparable worth" for economics. Most terms are interdisciplinary and could be of interest to scholars or students in sociology, psychology, economics, and/or social work.

Developing search strategy vocabulary for women's studies issues online is difficult. Hildenbrand, Drinkwater, Detlefsen, and Falk have documented a myriad of problems resulting from a lack of appropriate descriptors, poor indexing, new and changing terminology, variant spellings, difficulty in showing relationships, weaknesses in database construction, and the inability to focus on special populations (e.g., middle-aged women).[13] In order to contend with these problems, free text terms were used for the screening search. Some concepts were represented by truncated single word terms (feminis?, lesbian?), others required the use of one or more synonyms (housewi? or househusband? or homemaker?). Variants of the term "women" were used as a check to compare overall coverage of materials relating to women. Appendix I includes a complete list of the terms and search strategies for the screening search.

Table 1 shows the total postings per term(s) for each database. These are gross retrieval figures and will not make any fine distinctions between databases. The screening search identified the databases that appeared most promising and eliminated those with limited coverage. The seven databases with the greatest number of overall postings, *Social SciSearch*, *PsycINFO*, *ERIC*, *Sociological Abstracts*, *Family Resources*, *Social Sciences Index*, and *Agricola*, became the base for Part II of this study.

PART II

To ensure adequate subject coverage across disciplines, several databases were added to this core group of seven. The additional

TABLE 1. Screening Search

	AARP	AWPE	CAIN	ECON	ERIC	MHAB	NCFR	NCJRS	PSYC	SOCA	SSCI	SSI	SWAB
Feminism	12	0	17	7	719	153	509	116	610	4,578	1,207	780	63
Women	1,297	138	3,353	337	5,806	1,404	6,721	1,248	10,697	7,745	9,267	5,855	595
Females	3,390	114	6,186	1,216	23,554	33,619	2,614	5,072	31,179	14,670	9,968	618	967
Dual Careers	2	0	22	1	147	19	305	1	236	126	64	2	12
Displaced Homemakers	17	0	2	1	114	1	14	0	13	2	9	4	0
Housewife	155	0	90	5	320	38	102	16	256	177	89	76	23
Sex Bias	0	0	2	2	820	16	33	14	136	36	88	33	5
Incest	1	0	16	0	69	73	483	217	512	132	273	130	58
Rape	11	0	693	0	169	89	535	781	586	284	431	256	25
Homeless Women	1	0	0	0	2	1	8	2	7	15	6	7	6
Comparable Worth	6	8	10	27	102	0	37	0	32	33	221	57	4
Sexism	60	5	15	18	885	71	108	140	382	477	206	329	26
Marriage	378	85	359	133	1,284	588	4,013	226	7,132	2,515	1,642	13	311
Mothers	117	25	1,280	16	2,485	685	2,896	260	7,047	1,690	2,174	1,028	330
Prostitution	2	0	8	0	28	23	89	226	95	167	231	85	12
Matriliny	2	0	4	1	10	11	16	0	67	52	48	6	2
Lesbians	0	0	4	0	55	49	205	20	281	127	210	129	20
total	5,451	375	12,061	1,764	36,569	36,840	18,688	8,339	59,268	32,826	26,134	9,408	2,459

databases differed according to the topic, and included *PsycALERT*, a current extension of *Psychological Abstracts*, *Mental Health Abstracts*, *National Criminal Justice Reference Service*, *Economic Literature Index*, *Abstracts of Working Papers in Economics*, and *Ageline*. ERIC, recognized as the predominant database in education, was included to evaluate its coverage of other social science disciplines. For the purpose of comparison, *ERIC* searches were limited to journal articles as *ERIC* documents are rarely found in other databases. *ERIC* documents are, however, often relevant and useful, and a searcher seeking comprehensiveness will want to keep them in mind.

Three interdisciplinary profile searches were chosen for Part II of the study: divorce, battered women, and salary equity. *The Thesaurus of ERIC Descriptors*, *The Thesaurus of Psychological Index Terms*, *Women in LC's Terms: A Thesaurus of Library of Congress Subject Headings Relating to Women*, and *A Women's Thesaurus: An Index of Language Used to Describe and Locate Information by and about Women* were all consulted during the vocabulary development process.[14] Appendix II lists complete search strategies for the three topics. The same search strategy was used in all databases, and thus included both descriptors and free text terms.

Retrieval for these profile searches was large enough to justify limiting the time period to the years 1987 through 1989. Book reviews, editorials, letters, names of individuals, and ERIC documents were all excluded from retrieval. While these sources might be useful to researchers, they were excluded from this study for two reasons: to make the number of citations retrieved manageable, and to make the databases more comparable. Part II examined the total recall in each database, the percentage of that recall that was relevant, and the overlap between databases.

The retrieval was sorted by author, and full citations and descriptors were printed. Each citation was reviewed to determine whether or not it was relevant to the topic. If titles and descriptors were not enough to indicate relevance, abstracts were obtained. Relevance was defined as a primary focus on the search topic. As an example from the divorce search, if an article focused on why children fail in school, and divorce was only one of a number of factors, the citation was marked irrelevant. If the central purpose of the article was a study of school failure in children from divorced families, the citation was considered relevant. Tables 2, 3, and 4 show the total number of citations retrieved from each database, and the number and percentage considered relevant. The irrelevant citations were set aside, and the rest of this study focused on the relevant items.

The Relative Index of Uniqueness, devised by Daniel E. Meyer et al. for an overlap study on pesticide information, was used as a method of comparing and ranking the databases according to the percentage of unique documents retrieved.[15] To develop this index, the relevant citations were color-coded by database and taped to cards. All of these cards were then interfiled by author in order to place duplicate (identical) citations next to each other. Duplicate citations were banded together and counted as one card. A spreadsheet was constructed to tabulate and analyze the data. To compare the number of unique citations to the total number of cards, cards containing single citations were scored with a numerical weight of one in the spreadsheet column for that database. A citation that appeared in two databases was scored as 1/2 in each database column on the spreadsheet; citations appearing in three databases received 1/3 in three database columns, etc. Fractioning weighted each citation equally, regardless of the number of times it had been duplicated (each citation row had a sum of one '1'), and gave relatively greater weight to databases that generated more unique citations. The sum of each database column was divided by the total relevant citations to obtain the uniqueness factor (point percentage) for each database. A large point percentage total suggests a database with either (1) many citations (with duplicates in only a few databases), (2) multiple unique citations, or (3) a combination of the two.

Tables 2, 3, and 4 show the citation distributions which include the Uniqueness Factor, and the database rankings. The last line of the citation distribution chart labeled Percent Coverage is a recall figure or the percentage of the total number of relevant documents retrieved by the individual databases. The database rankings show (1) percentage of relevant retrieval, (2) uniqueness factor, and (3) percent coverage, with number one being the database that scored best for that particular factor.

TABLE 2. Battered Women

CITATION DISTRIBUTIONS

	CAIN	ERIC	MHAB	NCFR	NCJRS	PSAL	PSYC	SOCA	SSCI	SSI
Total Documents	12	43	20	184	167	22	93	73	50	47
Number Relevant	11	35	11	147	98	22	87	69	49	46
Percent Relevant	92%	81%	55%	80%	59%	100%	94%	95%	98%	98%
Uniqueness Index	0.015	0.053	0.015	0.269	0.183	0.043	0.145	0.106	0.064	0.062
Percent Coverage	3%	10%	3%	43%	28%	6%	25%	20%	14%	13%

DATABASE RANKINGS

Percent Relevant	Uniqueness	Percent Coverage
1. PSAL	1. NCFR	1. NCFR
2. SSCI & SSI	2. NCJRS	2. NCJRS
3. SOCA	3. PSYC	3. PSYC
4. PSYC	4. SOCA	4. SOCA
5. CAIN	5. SSCI	5. SSCI
6. ERIC	6. SSI	6. SSI
7. NCFR	7. ERIC	7. ERIC
8. NCJRS	8. PSAL	8. PSAL
9. MHAB	9. CAIN & MHAB	9. CAIN & MHAB

TABLE 3. Divorce

CITATION DISTRIBUTIONS

	CAIN	ERIC	MHAB	NCFR	NCJRS	PSAL	PSYC	SOCA	SSCI	SSI
Total Documents	59	118	14	452	62	55	250	197	168	123
Number Relevant	47	100	9	247	29	45	199	137	162	102
Percent Relevant	80%	85%	64%	55%	47%	82%	80%	70%	96%	83%
Uniqueness Factor	0.037	0.082	0.006	0.257	0.035	0.048	0.192	0.132	0.141	0.069
Percent Coverage	8%	16%	1%	39%	5%	7%	32%	22%	26%	16%

DATABASE RANKINGS

Percent Relevant
1. SSCI
2. ERIC
3. SSI
4. PSAL
5. PSYC & CAIN
6. SOCA
7. MHAB
8. NCFR
9. NCJRS

Uniqueness
1. NCFR
2. PSYC
3. SSCI
4. SOCA
5. ERIC
6. SSI
7. PSAL
8. CAIN
9. NCJRS
10. MHAB

Percent Coverage
1. NCFR
2. PSYC
3. SSCI
4. SOCA
5. SSI
6. ERIC
7. CAIN
8. PSAL
9. NCJRS
10. MHAB

TABLE 4. Salary Equity

CITATION DISTRIBUTIONS

	AARP	AWPE	CAIN	ECON	ERIC	NCFR	PSYC	SOCA	SSCI	SSI
Total Documents	10	13	14	39	68	46	55	58	168	68
Number Relevant	8	10	12	37	57	38	45	46	157	67
Percent Relevant	80%	77%	86%	95%	84%	83%	82%	79%	93%	99%
Uniqueness Factor	0.02	0.02	0.03	0.06	0.14	0.06	0.09	0.11	0.33	0.11
Percent Coverage	2%	3%	3%	11%	17%	11%	13%	13%	46%	20%

DATABASE RANKINGS

Percent Relevant

1. SSI
2. ECON
3. SSCI
4. CAIN
5. ERIC
6. NCFR
7. PSYC
8. AARP
9. SOCA
10. AWPE

Uniqueness

1. SSCI
2. ERIC
3. SOCA & SSI
4. PSYC
5. ECON & NCFR
6. CAIN
7. AARP & AWPE

Percent Coverage

1. SSCI
2. SSI
3. ERIC
4. SOCA
5. PSYC
6. ECON & NCFR
7. CAIN
8. AWPE
9. AARP

RESULTS

Social SciSearch (*SSCI*) stands out as the only database in which more than ninety percent of the recall was judged relevant in all searches. Subject searching in *SSCI* is limited to keywords in titles which, in these examples, accounted for the high percentage of relevance. *SSCI* fell behind other databases in uniqueness and percent coverage for the divorce and battered women searches. Descriptors and abstracts, available in many other databases, provide additional access points thereby increasing retrieval. *SSCI* was the best database overall for the salary equity search.

Social Sciences Index (*SSI*) and *SSCI* provide similar journal coverage, both in titles included and individual articles retrieved. These two were also the most fruitful sources for book reviews. *Social SciSearch* does include meeting abstracts, editorials, and several other publication types, although all of these were greatly outnumbered by journal articles in the retrieval. Publication type codes can be used to exclude any unwanted materials.

The *Family Resources* (NCFR) database ranked first for the divorce and battered women searches in both total recall and relative uniqueness. This can be attributed to the fact that *NCFR* indexes a wide variety of materials including books, journal articles, government documents, media, conference proceedings, and reports. The high marks in recall and uniqueness are offset, however, by several problems. Broad indexing lowers the precision (relevance). Forty-five percent of the divorce citations and twenty percent of the battered women citations were judged irrelevant. Poor authority control results in more internal duplication than found in any other database. Slight variations in the entry form of an author's name caused the same article to appear more than once, and many book entries were duplicated with only the pagination differing between entries. Journal indexing appears to be very selective. In several instances similar articles from two different issues of the same journal were both picked up by other databases, but only one of the articles showed up in *NCFR*. This database, nonetheless, is a gold mine for books, ephemera, fugitive publications, and other non-mainstream materials. Twenty-five percent of the items retrieved in the divorce search were not journal articles. Publication type codes should be used to exclude unwanted materials such as newsletters, professional agencies and organizations, and filmstrips.

PsycINFO ranked above *SSI* and *SSCI* for the divorce and battered women searches according to the uniqueness factor and percent coverage. As expected, it fell much lower in the salary equity search, an economic issue. *PsycALERT* is an in-process file for *PsycINFO* containing mostly very current citations. Late issues and newly acquired backfiles are also entered into *PsycALERT*. Several citations retrieved from *PsycALERT* were two or three years old, so both files should routinely be searched for retrospective materials. *Sociological Abstracts* and *PsycINFO* retrieved the greatest number of dissertations, a document type rarely included in other databases. *Sociological Abstracts* also includes many association papers and conference reports which are picked up only sporadically or not at all by most other databases.

National Criminal Justice Research Service was strong in its social science treatment of the battered women issue. The uniqueness factor placed *NCJRS* second to *NCFR* for this search. It should be noted that the percentage of irrelevant documents retrieved was high at forty-one percent. *NCJRS*, nonetheless, should certainly be included as an important database for criminal justice topics.

Mental Health Abstracts contributed very little to the results of any search. Recall was low, relevance was only at midrange, and *MHAB* ranks last in the uniqueness factor. *MHAB* was searched to determine if it would supplement *PsycINFO*, but there was almost complete overlap between the two. Although this sample is small, it may be safe to assume that *MHAB* would contribute only a small number of unique citations to most searches.

ERIC's journal coverage falls somewhere in the middle for the divorce and battered women searches, but very interestingly comes in second on the salary equity issue in terms of uniqueness. ERIC will be most useful for those family issues that overlap with schools such as day care or pregnant teens, and for workplace issues represented in the education profession. The *ERIC* database would undoubtedly move up in all rankings if ERIC documents had been included.

Abstracts of Working Papers in Economics (*AWPE*) and *Economic Literature Index* (*ECON*) were searched only for the salary equity issue, and the results were interesting. They did not rate highly in uniqueness, because the uniqueness factor shows which databases will retrieve the greatest amount of unique documents. Those databases that contribute a very small number of unique documents make a poor showing in this category. When time and cost are factored in, most searches are designed to retrieve the greatest number of unique citations. *AWPE* and *ECON*, however, include a number of very important economic documents and journals that are not picked up by the other social science databases. Although the actual retrieval was low, most of the documents retrieved were relevant and most were not duplicated in other social science databases. *AWPE* had some overlap with *Agricola*. No other database picked up these working papers issued by economic research organizations.

Ageline, likewise, produced only eight relevant documents but they were all unique citations. *Ageline* covers a variety of non-mainstream literature and selected journal articles on topics related to aging and the aged.

PART III

Part III of this study was an analysis of the inclusion (or lack thereof) of women's studies journals in the individual databases. Although the Futas study found that women's studies journals carry only a fraction of the total literature of the field, they are still an essential resource for women's studies scholars. Online access to the core journals also means that other social scientists studying women related issues will be exposed to women's studies scholarship and research. This part of the study was designed to determine which of the major women's studies periodicals are accessible online. A list of the academic journals recommended for inclusion in the forthcoming edition of *Magazines for Libraries* was obtained.[16] To this list were added social science journals recommended in Susan Searing's *Introduction to Library Research in Women's Studies*[17] (see Appendix III for the journal list). These journal titles were then searched across all of the original files except *AWPE* (it does not index journals). For these searches, BRS was the vendor of choice. It was easiest to search journal titles by limiting a free text version of the title to the source field on BRS. On DIALOG it is necessary to expand on the journal field to identify the correct journal titles. The most recent citations were printed to determine currency of coverage, and accuracy of the journal title. *ERIC*, for example, indexes several journals with the word "Frontiers" in the title. A special search strategy for *Frontiers* had to be devised to exclude the incorrect titles.

One journal, *Women's Studies Quarterly*, did not appear in any databases. Table 5 lists by journal title the databases in which the remaining eleven titles were located. The number on the first line is the total number of postings for that title. The number on the second line indicates the volume, issue number in parenthesis, and year of the most recent citation. While it is difficult to determine whether each journal included was indexed selectively or comprehensively, it is certainly easy to note when few articles from a journal title were retrieved. Different databases cover different periods of time, a low number of postings indicates an extremely selective coverage of the journal. In order to compare coverage, one must consider the time period covered by each database (listed in the database matrix). Because *SSCI* also includes letters to the editor, books reviews, and editorials for each title, the search was limited to retrieve journal articles only. Book reviews were also eliminated from the retrieval in the *Social Sciences Index*.

Agricola and *Economic Literature* are noteworthy for their total exclusion of the core journals, while *Social Work Abstracts*, *Ageline*, and *NCJRS* list fewer than fifteen articles per journal title. *ERIC* indexes several titles, but each very selectively as indicated by the variations in the total number of citations. The same is true for *NCFR*. The depth of coverage provided by *NCFR* must be questioned considering that its coverage of six current titles is noticeably selective.

As for the journals themselves, *Signs* and *Psychology of Women Quarterly* are well covered, and so, to a lesser extent, are *Sex Roles*, *Frontiers*, and *Feminist Studies*. Some journals are dropped from comprehensive to selective indexing or dropped altogether over time. *Women's Studies International Forum* has not been indexed since 1983. The same is true of *Connexions* and *Feminist Studies*, found in *PSYC* only through 1985 and 1980 respectively.

TABLE 5. Journal Title Search

	AARP	ERIC	MHAB	NCFR	NCJRS	PSYC	PSAL	SOCA	SSCI	SSI	SWAB
CONNEXIONS						100 (46)85					
FEMINIST REVIEW										63 30(aut)88	
FEMINIST STUDIES	1 12(3)86			81 14(1)88		5 6(2)80		108 13(3)87	224 14(3)88	209 14(3)88	
FRONTIERS		1 1(3)76		13 4(3)79				64 9(3)87	39 10(2)88		
PSYCHOLOGY OF WOMEN Q	4 12(1)88	344 12(1)88	30 7(1)82	108 12(2)88	1 10(2)86	381 12(1)88		182 11(3)87	399 12(4)88	198 12(3)88	15 7(4)83
RFR/DFR	1 11(2)82	2 9(4)81						36 16(4)87			
SEX ROLES		518 18(7/8)88	347 18(3/4)88	578 18(11/12)88	6 17(1/2)87	799 18(11/12)88	47 19(3/4)88	537 17(9/10)87	1021 19(7/8)88	716 19(5/6)88	
SIGNS	1 5(1)80	106 13(4)88		174 13(4)88	10 8(3)83	179 13(2)88	3 13(4)88	292 13(2)87	452 14(1)88	267 14(1)88	
WOMEN & POLITICS				26 7(4)87				52 7(2)87			
WOMEN & THERAPY			38 6(3)87	61 6(3)87		197 6(3)87	8 7(1)88		439 11(6)88		
WOMEN STUD INTL FORUM			10 6(4)83								

The top line of each entry indicates the the total number of postings and the second line indicates the volume, issue and year of the most recent citation.

The two comprehensive social science databases, *Social Sciences Index* and *Social SciSearch*, index more comprehensively and more rapidly than any of the other databases. Their overlap in coverage is considerable. Of the seven journals covered by the two indexes, four are covered by both, one is unique to *SSI* and two unique to *SSCI*. *SSCI* contains the most current citations with *SSI* a close second. Since they also index more of the core journal titles, one or the other should be part of a comprehensive search in the social sciences when including the greatest number of key women's studies journals is important.

CONCLUSION

The results of this pilot study suggest that no one database will provide comprehensive coverage for women's studies topics in the social sciences. Generally, searches on interdisciplinary topics should include a combination of databases beginning with either the *Social Sciences Index* or *Social SciSearch*. The overlap between these two databases is considerable in both retrieval of relevant citations and coverage of women's studies journals. Psychology topics provide the exception to this generalization. *PSYC* outperformed both *SSI* and *SSCI* on issues related to psychology. The most productive psychology searches will combine *PSYC* with an another appropriate specialty database.

With the exception of *PSYC*, the specialty databases do not stand out as more comprehensive or unique than their broader counterparts overall. For certain focused topics, especially in economics, searching one or two of the specialty databases in addition to the broader sources would be productive in terms of finding unique documents. In these cases, the searcher should be prepared to retrieve a significant number of irrelevant documents in addition to a few unique sources. For example, *NCJRS* ranked second in terms of uniqueness for the battered women search, but 41% of the documents retrieved were irrelevant.

Lacking a comprehensive women's studies database, multiple file searching will continue to be a necessity for online literature retrieval in the social sciences. The National Women's Studies Association, in conjunction with several other groups such as the National Council for Research on Women, has taken the first step toward meeting the needs of scholars with their development of a work-in-progress database which will include research, articles, working papers, research and policy resources, curricula, art, media, planning documents, and reports of innovative social service projects, all relating to, by and about women. This database is scheduled to be publicly available through the Research Libraries Information Network (RLIN) in 1989.[18] At present, this database will complement existing resources; it is hoped that this new project will expand in the future to become a comprehensive core database for women's studies.

REFERENCES

1. Suzanne Hildenbrand, "Women's Studies Online: Promoting Visibility." *RQ* 26 (Fall 1986) :63-74.

2. Elizabeth Futas, *Communication and Information Patterns in the Emerging, Interdisciplinary Area of Women's Studies*. New Brunswick, NJ: Graduate School of Library Science, 1980. Dissertation.

3. Claire Drinkwater, "Social and Behavioral Sciences." *Manual of Online Search Strategies*, ed. Chris J. Armstrong and J. A. Large (Aldershot, England: Gower, 1988) :120-133.

4. Trudy Gardiner and Mary Lou Goodyear, "The Inadequacy of Subject Retrieval." *Special Libraries* 68(May/June 1977) :193-197.

5. Drinkwater, "Social and behavioral sciences," 469.

6. Hildenbrand, "Women's Studies Online," 70.

7. David Levinson and Richard A. Wagner, "From Microfiche to CD-ROM: Converting the Human Relations Area Files Full-Text Database," *12th International Online Information Proceedings*, (Oxford: Learned Information, 1988), 671-677.

8. "Guide and Lists of Source Publications," *Social Sciences Citation Index*, (Philadelphia: ISI, 1986), 8.

9. Carol Tenopir, "Evaluation of Database Coverage: a Comparison of Two Methodologies." *Database* 2 (March 1979) :423-439.

10. Vidya S. Sharma, "A Comparative Evaluation of OnlineDatabases in Relation to Welfare and Corrective Services and Community Development." *Online Review* 6 (August 1982) :297-313; Daniel E. Meyer et al., "Comparison Study of Overlap Among 21 Scientific Databases in Searching Pesticide Information." *Online Review* 7 (January 1983) :33-43; Donna R. Dolan and Carol Heron, "Criminal Justice Coverage in Online Databases." *Database* 2 (March 1979) :10-32; Henry N. Mendelsohn, "Social Work Online." *Database* 7 (August 1984) :36-49.

11. Hildenbrand, "Women's Studies Online," 65.

12. *PsycAlert* was not used in the screening search but was used in the more extensive search.

13. Hildenbrand, "Women's Studies Online" 66-71; Drinkwater, "Social and Behavioral Sciences" 491-492; Ellen Gay Detlefsen, "Issues of Access to Information about Women," *Special Collections* 3 (Spring-Summer 1986) :165-167; Joyce Duncan Falk, "The New Technology for Research in European Women's History: Online Bibliographies," *Signs* 9 (Autumn 1983) :120-133.

14. *Thesaurus of ERIC Descriptors*, 11th ed. (Phoenix : Oryx, 1987); *Thesaurus of Psychological Index Terms*, 5th ed. (Washington: American Psychological Association, 1988); May Ellen S. Capek, ed. *A Women's Thesaurus: An Index of Language Used to Describe and Locate Information By and About Women*. (New York: Harper & Row, 1987); Ruth Dickstein, Victoria A. Mills, and Ellen J. Waite, *Women in LC's Terms: A Thesaurus of Library of Congress Subject Headings Relating to Women*. (Phoenix: Oryx, 1988).

15. Meyer, "Comparison Study of Overlap," 34.

16. Bernice Lacks, Vassar College Library is the consultant on Women's Studies for William Katz and Linda Sternberg Katz, *Magazines for Libraries*. Sixth edition. (New York: Bowker, in progress)

17. Susan Searing, *Introduction to Library Research in Women's Studies*, (Boulder: Westview Press, 1985).

18. "NWSA Collaborates With The National Council for Research on Women in Database Project," *NWSAction* 2 (Spring 1989) :4.

APPENDIX I. Search Strategy -- Screening Search

DIALOG	BRS	WILSON
feminis??	feminis$2	feminism or feminist#
wom?n	wom#n	wom#n
dual()career? ?	dual adj career$1	dual adj career#
displaced() (homemaker? ? or housewi??? or househusband? ?)	displaced adj (homemaker$1 or housewi$3 or househusband$1)	displaced adj homemaker# or displaced adj housewife or displaced adj housewives or displaced adj househusband#
(gender or sex)()bias	(gender or sex) adj bias	gender adj bias or sex adj bias
incest or incestuous	incest or incestuous	incest or incestuous

rape? ? or rapist? ?	rape$1 rapist$1	rape# or rapist#
comparable()worth	comparable adj worth	comparable adj worth
sexism or sex()discrimination	sexism or sex adj discrimination	sexism or sex adj discrimination
marriage? ? or marry or married	marriage$1 or marry or married	marriage# or marry or married
mother????	mother$4	mother# or motherhood
lesbian????	lesbian$3	lesbian# or lesbianism
prostitut???	prostitut$3	prostitute# or prostitution
matrilin? or matriarch?	matrilin$ or matriarch$	matrilin: or matriarch:
homeless()wom?n	homeless adj wom$n	homeless adj wom#n

93

APPENDIX II. Search Strategy for Divorce

divorce or   alimony or palimony or child()(custody or support) or
spousal()support   or   annulment   or   prenuptial()agreement   or
displaced()homemaker? ? or joint()custody or marital()separation

Search Strategy for Battered Women

1. battered()(wom?n or spouse? ? or wife or wives or husband?
   ? or lesbian? ?)

2. (spous? ? or wife or husband or lesbian)()abuse

3. (lesbian or spouse or wife or husband)()battering

4. (domestic or marital)()violence

5. abused()(wife or wives or husband? ? or spouse? ? or lesbian?
   ?)

6. crisis()shelter? ?

7. s1 or s2 or s3 or s4 or s5 or s6

Search Strategy for Salary Equity

1. comparable()worth

2. pay()equity

3. ((equal()pay or economic()equity or wage()discrimination or
   salary()differential)) and (wom?n or female? ?)

4. s1 or s2 or s3

APPENDIX III. Titles Included in the Journal Search (Part III)

Connexions

Feminist Review

Feminist Studies

Frontiers

Psychology of Women's Quarterly

RFR/DRF (Resources for Feminist Research/Documentation sur la
Recherche Feministe)

Sex Roles

Signs

Women & Politics

Women & Therapy

Women's Studies International Forum

Women's Studies Quarterly

Exploring the Coverage
of Women
in Biomedical Databases

Donna R. Dolan

SUMMARY. The coverage of women in major biomedical databases was analyzed subjectively by means of a profile of "hot topics" representing current issues and a searching hedge for women. The hedge classified terms for women in several categories: gender, occupational, positive, negative or biomedical. *MEDLINE, EMBASE, Comprehensive Core Medical Library, BIOSIS Previews, SCISEARCH*, and *PsycINFO* offer the best coverage of women in biomedicine, but specialized databases, such as *MEDLINE References on AIDS*, should be considered for some topics.

Conceptual issues in the online searching of women in biomedicine discussed in this paper include:

- the use of controlled vs. free text terms as represented in thesauri and the jargon of the discipline;
- the distinction between "women" (i.e., human females) as cultural, sociological, political, and psychological beings and "females" (a term which applies to all species) identified by their sexual and reproductive functions;
- the differentiation of women from men, especially important in professions dominated by one sex or the other and in diseases or processes which occur primarily in one sex or the other;

Donna R. Dolan is Quality Control Specialist, BRS Information Technologies, Inc., Latham, NY 12110.

- the identification of women as authors/researchers or women as subjects; and
- the accessibility of alternative opinions/controversial literature on women.

System features that aided in the compilation of this chapter are mentioned in the text, most notably the BRS hypertext LINK between databases with a commonality of subjects, coverage, or vocabulary. More hypertext features are expected in the future. The author speculates that more could be determined about the online coverage of women by exploring the coverage of men.

APPROACH TO THE TOPIC

This chapter focuses on the biological and psychological woman: woman as the subject (both literally and figuratively) of biomedical databases; woman as mother, as female, as wife and as wage-earner; woman in both positive and negative roles. Since this chapter focuses on women as subjects, it makes no attempt to uncover women as authors or contributors to the discipline. The approach is dual. Through a sampling of "hot topics" about women the chapter attempts to investigate the topicality of biomedical databases. Those databases that provide the best coverage of "hot topics" are further examined through a search strategy incorporating gender, occupational, positive, negative and biomedical terms for women.

HOT TOPICS

A "hot topic" is a subject, such as abortion rights, that seems to be ubiquitous in the media. A profile incorporating six "hot topics" from "women physicians" to "PMS" was strategized (Figure 1). This profile of biomedical issues concerning women was run on BRS. The purpose of this procedure was to determine which databases to consult on a new or novel topic, and secondarily to decide which databases to focus on. The assumption was that if a database covered a women's "hot topic," it would offer broad coverage of the sex as a whole.

Figure 2 summarizes the results of running the "hot topics" pro-

Figure 1

Hot Topics Profile for Women in Biomedicine

    1   (WOM$N FEMALE$1) WITH (MD MDS PHYSICIAN$1 DOCTOR$1)

    2   (MOTHER$4 MATERNAL LACTATI$ PREGNAN$4 BREASTFEED$3 (BREAST
ADJ (FEED$3 FED))) SAME (SMOKE SMOKING CIGARETTE$ TOBACCO)

    3   PMS OR (PREMENSTRUAL ADJ (SYNDROME$1 TENSION$1))

    4   (AIDS (ACQUIRED ADJ (IMMUNE IMMUNDEF) WITH SYNDROME)) SAME
(BABY BABIES INFANT$1 INFANCY NEONAT$4 NEWBORN$1)

    5   GAIA

    6   (SURROGA$4 HOST$1) WITH MOTHER$4

    7   1 OR 2 3 4 5 6
        RESULT

NOTES:

$ - indicates truncation
$n - indicates number of terms in a word ending.

file against a range of thirteen biomedical databases. Figure 3 lists and ranks the top eleven biomedical databases for women's "hot topics," while Figure 4 summarizes this data into a handy chart. The remainder of this chapter concentrates on those databases that were consistently in the top five, not suprisingly, the omnibus biomedical databases.

The "hot topics" results have implications for selective dissemination of information (SDI) searches. *Medical and Psychological Previews*, *PsycALERT*, *Comprehensive Core Medical Library*, and *Current Contents* should always supplement a "hot topical" search because documents will percolate there before they appear in the omnibus databases. In fact, *Previews* and *PsycALERT* were designed as companion files to *MEDLINE* and *PsycINFO*, respectively, to provide timely online access to newly published literature. Consulting these two current sources is like running an SDI on your biomedical topic *at the same time as the retrospective search*.

In some cases, the "hot topic" itself suggests the use of a specialty database. The case of the "AIDS babies" search provides an example. Choosing the hot issues subset of *MEDLINE, MEDLINE*

Figure 2
Results of Hot Topics Profile Run on
Selected Biomedical Databases
February 12, 1989

DATABASE	NO. OF CITATIONS ON ALL HOT TOPICS	TYPE OF DATABASES (A)ABSTRACT, (C)ITATIONS, (F)ULL TEXT	TIME SPAN	EARLIEST CITATION	LATEST CITATION
BIOSIS (BIOZ)	2959	A	1970-Feb.1989	1969	Nov. 1988
CANCERLIT (CANR)	1169	A	1980-Feb.1989	1978	Dec. 1988
CA Search (CHEM)	245	C	1977-Jan.1989	1976	1988
Comprehensive Core Medical Library (CCML)	2243	F	Varies by source journal generally mid-1985 to Feb. 89	1981	Feb. 9, 1989
Current Contents	171	Tables of Contents	12 month rolling file	Jan. 1988	Dec. 1988
EMBASE (EMEZ)	4094	A	1974-Iss. 4 1989	1973	1988
Health Planning & Administration (HLTH)	1914		1975-Dec. 1988	July 1974	July 1988
International Pharmaceutical Abstracts (IPAB)	265	A	1970-Jan. 1989	April 1970	May 1988
MEDLINE (MESZ)	7175	A	1966-Mar. 1989 (2nd update)	Oct. 1965	Sep. 1988
Medical and Psychological Previews (PREV)	37	C	Jul.1988-Feb.9,1989	June 1988	Jan-Feb. 1989
PsycINFO (PSYC)	1148	A	1966-Mar. 1989	1967	Sep. 1988
PsycALERT (PSAL)	52	C	Feb. 6, 1989	April 1988	Dec. 1988
SCISEARCH (SCIS)	2263	C with references	1974-1989 Week 4	1973	Jan. 1989

Figure 3
Zeroing in on the Hot Topics:
Where to find what

TOPIC	BIOZ	CANR	CCML	CHEM	EMEZ	HLTH	MESZ	PREV	PSAL	PSYC	SCIS
Women Physicians			2		4	3	1			5	
Maternal Smoking	3		4		2	6	1				5
PMS	3		5		2		1				4
AIDS Babies	6	2	3		4		1				5
Gaia	3		4				1				2
Surrogate Mothers	2		4		3		1				5
TOTAL RANKING	4		3		2	6	1				5

NOTES: Abbreviations are expanded in Figure 2.
Complete retrospective files searched for BIOSIS, EMBASE, MEDLINE and SCISEARCH.

99

Figure 4
Recommended Databases for Women's Hot Topics
(Searches Run February 12, 1989)

Characteristic	Databases	Postings
Highest Postings	MEDLINE	7175
	EMBASE	4094
	CCML	3343
	BIOSIS	2959

Characteristic	Databases	Citation Date
Most Current Citations	CCML	Feb. 9, 1989
	SCISEARCH	Jan. 1989
	Medical and Psychological Previews	Jan.- Feb.1989
	Current Contents	Dec. 1988
	CANCERLIT	Dec. 1988
	PsycALERT	Dec. 1988

Characteristic	Databases	
Earliest Citations	MEDLINE	Oct. 1965
	BIOSIS	1969
	Intl. Pharmaceutical Abstracts	Apr. 1970

References on AIDS, actually substitutes for the AIDS concept of
the search. Only the "infant" concept of the search need be formulated because of the database selection:

```
MRAI 1983-MAR 1989 (89032)       (Turn on automatic plurals
BRS SEARCH MODE - ENTER QUERY     feature so that only singular
   1_:  ..set plurals=on           form of terms need be entered.)

SET HAS BEEN COMPLETED
BRS SEARCH MODE - ENTER QUERY
   1_:  baby infant neonat$ newborn (new adj born)
   RESULT       995 DOCUMENTS
   2_:  pregnan$4 perinatal$       (Bare bones strategy representing
   RESULT       545 DOCUMENTS      "infant" run against the
   3_:  1 or 2                     specialty database, MEDLINE
   RESULT      1254 DOCUMENTS      REFERENCES on AIDS.)
   4_:  (1 or 2).ti,mj.
   RESULT       294 DOCUMENTS
   5_:  ..p 4 ti/1-5
*SEARCH 4              MRAI           SCREEN 1 OF 2*
           1 OF 294
TI  [AIDS AND RELATED SYNDROMES IN INFANTS IN BRAZZAVILLE (LETTER)].
```

TI DRUG USE IN PREGNANCY: PARAMETERS OF RISK.

TI OBSERVATIONS ON BREAST FEEDING AND THE RISK OF INFANT HIV
INFECTION [LETTER].

TI [AIDS, ATL AND STD: STD AND VERTICAL INFECTION FROM THE MOTHER
TO THE INFANT].

· TI [PREVALENCE OF HTLV-1 VIRUS IN PREGNANT WOMEN IN BLACK AFRICA].

MAJOR BIOMEDICAL DATABASES

The following databases were chosen for in-depth consideration because of the results of the "hot topics" profile and because they dominate the biomedical field:

DATABASE	PRODUCER	SYSTEM
Biosis Previews	BIOSIS	BRS, DIALOG
Comprehensive Core Medical Library (CCML)	BRS	BRS
EMBASE	Excerpta Medica	BRS, DIALOG
MEDLINE	National Library of Medicine	BRS, DIALOG
PSYCINFO	American Psychological Association	BRS, DIALOG
SCISEARCH	Institute for Scientific Information	BRS, DIALOG

The BRS system was searched almost exclusively because of the author's familarity with it and because it offers most of the omnibus as well as several specialty biomedical databases. BRS also offered several system features which simplified the retrieval and analysis of women's biomedical literature. These features are discussed below where relevant. It should be emphasized that this chapter focuses on the databases' coverage of women and are not on a comparison of search services. As the matrices indicate, these databases are generally available on other vendors as well.

A HEDGE FOR WOMEN
IN BIOMEDICAL DATABASES

A hedge, a group of related terms on the broad subject of women, was developed (Figure 5) and cross-searched on *MEDLINE*, *BIOSIS*, *EMBASE*, *SCISEARCH*, and *CCML*. The hedge for women was compiled from the following sources:

- controlled vocabularies for *MEDLINE*, *BIOSIS*, *EMBASE*, and *PsycINFO*;
- *Women's Thesaurus: An Index of Language Used to Describe and Locate Information by and about Women* (Capek, 1987);
- strategic system features; and
- several biomedical searchers who reviewed the hedge.

The hedge underwent several revisions over the course of the project and should continue to be revised. The hedge is an organized array of terms—an approach to searching women—not a strategy per se. The hedge is not comprehensive in scope but only indicative of the ways to describe women.

The Hedge and the BRS System

The hedge uses BRS searching conventions. A dollar sign ($) indicates internal or word ending truncation; a dollar sign followed by a number indicates how many characters may follow a truncation.

The BRS system features ROOT and PREF were instrumental in the formulation of the hedge. ROOT displays for selection in a search all terms beginning with the same root, such as *wife*:

```
PSYC PSYCINFO 1966-JUN 1989
BRS SEARCH MODE - ENTER QUERY
1_:   root wife

R1    WIFE                    1435 DOCUMENTS
R2    WIFEBEATERS                1 DOCUMENT
R3    WIFEBEATING                2 DOCUMENTS
R4    WIFEHOOD                   3 DOCUMENTS
R5    WIFELY                     3 DOCUMENTS
R6    WIFES                    344 DOCUMENTS

END OF ROOT OR PREF
1_:   r1 or r4-r6
      RESULT          1660 DOCUMENTS
```

Figure 5

A Hedge for Women
Gender, Occupational, Positive, Negative and Biomedical Terms

I.   Gender Terms That Imply Women (Human Females)

      Woman Women
      @Female$1 Femini$
      Wife Wives @Mother$4 @Maternal$2 Mom Moms
      Stepmother$1 Stepdaughter$1
      Daughter$1 Sister$4 Grandmother$2 Grandaughter$2 Aunt$1
      Niece$1 Girl$1 Girlhood
      Widow$1 Widowhood Matron$1 Madam$2
      Maternity Childbirth
      Gyn$2colog$ Obstetric$2
      Lesbian$3 *Prostitut$3

II.   Occupational Terms

      Midwi$ Housewi$ Homemak$3 Housekeeper$1 Laywom$n
      Businesswom$n Barmaid$1
      *Nurse$1 Secretar$3 Waitress$ Seamstress$ Governess$ Coeds
      *Librarian$4 (*Social adj Worker$1) (*Dental adj Hygienist$1)
      Debutante$1 (Prima adj Donna$1)

III. Postive Terms

      Goddess$2 Madonna$1 Priestess$ Diva Divas Heroine$1
      Matriarch$ Virgin$1 Nun$1 Bride$1 Bridal
      Mail$3 Mermaid$1
      Lady Ladies @Queen$2 Princess$2 Duchess$2 Countess$2
      Baroness$2

IV.   Negative Terms

      @Bitch$2 Hausfrau
      Gypsy Gypsies *Witch$ Sorceress$ Wench$2 Crone$1 Spinster$1
      Mistress$2 Hooker$1 Slut Sluts
      Whore$1 Harlot$1 Concubine$1 @Vixen$1
      Matricid$ Misogyn$
      Sexis$1
      Butch adj Femme

V.   Biomedical Terms (@: most terms may also apply to animals)

      Abortion$1
      Breastfe$ (Breast adj (Feed$3 Fed)) Lactat$3
      Milk with Human
      Mastectom$
      Mammar$3 Mamma$1
      Menstru$ Menses   May refer to other primates
      Premenstru$ PMS
      Menarche Menopaus$ Estr$2s
      Climacteric Amenorrh$ @Pregnant @Pregnanc$3
      Gravid$2 Primigravid$2 Puerper$
      Luteal Luteum (Fallopian adj Tube$1) (Tubal adj Ligation$1)
      Ovary Ovarian Anovulat$ Ovum Ovulat$
      Uterine Uterus Utero$ Womb$1 Vagina$1 Endometri$4
      Hysterect$ Hystero$

Consider Also: Reproductive Issues: Fertility, Infertility,
Conception, Contraception, Abortion, Birth Control, Genetics,
Sterilization, Voluntary & Involuntary.

Figure 5 (continued)

```
VI.     Non-Sexist Terms

        Human$3 Person$1 People
        @Mate$1 Spous$2 Partner$1
        Parent$2 Adult$1 Elderly (Middle adj (Age Aged)
        Child Children
        Family Families Familial
        Homeless
        Inmate$1 Incarcerated Criminal$1 Prisoner$1 Inpatient$1
        Patient$1 Student$1
        Subjects SS
        Worker$1 Employee$2
        Disabled Handicapped Retarded
        @Gender$1
        Sex adj Role$1
        Consider other collective nouns, e.g.: Crowd$1, Group$1,
           Voter$1, Legislator$1

Key:    $    Indicates truncation
        $#   Indicates number of letters following truncation
        @    May be animal
        *    May be male, but are traditionally female-dominant
        adj Adjacent

Note:   For more precision, exclude author fields.
```

PREF is the inverse of ROOT and displays for later search selection terms ending in the same suffix. For this chapter, the feature was especially useful when the suffix indicated sex, as in the case of *ess*. When "PREFed," *ess* unearthed such unusual terms as *murderess*, *authoress*, *foundress* and even *laundress*, which were not included in the hedge for women.

The ROOT and PREF features, used in tandem, are powerful tools for supplementing search terms and uncovering like terms:

```
PSYC PSYCINFO 1966-JUN 1989
BRS SEARCH MODE - ENTER QUERY
      1_:   root woman
R1       WOMAN                                   4076 DOCUMENTS
R2       WOMANCHILD                                 1 DOCUMENT
R3       WOMANHOOD                                 45 DOCUMENTS
R4       WOMANISM                                   1 DOCUMENT
R5       WOMANIST                                   1 DOCUMENT
R6       WOMANIZER                                  1 DOCUMENT
R7       WOMANIZING                                 2 DOCUMENTS
R8       WOMANKIND                                  1 DOCUMENT
R9       WOMANLESS                                  1 DOCUMENT
R10      WOMANLINESS                                4 DOCUMENTS
R11      WOMANLY                                    2 DOCUMENTS
R12      WOMANS                                  1206 DOCUMENTS

END OF ROOT OR PREF
      1_:   r1-r12
         RESULT         5167 DOCUMENTS
      2_:   root women
R1       WOMEN                                  21344 DOCUMENTS
R2       WOMEN-ENDORSING-DISCRIMINALIZAT            1 DOCUMENT
R3       WOMENS                                  3761 DOCUMENTS
```

```
R4       WOMENS-LIBERATION-MOVEMENT          351 DOCUMENTS

END OF ROOT OR PREF
         2_:  r1-r4
         RESULT           22802 DOCUMENTS
         3_:  1 or 2                         (Terms resulting from both
         RESULT           26604 DOCUMENTS     ROOTs are ORed.)
         4_:  pref woman                     (Same term is PREFed.)
R1       WOMAN                               4076 DOCUMENTS
R2       WOMEN                              21344 DOCUMENTS
R3       WOMANS                              1206 DOCUMENTS
R4       WOMENS                              3761 DOCUMENTS
R5       AIRWOMEN                               1 DOCUMENT
R6       ANTIPOLICEWOMEN                        1 DOCUMENT
R7       ANTIWOMAN                              1 DOCUMENT
R8       ANTIWOMEN                              1 DOCUMENT

             .
R39      TOWNSWOMEN                             1 DOCUMENT
R40      TRIBESWOMAN                            1 DOCUMENT
R41      UNDERCLASSWOMEN                        1 DOCUMENT
R42      UPPERCLASSWOMEN                        1 DOCUMENT
R43      WORKING-WOMEN                       1218 DOCUMENTS
R44      WORKWOMEN                              1 DOCUMENT

END OF ROOT OR PREF
         4_:  r1-r44
         RESULT           26625 DOCUMENTS
         5_:  3 or 4                         (For a final
         RESULT           26638 DOCUMENTS     result, the ROOTed
                                             and PREFed terms
                                             are ORed.)
```

The majority of the terms included in the hedge are biomedical. Terms such as *Mrs.* (magnetic resonance spectrum), which cause obvious false drops or terms such as *wifely* or *virago*, which cause zero results have been left out of the hedge or eliminated strategically. Terms such as *Equal Rights Amendment* and *suffrage* which slant toward other disciplines are excluded. Avoiding terms in the author (*Hooker*, E.Z.) or institution paragraphs (Our *Lady* of Lourdes Medical Center) provides more precise results. Searchers must make judgements about the array of terms offered depending upon the context of the search. Searchers are advised to evaluate the hedge for their own use, supply their own operators and consult controlled vocabularies when appropriate.

CLASSIFICATIONS FOR WOMEN: THE POSITIVE AND THE NEGATIVE

The hedge classifies terms for women according to gender and includes occupational terms, as well as positive and negative epithets. Depending upon the slant of a search request, searchers may want to choose terms selectively from each group. Although searchers may disagree with the placement of terms in the various categories, the objective behind the categories—to explore the presentation of women in the biomedical databases—was accomplished. On the whole, women are presented objectively in biomedical databases, probably more so than in humanities and social sciences files. In *BIOSIS*, the only *gypsy* is the moth, *witches* are brooms (the plant), and *Crone* is an author. The hedge may also be useful for searches on databases in the humanities and social sciences. On those databases, however, terms such as *virgin, bride, priestess*, and *goddess* are much more heavily posted. For humanities and social science databases, searchers may want to add terms peculiar to those disciplines such as *supermom, amazons, second sex*, or *fair sex*. On *ARTS AND HUMANITIES SEARCH* (AHCI), even the names of specific goddesses, terms such as *Athena, Artemis*, and *Aphrodite*, may be relevant (Bolen, 1984).

In biomedical databases the terms *bitch, vixen*, and *shrew* are used in their precise animal senses; in *AHCI* they retrieve negative references to human females:

- THE DOVER BITCH, VICTORIAN DUCK OR MODERN-IST DUCKRABBIT.
- SWINBURNE'S DIVINE BITCHES—AGENTS OF DE-STRUCTION AND SYNTHESIS.
- CLIO AND THE BITCH GODDESS—QUANTIFICATION IN AMERICAN POLITICAL HISTORY—BOGUE, GA.

In *SOCIAL SCISEARCH*, on the other hand, these pejorative terms for women retrieve a mixed bag of references:

- A BEHAVORIAL STUDY OF A BEAGLE BITCH AND HER LITTER DURING THE 1ST 3 WEEKS OF LACTA-TION.
- CLIO AND THE BITCH GODDESS—QUANTIFICATION IN AMERICAN POLITICAL HISTORY—BOGUE, GA.
- VIRGINS, WHORES, AND BITCHES—ATTITUDES OF RAPISTS TOWARD WOMEN AND SEX.
- PARTIAL ABORTION ASSOCIATED WITH GENITAL ESCHERICHIA-COLI INFECTION IN A BITCH.

- FELA, FELA – THIS BITCH OF A LIFE – MOORE, C.
- GENE-MAPPING OF THE TREE SHREW (TUPAIA GLIS).

One of the most derisive terms for women must be *butch-femme*. On *MEDLINE*, however, this term is used only in the context of "Role Relationships: Lesbian Perspectives." Perhaps the study of negative terms provides a glimpse of the interdisciplinary nature of the social sciences. Social science terminology combines the precision of biomedical terms with the ambiguity of humanities terms.

The whole strategy can be simplified by turning on the BRS PLURALS feature and entering *either* the plural or singular of a term. The system automatically retrieves the other form (even if it is irregular, as in the case of woman/women) and ORs both. This feature not only reduces keying but also increases precision, because *only* the singular and plural forms of *hooker*, for example, will be retrieved and not the false drop Hookeri (species name), which results from the truncated term hooker$1. To facilitate use of the hedge on more than one system, however, both singular and plural forms are accommodated in the profile. Searchers who use the hedge for women should consider adding more biomedical terms and codes specific to particular biomedical databases to be searched. On *MEDLINE* for instance, consider Female Genital Diseases and Pregnancy Complications (C13 +) or Contraceptive Devices, Female (E7.190.250 +).

Many terms, although not explicitly female in character, do connote gender (e.g., lactation, menarche). These terms, which appear frequently in biomedical databases, define the essence of femaleness by describing female organs or processes. The biomedical databases seem to employ the literary device of synecdoche in which a part stands for the whole or an action represents the actor. Womb, for instance, implies woman, and breastfeeding a mother.

COMING TO TERMS WITH HUMAN

Because the hedge includes "female" terms, the results include references to animal as well as human females. Animal terms, such as *bitch* and *vixen*, which have negative connotations when applied to humans, have already been noted. The gender, occupational, and

positive terms in the hedge are by definition human in character.
Biomedical terms, however, should be combined with terms indicating "human" to limit retrieval. Figure 6 lists the ways to limit
retrieval to human females in the omnibus biomedical databases.
Only *MEDLINE* offers a consistent (1966 +) method of searching
for females with its check tags. As stated in the *MEDLARS Indexing
Manual* (Charen, 1980):

> Following the principle of obvious redundancy, even when an
> indexed term is obviously exclusively male or female, index
> also under MALE or FEMALE. . . . In most instances the tags
> are required for retrieval of the other terms under which the
> article was indexed, and these other terms may not necessarily
> clearly indicate sex.

Because the FEMALE tag is used for both humans *and* animals,
it must be combined with the HUMAN tag. The manual continues:

> Check this tag [HUMAN] even when clinical or physiological
> headings are used which are inherently "human" as INFANT
> (as opposed to ANIMAL, NEWBORN) or PREGNANCY (as
> opposed to PREGNANCY, ANIMAL). . . . HUMAN must be
> stated by the indexer to assist the searcher in including it or
> excluding it in relation to ANIMAL.

MEDLINE also distinguishes the use of the routine FEMALE tag
from the heading WOMEN:

> MEN and WOMEN are used only for articles on men and
> women as distinct social groups, as sociological, cultural, po-
> litical, economic or psychological entities apart from physiol-
> ogy or genetic sex. Articles on organs, diseases, physiological
> processes and the like . . . on WOMEN are indexed under the
> specific heading (IM) and the check tags HUMAN and FE-
> MALE . . . Most articles will be clearly the physiological male
> or female (the check tags MALE and FEMALE) or the non-
> physiological man or woman (MEN and WOMEN).

It *is* possible that a *MEDLINE* article could be tagged HUMAN
without the additional tag, MALE or FEMALE, if the article does

Figure 6
SEARCHING FOR HUMAN FEMALES IN THE MAJOR
BIOMEDICAL DATABASES

Database	Terms/Codes For Female	Terms/Codes For Human
BIOSIS	Consult Hedge for Women.	BC86215 (Hominidae)
	Consider: Reproductive System CC1650$ Gonads & Placenta CC17006 Reproductive System CC22028	
	Above codes include male.	
EMBASE	Consult hedge.	
	Female.ii. (1988+) 010# Gynecology section code.	0888.ii. (human) 0800.ii. (normal human)
MEDLINE (also Health Planning & Administration; CANCERLIT)	FEMALE check tag. FEMALE indexed routinely.	HUMAN check tag. HUMAN indexed routinely.
PsycINFO	Has descriptor 'Human Females' (1973+) but not routinely assigned. Consider also Human Sex Differences (1967+).	
SCISEARCH	No controlled vocabulary. Consult hedge.	
CCML	Full text. Consult hedge.	

Also: Consider descriptors/codes which imply human, as in the BIOSIS Category Code, CC37013 (Occupational Health) and the MESH terms 'homeless persons,' 'politics,' or 'patient advocacy.'

not specifically identify the sex of the subjects studied. When the term *human*—or even *man* or *men*—is used in this generic sense, the addition of gender terms is redundant and may in fact eliminate relevant references.

Searching on *BIOSIS* and *EMBASE* is not as clear cut as searching on *MEDLINE*. *BIOSIS*, of course, offers the Biosystematic Code for Hominidae (BC86215), which can be effectively combined with any of the female terms. In fact, *BIOSIS necessitates* the use of the keyword approach to women because its concept codes, such as Social Biology/Human Ecology (CC05500), encompass both male and female populations. *EMBASE*, likewise, offers EM-TAGS for Human (0888) and Normal Human (0800).

In order to restrict searches to human populations, the search should AND the human tags rather than NOTing the animal tags so as not to *exclude* studies which encompass *both* humans and animals. Ambiguous terms such as *mother*, which might refer to humans or animals should be combined with human indicators. (See Figure 6.)

THE SUBJECT IS SEX

In addition to the hedge for women in Figure 5, there are a few other tactics for searching women to consider. It is conceivable that terms such as *hermaphrodite*, *androgyny* or *unisex*, describing subjects that cannot be classified as either male or female, might figure in a search. Terms such as *sex factors* (1968 +) on *MEDLINE* and *human sex differences* (1967 +) on *PsycINFO* are essential for accessing the many studies that compare or contrast the sexes. The *PsycINFO* Help Desk indicated that the indexers only assign the tag male or female when the sex of the population under study is notable, as in the case of males suffering from anorexia.

When the concept of sex differences is central to a search, it might be helpful to consult the forthcoming print vocabulary aid, *Social Science Synonyms and Search Terms*, from Oryx Press, based in part on the former BRS *TERM* database. This volume is a collection of social science free text synonyms arranged by concepts. The entry for sex differences lists more than thirty synonyms:

SEX DIFFERENCES. GENDER DIFFERENCES. SEX LINKED DEVELOPMENTAL DIFFERENCES. GENDER COMPARISON. SEX DIFFERENTIALS. INFLUENCE OF SEX. MALE VS FEMALE. MALES VS FEMALES. SEX COMPOSITION. SEX OF PATIENTS. SEX OF SUBJECTS. FEMALES VS MALES. FEMALE VS MALE. GENDER COMPOSITION. GENDER OF SS. SEX OF SS. SEX OF SUBJECTS. MALE FEMALE DIFFERENCES. WOMEN VS MEN. GIRLS VS BOYS. DIFFERENCES

BETWEEN MEN AND WOMEN. DAUGHTERS VS SONS. MOTHERS VS FATHERS. DIFFERENCES BETWEEN THE SEXES. MALE VS FEMALE. MALE FEMALE COMPARI- SONS. DISTINCTIONS BETWEEN THE SEXES. DISSIMILAR- ITIES BETWEEN MEN AND WOMEN. SEXUAL INEQUALI- TIES. SEX DISTRIBUTION. GENDER SPECIFIC. RATES WITH SEX. CONSIDER ALSO: MALE FEMALE. FEMALE MALE. MEN WOMEN. WOMEN MEN.

When searching for sex differences, it is also useful to include the phrase *his/her(s)* (with and without the slash) in the strategy. A search on the differences between male and female tolerance of pain combined the *PsycINFO* controlled vocabulary with the free text approach:

```
PSYC PSYCINFO 1966-MAR 1989
BRS SEARCH MODE - ENTER QUERY
    1_:     ..set plurals=on
            SET HAS BEEN COMPLETED
    1_:     (pain painful$2).ti,de.
    RESULT          4009 DOCUMENTS
    2_:     gender
    RESULT          5445 DOCUMENTS
    3_:     human-sex-differences
    RESULT         22462 DOCUMENTS
    4_:     human-males
    RESULT          4158 DOCUMENTS
    5_:     human-females
    RESULT         11594 DOCUMENTS
    6_:     sex
    RESULT         50010 DOCUMENTS
    7_:     1 same 3
    RESULT            32 DOCUMENTS
    8_:     1 and 4 and 5
    RESULT             1 DOCUMENTS
    9_:     1 same (2 or 6)
    RESULT            86 DOCUMENTS
   10_:     9.ti.
    RESULT            17 DOCUMENTS
   11_:     7 or 8 or 10
    RESULT            48 DOCUMENTS
   12_:     ..p 11 ti,de/1-4


   1
TI DAILY REPORTS OF DISTRESS: NOT FOR WOMEN ONLY.  SPECIAL ISSUE:
   WOMEN AND WORK.
DE OCCUPATIONAL-STRESS.  PSYCHOLOGICAL-STRESS.  DISTRESS.  ARMY-
   PERSONNEL.  PAIN.  SEX-ROLES.  JOB-CHARACTERISTICS.
   EXPERIENCE-LEVEL.  VALUES.  ADULTHOOD.


   2
TI PEDIATRIC RESIDENTS' ASSESSMENT OF ADOLESCENTS' EXPERIENCES
   DURING PELVIC EXAMINATION.  SOCIETY FOR ADOLESCENT MEDICINE
   (1986, DENVER, COLORADO).
```

```
DE PHYSICAL-EXAMINATION.  HUMAN-SEX-DIFFERENCES.  PEDIATRICIANS.
   GYNECOLOGY.  HEALTH-PERSONNEL-ATTITUDES.  THERAPEUTIC-PROCESSES.
   PAIN.  EMBARRASSMENT.  HUMAN FEMALES.


   3
TI SEX SIMILARITIES AND DIFFERENCES IN THE BIOFEEDBACK TREATMENT
   OF CHRONIC PAIN.
DE PERSONALITY-TRAITS.  ELECTROMYOGRAPHY.  BIOFEEDBACK-TRAINING.
   HUMAN-SEX-DIFFERENCES.  CHRONIC-PAIN.  ADULTHOOD.  HEADACHE.


   4
TI ALEXITHYMIA AND PAIN IN AN OUTPATIENT BEHAVORIAL MEDICINE CLINIC.
DE ALEXITHYMIA.  PAIN.  OUTPATIENT-TREATMENT.  AGE-DIFFERENCES.
   HUMAN-SEX-DIFFERENCES.  CLIENT-CHARACTERISTICS.  ADOLESCENCE.
   ADULTHOOD.
```

When investigating women in the larger societal context of parental, familial, conception, contraception, fertility, sterility, sex discrimination, and equal pay or sex discrimination issues, searchers should consult the social science controlled vocabularies. These thesauri may help to supplement descriptors with free text terms on the biomedical databases.

ON EQUAL TERMS

One of the difficulties in searching for the concept of women, according to Detlefsen (1984), is that "the standard terminologies and thesauri are frequently sexist or gender-stereotyped, and lack feminist terms altogether." She comments on the "women as syndromes" — descriptors which pair women with their roles, such as "women as lawyers," instead of the non-sexist "lawyers." Even such a paragon of controlled vocabularies as *MEDLINE* employs terms such as *physicians, women* and *nurses, male*.

In the 15,000 term *Medical Subject Headings*, such precoordinated terms may make the difference between flawed and fine retrieval. For example, by using the controlled term *physicians, women* in a search on dual addiction in female doctors, the searcher avoids unwanted references on the treatment of substance-dependent women. Perhaps *MEDLINE* should add the corresponding terms *physicians, men* and *nurses, female* for balance and precision in searching.

WOMEN AS AUTHORS

Because the biomedical databases use standardized author initials instead of full first names and middle initials, it is nearly impossible to determine their coverage of women as authors. *PsycINFO, CA SEARCH* and *CCML*, which supply full first names, if available, are among the exceptions. Full first names (of course there are always the problematic unisex names such as Kim, Lynn, Adrian, etc.) would make it possible to do bibliometric studies, such as the publishing output of women in ob/gyn journals.

If the Institute for Scientific Information's files (*SCISEARCH, SOCIAL SCISEARCH, ARTS AND HUMANITIES SEARCH*) specified the sex of the authors of documents as well as the sex of authors in cited references, it might be possible to identify schools of thought defined by sex and trace patterns in the reputation of women authors. At present, however, the only databases that seem to be searchable by sex are online directories such as *American Men and Women of Science*.

Figure 7 presents the BRS author format for biomedical databases and indicates whether the database producer supplies full first names or initials. *MEDLINE, Health Planning and Administration, Nursing and Allied Health Literature* and *MEDLINE References on AIDS* offer a Personal Name field for searching prominent women as subjects. Note the Pandora's box of personages (as well as the omissions) culled from this field in *MEDLINE*:

```
MESZ 1966-APR 1989 (89042)
BRS SEARCH MODE - ENTER QUERY
1_:  blackwell-e$.pn.
RESULT              9 DOCUMENTS
2_:  freud-a$.pn.
RESULT             38 DOCUMENTS
3_:  woolf-v$.pn.
RESULT             13 DOCUMENTS
4_:  fitzgerald-z$.pn.
RESULT              0 DOCUMENTS
5_:  elizabeth-i$.pn.
RESULT              2 DOCUMENTS
6_:  monroe-m$.pn.
RESULT              0 DOCUMENTS
7_:  nightingale-f$.pn.
RESULT            274 DOCUMENTS
8_:  mary-queen-of-scots.pn.
RESULT              4 DOCUMENTS
```

MEDLINE offers the headings *historical biography*, *famous persons*, *current biog-obit*, and *portraits*, which may be combined with the check tag FEMALE to locate notable women as subjects.

CONTROVERSIAL TOPICS IN DATABASES

An attempt was made to look at controversial topics in databases in order to determine both *whether* they are covered and how they are uncovered in biomedical databases. Most of the "hot topics" are controversial. Other controversial topics were searched through known issues or papers or discovered by running a brief strategy of terms that imply controversy.

Given a known — and in this case controversial paper — *SCISEARCH*, *SOCIAL SCISEARCH*, or *ARTS AND HUMANITIES SEARCH* can turn up other papers that cite it, as in the case of the Cann paper. Rebecca Cann and her colleagues concluded in 1987 that the most likely ancestor of us all, "Eve," was an African woman who lived 140,000-290,000 years ago. They based their case on a study of mitochondrial DNA, which is transmitted generation to generation only from the mother. Their work caught the attention of both the popular and academic presses. This interdisciplinary paper was searched by cited reference with the following results: *SCISEARCH* (62), *SOCIAL SCISEARCH* (7), *COMPUTERS AND MATHEMATICS SEARCH* (2), and *ARTS AND HUMANITIES SEARCH* (4). The assortment of papers retrieved either support or controvert Cann:

TI COMPUTERIZED PHYLOGENETIC ANALYSES - A REVOLUTION IN PHYSICAL ANTHROPOLOGY. [CMCI]
TI RECONSTRUCTION OF HUMAN EVOLUTION - BRINGING TOGETHER GENETIC, ARCHAEOLOGICAL, AND LINGUISTIC DATA. [AHCI]
TI MAJOR ISSUES IN THE EMERGENCE OF MODERN HUMANS. [SSCI]

This citation recycling procedure can locate references to *any* paper of course, but it provides an especially convenient way to locate controversial schools of thought.

Figure 7
SEARCHING AUTHOR NAMES

Database	Example	Initials	Full	As on Document
BIOSIS	cann-r-1	X		
CA SEARCH	cann-r-1 or cann-rebecca-1	X	X	X
CANCERLIT	cann-r-1 or cann adj r adj 1	X		
CCML	cann-rebecca-1 or cann adj rebecca 1	X	X	X
Current Contents	cann-rl	X (fused)		
EMBASE	cann-r-1	X		
Health Planning	cann-r-1 or cann adj r adj 1	X		
International Pharmaceutical Abs.	cann-r-1	X		
MEDLINE	cann-r-1 or cann adj r adj 1	X		
Medical and Psychological Previews	cann-r-1 or cann adj r adj 1	X		
PsycINFO and PsycALERT	cann-r-1 or cann-rebecca-1	X	X	X
SCISEARCH	E AU=CANN RL	X		

The *MEDLINE* document below also refers to the Cann study but gives no suggestion of the disputes surrounding the topic. *More importantly*, the citation does not explicitly indicate that the document concerns females.

```
AN 87090390.    87000.
AU WAINSCOAT-J.
TI HUMAN EVOLUTION: OUT OF THE GARDEN OF EDEN [NEWS].
SO NATURE. 1987 JAN 1-7. 325(6099). P. 13.
JT NATURE.
LG EN.
MJ EVOLUTION.
MN ANIMAL. DROSPHILA: GE.  DNA: AN.  DNA-MITOCHONDRIAL: AN.
   HUMAN.
RN 9007-49-2 -- DNA.
SB M, X.
YR 87.
IS 0028-0836.NSC.
ZN Z1.542.363.300.
IM 8704.
ED 870219.
FT THE FULL TEXT OF NATURE IS AVAILABLE IN CCML BEGINNING WITH THE
   OCT 1985 ISSUE.
```

The user must be aware that mitochondrial DNA implies "female" since the indexer did not assign the FEMALE check tag. This example emphasizes the importance of the different approaches to searches on women as discussed above.

Note that the new FULL TEXT (FT) paragraph appears and is limitable on BRS *MEDLINE* for documents whose full text is available in another database, the *Comprehensive Core Medical Library*. A somewhat broader search demonstrates the FT feature and the link between *MEDLINE* and *CCML*:

```
MESH 1983-MAR 1989 (89031)
BRS SEARCH MODE - ENTER QUERY
1_: evolution.mj. and dna-mitochondrial
RESULT          70 DOCUMENTS
2_: ..1/1 hu=y                    (Limits results to HUMAN.)
RESULT          31 DOCUMENTS
3_: ..1/2 ft=y                    (Limits results to FULL TEXT.)
RESULT           5 DOCUMENTS
4_: ..p 3 au,ti,so,ft/1-4

        1 OF 4
AU SAITOU-N.  OMOTO-K.
TI TIME AND PLACE OF HUMAN ORIGINS FROM MT DNA DATA [LETTER].
SO NATURE. 1987 MAY 28-JUNE 3.  327(6120). P 288.
FT THE FULL TEXT OF NATURE IS AVAILABLE IN CCML BEGINNING WITH
   THE OCT 1985 ISSUE.

        2 OF 4
AU ECKHARDT-R-B.
TI EVOLUTION EAST OF EDEN [LETTER].
SO NATURE. 1987 APR 23-29. 326(6115).  P 749.
FT THE FULL TEXT OF NATURE IS AVAILABLE IN CCML BEGINNING WITH
   THE OCT 1985 ISSUE.
```

```
                  3 OF 4
AU CANN-R-L.   STONEKING-M.   WILSON-A-C.
TI MITOCHONDRIAL DNA AND HUMAN ·EVOLUTION.
SO NATURE.   1987   JAN 1-7.   325(6099).   P 31-6.
FT THE FULL TEXT OF NATURE IS AVAILABLE IN CCML BEGINNING WITH
   THE OCT 1985 ISSUE.

                  4 OF 4
AU WAINSCOAT-J.
TI HUMAN EVOLUTION:   OUT OF THE GARDEN OF EDEN [NEWS].
SO NATURE.   1987   JAN 1-7.   325(6099).   P 13.
FT THE FULL TEXT OF NATURE IS AVAILABLE IN CCML BEGINNING WITH
   THE OCT 1985 ISSUE.

   :   link 4 ft

LINK                     CCML          SCREEN 1 OF 10

AN MJEA-325025.   87012.
AU WAINSCOAT, JIM.
IN DEPARTMENT OF HEMATOLOGY, JOHN RADCLIFF HOSPITAL,
   HEADINGTON, OXFORD OX3 9DU,   UK.
TI NEWS AND VIEWS:   HUMAN EVOLUTION:   OUT OF THE GARDEN OF EDEN.
SO NATURE.   1987   JAN 1.   325(6099).   P 13.
PU COPYRIGHT 1987 BY MACMILLAN JOURNALS LTD., LONDON.
PD 870101.
PT MISCELLANEOUS ARTICLE   (MIS).
IS 0028-0836.
LG ENGLISH (EN).
TX 1 OF 11.
   A PAPER BY R.L. CANN, M. STONEKING AND A.C. WILSON ON PAGE
   39 OF THIS ISSUE *rf 1 * REPORTS THAT EVE WAS ALIVE AND WELL
   AND PROBABLY LIVING IN AFRICA AROUND 200,000 YEARS AGO.   IN
   CONSIDERING THIS STRIKING CLAIM WE SHOULD BEAR IN MIND THE
   WORDS OF THOMAS HOOD IN THE FIRST STANZA OF 'A BLACK JOB':
            THE HISTORY OF HUMAN-KIND TO TRACE
            SINCE EVE - THE FIRST OF DUPES - OUR DOOM UNRIDDLED
            A CERTAIN PORTION OF THE HUMAN RACE
            HAS CERTAINLY A TASTE FOR BEING DIDDLED.
      CANN ET AL. BASE THEIR PROPOSED IDENTIFICATION OF EVE ON A DETAILED
   ANALYSIS OF THE MITOCHONDRIAL DNA TYPES IN A DIVERSE GROUP OF HUMAN
   POPULATIONS.   HUMAN MITOCHONDRIAL DNA, A CIRCULAR MOLECULE OF ABOUT
   16,500 BASE PAIRS *rf 2,3 *, HAS A STRICTLY MATERNAL INHERITANCE
   PATTERN.   THUS, THE MITOCHONDRIAL DNA TYPE OF AN INDIVIDUAL IS
   INHERITED FROM THEMOTHER, THE MATERNAL GRANDMOTHER AND SO ON...
   (Rest of text prints.)
```

Once a *MEDLINE* search has been limited to those articles available in full text in CCML (or the FT paragraph indicating availability of full text has been printed), a true hypertext link between these two databases may be invoked, as illustrated technically above and conceptually in Figure 8.

The *MEDLINE* reference that mentions the full text availability of the document in CCML (note the holdings date in FT) provides the starting point for the hypertext link between the citation and the full text document. A behind-the-scenes algorithm then matches

Figure 8

The MEDLINE to CCML
Full Text LINK*

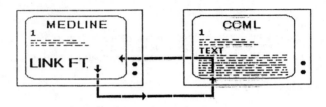

o MEDLINE references which are tagged with an FT field are most
   likely to have their corresponding FULL Texts available in
   CCML.

o A LINK from a tagged reference opens the text of the CCML
   document while holding your place in MEDLINE.

o The MEDLINE search remains intact.

o Resume the MEDLINE search after reading, printing or
   downloading the CCML document.

o LINK out to CCML as many times as desired duringt a MEDLINE
   search.

* The author gratefully acknowledges the use of this diagram
created by John Schumacher of BRS Information Technologies.

source and author data (although it is formatted quite differently in
MEDLINE and CCML) to the identical reference in CCML. The
CCML text is "opened" on top of the *MEDLINE* search so that the
article may be browsed or printed. This link breaks out of the search
process to page through relevant textual material while marking the
user's place in the *MEDLINE* search.

The LINK feature points out the logical similarities between
databases so that the user does not bear the burden of constructing
compatible strategies for databases that would ordinarily have to be
cross-searched. LINKs between other databases will undoubtedly
become available in the future.

Approximately 7.2% of the articles in the complete *MEDLINE*
file (1966+) can be LINKed to their full texts in CCML. Nine

percent of the articles about women in *MEDLINE* (as determined by the hedge for women strategy) are available on CCML.

The following terms indicating controversy, collected while browsing the "hot topics" mentioned above, work well in combination with women's terms/topics on the major biomedical files:

argue$1	argument$1	arguing
ban	bans	banned
contend$1	contention$1	
controve$5		
critique$1		
debat$3		
dichotom$3		
disput$5		
issue	issues	
reviewer$1	reviewed	reviewing
point adj view		
school$1 adj thought		
viewpoint$1		

A few sample titles from *EMBASE* illustrate the combination of the controversial and female terms:

TI MALE AXILLARY SECRETIONS INFLUENCE WOMEN'S MENSTRUAL CYCLES: A CRITIQUE.

TI ORAL CONTRACEPTIVES AND BREAST CANCER IN YOUNG WOMEN. SOME NOTES ON A CURRENT CONTROVERSY.

TI FAMILY SYSTEMS APPROACHES TO WIFE BATTERING: A FEMINIST CRITIQUE.

TI THE POLITICS OF FUNCTIONAL FAMILY THERAPY: A FEMINIST CRITIQUE.

TI SURVEY OF WOMEN PHYSICIANS ON ISSUES RELATING TO PREGNANCY DURING A MEDICAL CAREER.

Variants of the terms "feminism" and "sexism" will retrieve controversial articles or alternative literature about human females. These terms can retrieve citations on the feminist perspective on

topics such as mastectomy, abortion, professional status, etc. Some
examples from the major databases include:

TI WOMEN'S HEALTH – THE FEMINIST CONTRIBUTION.
[EMBASE]
TI AN ESSAY ON SURROGACY AND FEMINIST THOUGHT.
[MEDLINE]
TI DEEPENING AWARENESS – A PRIVATE STUDY GUIDE
TO FEMINISM AND FAMILY THERAPY. [PSYCINFO]
TI TOWARD A DEFINITION OF FEMINIST SOCIAL WORK
– A COMPARISON OF LIBERAL, RADICAL AND SO-
CIALIST MODELS. [CURRENT CONTENTS]
TI THE BIRTH MOTHER: A FEMINIST PERSPECTIVE FOR
THE HELPING PROFESSIONAL. [BIOSIS]

CONCLUSIONS

Because women constitute a clearly identified patient group and
research population in biomedicine, biomedical databases provide
more controls for online searches about women than social science
and humanities databases. *MEDLINE* offers the dependable check
tag FEMALE for the entire span of the database. The hedge for
women utilized in this paper offers guidance for searches on databases without controlled vocabularies or for extensive retrieval on
biomedical databases. For instance, terms from the hedge can be
selected to represent the "women" concept in searches. The hedge
can be adapted by the searcher and saved on a system for future use.

The biomedical databases exhibit the use of organs, systems,
processes and technics to represent females, as in the cases of ova-
ries, menstrual cycle, first trimester and hysterectomy. The hedge
for women needs the most expansion in this area. Since the biomedical databases tend to represent primarily the viewpoint of the
medical establishment, a strategy to ferret out alternative literature
was also suggested.

Searchers can expect the development of more hypertext links
between databases, making it possible, for instance, to restrict
searches to women only by means of a behind-the-scenes strategy
applicable to several files. These hypertext links will minimize the

differences between databases and simplify cross-database and cross-discipline searching. Technical information about women and *for* practitioners is already available online. In the future information *for* women themselves about their health issues will probably appear in new online sources. Finally, more can be determined about the online coverage of women in biomedical databases by exploring the online coverage of men.

REFERENCES

Bolen, Jean Shinoda. *Goddesses in Everywoman*. New York: Harper & Row, 1984.

Capek, Mary Ellen S., ed. *A Woman's Thesaurus: An Index of Language Used to Describe and Locate Information by and About Women*. New York: Harper & Row, 1987.

Charen, Thelma. MEDLARS Indexing Manual (Part II). Bethesda: National Library of Medicine, December 1980.

Detlefsen, Ellen Gay. "Issues of Access to Information About Women." *Special Collections* Vol. 3: 163-171 (Spr. 1984).

Women's Issues
and Online Legal Research

Richard Irving
Mary Jane Brustman

SUMMARY. Online legal databases — cases, statutes, regulations and periodicals (both bibliographic and non-bibliographic) — were searched free-text to determine the usefulness of computerized legal searching for research on women's issues. Results indicate that: (1) There is a wealth of information on women's issues available on primary and secondary legal databases. (2) There is considerable variation among topics and databases in the effectiveness of free-text searching. Free-text searching presents a number of difficulties in legal databases — first and foremost, the language used in legal documents. In many cases, the combination of free-text and full-text searching produces too low a precision rate to be considered effective. (3) While this study did not identify one particular strategy as the most effective approach to accessing information on women's issues, a number of factors to be considered in developing search strategies were identified. These factors are the purpose of the search, standardization and uniqueness of terminology, size of database being searched, expected number of relevant documents, searchable field available, and content and format of the search fields. (4) Bibliometric analysis was seen as useful in looking at trends of particular women's legal issues.

Why study the legal aspects of women's issues? What is the significance of gender in United States law? Throughout the body of American law — federal, state and local — differences based on gen-

Richard Irving is Bibliographer for Political Science, Public Administration, and Law and Reference Librarian, University at Albany, State University of New York 12222. Mary Jane Brustman is Bibliographer for Reference and Information Science and Policy, and Reference Librarian, University at Albany, State University of New York 12222.

der exist. The most obvious differences center around employment issues of hiring, benefits, leaves, harassment, comparable worth, and pensions, as well as on issues of women as victims of sexual assault or domestic violence. As Elizabeth Holtzman has asserted, the inequality of women is ". . . a glaring injustice still enshrined in our Constitution and mirrored in some of our laws . . . women are not entitled to the same protection against discrimination as other groups in society" (Holtzman, p. 1429).

These differences in the law reflect differential treatment of men and women in society. What some courts and legislatures are doing to address these differences reflects a broad based societal interest in resolving gender inequities. Statutes, court cases, and legal periodical articles constitute a rich source of information for research on women and their rights, opportunities, and roles in American society. This information can be used for substantive legal research (i.e., seeking primary and secondary sources of law that are applicable to a particular legal situation) or as raw data in bibliometrics, "the application of mathematics and statistical methods to books, and other media of communication" (Pritchard 1986:349).

This article addresses one aspect of legal research on women, the use of online legal databases as an effective tool for research on selected women's issues. Women's issues are here defined as legal issues whose impact is predominantly on women. Effectiveness is determined by the quantity of relevant documents retrieved and the precision of results for each of the issues searched.

Detlefson (p. 163) has noted several obstacles to accessing information on women's issues. Of particular relevance here is her point concerning the lack of standard, non-sexist subject descriptors. This study considers the extent to which this factor impedes searching as well as whether legal databases pose additional difficulties uniquely their own.

A secondary concern is to determine whether the data produced by online legal research is appropriate for bibliometric analysis. Lancaster (p. 389) and Raisig (p. 450) have noted that bibliometrics can be used to track the development of social movements and issues. While this study differs from Lancaster's in methodology, one goal of the study is to determine if legal databases, non-bibliographic or bibliographic, lend themselves to Lancaster's type of analysis. Bibliometric analysis may indicate that non-bibliographic legal databases can be used for historical and comparative studies as well as for substantive legal information on women's issues.

METHODOLOGY

Selection of Issues

Recent literature on women and the law was scanned in order to identify women's issues. Numerous books and articles were reviewed during this process. *Women's Legal Rights in the United States: A Selective Bibliography* and *Women's Annotated Legal Bibliography* were particularly useful. The final list included eight topics: Pregnancy Discrimination, Rape, Reproductive Rights, Sexual Harassment, Spouse Abuse, Inequities in Women's Pensions and Insurance, Affirmative Action, and Comparable Worth.

Databases

Databases were narrowly limited to legal databases, those including only primary or secondary law or law-related materials. Social sciences and public policy sources which contain legal references but do not specialize in law materials were excluded.

Legal databases provide access to a vast array of both primary and secondary legal documents. The primary databases contain the full text of cases, statutes, and administrative law materials. Secondary databases include bibliographic and full-text periodical databases, current awareness services and files containing abstracts of documents such as the *Congressional Record* and *Federal Register*. The online database field is dominated by two legal information vendors, WESTLAW and LEXIS, who specialize in providing access to the full-text legal databases. Other less specialized vendors such as BRS, DIALOG and WILSONLINE offer legal bibliographic databases.

On both LEXIS and WESTLAW the first group of databases selected were four full-text case law databases, U.S. Supreme Court, U.S. Court of Appeals, U.S. District Courts, and a database combining the court decisions of all the states. Each database is divided into different fields (referred to as segments on LEXIS). For the

Supreme Court these fields are comparable to sections found in the corresponding *Supreme Court Reporter* for WESTLAW and *U.S. Supreme Court Reports* for LEXIS. WESTLAW offers fields for synopsis, digest, headnote, topic, citation, title, date, court, judge and opinion. With the exception of the synopsis, digest, topic, and headnote fields, LEXIS has all these WESTLAW fields. LEXIS also provides argued date, syllabus, appeal statement, and a breakdown of opinions and authors of opinions by majority, dissenting or concurring.

On all four WESTLAW case law databases the searches were limited to a combined search of the synopsis and digest fields (the editorial features summarizing the case). On LEXIS, the U.S. Supreme Court database was searched twice, with the first search limited to the syllabus field (an abstract of the case provided by the court) and the second search limited to the opinion field. On the other three LEXIS databases only the opinion field was searched, as lower federal court and state court decisions often lack syllabuses. All of the case law searches were limited to the time period 1945-1988.

A second group of primary sources searched on both LEXIS and WESTLAW included the United States Code, Code of Federal Regulations and the state law codes. Both WESTLAW and LEXIS have added editorial features to their United States Code databases (WESTLAW's corresponds to the printed *United States Code Annotated* and LEXIS's to the *United States Code Service*). The full-text plus the editorial enhancements were searched for this group. The *Code of Federal Regulations* is available from both vendors without enhancements. CFR was searched full-text.

Neither the LEXIS nor WESTLAW state code databases provide coverage of all the states. At the time the searches were made WESTLAW covered 28 states and LEXIS 28 states, with considerable overlap between them. State law can be searched on both vendors' systems either by individual states or on a combined state code database. On both systems the latter was searched. WESTLAW offered the choice of searching the combined statutes with or without editorial enhancements (annotations). Searches were conducted both ways in order to allow for some evaluation of the editorial enhancements for online searching purposes. These enhancements are not available on LEXIS.

A third group of databases includes legal periodical databases, both bibliographic and full-text. LEXIS and WESTLAW each have full-text legal periodical databases: *WESTLAW-Text and Periodicals* and *LEXIS-Law Reviews*. At the time of this study WESTLAW covered over 200 titles and LEXIS 53 titles. Searches on WESTLAW and LEXIS were run on the full-text of documents. Also searched were two bibliographic databases: *Index to Legal Periodicals* on WILSONLINE and *Legal Resource Index* on BRS. *Legal Resource Index* covered 750 titles and *Index to Legal Periodicals* 500. All four databases have different time spans, with *Legal Resource Index* being the most retrospective. With the other three databases the period of coverage varies from title to title.

While *Index to Legal Periodicals* and *Legal Resource Index* have subject descriptor fields that can be searched using controlled vocabulary, this was not done. Searches were free-text on *Legal Resource Index* and limited to the title, subject descriptor, and note fields. On *Index to Legal Periodicals* free-text searches were made in the Basic Index which includes title, subject descriptor and note fields. WESTLAW and LEXIS periodicals databases do not use subject descriptors. The different periodical search strategies were intended to generate results which would allow for a comparison of the efficacy of searching free-text in a bibliographic database versus free-text searching in a full-text database.

Search Queries

Recall, the percentage of relevant documents retrieved in relation to the total number of relevant documents in the database, was emphasized in designing the search queries. Effective recall depends upon construction of a search strategy which includes all the synonymous terms representing a particular concept. The inclusion of all synonymous terms is particularly important in searching primary document databases, such as statutory and case law databases, which make limited or no use of controlled vocabulary. Synonymous terms were compiled from several sources including Burton's *Legal Thesaurus* and the *TERM* database on BRS.

As noted above, all queries were designed and run as free-text searches. No attempt was made to identify appropriate subject descriptors in databases where controlled vocabulary was available. The same terminology was used for bibliographic databases which offer controlled vocabulary searching as was utilized for WESTLAW and LEXIS which, generally, do not. The one case where legal vendors do offer a limited form of controlled vocabulary is in WESTLAW's case law databases.

While an effort was made to keep search strategies as consistent as possible when searching different databases, under some circumstances search statements had to be modified. Three factors led to these modifications. First, queries had to be adapted to four different search systems, WILSONLINE, BRS, WESTLAW and LEXIS. Second, queries had to take into account differences in structure from database to database within the same system as well as changes in the structure of a particular type of database from vendor to vendor. For example, case law databases are organized into different fields and statutory databases on WESTLAW. Changes in fields also occur when switching from WESTLAW to a comparable database on LEXIS. Third, searching the larger databases, especially in full-text, required restrictions on the use of truncation and the use of character limitations on proximity operators. For instance, in some databases a search strategy that required two terms to be in the same field produced many times more documents (including irrelevant ones) than a strategy that required two words to be positioned within three words of each other.

-SAMPLE SEARCH-

SEXUAL HARASSMENT

WESTLAW (Searches performed 1/89)

U.S. Supreme Court Database:
Synopsis, Digest ((Sex Sexual Gender /3 Harass!) (Treat! /3 "Sex Object" "Sexual Object") (Sexual /10 Work! Hostile! /5 Environment)) & Date (BEF 1989)

U.S. Court of Appeals Database:
[Same as U.S. Supreme Court Database.]

U.S. District Court Database:
[Same as U.S. Supreme Court Database.]

(Combined) State Court Database (ALLSTATE):
**Synopsis, Digest ((Sex Sexual Gender /3 Harass!)
(Treat! w/3 "Sex Object" "Sexual Objective") (Sexual /
10 Work! Hostile! /5 Environment)) & Date (AFT 1944
& BEF 1989)**

U.S. Code Annotated Database:
**(Sex Sexual Gender /3 Harass!) (Treat! /3 "Sex Object"
"Sex Objective") (Sexual /10 Work! Hostile! /5 Envi-
ronment)**

Code of Federal Regulations Database:
[Same as U.S. Code Annotated Database.]

(Combined) State Statutes Unannotated Database:
[Same as U.S. Code Annotated Database.]

(Combined) State Statutes Annotated Database:
[Same as U.S. Code Annotated Database.]

Texts and Periodicals Database:
**TE((Sex Sexual Gender /3 Harass!) (Treat! /3 "Sex Ob-
ject" "Sexual Object") (Sexual /10 Work! Hostile! /5
Environment))**

LEXIS (Searches performed 12/88)

U.S. Supreme Court Database (Syllabus field):
**Syllabus ((Sex or Sexual or Gender w/3 Harass!) or
(Treat! w/3 Sex Object or Sexual Object) or (Sexual w/
10 Work! or Hostile! w/5 Environment))
and
Date AFT 1944**

U.S. Supreme Court Database (opinion field):
Opinion ((Sex or Sexual or Gender w/3 Harass!) or (Treat! w/3 Sex Object or Sexual Object) or (Sexual w/ 10 Work! or Hostile! w/5 Environment))
and
Date AFT 1944

U.S. Court of Appeals Database:
[Same as U.S. Supreme Court Database (opinion field).]

U.S. District Court Database:
[Same as U.S. Supreme Court Database (opinion field).]

(Combined) State Court Database:
[Same as U.S. Supreme Court Database (opinion field).]

U.S. Code Service Database:
(Sex or Sexual or Gender w/3 Harass!) or (Treat! w/3 Sex Object of Sexual Object) or (Sexual w/10 Work! or Hostile! w/5 Environment)

Code of Federal Regulations Database:
[Same as U.S. Code Service Database]

(Combined) State Statutes Database:
[Same as U.S. Code Service Database]

Law Review Database:
Text (Sex or Sexual or Gender w/3 Harass!) or (Treat! w/3 Sex Object or Sexual Object) or (Sexual! w/10 Work! or Hostile! w/5 Environment))

Legal Database Searching

Since many of the primary source databases searched include tens of thousands of records, full-text searching is likely to lead to the retrieval of a large number of irrelevant documents. These irrelevant documents are referred to as fallout. Fallout problems are exacerbated in legal databases where terms or phrases may appear in the titles of cited references or in footnotes that are included for procedural rather than substantive reasons. Although procedural type fallout in legal databases may be akin to methodological type fallout in social science and science databases, the problem is likely to be more acute in legal databases due to emphasis on precedence (stare decisis) in decision making. The multiple search strategies performed on some databases allow a comparison of efficacy of the strategies in terms of the relevancy of documents retrieved.

Three variables may account for differences in results for the same search on the same database depending upon whether WEST-LAW or LEXIS is searched. First, differences in search systems can affect results, especially in situations involving free-text searching. This may occur when there are different uses of proximity operators.

Secondly, both LEXIS and WESTLAW have added editorial features to the original document in some databases. For example, WESTLAW adds a synopsis and headnotes to each of the cases in its case law database. There has been debate on the merits of searching WESTLAW's editorial features to enhance search results. Gott (1987) found value in the editorial features as additional access points; Coco (1984) found that searching full-text plus i.e., the text of a decision plus WESTLAW's editorial features, increased recall; Runde (1986) argued that not only can the editorial features enhance recall, but they may in some cases prove adequate to search by themselves. It could also be argued that limiting the searches to the editorial features reduces the chance of retrieving irrelevant documents.

Dabney has noted the problems associated with free-text full-text searching on large databases. Most significantly, fallout, i.e., "the proportion of the total number of irrelevant documents in a collection retrieved by a search" (Dabney, 1986, p. 16), reaches unmanageable proportions in a large database. This is a serious problem in large legal databases where determining relevancy can be an overwhelming process. Dabney does not see searching editorial features as an answer to this problem, and in fact, has maintained that there is little to be gained in searching editorial features (Dabney, p. 32-34). He contends that editorial features do not enhance recall because they merely repeat terminology used in the decision and, as selective summaries, are not adequate to search by themselves.

As mentioned above, WESTLAW attempts to provide subject access in its case law databases through the inclusion of a "Topic" field. Topics are limited to the 480 topics plus subheadings making up the key number system in West's printed digests (indexes to published court cases). Furthermore, the hierarchial structure of the key number system inhibits the integration of new concepts, especially social concepts that are not legal issues per se. For example, neither "comparable worth" nor "sexual harassment" appear in the "Topic" field. Therefore, controlled vocabulary searching has limited value, as least for social science topics.

A third variable is the difference in fields that WESTLAW and LEXIS use to break down the documents in their case law databases. In some instances the fields refer to editorial features only available on WESTLAW, e.g., synopsis, digest, headnote, topic. Only certain editorial fields and the text of the decision lend themselves to free-text searching. These include the synopsis, digest, headnote, opinion, concurring opinion, dissenting opinion, syllabus and appeal statement. None of the free-text searchable fields on LEXIS match up exactly with the free-text fields on WESTLAW. For instance, WESTLAW's opinion field incorporates the opinion, concurring opinion, dissenting opinion and syllabus fields on LEXIS.

By using a variety of search options made possible by the unique features and different fields of each vendor, searches were conducted which allowed for some comparisons of the efficacy of free-text searching on full-text versus free-text searching of syllabus or digest and synopsis fields. The latter could be considered somewhat akin to searching the abstract field on bibliographic databases.

WESTLAW and LEXIS are designed to facilitate legal research for practitioners. Although Irving and Mendelsohn (1987) have suggested ways in which online legal database systems, specifically WESTLAW, can be used by social scientists, the systems were not designed to assist social science research. The present study's results and analysis should not be interpreted as a comparative evaluation of WESTLAW and LEXIS, but rather as observations on the effectiveness of various strategies for determining the occurrence of relevant documents on women's issues.

RESULTS

The results and analyses focuses on two assessments. First, the quantity of information on each topic in each database searched. Second, the effectiveness of alternative strategies for accessing relevant information for each search topic on the same or comparable databases. The assessments were arrived at by taking a sample of each search result and determining from that sample a rate of precision for the search, i.e., the proportion of the retrieved documents that were relevant to the topic. Using the precision rate, the likely number of relevant documents and fallout (irrelevant documents) were projected for each topic on each database. The precision rate, number of relevant documents retrieved, and fallout were used to compare the effectiveness of alternative search strategies.

Preliminary Results

Tables 1, 2, and 3 present the total number of documents retrieved for all topics, on each database, before precision rates and projected numbers of relevant documents were determined. Table 1 includes the results for all the secondary source databases, Table 2 the primary source databases on WESTLAW and Table 3 the primary source databases on LEXIS. While there was a considerable spread in the number of documents retrieved, depending on the topic and database, the preliminary results indicate a wealth of information for all topics on both primary and secondary databases. For some topics, e.g., "Rape," "Spousal Abuse," and "Reproductive Rights," the number of documents retrieved on some databases was so large as to indicate that online searches should be limited to a particular aspects of these topics.

The retrieval totals for the statutory databases were much smaller than those for either the periodical or case law databases. Statutory laws tend to be written with broad brush strokes that are left to be interpreted by the courts. A single section of statutory law may result in hundreds of court cases interpreting the meaning and application of the law. Therefore, the fact that few documents were retrieved for some topics, e.g., "Comparable Worth" and "Pregnancy Discrimination," in the U.S. Code databases, does not by itself indicate a lack of federal statutory law on those topics. How-

Table 1. Total Number of Hits—Secondary Sources.

TOPICS	Rape	Pension Insurance	Spousal Abuse	Pregnancy Discrim.	Comparable Worth	Affirmative Action	Reproductive Rights	Sexual Harassment.
DATABASES								
Legal Resources Index	1130	98	662	303	747	151	1621	393
Index to Legal Periodicals	238	15	140	82	179	22	417	155
LEXIS—Periodicals	1141	93	288	235	142	242	1339	161
WESTLAW—Periodicals	734	97	166	251	166	68	976	178

Table 2. Total Number of Hits--Primary Sources--WESTLAW

TOPICS	Rape	Pension Insurance	Spousal Abuse	Pregnancy Discrim.	Comparable Worth	Affirmative Action	Reproductive Rights	Sexual Harassment
DATABASES								
US SUPREME COURT CASES	80	4	3	17	3	12	82	3
US COURT OF APPEALS CASES	1113	25	78	113	112	218	337	81
US DISTRICT COURT CASES	571	54	52	186	174	384	445	206
STATE COURT CASES	22460	50	4772	357	58	48	2844	156
US CODE ANNOTATED	21	1	3	4	1	7	61	0
CODE OF FED. REGULATIONS	47	4	17	37	23	224	223	14
STATE STATUTES UNANNOTATED	1193	45	146	137	91	104	1351	34
STATE STATUTES ANNOTATED	3391	70	783	340	127	127	2259	96

Table 3. Total Number of Hits--Primary sources--LEXIS

TOPICS: DATABASES	Rape	Pension Insurance	Spousal Abuse	Pregnancy Discrim.	Comparable Worth	Affirmative Action	Reproductive Rights	Sexual Harassment
		.788						
US SUP. CT. CASES SYLLABUS	69	6	3	15	4	11	40	2
US SUP. CT. CASES OPINION	218	20	22	32	11	25	125	3
US COURT OF APPEAL CASES	3223	121	407	369	210	653	985	205
US DISTRICT COURT CASES	2502	230	310	795	561	1599	1586	642
STATE COURT CASES	34938	184	7921	978	135	218	4139	302
US CODE SERVICE	10	0	3	3	3	15	68	11
CODE OF FED. REGULATIONS	61	9	17	27	13	210	231	12
STATE STATUTES ANNOTATED	2061	42	434	148	43	96	1583	59

ever, for topics, such as "Pension/Insurance" and "Sexual Harass-ment" where we had zero results on one of our searches, it is rea-sonable to conclude that there is no federal statutory law.

The state statutory databases yielded more documents than the federal statutory databases for all topics. It is not clear whether this indicates greater legislative activity at the state level regarding women's issues or merely reflects the fact that the state databases are multijurisdictional.

The *Code of Federal Regulations* (CFR) contains the rules and regulations promulgated by federal executive agencies. Usually, the regulations detail the manner in which statutory laws are to be im-plemented. Interestingly, even those topics, "Sexual Harassment" and "Pension Insurance," that yielded zero results on a U.S. Code search retrieved documents in the CFR databases. The results indi-cate that federal agencies are cognizant of women's issues in estab-lishing the process for the implementation of statutory law even if those issues are not addressed directly in the statutory law.

Periodicals

As mentioned above, Detlefson has stated that one of the factors inhibiting the retrieval of information on women's issues has been the lack of adequate subject access to documents dealing with wom-en's issues. The constraints imposed by controlled vocabulary searching can be avoided by using free-text searching in online databases. Thus online databases could mitigate the subject access difficulties for women's issues. In this search this proposition was tested by free-text searching both bibliographic and full-text period-ical databases.

The effectiveness of free-text searching depends to a considerable extent on the standardization and uniqueness of the terminology rep-resenting a topic. It also depends on the size, information provided, and structure of the database being searched. Table 4 presents the results for the topics for which the researchers examined samples of at least 10% of the results and then projected the total number of relevant documents retrieved for each search.

Relevant documents were retrieved for all three of the topics. The results indicate that *Index to Legal Periodicals* (ILP) lags behind the

TABLE 4. PERIODICAL DATABASES-TOTAL DOCUMENTS RETRIEVED, RELEVANT
DOCUMENTS AND FALLOUT FOR SELECTED TOPICS
(ROW PERCENTAGES IN PARENTHESES)

TOPIC DATABASE	TOTAL DOCUMENTS	RELEVANT DOCUMENTS	FALLOUT
PENSION/INSURANCE			
LRI	98	81 (83%)	17 (17%)
WEST-TP	97	51 (53%)	46 (47%)
LEXIS-LR	93	74 (80%)	19 (20%)
ILP	15	15 (100%)	0 (0%)
SEXUAL HARASSMENT			
LRI	393	385 (98%)	8 (2%)
WEST-TP	178	84 (47%)	94 (53%)
LEXIS-LR	161	45 (28%)	116 (72%)
ILP	155	155 (100%)	0 (0%)
AFFIRMATIVE ACTION			
LEXIS-LR	242	65 (27%)	177 (73%)
LRI	151	133 (88%)	18 (12%)
WEST-TP	68	27 (40%)	41 (60%)
ILP	22	22 (100%)	0 (0%)

other databases in terms of recall for some topics. The "Pension/
Insurance" search yielded only fifteen relevant documents on ILP.
The same search on both of the full-text databases, *WESTLAW Text
and Periodicals* (WEST-TP) and *LEXIS-Law Reviews* (LEXIS-
LR), retrieved more relevant documents even though those databases contain fewer titles. However, for "Sexual Harassment" ILP
performed considerably better than either of the full-text databases
in terms of recall. The differences in the search results can be
explained by the fact that the concept of sexual harassment can be
represented by standardized and unique terminology, whereas the
"Pension/Insurance" search lacked standard and unique terms.
Consequently, the "Sexual Harassment" search worked well on a
bibliographic database because most relevant documents made use
of the phrase sexual harassment in either the subject or title field.
However, the "Pension/Insurance" search worked better in the

full-text databases, where the lack of standard terminology or appropriate subject descriptors was less of a burden.

Legal Resources Index (LRI) consistently outperformed ILP in terms of the number of relevant documents retrieved. The superior performance of LRI could be a function of better indexing on LRI; the greater scope of coverage of LRI; the slightly more information about each document provided by LRI; or a combination of all these factors. This study did not attempt to parcel out the responsibility among these factors.

The relatively low precision rates for the full-text searches were disappointing. Even for a topic such as "Sexual Harassment" with standardized terminology the precision rates were low; 47% on WEST-TP and 28% on LEXIS-LR. The low precision rates may be due to the nature of legal literature with its reliance on analogies and citations for procedural rather than substantive purposes. Full-text searching has limited utility in this genre of literature. It may be effective with some topics such as "Pension/Insurance," where there are relatively few documents to sift through in order to get at the relevant ones, but ineffective with topics such as "Sexual Harassment," where the few additional documents retrieved via full-text searching are at the expense of weeding through a considerable quantity of irrelevant documents.

Primary Sources

Cases

The lack of appropriate controlled vocabulary on case law databases is an endemic problem for searching all social science topics and not just women's issues. Even on WESTLAW, which provides controlled vocabulary searching in the "Topic" field of its case law databases, the controlled vocabulary represents principles of law rather than substantive topics such as "Comparable Worth" and "Sexual Harassment." Therefore, only free text searching was used on the caselaw databases, although for comparative purposes editorial fields (synopsis and digest fields on WESTLAW) and the text of the decision (opinion field on LEXIS) were searched separately. In addition, for U.S. Supreme Court cases the syllabus field on LEXIS was searched.

Table 5 presents the results for the U.S. Supreme Court searches. Relevant documents were retrieved for each topic with "Rape," "Reproductive Rights," and "Pregnancy Discrimination" producing the most relevant documents. In terms of recall the full-text searches (LEXIS OPINION) consistently performed better, with the exception of the "Comparable Worth" search. The editorial field searches (WESTLAW SYNOPIS & DIGEST) and summary field searches (LEXIS SYLLABUS) were remarkably similar in terms of the relevant documents retrieved. With the exception of the "Pregnancy Discrimination" and "Sexual Harassment" searches, the WESTLAW and LEXIS SYLLABUS searches performed better than the full-text searches in terms of precision.

There were a couple of anomalies. The "Reproductive Rights" search on WESTLAW produced an unusually high percentage of irrelevant documents. Our evaluation of the samples for the "Reproductive Rights" searches yielded a probable explanation. The word abortion is used along with assault, homicide, and kidnapping in some WEST key numbers under the topic "Criminal Law." The key numbers are included within the digest field. Consequently, documents that had these key numbers were retrieved even though most had nothing to do with abortion. The other anomaly occurred with the "Pregnancy Discrimination" search, where the LEXIS OPINION search had a better precision rate than the other two strategies. This phenomenon may be partially explained by the uniqueness of the terminology used in that search. "Pregnancy Discrimination" yielded the most precise results overall in the primary databases (see Table 11).

The U.S. Supreme Court is the ultimate authority for interpreting law in the United States. For that reason it is important to access all relevant cases decided by the court. Since full-text searching offers the highest recall of relevant cases and since the Supreme Court database is a relatively small database, full-text searching for women's issues is the preferred search option. In every instance except "Sexual Harassment" full-text searching on case databases produced additional relevant documents and without the precipitous drop off in precision rates that was evident with the full-text searches on the periodical databases.

Most of the search topics retrieved so many documents on the

TABLE 5. U.S. SUPREME COURT SEARCHES-TOTAL DOCUMENTS RETRIEVED,
RELEVANT DOCUMENTS AND FALLOUT
(ROW PERCENTAGES IN PARENTHESES)

TOPIC FIELD	TOTAL DOCUMENTS	RELEVANT DOCUMENTS	FALLOUT
SEXUAL HARASSMENT			
LEXIS OPINION	3	3 (100%)	0 (0%)
WEST SYNOPSIS & DIGEST	3	3 (100%)	0 (0%)
LEXIS SYLLABUS	2	2 (100%)	0 (0%)
AFFIRMATIVE ACTION			
LEXIS OPINION	25	16 (64%)	9 (36%)
WEST SYNOPSIS & DIGEST	12	10 (83%)	2 (17%)
LEXIS SYLLABUS	11	8 (73%)	3 (27%)
REPRODUCTIVE RIGHTS			
LEXIS OPINION	125	50 (40%)	75 (60%)
WEST SYNOPSIS & DIGEST	82	16 (20%)	66 (80%)
LEXIS SYLLABUS	40	32 (80%)	8 (20%)
COMPARABLE WORTH			
LEXIS OPINION	11	5 (46%)	6 (54%)
WEST SYNOPSIS & DIGEST	3	2 (67%)	1 (33%)
LEXIS SYLLABUS	4	3 (75%)	1 (25%)
SPOUSE ABUSE			
LEXIS OPINION	22	9 (41%)	13 (59%)
WEST SYNOPSIS & DIGEST	3	2 (67%)	1 (33%)
LEXIS SYLLABUS	3	1 (33%)	2 (67%)
RAPE			
LEXIS OPINION	218	159 (73%)	59 (27%)
WEST SYNOPSIS & DIGEST	80	64 (80%)	16 (20%)
LEXIS SYLLABUS	69	69 (100%)	0 (0%)
PENSION/INSURANCE			
LEXIS OPINION	20	16 (80%)	4 (20%)
WEST SYNOPSIS & DIGEST	4	4 (100%)	0 (0%)
LEXIS SYLLABUS	6	6 (100%)	0 (0%)
PREGNANCY DISCRIMINATION			
LEXIS OPINION	32	28 (88%)	4 (12%)
WEST SYNOPSIS & DIGEST	17	12 (71%)	5 (29%)
LEXIS SYLLABUS	15	11 (73%)	4 (27%)

other case law databases that we were unable to evaluate a sufficiently large sample size of the results to project, with confidence, the number of relevant documents (see Tables 2 and 3).

Some topics, e.g., "Rape," retrieved so many documents in both the lower federal and state courts as to indicate that online searching should focus in on an aspect of the topic and not search it full-text. With other search topics such as "Pension/Insurance" relatively few documents were retrieved, indicating that full-text searching is appropriate. Other topics, most noticeably "Spousal Abuse," yielded relatively few cases in the lower federal court databases but a large number of cases in the state court databases. Searchers interested in the latter topic should adjust their strategies as they move from state to federal jurisdictions.

Tables 6 and 7 depict the results for those searches where we were able to project the total number of relevant documents. The results indicate a familiar pattern. Full-text searching produced more relevant documents but at the cost of a lower precision rate. The "Pension/Insurance" results on Table 5 indicate that full-text searching retrieved four times as many documents with only a slight drop off in precision rate. These results reinforce the conclusion that the "Pension/Insurance" topic should be searched full-text. The "Comparable Worth" results depicted on the same table are less conclusive. The full-text search produced approximately 50% more relevant documents but at a 22% drop-off in the precision

TABLE 6. U.S. COURT OF APPEALS SEARCHES-TOTAL DOCUMENTS RETRIEVED, RELEVANT DOCUMENTS AND FALLOUT FOR SELECTED TOPICS (ROW PERCENTAGES IN PARENTHESES)

TOPIC FIELDS	TOTAL DOCUMENTS	RELEVANT DOCUMENTS	FALLOUT
COMPARABLE WORTH			
LEXIS-OPINION	210	164 (78%)	46 (22%)
WEST SYNOPSIS & DIGEST	112	112 (100%)	0 (0%)
PENSION/INSURANCE			
LEXIS OPINION	121	97 (80%)	24 (20%)
WEST SYNOPSIS & DIGEST	25	23 (92%)	2 (8%)

TABLE 7. STATE COURT SEARCHES-TOTAL DOCUMENTS RETRIEVED,
RELEVANT DOCUMENTS AND FALLOUT FOR SELECTED TOPICS
(ROW PERCENTAGES IN PARENTHESES)

TOPIC FIELDS	TOTAL DOCUMENTS	RELEVANT DOCUMENTS	FALLOUT
AFFIRMATIVE ACTION			
LEXIS OPINION	218	113 (52%)	105 (48%)
WEST SYNOPSIS & DIGEST	48	32 (67%)	16 (33%)
COMPARABLE WORTH			
LEXIS OPINION	135	70 (52%)	65 (48%)
WEST SYNOPSIS & DIGEST	58	46 (79%)	12 (21%)

rate. In addition, the "Comparable Worth" search started with a larger pool of documents to be sifted through.

The results for searching women's issues on case law databases do not lend themselves to generalizations regarding appropriate search strategies. Rather, they suggest that search strategies should be devised on an ad hoc basis and take into account the following factors:

Purpose of the Search
Standardization and Uniqueness of Terminology
Size of the Database being Searched
Expected Number of Retrieved Documents
Searchable Fields Available
Contents and Format of Searchable Fields

Primary Sources

Statutes

In terms of quantity the U.S. Code databases were the least productive of the databases searched. As Table 8 indicates, with the exceptions of the "Reproductive Rights" searches and the "Rape" search on WESTLAW, the search topics all yielded fewer than ten relevant documents. The low search results were not entirely surprising. As noted above statutory law can be written in general lan-

TABLE 8. UNITED STATES CODE DATABASES-TOTAL DOCUMENTS RETRIEVED,
          RELEVANT DOCUMENTS AND FALLOUT

TOPIC DATABASE	TOTAL DOCUMENTS	RELEVANT DOCUMENTS	FALLOUT
REPRODUCTIVE RIGHTS			
LEXIS-USCS	68	63	5
WEST-USCA	61	61	0
COMPARABLE WORTH			
LEXIS-USCS	3	3	0
WEST-USCA	1	1	0
SEXUAL HARASSMENT			
LEXIS-USCS	11	1	10
WEST-USCA	0	0	0
AFFIRMATIVE ACTION			
LEXIS-USCS	15	9	6
WEST-USCA	7	7	0
PREGNANCY DISCRIMINATION			
LEXIS-USCS	3	1	2
WEST-USCA	4	2	2
PENSION/INSURANCE			
LEXIS-USCS	0	0	0
WEST-USCA	1	1	0
RAPE			
LEXIS-USCS	10	5	5
WEST-USCA	21	13	8
SPOUSE ABUSE			
LEXIS-USCS	3	3	0
WEST-USCA	3	3	0

guage with a single section of the code governing a wide range of
activities, whereas case law tends to be narrower in focus interpreting the finer points of law. A single section of the code could result
in hundreds of court cases interpreting that section. Consequently,
the few relevant documents retrieved for topics such as "Compara-

ble Worth," "Sexual Harassment," "Pregnancy Discrimination" does not mean by itself that there is a paucity of federal statutory law regarding these topics, although that is certainly a possibility not ruled out by the results. It is unlikely that the low number of documents retrieved was due to an inadequate search strategy, since the searches were performed full-text plus the annotations added by WEST and LEXIS.

The state codes produced considerably more relevant documents. (See Tables 2 and 3.) On WESTLAW the codes were searched with (WEST-TEXT PLUS) and without the annotations (WEST-TEXT). On LEXIS the searches were limited to the actual text of the code (LEXIS-TEXT).

Table 9 presents the results of the state code searches for the two topics where we were able to examine sufficient sample sizes. Although the state code databases both cover 28 states, the states covered are not identical. Therefore, the LEXIS-TEXT and WEST-TEXT search results are not comparable. However, comparison of the text only with the text plus annotation searches on WESTLAW clearly indicates that searching text plus does not significantly increase the number of relevant documents retrieved but does reduce the precision rate. The results also indicate that there has been more legislative activity regarding women's issues on the state level than the federal level (see Tables 2, 3, 9 and 10).

TABLE 9. STATE CODE DATABASES-TOTAL DOCUMENTS RETRIEVED, RELEVANT DOCUMENTS AND FALLOUT FOR SELECTED TOPICS (ROW PERCENTAGES IN PARENTHESES)

TOPIC FIELDS	TOTAL DOCUMENTS	RELEVANT DOCUMENTS	FALLOUT
COMPARABLE WORTH			
WEST-TEXT PLUS	127	67 (53%)	60 (47%)
WEST-TEXT	91	66 (72%)	25 (28%)
LEXIS-TEXT	43	31 (72%)	12 (28%)
PENSION/INSURANCE			
WEST-TEXT PLUS	70	37 (53%)	33 (47%)
WEST-TEXT	45	33 (67%)	15 (33%)
LEXIS-TEXT	42	28 (67%)	14 (33%)

Administrative Law

Table 10 presents the data from the *Code of Federal Regulations* (CFR) searches. The results indicate that there has been some concern on the part of federal executive agencies in addressing wom-

TABLE 10. CODE OF FEDERAL REGULATIONS DATABASES-TOTAL
DOCUMENTS, RELEVANT DOCUMENTS AND FALLOUT
(ROW PERCENTAGES IN PARENTHESES)

TOPIC FIELDS	TOTAL DOCUMENTS	RELEVANT DOCUMENTS	FALLOUT
REPRODUCTIVE RIGHTS			
LEXIS-CFR	231	169 (73%)	62 (27%)
WEST-CFR	223	178 (80%)	45 (20%)
COMPARABLE WORTH			
LEXIS-CFR	13	13 (100%)	0 (0%)
WEST-CFR	23	23 (100%)	0 (0%)
SEXUAL HARASSMENT			
LEXIS-CFR	12	12 (100%)	0 (0%)
WEST-CFR	14	13 (93%)	1 (7%)
AFFIRMATIVE ACTION			
LEXIS-CFR	210	210 (100%)	0 (0%)
WEST-CFR	224	208 (93%)	16 (7%)
PREGNANCY DISCRIMINATION			
LEXIS-CFR	27	27 (100%)	0 (0%)
WEST-CFR	37	30 (81%)	7 (19%)
PENSION/INSURANCE			
LEXIS-CFR	9	5 (56%)	4 (44%)
WEST-CFR	4	4 (100%)	0 (0%)
RAPE			
LEXIS-CFR	61	12 (20%)	49 (80%)
WEST-CFR	47	13 (28%)	34 (72%)
SPOUSE ABUSE			
LEXIS-CFR	17	14 (82%)	3 (18%)
WEST-CFR	17	12 (70%)	5 (30%)

en's issues. Regulations dealing with "Reproductive rights" and "Affirmative Action" were the most prevalent with a significant drop off for the rest of the topics.

CFR was searched full-text on both LEXIS and WESTLAW. Since neither LEXIS nor WESTLAW provide editorial enhancements to their CFR databases, the differences in the number of documents retrieved were due to differences in software. The precision rates were excellent for all the topics except "Rape." Most of the irrelevant documents retrieved for the "Rape" topic dealt with agricultural issues such as the use of "rape seed." In general, full-text searching was very effective for accessing information on women's issues in the CFR databases.

PERILS OF FREE-TEXT
AND FULL-TEXT SEARCHING

An important consideration in free-text searching is the uniqueness of the terms or phrases being searched. If common terms are used then in some instances the proper use of proximity operators may still restrict the fallout ratio. However, with some topics the terms may be too common for effective free-text searching. As a means of evaluating the appropriateness of the topics in this study for free-text searching we calculated an overall precision rate for each topic. The overall precision rate was derived from the sample of documents retrieved from the primary database searches. The results are displayed in Table 11. As the table indicates, topics with unique and standardized terminology, such as "Pregnancy Discrimination," "Sexual Harassment," and "Comparable Worth," fared better in terms of precision than topics such as "Reproductive Rights" and "Spouse Abuse" which relied on common terms used in a variety of contexts.

One of the problems associated with the "Reproductive Rights" topic was mentioned above. A second problem encountered with the same topic was the retrieval of documents including the use of the phrase "reproductive rights" in a copyright context. Other examples of the perils of free-text searching include the retrieval of the phrase "abuse of discretion" in marital and child custody cases that affected the "Spouse Abuse" results. In addition to the prob-

TABLE 11. SEARCH TOPICS RANKED BY PRECISION
FOR PRIMARY DATABASES

TOPIC	PRECISION RATE
PREGNANCY DISCRIMINATION	.788
SEXUAL HARASSMENT	.771
COMPARABLE WORTH	.753
AFFIRMATIVE ACTION	.725
PENSION INSURANCE	.707
RAPE	.698
REPRODUCTIVE RIGHTS	.591
SPOUSE ABUSE	.547

lems with the "Rape" search on the CFR databases, irrelevant documents were retrieved from the case law databases referring to persons named Raper and where rape was listed as one of a series of "heinous" crimes although it was not the subject matter of most of those cases. Even with the "Pregnancy Discrimination" topic, which had the highest overall precision rate, we retrieved irrelevant documents containing the phrase "pregnant with discrimination."

The potential problems associated with free-text searching are exacerbated when free-text searching is combined with full-text searching. In weighing the utility of full-text searching the nature of the text and the manner in which the text is broken down into searchable fields are important considerations. The text fields in the statutory and regulatory (CFR) databases were relatively short and made use of simple, straightforward language. Full-text searching on the statutory and regulatory databases were generally effective. The text fields on the periodical and case law databases tend to be verbose due to their analytical and explanatory nature. In addition, both cases and articles reflect the individual writing styles of their principal authors. For these reasons they are likely to produce a higher percentage of irrelevant documents than the statutory or regulatory databases. Deciding whether or not to search periodical and case law databases full-text depends upon a multitude of factors that have been mentioned above, but precision rates on these databases are almost certain to be lower than on the statutory or regulatory databases.

BIBLIOMETRICS

The raw data (number of documents) retrieved from a database search can be manipulated to indicate social trends, or for other types of social or legal analysis. This process is called bibliometrics. Table 12 depicts a very rudimentary manipulation of the data retrieved in this study. From Table 12, it is possible to make some preliminary observations as to whether a particular topic has been primarily a state or federal issue, and whether it has been dealt with primarily through legislation or litigation.

TABLE 12. TOTAL NUMBER OF PRIMARY SOURCE HITS, WESTLAW AND LEXIS, BY FEDERAL AND STATE, CASE LAW OR LEGISLATION

TOPIC DATABASE	FEDERAL CASES	STATE CASES	FEDERAL STATUTES	STATE STATUTES
REPRODUCTIVE RIGHTS				
WESTLAW	964	2844	61	2559
LEXIS	2596	4139	68	1583
COMPARABLE WORTH				
WESTLAW	289	58	1	127
LEXIS	782	135	3	43
SEXUAL HARASSMENT				
WESTLAW	443	156	0	96
LEXIS	850	302	11	59
AFFIRMATIVE ACTION				
WESTLAW	614	48	7	127
LEXIS	2277	218	15	96
SPOUSE ABUSE				
WESTLAW	133	4772	3	783
LEXIS	741	7921	3	434
RAPE				
WESTLAW	1764	22460	21	3391
LEXIS	5943	34938	10	2061
PENSION/INSURANCE				
WESTLAW	83	50	1	70
LEXIS	371	184	0	42
PREGNANCY DISCRIMINATION				
WESTLAW	316	357	4	340
LEXIS	1196	978	3	148

The bulk of case law on "Comparable Worth," "Sexual Harassment," and "Affirmative Action" has been at the federal rather than the state level. However, for the same topics the bulk of the statutory law has been at the state rather than federal level. We should note that these observations deal with quantity of documents retrieved and not with the impact of federal versus state, or legislative versus litigation activity. "Pregnancy Discrimination" cases are equally prevalent in federal and state courts, but the bulk of statutory activity has been at the state level. "Spouse Abuse" and "Rape" appear to be topics primarily addressed by state courts and statutes, although there is a large quantity of documents in the federal databases as well. The table indicates that there has been a high level of activity concerning "Reproductive Rights" across the board. Information regarding "Pension/Insurance" issues as they relate to women is the scarcest. There has been more federal case law on the topic, but almost all of the statutory law has been at the state level.

The preliminary data manipulation, displayed in Table 12, indicate that legal databases can be a source for bibliometric analysis. It would be easy through the use of date, court, and other modifications of search strategies to plot trends in the development of each of the women's issues searched in this study.

CONCLUSION

The results indicate that online legal databases contain an abundance of information on women's issues. However, there is not a particular strategy which can be identified as the best approach to accessing information on women's issues.

By necessity as well as design, free-text searching, rather than controlled vocabulary searching, was used in all the searches. By necessity, because many of the databases lacked controlled vocabulary capabilities. By design, because access to information on women's issues has been generally hampered by the unavailability of appropriate controlled vocabulary. Free-text searching compensates for both of these deficiencies.

The results indicate a considerable variance in the effectiveness of free-text searching as a means of providing access to the women's issues searched in this study. Topics such as "Sexual Harassment," "Pregnancy Discrimination," and "Comparable Worth," which are represented by relatively standardized and unique terminology, generally fared better than topics such as "Rape" and "Spousal Abuse," which rely on common terms capable of being used in many contexts. The effectiveness of the searches also depended on the type of documents being searched and whether the full-text or a summary field of the documents was searched. These three variables, i.e., terminology, type of document, field of document, interacted in such a manner as to preclude a conclusion that a particular optimal strategy exists for searching online legal databases.

Free-text full-text searching, in most instances, produces too low a precision rate to be considered effective. However, for obscure topics such as women's issues regarding "Pension/Insurance" free-text full-text searching is preferred. The bibliographic periodical databases performed better in terms of precision but suffered in terms of recall except for those topics such as "Sexual Harassment" that make use of standardized and unique terminology.

Text searching of the case law databases fared moderately better in terms of precision rates. Text searchers produced more relevant documents than summary field searching but with lower precision rates. There were exceptions. The "Pregnancy Discrimination" full-text search on the U.S. Supreme Court database produced more relevant documents and with a higher precision rate than either of the two summary field searches.

The results demonstrated that the size of a database should be considered in developing a search strategy. On the larger databases the topics "Rape" and "Spousal Abuse" retrieved thousands of documents, whereas on the smaller U.S. Supreme Court databases the same topics retrieved a manageable number of documents. On the larger databases these topics should probably be narrowed in terms of subject focus and not searched full-text. However, on the Supreme Court database full-text searching of these topics would be appropriate both because of the limited size of the databases and the importance of not missing any relevant decisions issued by the nation's highest court.

Full-text searching of the statutory (federal and state codes) and regulatory *(Code of Federal Regulations)* databases was very effective with a few exceptions, most noteworthy the "Rape" search on CFR, which produced a high percentage of irrelevant documents.

Finally, some very preliminary manipulations of the data indicate that the legal databases can produce data appropriate for bibliometric analysis. Enough data exists for all of the women's issues examined in the study to perform bibliometric analysis on each.

While the study failed to produce a consensus regarding a standard strategy for accessing information on women's issues in legal databases it did lead to the conclusion that six factors should be considered in developing strategies: purpose of the search, standardization and uniqueness of terminology, size of the database being searched, expected number of relevant documents, searchable fields available, contents and form of search fields.

BIBLIOGRAPHY

Ariel, Joan, Ellen Broidy and Susan Searing, comps. *Women's Legal Rights in the United States: A Selective Bibliography*. Chicago: American Library Association, 1985.

Brody, Fern and Maureen Lambert. "Alternative Databases for Anthropology Searching." *Database* 7 (February 1984):28-33.

Coco, Al. "Full-Text vs. Full-Text Plus Editorial Additions: Comparative Retrieval Effectiveness of the LEXIS and WESTLAW Systems." *Legal Reference Services Quarterly* 4, no. 2 (Summer 1984):27-37.

Dabney, Daniel P. "The Curse of Thamus: An Analysis of Full-Text Legal Document Retrieval." *Law Library Journal* 78, no. 1 (Winter 1986):5-40.

Detlefsen, Ellen Gay. "Issues of Access to Information about Women." *Special Collections* 3, no. 3/4 (Spring/Summer 1986):163-171.

Dolan, Donna R. and Carol E. Heron. "Criminal Justice Coverage in Online Databases." *Database* 2, no. 1 (March 1979):10-32.

Gott, Gary D. and Gary R. Hartman. "Law: North American Legal Systems," in *Manual of Online Search Strategies*, edited by C. J. Armstrong and J. A. Large. Aldershot, England: Gower, 1988, 537-558.

Hildebrand, Suzanne. "Enduser Satisfaction with Computerized Bibliographic Searches in Women's Studies: Preliminary Report," in *Proceedings of the National Online Meeting*. Medford, N.J.: Learned Information, 1985, 215-219.

Hildebrand, Suzanne. "Women's Studies Online: Promoting Visibility." *RQ* 26, no. 1 (Fall 1986):63-74.

Holtzman, Elizabeth. "Women and the Law." *Villanova Law Review* 31 (1986): 1429-1438.

Irving, Richard and Henry Mendelsohn. "Westlaw: Online Legal Reference Searching in a Social Science Library." *The Reference Librarian* no. 18 (Summer 1987):291-305.

Lancaster, F. W. and Ja-Lih Lee. "Bibliometric Techniques Applied to Issues Management: A Case Study." *Journal of the American Society for Information Science* 36, no. 6 (November 1985):389-397.

Mendelsohn, Henry N. "Social Work Online." *Database* 7 (August 1984):36-49.

Nicholas, Susan Cary, Alice M. Price and Rachel Rubin. *Rights and Wrongs: Women's Struggle for Legal Equality*. Old Westbury, N.Y.: Feminist Press and New York: McGraw-Hill Book Company, c1979.

Pritchard, Alan. "Statistical Bibliography or Bibliometrics?" *Journal of Documentation* no. 25 (December 1986):348-349.

Pritchard, Sarah M. "Developing Criteria for Database Evaluation: The Example of Women's Studies." *The Reference Librarian* no. 11 (Fall/Winter 1984):247-261.

Pritchard, Sarah M. "Linking Research, Policy, and Activism." *The Reference Librarian* no. 20 (1987):89-103.

Raisig, L. Miles. "Statistical Bibliography in the Health Sciences." *Bulletin of the Medical Library Association* 50, (July 1962):450-461.

Rhode, Deborah L. "Gender and Juisprudence: An Agenda for Research." *University of Cincinnati Law Review* 56, no. 2 (1987):521-534.

Runde, Craig E. and William H. Lindberg. "The Curse of Thamus: A Response." *Law Library Journal* 78, no. 2 (Spring 1986):345-347.

Sharma, V. S. "A Comparative Evaluation of Online Databases in Relation to Welfare and Corrective Services and Community Development." *Online Review* 6, no. 4 (August 1982):297-313.

Tenopir, Carol. "Evaluation of Database Coverage: A Comparison of Two Methodologies." *Online Review* 6, no. 5 (October 1982):423-439.

Tong, Rosemarie. *Women, Sex and the Law*. Totowa, N.J.: Rowman and Allanheld, c1984.

Voges, Mickie A. "Information Systems and the Law," in *Annual Review of Information Science and Technology*, Vol. 23, edited by Martha E. Williams. Amsterdam: Published for the American Society for Information Science by Elsevier Science Publishers, 1988, 193-216.

Women's Annotated Legal Bibliography. New York: Clark Boardman Co., c1984.

Bibliometric Techniques Applied to Women's Issues in Business Databases

Geraldene Walker
Ruth A. Palmquist
Steven D. Atkinson

SUMMARY. The patterns of production in the literature on women's issues in business databases are investigated by analyzing the postings produced by six topical searches and comparing the results with overall growth between 1976 to 1987 in the files included in the study. Overall file growth is linear, while the pattern for postings on women's issues is curvilinear. This pattern peaked around 1985 or 1986 and has dropped since. The curvilinear model is confirmed by its successful prediction of the number of postings for the year 1988. The sharp decrease in postings for the year 1982 invites speculation regarding the social factors which might have contributed to this finding. Clusters of business, government, and general/interdisciplinary databases are investigated to measure differences in the numbers and patterns of postings on women's issues. All three clusters fit the curvilinear model. The business and government groups show a slow start, modest growth, and slight dropoff in recent years. The general/interdisciplinary group shows more spectacular growth, peaking in 1983 and declining since. Patterns displayed by these clusters resemble patterns in the overall growth in the databases included in the study.

Geraldene Walker is with the School of Information Science and Policy, University at Albany, State University of New York. Ruth A. Palmquist is with the School of Library and Information Science, University of Tennessee, Knoxville. Steven D. Atkinson is with University Libraries, University at Albany, State University of New York.

INTRODUCTION

Although women's contributions to American business enterprise date back to colonial days, they have remained largely unrecognized. A variety of social, economic, educational and legal factors have combined to expand their role in the workforce. The growth in the number of wage-earning women is regarded as "one of the most striking phenomena of modern American society." Most women workers, though, remain clustered in traditional "female" jobs. Only 5% work in managerial/administrative positions (Brown 1981, p. 13). The integration of women into positions of authority within business organizations has been limited by occupational sex typing and the male-dominated culture of most large companies. The disparity between women's expectations and the reality of discrimination has encouraged some to develop mentor relationships within the traditional corporate culture and others to leave this environment and organize their own enterprises. This investigation explores the coverage of women's issues in the online literature of business and management in order to identify trends in publication patterns between 1976 and 1987. The growing recognition within the business community of the importance of information as a corporate resource has been reflected in the simultaneous expansion of all types of information resources. The proliferation of machine readable bibliographic databases has made it possible to monitor patterns in the business and management literature and identify points at which the rate of growth in the number of publications on a given topic has changed.

A sizeable amount of business and management information is available online in the form of statistics included in non-bibliographic databases offering company, product, financial and demographic data. This analysis, however, concentrates on bibliographic and full-text files that provide access to the secondary literature in the field. These databases include bibliographic records on such topics as finance, marketing, personnel, management and working conditions from business journals, newspapers, popular magazines, and dissertations. The core business files selected for this study are *ABI/INFORM*, *Management Contents*, *Economic Abstracts*, *Harvard Business Review Online*, and *Foreign Trade and Economic*

Abstracts International. These files have all been recommended as useful sources of business information (Donati 1981, Meredith 1986, Roan 1984, and Shorthill 1985). The business files are supplemented by interdisciplinary and popular databases — *Dissertation Abstracts International, Magazine Index, National Newspaper Index,* and *Social Scisearch* — in order to estimate public awareness of the issues investigated. A third group of databases — *Congressional Information Service* (CIS), *PAIS, GPO Monthly Catalog,* and *Legal Resource Index* — was consulted in order to measure Congressional interest in and action on these issues. (See Figure 1.)

SEARCH TOPICS

Six topics dealing with women in business were selected for searching:

1. Affirmative Action;
2. Equal Pay;
3. Entrepreneurs;
4. Women in Management;
5. Mentors and Proteges; and
6. Sexual Harassment.

These topics were profiled across the databases from 1976 through 1987. Postings figures for each topic were isolated in every database for each year, in order to record the yearly coverage provided by the different files. Online searches were performed using the OneSearch feature on DIALOG with the option of SET DETAIL ON. By combining terms with years of publication it was possible to generate a listing of the number of items published in each year in each database for each topic.

Terms selected for the search strategies used natural language vocabulary and were as explicit as possible. They were either single phrases representing key women's issues (e.g., affirmative action) or combinations of more general terms with terms representing the female sex (e.g., entrepreneurs and women). The selection of terms was guided by Lancaster and Lee's conclusion that the choice of

FIGURE 1. Databases Used by Database Group

Business

ABI/INFORM: Aimed at business executives and covers all aspects of management and administration. Indexes approximately eight hundred primary publications in business and related fields. File size: 422,290 records.

Economic Literature Index: Indexes approximately 260 journals covering articles and book reviews and approximately 200 monographs per year in all areas of economics. File size: 164,429 records.

Foreign Trade and Economic Abstracts: Covers all areas of economics, including markets, industries, and international economic data in the fields of economic science and management. Abstracts approximately 1800 journals in addition to books, directories, and reports. File size: 193,184 records.

Harvard Business Review: Provides full-text of the Harvard Business Review, which includes articles on accounting, automation, business ethics, industry analysis, strategic planning, and trade. File size: 3,000 records.

Management Contents: Indexes articles from over 120 U.S. and international journals, as well as proceedings, transactions, business course materials, newsletters, and research reports. Covers accounting, decision sciences, finance, industrial relations, managerial economics, marketing, operations research, organization behavior, and public administration. File size: 269,544 records.

General

Dissertation Abstracts: Comprehensive coverage of American Doctoral Dissertations, plus increasing numbers from abroad. Includes all subject areas. File size: 988,740 records.

Magazine Index: Covers more than 435 popular magazines, providing coverage of current affairs, the performing arts, business, sports, recreation and travel, consumer product evaluations, science and technology, leisure time activities, etc. File size: 2,785,827 records.

National Newspaper Index: Provides front-to-back index to the Christian Science Monitor, the New York Times, and The Wall Street Journal. Also includes the Los Angeles Times and the Washington Post since 1982. File size: 1,671,069 records.

Social SciSearch: Indexes every significant item from 1500 social science journals throughout the world and selected articles from 3000 additional journals in the natural, physical, and biomedical sciences.

Includes monographs and covers every area of the social and behavorial sciences. File size: 2,424,850 records.

FIGURE 1 (continued)

Government

CIS: Provides current, comprehensive access to the contents of the entire spectrum of Congressional working papers published by House, Senate, and Joint Committees and Subcommittees each year. File size: 257,849 records.

GPO Monthly Catalog: Indexes reports, studies, fact sheets, maps, handbooks, conference proceedings, etc., issued by all U.S. federal government agencies and the U.S. Congress. Includes records of all House and Senate hearings on private and public bills and laws. File size: 297,700 records.

Legal Resource Index: Indexes more than 750 key law journals, six law newspapers, and legal monographs. File size: 360,880 records.

PAIS International: Indexes public policy issues in business, economics, finance, law, international relations, government, political science, and other social sciences worldwide. Includes printed material in all formats in six languages. File size: 311,057 records.

unambiguous terms is more important than the completeness of the search (Lancaster and Lee 1985). Searches were performed on both Title (TI) and Descriptor (DE) fields in order to enhance specificity and limit false drops. This strategy yielded two types of information useful for evaluating coverage of women's issues as represented by the six topics: statistics on the overall growth of the literature and figures on the differences between the three clusters of databases (business, general, and government). The following search statements, limited to the years 1976 through 1987, were profiled for each of the topics under consideration:

(wom?n? OR female?)/TI,DE AND (pay()equity OR equal()pay
OR
comparable()worth?/TI,DE

(wom?n? OR female?)/TI,DE AND entrepreneur?/TI,DE

(wom?n? OR female?)/TI,DE AND (mentor? OR protege? OR
role()model?)/TI,DE

affirmative()action/TI,DE

sex?()harass?/TI,DE

(wom?n? OR female?) AND (executiv? OR president? OR ceo?
OR (high? OR
top)(1W)(manag? OR administrat?))/TI,DE

TREND ANALYSIS

The availability of bibliographic records in machine readable form not only permits fast and inexpensive searching but also allows for analysis of trends in the literature. Online bibliographic databases make it possible to document changing patterns of interest in various topics and to track the diffusion of issues in online indexes and abstracts over time. It might be the case, for example, that coverage of issues concerning women in business spread from the specialized business literature (professional journals) to more general publications (newspapers and magazines) to government sources (Congressional testimony and legislation). This type of trend analysis was pioneered by Lancaster and Lee, who suggested that

> if an . . . issue begins to appear in the popular press at some significant level, a high probability exists that it will later become of concern to Congress or the Executive Branch. (Lancaster and Lee 1985, p. 390)

It is possible to test hypotheses about diffusion of women's issues in business, general, and government publications by tracking the coverage of these issues through the three clusters of databases. The methodology utilized in this research is adapted from Lancaster and Lee's case study analyzing the coverage of "acid rain" in bibliographic files (Lancaster and Lee 1985) and from the statistical techniques used by both McNeil (McNeil 1975) and Bobner (Bobner 1982). This bibliometric approach provides a somewhat crude reflection of interest in women's issues over time. Crude because this technique cannot compensate for the time lag in the writing, editing and publishing of manuscripts. Since relationships are not easy to detect when the information is in table format, it is presented here in the form of graphs. While these graphic presentations can be used to identify the broad pattern of overall interest in women's issues and in each search topic from 1976 to 1987, it was also deemed necessary to test whether the suggested relationships are statistically significant through the use of multiple linear regression techniques.

DATA EVALUATION

Research Question 1: How has the coverage of women's studies topics evolved — according to a linear or curvilinear model — in the selected databases during the period 1976-1987?

In order to answer this question, a visual examination of the graphs of the yearly totals was made. Once a visual trend was detected, a statistical technique known as trend analysis was used to fit a line or curve through the points representing these yearly totals. This type of statistical analysis provides an understanding of changes in the production of literature on selected topics that can be attributed to factors other than chance. The research may then attempt to correlate the documented fluctuations with social developments.

A summary of the total postings for all thirteen databases for all six search topics is shown in Figure 2.

Visual inspection suggests a curvilinear pattern, rising to 1984 and then dropping off. The drop in the total for 1982, which stands out clearly, seems atypical, so the 1982 data was omitted from the multiple linear regression analysis shown below. The omission of such outlier data is a commonly used technique in the aggregation of nonresistent summary statistics (Hartwig and Dearing 1979, pp. 27-28). Possible changes in the lag time between writing and publication, the erosion of support for the Equal Rights Amendment after 1978 (Berry 1986 and Mansbridge 1986), and the nomination of Ronald Reagan for the Presidency in August, 1980 might help to explain the drop in 1982. Inspection of the graph also suggests that a simple linear model may not provide an adequate estimation of the trend in the literature, because the total postings appear to diminish somewhat after 1984. Alternative quadratic and cubic models were assessed using a SAS general linear models program in order to determine the best fit model. The results (shown below) suggest that the quadratic model may be appropriate because the Type I Sum of Squares has an $F(1,8) = 31.34$ (p > .0005) and indicates that a quadratic term (Time*Time) added to the model accounts for a significant share of the variance.

QUADRATIC MODEL FOR TOTAL POSTINGS

SOURCE	DF	Sum of Sq	Mean Sq	F
Model	2	1464828.204	732414.102	87.21
Error	8	67186.34	8398.293	P = .0001
Total	10	1532014.544		

R-Square = .9561

SOURCE	DF	TYPEI SS	F Value	PR > F
Time	1	1201645.536	143.08	.0001
Time*Time	1	263182.668	31.34	.0005

These figures suggest that a reasonable model for the estimation of future trends in the production of literature on women's issues would look like:

$$TOTAL(postings) = A(Time*Time) + B(Time) + C$$

where A, B, and C are constants computed by the SAS multiple linear regression routine. A t-test was performed on the estimates of these parameters (A, B, and C) to determine whether each of them differs significantly from zero. The following results provide the numeric estimate for each parameter given in the model above.

Parameter	Estimate	t-Value	p > ltl
A	− 17.514	− 5.60	0.0005
B	314.69	8.16	0.0001
C	− 121.11	− 1.20	0.2632

While the t-test value for the C estimate was higher than the usual 0.05 level of significance used in most regression analyses, many authorities (Moore 1988) recommend the use of a liberal level of significance, because the less liberal 0.05 tends to lead to models that do not have enough parameters and are often biased as a result.

Research Question 2: Do the three clusters of databases (business, general, government) reveal differences in the patterns of coverage of women's issues? (See Figure 3.)

Visual inspection of the graphs suggests that both the business and government groups have a somewhat slowed level of production, with the government group making a very slow start. The general group has experienced some sizable leaps but appears to have tailed off over the last four or five years. This visual analysis of grouped databases suggested that descriptions of their trends might require different statistical models.

For both the business and the government groupings, a quadratic model fit the data best.

BUSINESS GROUP F TEST OF THE QUADRATIC MODEL

MODEL	2	17768.295	884.148	7.67
ERROR	9	10423.372	1158.152	p = .0114
TOTAL	11	28191.667		

R-Squared = 0.6303

	df	TYPE I SS	F VALUE	p
Time	1	9232.175	7.97	0.02
Time*Time	1	8536.120	7.37	0.02

BUSINESS GROUP – MODEL

BUSN (Totals) = -2.529(Time*Time) + 40.912(Time) + 117.2

GOVERNMENT GROUP – F TEST OF THE QUADRATIC MODEL

	df	SS	MS	F
MODEL	2	74743.209	37371.604	11.18
ERROR	9	30075.708	3341.745	p = .0036
TOTAL	11			

R-Squared = 0.713

	df	TYPE I	SS	F VALUE p
Time	1	57982.659	17.35	0.002
Time*Time	1	16760.550	5.02	0.0519

GOVERNMENT GROUP – MODEL

GOVT(totals) = -3.544(Time*Time) + 66.205(Time) + 0

(Note: The intercept term did not provide a significant t-value and is therefore assumed to be no different from zero.)

The third (general) grouping is described here with both the quadratic and linear models; it was close to significance in the quadratic form but was clearly significant in the linear form.

GENERAL GROUPING
Quadratic Model
GEN(totals) = -5.76(Time*Time) + 137.85(Time) - 98.82

Linear Model
GEN(totals) = 63.0(Time) + 75.83

To check the appropriateness of the models chosen for both the overall subject field and for the different groupings, a search of the thirteen databases for 1988 was conducted. The formula for the quadratic model was used to predict the expected postings for the year 1988 and did so with considerable success (predicted 1133, retrieved 1063). The results indicate that we can accept the quadratic model and predict with some certainty that the literature peaked around 1985 or 1986 and is continuing to drop. For the three different database groups, the quadratic model also provided rea-

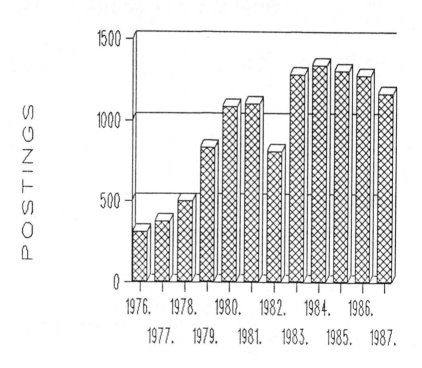

YEARS

FIGURE 2. Women's Issues Postings

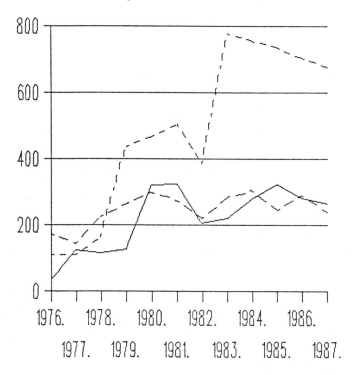

FIGURE 3. Group Postings

sonable predictions when compared with the actual figures for 1988, though postings are dropping more than expected. (See Figure 4.)

The initial impact of this specific trend analysis shows a striking leveling and decline in postings on the topics searched. This decline, if real, is a recent phenomenon and one which cannot be traced to any particular database.

Before accepting the finding that the number of postings on women's issues is declining both in the literature as a whole (as measured by the 13 databases examined) and in the database clusters (business, general, government), it was important to be certain that this decline occurred independently of the ups and downs of the total literature production in these 13 databases.

It was necessary to find the total number of documents included in the 13 databases from 1976 to 1987 (see Figure 5) and determine the multiple linear regression fit which most closely described the totals. If the best fit was a linear one, it would seem that the literature as a whole was still growing and that the decline in the emphasis on women's issues was real. To check the accuracy of the equation chosen as best fit, its ability to predict the postings figure for 1988 was tested. In a similar manner, the totals for each of the databases previously grouped under the three concentrations were assessed. Table 1 indicates which type of equation (linear or curvilinear) that best predicts the actual postings figures for 1988.

CONCLUSIONS

Trend analysis provides an effective methodology for bibliometric studies of online databases for women's issues in business because it accommodates noise within the aggregate data. In other words, the total of postings for all topics (affirmative action, equal pay, entrepreneurs, women in management, mentors and proteges, and sexual harassment) across multiple databases enables the particular biases in any one file or on any one topic to be much less detrimental to the analysis of the data in question. It is clear that after a period of exponential growth the literature on women's issues in business peaked around 1985 or 1986 and appears to have dropped since.

	Predicted	Actual
Government	263	225
Business	244	206
General	726	632
Total	1133	1063

FIGURE 4. Predicted and Actual Postings

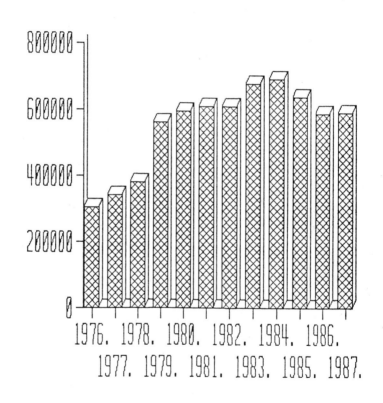

FIGURE 5. Total File Postings

TABLE 1. Database Total for 1988

	PREDICTED	ACTUAL
GOVERNMENT (curvilinear, quadratic)	65,446	64,100
BUSINESS (curvilinear, quadratic)	60,694	61,552
GENERAL (linear)	541,387	636,988
TOTAL (linear)	730,847	762,640

Trend analysis does have a number of limitations. The assumption that each article is of equal importance is obviously an oversimplification, as is the assumption that each search term or topic is of equal value. Databases under consideration differ in comprehensiveness, timeliness, and accuracy, which makes the initial selection of an appropriate range of files particularly important. Despite these drawbacks, trend analysis of online databases provides figures on patterns of literary production over time on topics such as women's issues and invites correlations between these patterns and social developments.

BIBLIOGRAPHY

Bechtel, H. "The Imperfections of Databases: How Gaps and Overlaps Can be Detrimental to the User." In *Proceedings of the 9th International Online Information Meeting.* pp. 453-460. Oxford: Learned Information, 1985.

Berry, Mary Frances. *Why ERA Failed: Politics, Women's Rights, and the Amending Process of the Constitution.* Bloomington: Indiana University Press, 1986.

Bobner, Ronald F. et al. *Historical Policy Capturing Through Use of Computerized Databases and Trend Analysis Techniques.* (March 1982): ED 216 957.

Brown, Linda Keller. *Woman Manager in the United States: A Research Analysis and Bibliography.* Washington, D.C.: Business and Professional Women's Foundation, 1981.

Budd, John M. "Bibliometric Analysis of Higher Education Literature." *Research in Higher Education* 28 (1988): 180-190.

Dolan, Donna. "Criminal Justice Coverage in Online Databases." *Database* 2 (March 1979): 10-32.

Donati, Robert. "Decision Analysis for Selecting Online Databases to Answer Business Questions." *Database* 4 (December 1981): 49-63.

Dou, Henri. "How to Use Online Databases as a Tool for Forecasting Fundamental and Applied Research." In *Proceedings of the 7th International Online Information Meeting.* pp. 175-183. Oxford: Learned Information, 1983.

Frohmann, Bernd. "A Bibliometric Analysis of the Literature of Cataloguing and Classification." *Library Research* 4 (Winter 1982): 355-373.

Gersh, Barbara. "Business and Economics." In *Online Search Strategies.* Edited by Ryan E. Hoover. pp. 305-330. White Plains, NY: Knowledge Industry Publications, 1982.

Grenier, M.T. "Business Databases – A Comparative Review." In *Online '85 Conference Proceedings.* pp. 125-128. Weston, CT: Online, Inc., 1985.

Hartwig, F. and Dearing, D.E. *Exploratory Data Analysis.* Beverly Hills, CA: Sage Publications, Inc., 1979.

Hawkins, Donald T. "Unconventional Uses of On-line Information Retrieval

Systems: On-line Bibliometric Studies." *Journal of the American Society for Information Science* 28 (January 1977): 13-18.

Hildenbrand, Suzanne. "Women's Studies Online: Promoting Visibility." *RQ* 26 (Fall 1986): 63-74.

Hoffman, Nancy Jo. "Feminist Scholarship and Women's Studies." *Harvard Educational Review* 56 (November 1986): 511-519.

Janke, Richard. "Business on BRS: Focus on Predicasts." *Database* 6 (August 1983): 33-50.

Keck, Bruce L. "An Investigation of Recall in the ABI/INFORM Database when Selecting by Journal." *Online Review* 5 (October 1981): 395-398.

Lancaster, F.W. and Lee, Ja-Lih. "Bibliometric Techniques Applied to Issues Management." *Journal of the American Society for Information Science* 36 (November 1985): 389-397.

Lawrence, Kathleen A. *"My Key to the Men's Room": Mentor and Protege Relationships in Business and Professional Organizations: An Overview.* (April 1985): ED 266 496.

McBroom, Linda. "Sensing the Right Database for Business and Financial Affairs." In *Online '85 Conference Proceedings*. pp. 205-209. Weston, CT: Online, Inc., 1985.

McNeil, K.A., Kelly, F.J., and McNeil, J.T. *Testing Research Hypotheses Using Multiple Linear Regression.* Carbondale, IL: Southern Illinois University Press, 1975.

Mansbridge, Jane J. *Why We Lost the ERA.* Chicago: University of Chicago Press, 1986.

Meredith, Meri. "Ten Most Searched Databases by a Business Generalist." *Database* 9 (February 1986): 36-40.

Moore, Geoffrey H. "The Development and Analysis of Economic Indicators." In *Statistics: A Guide to the Unknown.* Edited by Judith M. Tanur, et al. 3rd ed. pp. 227-238. Pacific Grove, CA: Wadsworth and Brooks/Cole, 1988.

Novarra, Virginia. "Women's Studies Management Education: A Case for Women's Studies?" *Women's Studies International Forum* 5 (1982): 69-74.

Ojala, Marydee and Bates, Ellen. "Business Databases." In *Annual Review of Information Science and Technology.* Edited by Martha E. Williams. pp. 87-117. White Plains, NY: Knowledge Industry Publications for American Society for Information Science, Volume 21, 1986.

Oppenheim, C. "Use of Online Databases in Bibliometric Studies." In *Proceedings of the 9th International Online Information Meeting.* pp. 355-364. Oxford: Learned Information, 1985.

Roan, Tattie W. "Meeting Business Needs Via Online Searching." In *Proceedings of the National Online Meeting.* Compiled by Martha E. Williams and Thomas H. Hogan. pp. 313-317. Medford, NJ: Learned Information, 1984.

Searing, Susan. "Business, Economics, and Labor Studies." In *Introduction to Library Research in Women's Studies.* (Westview Guides to Library Research) pp. 93-99. Boulder and London: Westview Press, 1985.

Sharma, V.S. "A Comparative Evaluation of Online Databases in Relation to

Welfare and Corrective Services, and Community Development." *Online Review* 6 (August 1984): 297-313.

Shorthill, Rachel R. "Unexpected Online Sources for Business Information." *Online* 9 (January 1985): 68-78.

Trubkin, Loene. "Building a Core Collection of Business & Management Periodicals: How Databases Can Help." *Online* 6 (July 1982): 43-49.

Wagers, R. "The Decision to Search Databases Full Text." In *Proceedings of the 10th International Online Information Meeting.* pp. 93-107. Oxford: Learned Information, 1986.

Wagers, Robert. "ABI/INFORM and Management Contents on Dialog." *Database* 3 (March 1980): 12-36.

Wallace, Danny P. "A Solution in Search of a Problem: Bibliometrics and Libraries." *Library Journal* 112 (May 1987): 43-47.

Researching Information About Women in Reference Databases: Advances and Limitations

Barbara Ammerman Durniak

SUMMARY. Several sources traditionally found in reference collections are now available online. The online versions of eight standard reference works were examined to determine whether or not they provide accurate and adequate information on women and women's issues.

Found in every library is a core collection known as the reference collection. Although the contents of this collection are partially dictated by such factors as the library's purpose, clientele, and budget, materials are placed in this collection as a rule because they provide convenient and accurate answers to a variety of questions. Authoritativeness, timeliness, and comprehensiveness are features librarians seek when evaluating and selecting sources for the reference collection, and if a source meets these criteria, it is likely to be consulted frequently to answer patron queries. Over time, certain titles become well-known and may be thought of as standards by librarians and users alike.

In the past twenty years, standards regarding women's place in and contributions to society have been challenged. As part of this challenge, popular media such as television, film, and children's literature have been examined with respect to their representation of women. Studies of print reference sources such as encyclopedias (Engle and Futas 1983) and dictionaries (Gershuny 1975) conclude

Barbara Ammerman Durniak is Database Searching Coordinator, Vassar College, Box 20, Poughkeepsie, NY 12601.

that there are fewer biographical entries for women than for men, that illustrations typically depict men as leaders and women as spectators or subordinates, and that language is not gender-neutral. What these media have in common is that (1) they reach a wide audience (2) they are frequently available in the home and are viewed/utilized by children as well as by adults and (3) because of ease of access, little or no guidance is provided in their use. As a result, it is unlikely that what the user sees or reads will be questioned. If it is assumed that the above sources reflect the conventional attitudes and wisdom of the society that produced them, then the idea that women are less visible, less important, and less likely to have made a contribution to society is perpetuated.

Some of the obstacles connected with researching women and women's issues are mentioned by Detlefsen (1986). It is difficult to locate feminist materials that portray women in a positive and non-sexist light. Another factor is the interdisciplinary nature of Women's Studies materials and the attendant problems with classification. The vocabulary used to describe women or women's roles is frequently sexist and/or non-specific.

The advent of online versions of standard reference sources opens up new avenues in reference service. Katz (1982) discusses the trade-off between the timeliness, speed, and increased access points offered by online files and the no-cost but at times tedious search required by print sources. Although reference databases may be used in the traditional manner, i.e., to answer ready-reference questions, the structure and interactive nature of online systems makes it possible to investigate patterns that would be difficult to trace in the print counterparts. The purpose of this paper is to find out whether standard online reference sources adequately and accurately reflect the experiences of women.

METHODOLOGY

Four types of reference databases were examined: encyclopedias, biographical sources, institutional directories, and trade bibliographies. Sample searches were devised and run on each file. All searches were run on the DIALOG Information Retrieval system, although many of the databases are available on other utilities such as BRS.

Encyclopedias: *Academic American Encyclopedia* and *Everyman's Encyclopedia*

Biographical: *Marquis Who's Who* and *Biography Master Index*

Institutional Directories: *American Library Association* and *Encyclopedia of Associations*

Trade Bibliographies: *Ulrich's International Periodical Directory* and *Books in Print*

ENCYCLOPEDIAS

The *Academic Encyclopedia (AAE)* and *Everyman's Encyclopedia (EE)* are general encyclopedias, providing information on a wide variety of topics. Both works are aimed at high school and college students as well as adults. The online files correspond to the latest editions of the printed versions, plus quarterly updates for the *AAE*. The *AAE* in print is updated yearly, while the latest edition of *EE* is the 6th, published in 1978.

Three tests were conducted to evaluate these databases in terms of their coverage of women and women's issues. First, the files were searched for the inclusion of biographical entries of selected women. Second, they were searched for information on events and issues important to women and women's history. Third, the use of non-sexist language was examined.

Biographical Entries

According to the preface of the *AAE*, 35% of the records in the database are biographies, while *EE* states that biographies account for approximately 25% of all records. The names of fifty women were searched in order to determine if information was available about them and to ascertain whether the information was in the form of a separate biographical entry or included in another record. Subjects were chosen on the basis of their inclusion in at least one of the following sources: *Notable American Women: 1607-1950, Notable American Women: The Modern Period, The Biographical Dictionary of British Feminists: Volume One: 1800-1930,* or *The Interna-*

tional Dictionary of Women's Biography. Approximately equal numbers of United States, British, and international figures were chosen, and historical as well as contemporary women were included. Subjects chosen reflected achievements in politics, social reform, women's rights, science, athletics, and the arts. See Appendix A for the names of women included in this sample.

Of the 50 names searched in the *AAE*, 35 (70%) were present. Thirty-one women, or 62%, were accorded biographical entries, and four were mentioned in the texts of articles on other subjects. In the *EE*, 34% of the names searched were located. Thirty-two percent of the subjects chosen were accorded biographical entries and one was mentioned in connection with other topics.

Of the names searched, 36% were American citizens, 32% were British, and the remainder were of other nationalities. The breakdown by nationality of women included was not uniform; in the *AAE*, U.S. women were found more frequently, while in the *EE*, entries for British and women from countries other than the United States were found in equal numbers. Table 1 illustrates the breakdown by nationality. (See Table 1.)

Of the women searched, nine, or 18%, are still living. Six of the nine women, or 67%, were found as biographical entries in the *AAE*, while in *EE*, only one name, or 11%, was found. Ten women included in the sample were women of color; 70% of these women were found in the *AAE* but only 11% were located in *EE*.

Since it is possible to search records in *EE* by article type, a further test of the number of biographical entries accorded to women was conducted. It was assumed that records about women tagged as BIOGRAPHY would also contain the pronouns "she" and "her" in their texts. Accordingly, records containing these two criteria were searched. Of the 15,002 records tagged as biographies, 1,301, or 9%, contained the pronouns "she" and "her" in

TABLE 1
ENTRIES BY NATIONALITY

	AAE	EE
British	28.5%	41%
American	43%	18%
Other	28.5%	41%

the text. If the above assumption is correct, then the majority of biographical entries are for men.

Events and Issues

Twenty topics relating to or of interest to women were searched. Topics selected were based on entries in the *Encyclopedia of Feminism* and *A Feminist Dictionary* as well as on contemporary issues frequently in the news. Included were concerns in the areas of health, law and legislation, labor, politics, women's rights, and sexuality.

Topics were first searched in all subject-conveying fields of the Basic Index; in the *AAE*, the Subject Heading, Title Text, and Cross-Reference fields were accessed, while in *EE*, the Descriptor, Title, and Text fields were searched. As recommended by the producers of both databases, proximity operators rather than the Boolean operator AND were employed to decrease the likelihood of false drops, especially when searching the Text field.

Of the twenty topics searched in the *AAE*, some mention was found of 10, or 50% of the topics. The following were accorded full entries as well as being included in related articles: DES, the Seneca Falls Convention, Lesbianism, the National Organization of Women, Suttee, and Roe v. Wade. The remaining 4 topics were mentioned at least once in the texts of related articles. The same search in *EE* yielded 6 hits, or 30%. Of these, two topics, Lesbian and Suttee, were full entries as well as parts of the texts of related articles. The remaining 4 topics were found in the texts of at least one article. Table 2 provides a breakdown of search topics and findings in each database.

Gender-Neutral Language

To determine whether or not there was a preponderance of masculine vs. feminine pronouns and words in the texts of the articles included in the two encyclopedias, masculine and feminine pronouns and terms were searched in the text fields. In the *AAE*, the words "him, his, he, man and men" were approximately 5.6 times as likely to appear as were the feminine counterparts. In *EE*, the masculine words were 8.3 times more prevalent. The ratio of male to female terms is given in Table 3.

As demonstrated previously, *EE* contains more biographical entries for men than for women. Even when biographical entries were eliminated, masculine terms were still more prevalent in *EE* articles. A total of 4,362 non-biographical articles were found that contained masculine terms but no feminine terms. When search terms were limited to feminine terms, only 449 records were retrieved.

A sampling of every 200th record from the first search revealed that usage of masculine terms fell into three categories. The first

TABLE 2
SEARCH TOPICS FOUND BY DATABASE

Topic	Full Entry AAE	Full Entry EE	Text AAE	Text EE	Not Found AAE	Not Found EE
Teen pregnancy			x	x		
DES	x					x
Seneca Falls	x		x	x		
Declaration of Rights of Women					x	x
Declaration of Sentiments			x			x
International Women's Day					x	x
International Women's Year					x	x
Cat & Mouse Act			x	x		
Contagious Diseases Act					x	x
Lesbian/ism	x	x				
Cable Act					x	x
NOW	x		x			x
Muslim women			x	x		
Suttee	x	x				
Matchgirls Strike					x	x
Triangle Shirtwaist Company					x	x
Date Rape					x	x
WSPU			x			x
WTUL					x	x
Roe v. Wade	x		x			

TABLE 3
PROPORTION OF MASCULINE V. FEMININE TERMS IN TEXT FIELD

Terms	Ratio of Male:Female AAE	Ratio of Male:Female EE
him/her	2637:1904	3443:1774
his/hers	11643:5	13788:5
he/she	10649:1402	13742:1293
man/woman	1327:535	1810:327
men/women	1154:1068	1368:714
Totals	27410:4914	34151:4113

was the use of pronouns to refer to a male individual mentioned in the article; for example, Clerk Maxwell and "his theory of electricity" in the articles on RADIOCOMMUNICATION and Bach and "his well-tempered clavier" in the article on TEMPERMENT. The second category reflected the use of masculine pronouns in connection with occupations traditionally associated with men, as evidenced by this sentence that appeared in the article on HELICOPTERS: "There are many types of flying . . . recently a number of one-man types have been built in which the pilot stands on a platform with . . . rotors revolving below him" and also by the articles entitled SALESMANSHIP. The third category included instances in which a masculine term was used to represent the whole of humanity. Examples of such usage were found in the article on CULCIDAE: "The anophelinae contains the genus Anopheles, species of which are vectors of malaria parasites to man" and in the article on BOOK-KEEPING: "Ever since man began trading it has been necessary to keep a record of transactions."

A sampling of every 25th record of the set containing solely feminine terms revealed a different pattern of usage. Feminine pronouns were commonly found in articles on mythological or folk figures (ANAHITA, a goddess; the nymph of STYX; and cailleach (old woman), a symbol of HARVEST CUSTOMS), but did not refer to actual women. Another use was to refer to the female of certain species of insects (GOLDEN-EYE FLY; QUEEN BEE). A third example was the use of feminine pronouns to refer to geographic locations, as evidenced by this sentence which appeared in an article on the DELIAN LEAGUE: ". . . Athens had no difficulty . . . until she lost the bulk of her fleet in the Sicilian disaster." This small sampling (21 records were viewed from the first set, and 18 were viewed from the second set) suggests that this database has not made an effort to raise the visibility of women or to eradicate sexist language and stereotyping.

BIOGRAPHICAL DIRECTORIES

Aside from the encyclopedias discussed above, there are several other online databases that contain biographies or provide access to biographies. Two of these are *Marquis Who's Who (WW)* and *Biog-*

raphy Master Index (BMI). The *WW* file commenced in 1982 and includes that year's and all subsequent editions of *Who's Who in America* as well as all published editions of *Who's Who in Frontiers of Science and Technology*. *BMI* corresponds to the second edition of the *Biography and Genealogy Master Index*. *WW* is reloaded biannually, while *BMI*, according to documentation, is updated "periodically." *WW* contains biographical profiles of prominent men and women residing in the United States, Canada, and Mexico, selected for inclusion by virtue of position held or as a result of outstanding accomplishment. *BMI* is international in scope and functions as an index to over 350 biographical works.

In order to determine the extent to which women are represented in these files, the following tests were conducted. In *WW*, the ratio of men's to women's entries was examined, and portions of the records listing civic or political activities and memberships were searched in order to identify individuals associated with particular organizations or causes. The ratio of men to women awarded various prizes or honors was examined, and a search was also conducted on the names of fifty contemporary women to determine if biographical entries for them were included. In *BMI*, the same fifty women searched in the encyclopedic databases were searched, and the number of sources accorded them was examined.

Marquis Who's Who

A factor complicating searching in this file is the fact that biographees supply their own data. If the individual chooses to omit certain information, it will not be available. Another complicating factor is the lack of a thesaurus that would allow standardization vis-à-vis form of entry. This lack of standardization results in variations in occupational titles, lack of uniformity in the use of abbreviations (which are heavily employed), and arbitrary categorization of various data. To allow for as precise retrieval as possible, it is necessary to use suffixes, prefixes, truncation and expansion.

Records are tagged by the sex of the biographee if this information was supplied. It was found that out of a total of 97,055 records, almost 90% were men, 6% were women, and 4% of the records did not specify gender. Searching by gender and 25 selected occupa-

tions yielded the results in Table 4. The highest percentages of
women were found in the following occupations: actor/actress
(37%), librarian (26%), editor (17%), artist (17%), author (16%),
state official (16%), and journalist (14%). In all categories, the percentage of men's biographies was higher than women's.

In order to determine whether or not this database could be used
as a means of identifying members of particular organizations, the
following test was conducted. Ten organizations, all but one having
at least 10,000 members, were searched. Organizations chosen included eight that were specifically concerned with women and/or
women's roles; however, in no case was membership restricted
solely to women. Organizations were searched as part of the identifier field because even though records have a "membership" tag,
retrieval by identifier field was more comprehensive.

Of the ten organizations searched, memberships for four were
retrieved. In all cases, relative to the number of potential members,
retrieval was low. The largest memberships were found for the
male-associated Kiwanis and the female-associated National Organization for Women. In both cases, however, the number of men

TABLE 4
PERCENTAGE OF WOMEN INCLUDED BY OCCUPATION

Occupation	Total	% Women
Actor/Actress	977	37%
Artist	1092	17%
Author	1706	16%
Banker	2306	1%
Biologist	890	13%
Chemist	1982	4%
College Dean	197	11%
College President	1569	12%
Clergy	599	1%
Congress Members	521	6%
Economist	806	6%
Editor	1727	17%
Engineer	3501	2%
Executive	18331	3%
Government Official	1115	8%
Journalist	791	14%
Judge	1102	6%
Lawyer	7618	2%
Librarian	689	26%
Physician	3547	4%
Playwright	117	10%
State Official	185	16%
Surgeon	809	1%
University Dean	784	6%
University President	473	3%

who reported belonging to these organizations was higher than the number of women who listed membership. Table 5 provides information of the organizations searched and membership by sex.

Oftentimes, achievement is recognized and commemorated by the bestowing of awards or honors. To ascertain the distribution of honors between men and women, the database was searched by award name and the sex of the recipient. For seven of the prizes searched, persons of either sex are eligible. The remaining three are only granted to women.

Recipients were located for all of the awards that are not gender-based; for the three that are awarded only to women, no recipients were found. Even taking into account the fact that in some instances the sex of the biographee was not stated, in all cases, the number of male recipients exceeded the number of females. Table 6 provides a breakdown of award by recipient.

The names of fifty women of achievement of the 1980s were searched for availability of their biographies. Subjects were selected on the basis of inclusion in at least one of the following sources: *International Dictionary of Feminist Biography*, *Current Biography*, *The Third Woman: Minority Women Writers in the United States*, or a survey of America's 100 most important

TABLE 5
ORGANIZATIONAL MEMBERSHIP BY SEX

Organization	Membership*	Members:WW	Male	Female
Eagle Forum	80000	2		100%
Kiwanis	315000	853	99%	1%
Natl. Fed. of Business & Professional Women	125000	0		
Natl. Gay & Lesbian Task Force	10000	0		
Natl. Organization for Women	260000	301	71%	25%
Natl. Political Congress of Black Women	10000	0		
Natl. Women's Political Caucus	75000	0		
Natl. Women's Studies Assoc.	3500	0		
Women Against Pornography	10000	0		
Women's Intl. League for Peace & Freedom	15000	1		100%

*Encyclopedia of Associations, 23rd ed., 1989

TABLE 6
COMPARISON OF MALE AND FEMALE AWARD RECIPIENTS

Award	Recipients	
	Male	Female
A. Einstein Peace Prize	80%	20%
American Book Award	81%	19%
Elizabeth Blackwell Medal		
Grammy Award	62%	20%
Ladies Prof. Golf Assoc. Hall of Fame		
Natl. Assoc. of Women Artists Annual Exhibition Award		
Nobel Prize	95%	2%
Pulitzer Prize	90%	7%
Spingarn Medal	13%	
Tony Award	64%	26%

women, conducted by the *Ladies' Home Journal.* Subjects represented achievements in the following areas: politics, business, science, the women's movement, and the arts and athletics. Since certain categories of persons such as governors or Nobel Prize winners are included in this database automatically, women who would have been included by virtue of their position from 1982 to the present were not chosen as part of the sample. Appendix B lists the names of the women included in this sample.

Names were searched using either the "name" prefix or the "name" suffix, depending on the complexity of the name. Truncation was used to retrieve variant forms of the name, and postings were verified by the subject's year of birth.

Of the fifty women searched, 23 (46%) had biographical entries in this database. The categories of women most likely to be included in this file were scientists and businesswomen, with 60% of the names in each of these categories located. Postings for the other categories were: arts and athletics — 50%, feminists and activists — 30%, and politicians and women connected with the legal system — 20%. Ten of the women chosen were women of color; of these, only one (Ntozake Shange) was included.

Biography Master Index

Since this database provides access to biographical entries appearing in approximately 375 sources, it was assumed that the likelihood of finding references to the fifty women searched in the encyclopedic databases would be increased. The names were searched in the Name field of the basic index and with the "name" prefix. Truncation was employed to retrieve variations of names and dates.

Records were retrieved for all fifty women. The average number of sources indexed per name was 7.2. For the ten women of color included in the sample, the number of sources average 5.4, while for the other forty women, the average number of sources was 7.6. There was also a difference in the number of sources listed for contemporary women and that for historical (deceased) women, the former group averaging 6.7 and the latter averaging 7.3.

INSTITUTIONAL DIRECTORIES

Institutional directories provide the names, addresses, background information and purposes of organizations. Arrangement and indexing of the print version may allow for a limited number of ways in which information can be located. Online, the same records are accessible in a number of different ways.

Two sources usually found in libraries and frequently consulted are the *Encyclopedia of Associations (EA)* and the *American Library Directory (ALD)*. Both are available online, with the online file corresponding to the latest print editions.

To test each file's coverage of women, the following tests were conducted. In the *EA*, the number and categorization of women-oriented associations, as well as the assignment of descriptors, was examined. In the *ALD*, the ease with which the database could locate libraries with collections of interest to women was examined.

Encyclopedia of Associations

The current file of *EA* provides basic information on 21,000 non-profit U.S. organizations that are national in scope. The first test examined the categorization of women's organizations as reflected by the eighteen broad subject headings used by *EA*. The words "woman," "women," and "feminist" (along with appropriate permutations) were searched in the following fields: Organization Name, Abstract, and Descriptor. The use of descriptors is not apparent from the file documentation, but a call to the database producer revealed that descriptors, which correspond to the keywords used in the print version, are assigned to records in which the keyword does not appear in the name of the organization. As there are no plans to publish a separate keyword list or thesaurus, searchers must have in hand Volume 1, Part 3 of the print version in order to use this field effectively.

Associations in both the online and print versions of *EA* are assigned to one of 18 categories, or Section Headings. To determine which Headings were most likely to be assigned to associations concerning women, the terms "woman" and "women" were searched in the Descriptor, Abstract, and Organization Name fields and were then "anded" with codes for the various Section Headings. The category with the largest number of records pertaining to women was Section 17, Greek and Non-Greek Letter Societies, Associations, and Federations, with 30% of the records assigned to this Section Heading also containing a reference to women. The second-largest category of associations for or about women was the section of Fraternal, Foreign-Interest, National and Ethnic Organizations, with 16%. The categories least likely to be concerned with women were those connected with traditionally male occupations, such as business, labor, and government. Table 7 lists the number and percentages of women-related organizations by category.

TABLE 7
WOMEN'S ASSOCIATIONS BY CATEGORY

Category	Hits	Percentage
Trade, Business, Commercial	141	4%
Agricultural, Commodity Exchanges	12	1%
Legal, Gov't., Public Admin., Military	25	3%
Scientific, Engineering, Technical	37	3%
Educational	85	1%
Cultural	79	4%
Social Welfare	210	13%
Health, Medical	69	3%
Public Affairs	264	11%
Fraternal, Foreign Interest, Nationality, Ethnic	88	16%
Hobby, Avocational	16	1%
Athletics, Sports	87	11%
Labor Unions, Associations, Federations	8	3%
Chambers of Commerce, Trade, Tourism	4	2%
Greek & Non-Greek Letter Societies	100	30%
Fan Clubs	5	1%

The same test was conducted using the terms "feminist" and "feminism." Since the terms only occurred a total of 67 times in either the Organization Name or Abstract fields, and not at all in the Descriptor field, the percentages by category were negligible. The largest number of feminist organizations was assigned to the Public Affairs Heading and amounted to less than 2% of all associations in this category. Associations assigned to this category included the Association of Libertarian Feminists (descriptor: Libertarianism); Women Against Violence Against Women (descriptor: Pornography); Radical Women (descriptor: Women); and the Sisterhood is Powerful Institute (descriptor: Women's Rights).

The second test examined the descriptors used to tag organizations concerned with issues of interest to women. The ten topics chosen were searched in the Organization Name, Abstract, and Descriptor fields. The print keyword index was not consulted prior to going online. Instead, terms were chosen by consulting *A Women's Thesaurus*, edited by Mary Ellen S. Capek. In some searches, commonly used synonyms were searched in addition to the phrases suggested by the thesaurus.

Of the 101 records retrieved, 86 (85%) were relevant. The average number of relevant records retrieved per topic was 8.6. The average number of descriptors assigned to relevant records was 1.1. In only one instance (Surrogate Mothers) was the term advocated by the *Women's Thesaurus* used as a descriptor. Assignment of descriptors was not consistent. For instance, the descriptor "Domestic Violence" was assigned to only two of the ten organizations dealing with battered women. Nor were certain descriptors specific; the Black Affairs Center, a management research organization and the only association addressing the issue of sexual harrassment, was assigned the descriptor "Social Problems." Another difficulty occurred when an appropriate descriptor such as "Reproductive Freedom" was ignored in favor of the emotion-laden term "Abortion." Table 8 illustrates the use of descriptors for the ten topics chosen. Shown are the topics searched, the total number of records retrieved, the number of records printed, the number of records viewed that were relevant, the descriptors assigned to relevant records, and the number of times that descriptor was used.

TABLE 8
ASSIGNMENT OF DESCRIPTORS IN THE Encyclopedia of Associations

Topic	Hits	Printed	Relevant	Descriptors	Used
antiabortion*,	59	31	31	right to life	28
prolife, right				ecumenical	1
to life				conservative	1
				obstetrics/gynecology	1
prochoice*	4	4	4	abortion	3
				family planning	1
				reproductive freedom	1
battered women*	12	12	10	domestic violence	2
				women	2
				women's rights	2
				Catholic	1
				housing	1
				Israel	1
				rape	1
displaced homemaker*	6	6	6	women	2
				civil rights	1
				Hispanic	1
				social change	1
feminist media					
groups	12	12	7	women	5
				pornography	2
surrogate mothers*	2	2	2	parents	2
				surrogate mothers	1
rape victims*	4	4	3	rape	2
				criminal justice	1
women and disarma-					
ment	20	10	3	peace	3
				disarmament	2
sexual harrassment*	1	1	1	social problems	1
women of color*,					
minority women,					
third world women	19	19	19	women	7
				business	3
				books	1
				domestic violence	1
				employment	1
				international dev.	1
				mathematics	1
				science	1
				social problems	1
				substance abuse	1
				women's rights	1

* terms chosen from A Women's Thesaurus

American Library Directory

This file contains over 37,000 entries on U.S. and Canadian libraries and related institutions. The following fields were determined to be subject-conveying and were examined with respect to locating libraries with women's studies or feminist collections: Subject Interest Code, Subject Interest, Special Collections, and Institution Name.

Subject Interest Codes are assigned by the database producer as an indication of the institution's collection focus. The code list is included as part of the file documentation. Nine codes, representing topics of interest to women, were searched. Table 9 lists the topics chosen and the number of records retrieved by code. Records were retrieved for all but the code Non-Sexist Literature. The code for Women's Studies successfully retrieved records for such libraries as the Arthur and Elizabeth Schlesinger Library on the History of Women in America (Radcliffe College), the Women's History Research Center (Berkeley), and the Sophia Smith Collection (Smith College).

Three terms were searched in the aforementioned subject-conveying fields in order to determine the correlation and consistency of Subject Interest Code assignment. The concepts searched were "women," "feminism," and "lesbianism." Truncation was employed to ensure retrieval of plurals and other closely-related concepts.

A total of 234 records were retrieved for the concept "women," 59 for "feminism," and 9 for "lesbianism." In all three searches, more records were retrieved by means of free-text searching than by use of the codes alone, as shown in Table 10. For some records, the above results can be attributed to the fact that the record did not contain a Code field. In other instances, the Code field existed, but an appropriate code was not assigned despite mention of the con-

TABLE 9
RETRIEVAL BY SUBJECT INTEREST CODES

Subject and Code	Hits
Abortion [4605]	5
Birth Control [4610]	14
Feminism [4655]	54
Gay Liberation [4660]/Homosexuality [4665]	8
Marriage [4690]	12
Non-Sexist Literature [2690]	0
Obstetrics and Gynecology [1905]	67
Sexuality [4720]	10
Women's Studies [4745]	79

TABLE 10
RETRIEVAL BY SUBJECT FIELD

Concept	Code	Name (NA= & /NA)	Identifier	Spec. Coll.
Woman/Women	79	15/54	110	99
Feminist/ism	54	0/2	56	2
Lesbian/ism	8*	2/4	7	2

*coded to Homosexuality or Gay Liberation

cept elsewhere in the record. Below are sample records illustrating the lack of consistent usage of the Subject Interest Code field.

NAME: Ann Carry Durland Memorial Alternatives Library
SUBJECT INTERESTS: alternative lifestyles; disarmament; ecol; energy; farming; gay & lesbian lifestyles
CODES: 0700 (energy); 0815 (ecology); 3000 (law)

NAME: College of Saint Elizabeth—Mahoney Library
SUBJECT INTERESTS: bus; educ; fashion; gerontology; hist; lit; nursing; nutrition; women
CODES: 0300 (business and mgmt); 0520 (fashion); 0530 (home economics); 0600 (education); 1895 (nursing); 1897 (nutrition); 2200 (history); 2280 (World War I)
SPECIAL COLLECTIONS: History of Women in America (Doris & Yisral Mayer Coll); among others

NAME: Front Range Community College-Library
SUBJECT INTERESTS: ethnic studies; feminism; natural sci; soc & behav sci; vocational mat
CODES: 0125 (art and architecture); 2205 (American history); 2300 (international relations); 4600 (social sciences and is-sues)

In another test of free-text searching, the ten concepts searched in the *EA* (Table 8) were also searched in the subject-conveying fields of the *ALD*. Of the ten search statements, only one yielded a hit: the term "third-world women" was found in the Subject Interest field of the Hartford Women's Center Hartford Feminist Library. The codes assigned to this record were for Feminism and Women's Studies.

TRADE BIBLIOGRAPHIES

The surge in feminist publishing reflects rejection of the traditional image of women so often depicted in the media. There are many print sources specializing in the identification of women's studies and feminist materials. The annual *Index/Directory of Women's Media* lists periodicals, publishers, bookstores, and other media pertaining to women. The *Annotated Guide to Womens' Periodicals in the United States and Canada* and Joan Ariel's *Building Women's Studies Collections: A Resource Guide* are other useful listings of little-known and alternative sources.

Standard trade bibliographies such as *Books in Print (BIP)* and *Ulrich's International Periodical Directory* are routinely used both as acquisitions tools and for verification purposes. How comprehensive are they with respect to the inclusion of feminist, alternative, and women-oriented pressed and titles, which were initiated primarily because of the dearth of such materials in mainstream, commercial publishing? Searches were run in these two databases to determine the extent of inclusion of women's presses and titles, and also to examine indexing policies that may facilitate or hinder identification of these materials.

Ulrich's International Periodical Directory

This database provides access to publication data on over 135,000 serial titles. Regularly published, irregularly published, and ceased titles are included. The database corresponds to the following print sources: *Ulrich's International Periodical Directory*, *Irregular Serials and Annuals*, and the *Bowker International Serials Database Update*.

In order to determine comprehensiveness of coverage, 50 titles were searched, forty chosen from the *1987 Index/Directory of Women's Media* and the remainder from the "General Women's Magazines" section of the 5th edition of *Magazines for Libraries*. The titles chosen from the *Index/Directory* can be considered feminist in nature and included 20 serials published in the United States and 20 published abroad; the 10 titles selected from *Magazines for Libraries* are "traditional" women's magazines, concerned with the home, cooking, beauty, and fashion. See Appendix C for titles selected.

Eighty percent of the titles searched were included in this database. All of the feminist titles published in the U.S. as well as all 10 of the general-interest women's magazines were found. Of the twenty foreign titles searched, 14 (70%) were included. Four of the 6 titles not included were published in underdeveloped nations.

Descriptors assigned to the 44 records found were examined. Descriptors are listed in the file documentation and are assigned and searchable as either phrases or codes. According to the database producer, the average number of descriptors assigned per record is 1.3. In this sample, the average was slightly higher at 1.5 descriptors per record.

The descriptor most appropriate to women-oriented periodicals, whether feminist or traditional, is "Women's Interests," and was assigned to a total of 1,258 records. Thirty-five (80%) of the 44 records examined contained this descriptor, and for 18 titles, it was the sole descriptor. Eight of these 18 titles were for journals published outside of the United States. Distinctively feminist titles, such as *Trouble and Strife: A Radical Feminist Journal, Feminist Studies*, and *Hypatia; A Journal of Feminist Philosophy*, were assigned only the descriptor "Women's Interests." In contrast, traditional women's magazines were likely to be assigned such descriptors as "Home Economics" *(Women's Day, Family Circle*, and *Good Housekeeping)*, "Clothing Trade-Fashions" *(Glamour; Vogue)* or "General Interest Periodicals" *(Redbook)*. Only four of the ten titles in this group were tagged with the descriptor "Women's Interests": *Cosmopolitan, Essence, Ladies' Home Journal*, and *Playgirl*.

Ideally, combining the descriptor or descriptor code for "Women's Interests" with other descriptors or codes would be a way of identifying women's periodicals in a particular field. Inconsistent assignment of descriptors or omission of appropriate descriptors, however, resulted in less than optimum recall. An example of the first problem was the record for the journal *Third Woman, Hispanic Woman: International Perspectives*, which was assigned the sole descriptor "Literature." Serials similar in scope and content, such as *Tulsa Studies in Literature* had both "Literature" and "Women's Interests'' as descriptors. In all, 71 titles were indexed to both of these descriptors, but there is no assurance that this number accurately reflects all titles having to do with women and literature. The problem of omission of appropriate descriptors was seen with the records for *Hypatia*, which was only indexed to "Women's Interests" and not to the descriptor for Philosophy.

A third problem with descriptors was the lack of specificity. For instance, the descriptor "Ethnic Interests" was used to describe all ethnic groups, as evidenced by its use for the journals *Lilith, the Jewish Women's Magazine, Sage, a Scholarly Journal on Black Women*, and *Essence* (but not, incidentally, for *Third Woman*). The broader "Homosexuality" was used; the more specific term Lesbian(ism) is not a descriptor. *Aegis: Magazine on Ending Violence Against Women*, was assigned the descriptors "Women's Interests" and "Political Science — Civil Rights." A more specific descriptor does not exist. These indexing practices make it advisable to use a combination of both controlled vocabulary and free-text searching for optimal retrieval.

It is interesting to note that at one point *Ulrich's* assigned identifiers to its records. A list of identifiers appears in the file documentation and includes such phrases as "Black Interests," "Midwifery," and "Women's Liberation Movement." However, this field is no longer used because, according to the vendor, the database producer was negligent in assigning terms to the majority of the records.

Books In Print

This database provides publication data on books published by over 22,000 publishers located in the United States. It corresponds to the latest print editions of 12 Bowker publications and includes books currently in print, forthcoming titles, and titles that have been out of print since 1979. This file was tested to determine the extent to which women's presses and series were included. The use of descriptors was also examined.

Twenty publishers, chosen from the *1987 Index/Directory of Women's Media*, were searched. The sample included fiction, nonfiction, lesbian, and special interest publishers. Expansion was used in order to identify such variations of company names as occurred with the Seal Press, which was listed variously as "Seal Pr," "Seal Pr Feminist," and "Seal Pr-Feminist." Fifteen (75%) of the publishers were found. The total number of titles retrieved was 598; the largest number (134) published by Feminist Press and the smallest number (3) by Margaretdaughters. Table 11 lists retrieval by publisher.

Of the ten series titles searched, 6, or 60%, were found, representing a total of 83 titles. The following series were included: *New Leaf* (Seal Press), *Women Composer Series* (DaCapo Press), *Women & Health* (Haworth Press), *Key Women Writers* (Indiana U. Press), *New Feminist Perspective Series* (Rowman & Littlefield), and *Women in Culture and Society* (U. of Chicago Press). Not included were: *Harvard Women's Studies in Religion* (Beacon Press), *Monographs in Women's Studies* (Eden Press), *Feminist Press Biography* (Feminist Press), and *Athene Series: An International Collection of Feminist Books* (Pergamon Press).

Descriptors for this file are chosen from the following sources: the ninth edition of *Library of Congress Subject Headings*, *Sear's List of Subject Headings* (children's titles), and subject lists developed by Bowker for paperback books *(PBIP)* and forthcoming

TABLE 11
RETRIEVAL BY PUBLISHER

Publisher	Hits
Acacia	0
Alicejamesbooks	60
Biblio Press	0
Bootlegger Press	0
Cleis Press	15
Coalition on Women and Religion	4
Down There Press	18
Feminist Press	134
Firebrand Books	28
Frog In Well	6
Kitchen Table	12
Margaretdaughters	3
Metis Press	7
Naiad Press	126
Seal Press	66
Shameless Hussy	43
Spinsters Aunt Lute	37
Volcano Press	39
Women for Art	0
Women's International Service Exchange (WIRE)	0

books *(FBIP)*. Depending on the work, a book may be assigned descriptors from more than one list; in this survey, however, records retrieved were assigned descriptors only from *LCSH* or *PBIP*. Ten records from each of the presses and series retrieved were printed out in the Title/Descriptor format in order to ascertain the depth of indexing and appropriateness of descriptor assignment. According to file documentation, titles may receive up to four assigned descriptors, but the average for this sample was 1.6.

LCSH descriptors were, on the whole, more specific than *PBIP* subject headings. For instance, the books *A Studio of One's Own* and *A World Without Men* both received the *LCSH* descriptor "Lesbians;" the *PBIP* equivalent was "Government and Political Science-Minority Group Studies." That same *PBIP* heading was also assigned to two books on domestic violence, *For the Latina in an Abusive Relationship* and *Chain Chain Change: For Black Women Dealing With Physical and Emotional Abuse*. The *LCSH* descriptor "Conjungal Violence" was more appropriate, and, in addition, a second descriptor was assigned to each record to describe the ethnic group in question. A third example of the poor quality of the *PBIP* descriptors occurred in the records for these two titles on AIDS, *Making It: A Woman's Guide to Sex in the Age of AIDS* and *AIDS: The Women*. Both titles received the *PBIP* descriptor "Medical Sciences-Medicine-General." The first title has two *LCSH* descriptors, "Women-Sexual Behavior" and "Acquired Immune Deficiency Syndrome," but the second title had no *LCSH* subject headings. It can be concluded that because the *PBIP* descriptors are so general, the likelihood of retrieving the maximum number of relevant records is diminished if the search is restricted to the descriptor field alone.

Although the *LCSH* descriptors are more specific, it was found that at times, valid descriptors were not assigned when they should have been, as illustrated by the three records below.

TITLE: *Home Girls: A Black Feminist Anthology*
LCSH: Afro-American Women; Women's Writings
PBIP: Government and Political Science-Minority Group Studies

TITLE: *Combahee River Collective Statement. Black Feminist Organizing in the Seventies and Eighties*
LCSH: same as above
PBIP: same as above

TITLE: *This Bridge Called My Back: Writings by Radical Women of Color*
LCSH: Women; Women's Writings; Feminists
PBIP: none

Even though the first two books had the word "feminist" in their titles, the descriptor "Feminists" was not assigned.

Another problem was the fact that at times, the *LCSH* assigned were not the most appropriate subject headings available. The book *Women, Sex and the Law* was assigned the descriptor "Women-Legal Status, Laws, etc." However, the OCLC record for the same title listed nine additional headings, including the more specific "Sex and Law-United States" and "Sex Discrimination Against Women-Laws and Legislation."

Most descriptors in this file are assigned a corresponding eight-digit descriptor code, which is also searchable. In 1984, Bowker published *The Subject Thesaurus for Bowker Online Databases*, an alphabetical list (with "see" and "see also" references) of descriptors and their codes. According to file documentation, some descriptor codes are assigned in a hierarchical arrangement, and truncation after the sixth digit may be used to retrieve related records. However, the nature of the hierarchical arrangement is not clear from the *Thesaurus* and not apparent at all online. An example of how codes are related can be seen by examining the code for the subject "Women-Suffrage." The code for this descriptor is (00507489), and is related to the headings "Women-Legal Status, Laws, etc." (00507416) and "Women's Rights" (00507441), both of which are "see also" references. However, books on women's suffrage in specific geographical locations are part of a different hierarchy, as seen by the following codes: "Women-Suffrage-Canada" (00684612), "Women-Suffrage-Great Britain" (00684624), and "Women-Suffrage-Mexico" (00684636). The need to search on two different truncated codes would not be apparent from file records alone, yet the *Thesaurus* is now out of print and there are no plans to issue a new edition. It would be assumed that the descriptors "Rape" and "Incest" would be related to "Sex Crimes," since they are "see also" references from that phrase. However, the code for "Sex Crimes" is (00425412), and the codes for "Rape" and "Incest" are (00396837) and (00229684), respectively.

The inadequacies of the Library of Congress classification scheme with respect to the terminology used to classify materials about women were manifested in this file as well. Women were far more likely than men to be defined in terms of their marital status, profession, or ethnicity, as was shown by the fact that the descriptors "Married Women," "Women Bankers," and "Afro-American Women" had no masculine counterparts. "Pregnant Schoolgirls" is used but the closest descriptor to the concept of "teenage fathers" is "Adolescent Parents." The term "Vasectomy" is a descriptor but "tubal ligation" is not; instead, "Sterilization of Women" is used. This pejorative phrase implies, as does the descriptor "Sterilization of Criminals and Defectives," involuntary sterilization.

CONCLUSION

The additional access points available on online reference databases can be used to garner information about women and women's issues that would be difficult to uncover in their printed counterparts. However, coverage of women and women's materials is not comprehensive. Biographical information about women, especially contemporary women, women of color, and non-English speaking women is not always available. *Biography Master Index*, because it indexes so many sources, was the only database to have records for all women included in the sample. The second-best source for biographical information was the *Academic American Encyclopedia*, which had fairly good coverage of women in general, contemporary women and women of color but fell down in its coverage of foreign women. Coverage of women in the *Marquis Who's Who* file would be greatly enhanced if data from the publication *Who's Who of*

American Women was also mounted online, or if the two sources were merged into one instead of treating women as though they were a separate species. The poor performance of *Everyman's Encyclopedia* may be partially attributable to the fact that the file has not been updated since 1978.

Despite the fact that both encyclopedias claim to be international in scope, cultural bias was apparent in their coverage of women's events and issues as well as in their inclusion of women's biographies. The *Academic American Encyclopedia* was more likely to include articles on British events and history than *Everyman's Encyclopedia* was to include articles related to the United States. The *Academic American* was also more likely to include articles on contemporary concerns such as DES and the National Organization of Women than was *Everyman's*. *Ulrich's* also displayed a bias by its exclusion of several third world periodicals.

The lack of gender-neutral language was seen in many databases, from the preponderance of masculine pronouns used in the encyclopedias to the sexist terminology exhibited in the trade bibliographies. A related vocabulary problem, that of non-specific terminology, was seen in the descriptors used by the *Encyclopedia of Associations*, the *American Library Director*, and *Ulrich's*. Even when appropriate vocabulary terms were available, inconsistent assignment of descriptors hindered retrieval of relevant records. The searchers cannot rely upon the database's standardized vocabulary alone, and instead must draw from other subject-conveying fields for optimal retrieval. There now exist several thesauri, such as *A Women's Thesaurus*, that promote specific yet non-sexist terminology that could be easily adapted by database producers to facilitate retrieval of information about women. It would also be helpful if producers assigned more descriptors per record and published up-to-date thesauri for their files.

The message given by online reference databases regarding women's achievements and professional status is that they are far behind men. They are less likely to be recognized for their contributions, they are not regarded as "power" players in the world of business or in the political or legal arenas, and their voices vis-à-vis the medium of publishing are not always heard. In short, women are still not as visible as men in standard reference sources. Until these problems are addressed, it is advisable to turn to more specialized sources to corroborate and/or supplement information pertaining to women found in standard reference sources.

REFERENCES

Detlefsen, Ellen Gay. "Issues of Access to Information About Women." In *Women's Collections: Libraries, Archives, and Consciousness*, edited by Suzanne Hildebrand. New York: The Haworth Press, 1986.

Engle, June L., and Elizabeth Futas. "Sexism in Adult Encyclopedias." *RQ* 23 (Fall 1983): 29-39.

Gershuny, H. Lee. "Public Doublespeak: The Dictionary." *College English* 36 (April 1975): 938-42.

Katz, William A. *Basic Information Sources*. Vol. 1 of *Introduction to Reference Work*. New York: McGraw-Hill, 1982.

BIBLIOGRAPHY

Allen, Martha Leslie. *1987 Index/Directory of Women's Media*. Forestville, MD: Anaconda Press, 1987.

Ariel, Joan. *Building Women's Studies Collections: A Resource Guide*. Middletown, CT: Choice, 1987.

Banks, Olive. *The Biographical Dictionary of British Feminists. Volume One: 1800-1930*. New York: New York University Press, 1985.

Capek, Mary Ellen S. *A Women's Thesaurus: An Index of Language Used to Describe and Locate Information by and About Women*. New York: Harper & Row, 1987.

Current Biography. New York: H.W. Wilson, 1980-1987.

Fisher, Dexter, ed. *The Third Woman: Minority Women Writers of the United States*. Boston: Houghton Mifflin, 1980.

James, Edward T., ed. *Notable American Women: 1607-1950*. Cambridge, MA: Belknap Press of Harvard University Press, 1971. 3 v.

Katz, Bill, and Linda Steinberg Katz. *Magazines for Libraries*. 5th ed. New York: R.R. Bowker, 1986.

Kramarae, Cheris, and Paula A. Treichler. *A Feminist Dictionary*. London: Pandora Press, 1982.

Ladies' Home Journal. CV (November 1988): 50-56; 221-26.

Mehlman, T., ed. *Annotated Guide to Women's Periodicals in the United States and Canada*. v. 4, no. 1. Richmond, IN: Women's Program Office, Earlham College, 1985.

Sicherman, Barbara, and Carol Hurd Green, eds. *Notable American Women: The*

Modern Period. Cambridge, MA: Belknap Press of Harvard University Press, 1980.

Subject Thesaurus for Bowker Online Databases. New York: R.R. Bowker Co., 1984.

Tuttle, Lisa. *Encyclopedia of Feminism.* New York: Facts on File, 1986.

Uglow, Jennifer S., ed. *International Dictionary of Women's Biography.* New York: Continuum Publishing Co., 1982.

Appendix A: NAMES SEARCHED IN ENCYCLOPEDIAC DATABASES

Name	AA	EE
Armatrading, Joan		
Augsburg, Anita		
Ballinger, Margaret		
Besant, Annie	x	x
Bethune, Mary McLeod	x	
Bhutto, Benazir	Pakistan	
Boupacha, Djamila		
Braun, Lily		
Callas, Maria	x	x
Carson, Rachel	x	x
Ch'ing, Chiang	x	Chiang Kai-shek; Taiwan
Decker, Mary Slaney	x	
Dix, Dorothea	x	
Dod, Lottie (Charlotte)		
Franklin, Rosalind	x	
Gilman, Charlotte Perkins	x	
Goldman, Emma	x	
Goodall, Jane	x	
Grasso, Ella	x	
Greer, Germaine	x	
Hepworth, Barbara	x	x
Hill, Octavia		x
Hopper, Grace		
Hurston, Zora Neale	x	
Hypatia		x
Jex-Blake, Sophia		
Kovalevsky, Sofia		
Lovelace, Ada (Augusta)	Ada	
Luxemburg, Rosa	x	x
Martineau, Harriet	x	x
Mayer, Maria Goeppert	x	
McClintock, Barbara	x	
Mistral, Gabriela	x	x
Montessori, Maria	x	x
Norton, Caroline		x
O'Keeffe, Georgia	x	
Paul, Alice	x	
Pelletier, Madeleine		
Perkins, Frances	x	x
Peron, Eva (Evita)	x	
Sarojini, Naidu	x	
Schneiderman, Rose		
Schreiner, Olive	x	x
Stone, Lucy	x	
Stopes, Marie	Birth Control	x
Strachey, Ray (Rachel)	Women's Rights Mov't.	
Tereskova, Valentina	x	x
Wells-Barnet, Ida		
Willard, Frances	x	
Zaharias, Babe Didrikson	x	x

Appendix B: NAMES SEARCHED IN <u>MARQUIS WHO'S WHO</u>

Name	Biography Included
Atwood, Margaret	x
Battle, Kathleen	
Beers, Charlotte	x
Bird, Rose	x
Black, Cathleen	x
Brody, Jane	x
Castillo, Ana	
Chicago, Judy	x
Daly, Mary	
Decker, Mary Slaney	x
Estrich, Susan	
Eu, March Fong	
Firestone, Shulamith	
Fisher, Anna	x
Frankenthaler, Helen	x
Freeman, Jo	
French, Marilyn	x
Fritz, Leah	
Gilligan, Carol	
Ginsburg, Ruth Bader	x
Grann, Phyllis	x
Griffith-Joyner, Florence	
Hefner, Christie	
Hopper, Grace	x
Horn, Karen	x
Johnson, Sonia	
Krim, Mathilde	
Kubler-Ross, Elisabeth	x
Lorde, Audre	
Mankiller, Wilma	
Marram, Ellen	
McNamee, Louise	x
Millett, Kate	
Mirikitani, Janice	
Morgan, Robin	
Navidad, Irene	
Reuss, Patricia	
Riley, Matilda White	x
Sauve, Jeanne	
Shange, Ntozake	x
Siebert, Muriel	
Silko, Leslie Marmon	
Steel, Dawn	x
Tharp, Twyla	x
Uhlenbeck, Karen	x
Wachner, Linda	x
Wallace, Michele	
Wattleton, Faye	
Yalow, Rosalyn	x
Yeager, Jeana	

Appendix C: JOURNALS SEARCHED IN ULRICH'S

Title	Descriptors
Aegis: Magazine for Ending Violence Against Women	WI; Poli Sci.-Civil Rights
Ahfad Journal	WI; Poli Sci.-Int'l. Relations
Backbone; a Journal of Literature	WI; Lit.-Poetry; Homosexuality

Title	Descriptors
Common Lives-Lesbian Lives	WI; Homosexuality
Cosmopolitan	WI
Essence	WI; Ethnic Interests
Family Circle	Home Economics
Fem	WI
Feminist	WI
Feminist Studies	WI
Glamour	Clothing Trade-Fashions; Beauty Culture
Good Housekeeping	Home Economics
Hecate, Women's Inter-disciplinary Journal	WI
Hertha	WI; Poli Sci.-Civil Rights
Hypatia; a Journal of Feminist Philosophy	WI
Hysteria	General Interest-Canada
Journal of Women and Religion	WI; Religion and Theology
Ladies' Home Journal	WI; Home Economics
Lilith; the Jewish Women's Magazine	WI; Ethnic Interests
Manushi	WI
Mulherio	WI
New Directions for Women	WI
Noga	WI
Off Our Backs	WI
Playgirl	WI
Psychology of Women Quarterly	WI; Psychology
Redbook	General Interest- U.S.
Revista	
Room of One's Own	WI; Literature
Sage: A Scholarly Journal on Black Women	WI; Ethnic Interests; Poli Sci.-Civil Rights
Samya Shakti	
Shifra	
Signs: Journal of Women in Culture and Society	WI
Sojourner; the Women's Forum	WI
Somos	WI
Third Woman; Hispanic Women	Literature
Through the Looking Glass	WI; Criminology & Law Enforcement; Children & Youth
Torajyva	
Trouble & Strife: A Radical Feminist Journal	WI
Tulsa Studies in Literature	WI; Literature
Turn of the Century Woman	WI
Vamos Mujer	
Viva	
Vogue	Clothing Trade-Fashions; General Interest- U.S.
Voice of Women	WI; Poli Sci.-Civil Rights
Woman's Day	Home Economics
Women & Environments	WI; Housing & Urban Planning; Environmental Studies
Women & Health; Journal of Women's Health Care	WI
Women & Politics	WI; Political Science
Women's Rights Law Reporter	WI; Law
Women's Studies International Forum	WI

Women in News
and Popular Databases

Andrea Weinschenk

SUMMARY. This article begins with a discussion of some of the "women's" headings used in indexing the IAC databases and Wilson's *Readers' Guide*. Several topics of interest to women are searched in the bibliographic news and popular databases. Search strategies and results are discussed and compared. A comparison between bibliographic and full text databases is made for the topics of states' laws on surrogate motherhood and women elected to office in the 1988 elections.

INTRODUCTION

The purpose of this paper is to profile news and popular online databases for their coverage of social, legal and economic issues which concern women. Five databases — *Magazine Index* (MI), *National Newspaper Index* (NNI), *Newspaper Abstracts* (NA), *Newsearch, Readers' Guide Abstracts* and the family of VU/Text files — are evaluated in three areas: (1) availability of relevant subject headings, (2) full text vs. bibliographic retrieval and (3) coverage of five "hot topics" searched across the files. The news and popular databases are highlighted for their currency which in many cases provide up-to-the-minute coverage.

SUBJECT HEADINGS FOR WOMEN
IN CONTROLLED VOCABULARY DATABASES

One method of evaluating online databases with controlled vocabularies is to examine the subject headings used. When one

Andrea Weinschenk is Coordinator of Computer Services, Boston University Libraries, Boston University, Boston MA 02215.

searches in the time-honored way, one begins by looking at the
thesaurus for terms related to the search topics.

In dealing with women's issues, however, many inconsistencies
in subject headings are found. Viewed in a positive light, these
inconsistencies might be seen as attempts to keep up with the
changing status, roles and issues which concern women. At worst,
they could lead the unwary searcher into omitting a relevant subject
heading because the concept is not expressed in the thesaurus in a
standard fashion.

The first database thesaurus, *The Subject Guide to IAC Databases* (Second edition, 1985), was examined for terms which expressed the concepts of woman or women. To begin at the most
basic biological level, the term "Females" is not used in the thesaurus and is not cross referenced to "Women," although the
searcher may make the connection from the cross reference "Female studies see Women's studies." To confuse the issue further,
"Female offenders" is used as a bona fide subject heading. While
browsing in the "Fem-" section of the thesaurus one does find
"Femininity of God," "Feminism" (with a number of "See also"
references), "Feminists" and "Femmes fatales."

The IAC indexers also use "Girls" with a number of "See also"
references and some subheadings. "Daughters" is used with "See
also" references to "Fathers and daughters" and "Mothers and
daughters." "Mothers" exists as a subject heading with twelve
"See also" references: There are seven more headings beginning
with the word "mother." If one looks up "Sisters," one finds
"Sisters and brothers" see "Brothers and sisters." "Aunts" is a
subject heading. "Wives" is used and has twenty four "see also"
references, but "Widows," which is a bona fide subject heading, is
not one of them. As might be expected for an index which serves
for news and magazine databases, a number of these cross-references are for wives of athletes, politicians and men in other news-
making occupations. Oddly enough, there is no "Presidents'
wives" or "First Ladies."

One finds "Woman see Women" and "Woman (Theology)."
"Women" has twenty-five "see also" references and subheadings
with "see also" references covering approximately a column and a
half on the page. There are many headings for women in specific

occupations or activities, e.g., "Women accountants," "Women broadcasters." IAC uses five of the "Women as" headings, such as "Women as diplomats" and "Women as jurors," a puzzling inconsistency since there are headings for "Women lawyers" and "Women judges." Indeed, there are many cross references from this type of subject heading format, such as "Women as artists" to "Women artists." Another inconsistency is the heading "Women as missionaries" which has a " see also" reference to "Missionaries, Women." There are many "Women in " headings: the fields include professions and religions, as well sociological concepts of women ("Women in popular culture") and artistic and literary portrayals of women.

Locating terms for ethnic women is confusing in this thesaurus. There are "Afro-American Women" as well as "Women, Black," following Library of Congress practice. There are headings for Mexican American and Hispanic American women.

There are no specific headings for Native American women and Asian American women. Items on these subjects are indexed under "Indians in North America" and "Asian Americans," respectively, with no "see" references in the "Women" section of the thesaurus.

As a concluding example of the inconsistencies of IAC indexing, one finds the term "Female offenders" as a subject heading. There is no "See" reference from the "Women" part of the thesaurus and, although, one will find "Women prisoners" as a valid subject heading, there is no "see also" reference to "Female offenders." Surely these two headings are logically related! A little farther down the page, one finds an entry "Women saints see Saints, Women." Apparently, if a woman is a criminal, then she is defined by her biological status – female. If apprehended and convicted, she is defined by her social status – woman. If she is canonized, however, then she is a saint first, gender and social status are secondary!

Another database with a controlled vocabulary, *Readers' Guide*, produced by the H.W. Wilson Co., does not have a thesaurus, and it would be helpful to the online searcher if one existed. For this discussion, the cumulated *Readers' Guide* for 1987 was used. As a result, some terms referring to women/females may be omitted if they were not used in the 1987 *Readers' Guide.* As in the IAC Thesaurus, there is no cross reference from "Females" to "Women." "Feminism" and its various aspects are found, as are headings beginning "Feminist." "Girls" is a subject heading. "Mothers" has a list of eleven "See also" subject headings, including "Stepparents and stepchildren" and "Surrogate mothers." The latter are evidence of the indexers' awareness of important current issues. "Mothers, Unmarried" has a "See" reference to "Single mothers." "Daughters and parents" is not a bona fide subject heading and has a "See" reference to "Parent Child relationship."

"Wives" as a subject heading has eighteen "See also" references listed, including "Presidents – Wives," "Widows" and "Wife abuse." "Woman" has a "see" reference to "Women." That heading has eighteen "See also" references including "Black women" and "Indians of North American – Women." There is no reference to Asian American women. There is a reference "Young women," but none to "Aged women": this concept is found via a reference from "Women, Aged" to "Aged." There are numerous subheadings under "Women," including "Crime" (i.e., women criminals), "Crimes against" and "Equal rights." There are a number of "Women and-" headings. There are no "Women as-" headings. "Women in-" covers women in various occupations and disciplines.

Controlled vocabularies have their inconsistencies, but they may be useful in locating information about women in their respective databases. They may also hinder access by being too broad or too narrow in scope or by being applied inconsistently. To use controlled vocabularies effectively, the searcher must be aware of their limitations and construct search strategies that take them into account.

WOMEN'S ISSUES IN NEWS
AND POPULAR DATABASES

A myriad of issues concerning women are found in the news and popular databases. Three current issues were searched across the files as a means of evaluating the coverage of social, legal and economic issues which concern women.

Abortion

The 1973 U.S. Supreme Court decision in the case of Roe v. Wade, which legalized abortion, has always been controversial. Recently the abortion controversy heated up again. Thus, the topic (abortion) was chosen because a substantial amount of material is available and the subject has many facets that might be searched. A search using terms from the IAC thesaurus ("Abortion," "Right to life," "Prochoice movement," "Prolife movement") retrieved almost two thousand documents in the *Magazine Index*. A hypothetical query was created: "What groups, both prochoice and prolife, have been involved in the abortion controversy?" It is desirable to divide the search into two parts to retrieve separate lists of articles dealing with prochoice groups and prolife groups. A simple search on the headings **ABORTION AND PROCHOICE MOVEMENT** retrieved sixty-three documents. This set included articles about the Abortion Rights Mobilization group. Browsing through the titles and subject headings revealed some organizations which were conspicuously absent. The next step was to combine **ABORTION AND NATIONAL ORGANIZATION FOR WOMEN OR PLANNED ADJ PARENTHOOD.** This step retrieved an additional thirty-one unique articles. A quick check of the print *Encyclopedia of Associations* revealed the names of additional organizations. Using some of these, the National Abortion Rights Action League, for example, in combination with the subject heading "Abortion," brought up an additional twenty-nine documents. The wary searcher must be creative; using only the printed subject headings does not provide as complete a search as the subject headings with the names of specific organizations. Indeed the organizations' names are given in the descriptor field, but they are not also automatically indexed with the "Prochoice Movement" subject heading. For organizations such as the National Organization for Women and the various Planned Parenthood groups, whose entire efforts are not devoted to the prochoice movement, such an omission is perhaps understandable. For an organization which has the words "abortion rights" in its name, IAC indexing policy is somewhat puzzling.

A similar strategy for prolife groups was used. Initially, **ABOR-**

TION AND PROLIFE MOVEMENT was entered: that statement retrieved two hundred documents. Entering the names of prolife groups such as National Right to Life Committee, Crusade for Life and Feminists for Life retrieved an additional seventeen documents. Indexing practice is again not clear, and the searcher must be creative.

Wilson's *Readers' Guide Abstracts* presents a different problem. A search on "Abortion" retrieved approximately twelve hundred articles since 1983. The subject heading "Pro life movement" was found (sixty-five articles), but the only comparable prochoice heading available, "Prochoice movement/United States," retrieved four book reviews published from 1983-1985. **PROCHOICE OR PRO-CHOICE OR PRO ADJACENT TO CHOICE** yielded forty-seven documents. By browsing some of the subject headings that "Prochoice" retrieved many articles also indexed with "Abortion/Moral and religious aspects" were found. Indexing prolife articles under the term "Pro life movement" as well as "Abortion/ Moral and religious aspects," seems to be accepted practice. The practice of indexing both prochoice and prolife articles under the term "Abortion/Moral and religious aspects" makes it difficult to create separate lists of articles about prolife and prochoice organizations in the *Readers' Guide Abstracts* database.

Another question on the topic of abortion concerning the U.S. Supreme Court's decision to hear *Webster v. Reproductive Health Services*, involves the 1986 Missouri abortion law. A hypothetical request might be, "I need to know about the Supreme Court's recent decision to hear a case involving a Missouri abortion law." Since this issue is very current, the wary searcher must use the news and popular databases. The *National Newspaper Index* and the *Magazine Index* are appropriate databases to search, using a straightforward strategy such as **ABORTION AND SUPREME COURT MISSOURI.** In reviewing the results of the search in the NNI (three postings), the latest article is from October 1988, but the Supreme Court's review of the Missouri law is much more recent than that. The same search performed in MI retrieves one document dated 1981. The next place the searcher might look is *Newsearch*, the update database containing IAC's most recent entries. The same search strategy retrieves eight postings of articles published in the month immediately prior to the search. On January 10, 1989 both the *Washington Post* and the *New York Times* ran front page articles on the Court's decision to hear the case. A search of *Newspaper Abstracts* retrieved nine postings, but only one had a 1989 dateline, the *Wall Street Journal* story on the Court's decision, dated January 10, 1989. When looking for recent news items the caveat is to be aware of the frequency of database update.

The same search strategy was entered in *Readers' Guide Abstracts*. Three postings were retrieved, none with a 1989 date. A review of the most recent postings retrieved under "Abortion" revealed that there were indeed articles on abortion published less than a week prior to the day of the search. One article, "Prochoicers gird for battle," published in *Time*, January 23, 1989, appeared to cover the decision, but Missouri was not mentioned. Since this citation, in its fullest form, did not have an abstract, but merely the citation and subject headings, the actual article was reviewed. It was found to concern the Supreme Court's decision to hear the Missouri case and the efforts of the prochoice movement to influence the Court. The only subject heading given to this half page article is "United States/Supreme Court: Decisions/Abortion decisions." There is also a reference to "Roe v. Wade decision." The exercise described above, on a very current topic, demonstrates the importance of selecting a database whose currency is appropriate to the topic and using a variety of headings, both specific and general, to search for the topic.

Post-Traumatic Stress and Women

Post-traumatic stress disorder experienced by soldiers who served in the Vietnam War has been much written about lately. The stories of lives disrupted by this disorder seem to concern only men. What about women who served in Vietnam? Have they experienced this disorder, too? A quick search of *Medline* confirmed that this material existed in the clinical literature. A review of the topic in the news and popular databases would reveal if these women's stories had reached the general public.

In the *Magazine Index* the strategy **WOMEN SOLDIERS AND VETERANS AND POST-TRAUMATIC STRESS DISORDER** resulted in one posting, a 1984 story in *Savvy*. Next the strategy **WOMEN SOLDIERS AND VETERANS AND VIETNAM OR VIETNAMESE** was entered. Three postings were retrieved, but none on the subject of post-traumatic stress syndrome. A simplified strategy, **POST-TRAUMATIC STRESS DISORDER AND WOMEN OR FEMALE(S)** retrieved the *Savvy* article, an article about rape and one about wives of Vietnam veterans. As a last resort, the thirty-five documens retrieved with "Post-traumatic stress-disorder" were reviewed. One study, done by the Veterans Administration and reported in *Science*, August 12, 1988, seemed promising. The article itself was reviewed and found to include not only statistics for male Vietnam veterans, but also the number of women who served in Vietnam (7,166) and the prevalence rate for post-traumatic stress disorder (9%) which they experienced. The relevant subject heading was "Veterans: psychology."

The same strategies were tried next in *National Newspaper Index*. One 1984 article from the *Washington Post* was retrieved. A review of nine articles retrieved by **WOMEN SOLDIERS AND VETERANS** resulted in several articles about women veterans' health and psychology published in the early 1980s which seemed to be relevant. Post-traumatic stress disorder first appeared in the publication of the *Diagnostic and Statistical Manual*, 3d ed., 1980 (Andreasen, 1985).

When a search of *Newspaper Abstracts* using strategies similar to the ones described above met with no results, the search terms **WOMEN AND INDOCHINA WAR AND STRESS OR PSY-CHOLOGY** were input. Three articles were retrieved, including an article discussing the effects of the Vietnam War on women at home.

Finally, the Wilson database *Readers' Guide Abstracts* was accessed. The original strategy was entered and one article from *Good Housekeeping*, May 1988, was retrieved. Browsing through the eight citations retrieved by "Women veterans" revealed articles about memorials for women Vietnam veterans, their lack of recognition and other problems they face. The set of articles retrieved by "Post-traumatic stress disorder" included a number of possibly relevant articles, but none of them were indexed with "Women veterans." Difficulty in finding information about women who served in Vietnam may be due to indexing practices.

Women Prize Winners

In 1988, Toni Morrison won the Pulitzer Prize for her novel, *Beloved*. What other women have won Pulitzer Prizes or Nobel Prizes? In the NNI database, a very simple search strategy was entered: **PULITZER ADJACENT PRIZE(S) AND WOMEN**. Four postings were retrieved, the first one concerning the 1988 Pulitzer awards. Other postings were about Alice Walker's 1983 award and Ellen Zwilich's 1983 award for composition. Changing the search strategy to **WOMEN NOVELISTS OR WOMEN AUTHORS AND AWARDS** (IAC subject headings) retrieved eleven unique articles on various literary awards won by women and included the induction of the first woman, Marguerite Yourcenar, into the Académie Française. A simple strategy to find women Nobel winners was employed: **NOBEL ADJACENT TO PRIZE(S) AND WOMEN**. That strategy retrieved nine postings, including Mother Teresa, Barbara McClintock and Alva Myrdal. Nobel Prizes is a subject heading, and the indexing consistently seems to include the "Women" terms ("Women scientists," "Women and peace," etc.) that enable the searcher to pull out articles on these women. The same strategy was employed in the *Magazine Index*, and eight documents were retrieved. The Nobel Prize winners strategy used in the NNI yielded fifteen postings. Again, the "Women" terms seemed to be applied consistently.

Newspaper Abstracts was the next database accessed. **PULITZER ADJACENT TO PRIZE(S) AND WOMEN** retrieved zero postings. **TONI ADJACENT MORRISON** retrieved fifty-three postings. In reviewing the descriptors for some of the articles, it became clear that individual authors' names are used with the descriptor "Pulitzer Prizes." **WOMAN OR WOMEN ADJACENT AUTHOR(S) OR NOVELISTS(S) OR WRITER(S)** retrieved twenty postings, but when combined with **AWARD(S) OR PRIZE(S)**, a zero posting resulted. The Nobel Prize strategy was the same one described above: it retrieved three postings. Only one of the articles was indexed with "Nobel Prizes" and "Women." If the searcher is looking for articles about known women in these areas, there should be no problem in entering a woman's name and the name of the award she received. *Newspaper Abstracts* is not useful when the searcher is looking for any women who won a Nobel, Pulitzer or other prize.

Readers' Guide Abstracts was the final database accessed. **PU-LITZER ADJACENT PRIZE(S) AND WOMAN OR WOMEN** was again used. Twenty-eight postings were retrieved, including a hodge podge of articles and many movie reviews of films that were based on "Pulitzer Prize winning novels" with "women" characters. When **WOMEN AUTHORS AND LITERARY PRIZES** was input, one posting resulted. The Nobel Prize strategy was entered and six postings were retrieved. Only one concerned a recent Nobel Prize winner (McClintock). Some of the others were about an award for women physicists in honor of Maria Goeppert-Mayer, a 1963 Nobelist. This database seems less useful when looking for prize-winning women.

FULL TEXT VS. BIBLIOGRAPHIC DATABASES

The coverage of women's issues in full-text and bibliographic databases is compared using two "hot topics," surrogate mothers and women elected to office in 1988. These topics are searched through two types of database.

Surrogate Mothers

The Baby M story received heavy coverage in the press and sparked controversy on all sides. Alerted by this controversy, several states proposed and/or passed legislation regarding surrogacy. In an attempt to identify the states, a search was run in the *National Newspaper Index*. NNI was a chosen as a good place to start since several major newspapers are indexed here and the database might provide insight into the state of surrogacy legislation across the country. The strategy **SURROGATE ADJACENT MOTHER(S) AND LAW(S) OR LEGISLAT (TRUNCATED) AND STATE(S)** was used. The search retrieved twenty-three postings. Of these, ten were about legislation in New York State and appeared in the *New York Times*. One story about New York State appeared in the *Washington Post*; and six stories about legislation in other states in the *Christian Science Monitor* and one in the *Washington Post* and the *New York Times* were also listed. One article about California legislation appeared in the *Los Angeles Times*. Presumably, one could determine which states were considering legislation on surrogacy by reading one of the latter articles; the *Monitor* article of August 1988 was the most current. The *Newsearch* database had five articles on the topic. Four articles were on New York or New Jersey; the fifth addressed the surrogacy problem as a whole. It should be noted that this database serves as the update file for all IAC databases. In this example, articles from legal journals were included in the retrieval.

Since the goal of this search was to look at the national picture of this legislation, the search was run in VU/TEXT, which provides full text coverage of forty regional newspapers as of the date of this writing. Years of coverage vary by newspaper. The papers with the longest coverage are the *Boston Globe* (1980-) and the *Philadelphia Daily News* (1978-). VU/TEXT has created global groups of newspapers to allow the searcher to access several papers with one search. There are globals for all papers for 1988 and 1987, globals by regions of the country and a global for a group of major newspapers — the top six circulation papers on VU/TEXT.

The search on surrogacy legislation was done on the Major global group, comprised of the *Boston Globe, Chicago Tribune, Los Angeles Times, Newsday, Philadelphia Inquirer* and *Washington Post*. The coverage of these papers, from 1987, is appropriate since the New Jersey Supreme Court ruling in the Baby M case was made in February, 1988. The search strategy was the same as the one used in NNI. VU/TEXT training staff recommend that a search be done initially in the headline and lead paragraph, since the major point of any news story should be mentioned there. That procedure was followed, and forty articles were retrieved and reviewed in full text. They all related to laws proposed or enacted by state legislatures. Twelve states in all were identified, as well as the U.S. Congress. New Jersey's Supreme Court decision figured prominently, since it was the site of the Baby M case. However, references to "several states" that were considering some sort of regulation of surrogacy were commonly found in the text of the articles. The states were not always specifically named. If a state passed a law regarding surrogate motherhood, as Michigan did in June 1988, that information was easy to find by scanning headlines. Since finding the ambiguous "several states" was not possible in this search, all VU/TEXT newspapers for 1988 were searched using the strategy described above to broaden the search to a more truly national basis. That search resulted in fifty-two postings, which were reviewed in full text. Although many of these were about the Baby M case, the name of one additional state considering surrogacy legislation was identified.

Given the way news stories are written, it may not be possible, even in a full text database to find the definitive answer to this question. Perhaps a legal source such as *Legal Resource Index* would provide the most authoritative answer for this question.

Women Elected to Office in 1988 Elections

News databases should be the source of up-to-the-minute information such as the number of women who were elected to office in the last election. A search strategy was devised and run in both bibliographic and full text databases to test this hypothesis.

For the *National Newspaper Index*, the strategy was **WOMAN OR WOMEN OR FEMALE(S) AND LEGISLATOR(S) OR POLITICIAN(S) OR MAYOR(S) OR GOVERNOR(S) OR REPRESENTATIVE(S) OR SENATOR(S) OR JUDGE(S) OR BENCH AND WITH ELECT (TRUNCATED).** Seven postings were retrieved from NNI, but none were stories about the 1988 elections.

Indeed, the first citation viewed, dated 1981, was about Houston's first woman mayor. The second was dated 1987. Searchers accustomed to seeing the familiar "last in, first out" should be aware that this database apparently has loaded some retrospective tapes.

Since a search in a full text database might answer the question, the *Washington Post* for 1988 was searched on VU/TEXT using a modified search strategy with proximity operators: **WOMAN OR WOMEN OR FEMALE(S) SAME LEGISLATOR(S) OR POL-**

ITICIAN(S) OR MAYOR(S) OR GOVERNOR(S) OR REPRE-
SENTATIVE(S) OR SENATOR(S) OR JUDGE(S) OR BENCH
SAME ELECT (TRUNCATED). The search was limited to the
headline and lead paragraph. News items about Senator Warner's
recommending women for appointment to federal judiciary, items
about the investigation of Senator Tower's relationships with women
and a story about Mayor Koch's boasts of appointing many women
to high office appeared, as did articles on Benazir Bhutto and the
sixteen women who were elected with her in Pakistan. Little was
found, however, about the advance or decline of women in politics
in America.

For geographic diversity, a search was run in the *Los Angeles
Times* for 1988. To broaden the search, the strategy was changed to
**WOMEN OR WOMAN OR FEMALE(S) SAME ELECTED
OR ELECTION(S)**. These terms were to be in the headline or the
lead paragraph. Articles were found about Elizabeth Dole's selection as Secretary of Labor and Carla Hills' selection as special trade
representative by President-Elect George Bush, and stories on
Benazir Bhutto and Barbara Harris appeared. There were many
items about women elected to offices in social, professional or trade
organizations; usually, they were the first or second women to hold
these positions. There was even a story about a male student who
was elected Homecoming Queen at Rice University; his opponent
was a woman. Finally, on November 16, 1988, a very brief article
on a report issued by Women's Research and Education Institute
appeared. The report gave statistics for women in state legislatures
and the Congress in 1988 compared to 1983. Unfortunately, no
mention was made of gains or losses in the 1988 election.

It is interesting to note the differences in retrieval between bibliographic and full-text databases. Both the *Washington Post* and the
Los Angeles Times are indexed in the NNI and in full-text. The
difference in the number of citations retrieved is notable. Fewer
than fifty citations were found in the bibliographic databases, while
more than two hundred citations were found in the *Post* and *Times*
in 1988. A comparison of the types of material included in the full-
text files with the bibliographic databases is even more interesting.
The small item which almost answered the hypothetical question
was not found in the bibliographic database. Even double checking

for the name of the organization which issued the report did not
locate it.

There are both advantages and disadvantages to be gained by
searching in one of these large full-text databases. One can retrieve
a great deal of information, but much of it may be irrelevant.

CONCLUSION

One cannot rely on subject headings alone to search for women's
issues in these databases because subject headings may not exist for
the concepts one wishes to find. The searcher must be creative and,
as in the case of prochoice groups, add names or terms which she
knows to relevant to the search. Even when the subject headings for
a concept do exist, they may not be used or they may be applied
inconsistently. It is important to compensate for this deficiency by
adding relevant free text terms. For news items, currency is important. Therefore, searchers should check the update files to insure
retrieval of the latest information on their topics. Retrieval varies
from database to database. A strategy (even free text) which works
well in one database will not necessarily work well in another database with comparable coverage.

Full text databases can provide additional information since the
entire text of an article can be accessed. Due to the way news stories
are written, however, the searcher may not be able to find precise
facts. For example, if the reporter does not name the "several
states" where legislation on surrogate motherhood has been enacted
or is pending, that factual information will not be found. The
searcher may have to search for information on surrogate motherhood legislation in all forty newspapers for 1988. Some results will
be redundant, but she may be able to cull out the names of the states
from the articles retrieved.

In some sense, finally, searching for information about women is
like searching for information about anything else. One can never
be sure that all relevant information has been retrieved. The
searcher must be suspicious of all results and, as a matter of course,
try alternate strategies to retrieve that one important article which,
through inconsistent indexing or its author's use of language, has
escaped her best attempts to find it.

BIBLIOGRAPHY

Nancy C. Andreasen, "Posttraumatic Stress Disorder" in Harold I. Kaplan and Benjamin J. Sadock, eds., *Comprehensive Textbook of Psychiatry* (Baltimore, London: Williams & Wilkins, 1985) vol. 1, p.918-924.

Feminist Perspectives
Through Cited Reference Searching

Barbara J. Via

SUMMARY. This paper explores the use of cited reference searching for research on women. The online versions of the Institute for Scientific Information's three citation indexes provide the women's studies researcher with more comprehensive access to feminist publications than the traditional online bibliographic databases. Particular benefits of citation searching are currency of retrieved documents, retrieval of expanded journal contents, including letters and brief communications, and relevancy of retrieved items. Cited reference searching is recommended as a useful tool for gaining access to feminist scholarship.

FEMINIST SCHOLARSHIP

The past 10 to 15 years have seen an outpouring of feminist scholarship on every conceivable aspect of women's lives and thought. History, politics, literature, anthropology, religion, biology, in fact, virtually every area of knowledge has been reinterpreted by women seeking to modify a heretofore patriarchal world view. Feminist writing has been with us for a long time, but it is only since the advent of the women's movement in the late 1960s that it has swelled into a virtual deluge of scholarship. Although we know that this mass of scholarship exists, locating it through conventional library searching techniques is difficult, at best. Women have therefore tended to rely on the informal sharing of knowledge and resources in the pursuit of women's studies. With the develop-

---

Barbara J. Via is Reference Librarian and Bibliographer for Information Science and Policy, University at Albany, University Libraries, State University of New York, Albany, NY 12222.

ment of increasingly sophisticated online retrieval systems, however, searching for feminist scholarship has become a more fruitful endeavor. This paper will discuss how cited reference searching can aid in the retrieval of feminist scholarship. Feminist perspectives as used in the title of this paper means the viewpoint expressed by feminists on any area of knowledge.

In her introduction to *Women's Studies: A Recommended Core Bibliography*, Esther Stineman provides a definition of Women's Studies as "the study of traditional disciplines from a feminist perspective" (Stineman 1979). She provides a list of typical women's studies courses offered in colleges across the United States that exemplify her definition. "Black Women in American Society" and "Women and Literature" are two she mentions. Other women's studies courses bear titles like "Women and the Law," "Feminist Thought and Public Policy," "Sociology of Sex Roles," "Anthropology of Gender," "Women Writers," "Philosophy and Feminism," and "Feminist Historical Methodology." Clearly, then, the objective of much of women's studies is to confront the traditional patriarchal bias in all areas of knowledge and counteract it with research from a feminist perspective. The goal is to achieve equality between the sexes in theory and policy.

FINDING FEMINIST PERSPECTIVES THROUGH ONLINE SEARCHING: THE PROBLEM

Many articles have been written about the difficulties of conducting research on feminist issues and/or feminist perspectives. Ellen Gay Detlefsen, for example, discusses problems that confront women's studies scholarship. She makes the point that interdisciplinary approaches to women's and feminist information are necessary, and that massive vocabulary problems make searching for women's information exceedingly difficult (Detlefsen 1986). Scholarship written from a feminist viewpoint is scattered in journals of every kind, in many disciplines, including mainstream journals not devoted exclusively to women's issues. Furthermore, not every article title that includes the word women/woman, female, or feminine in the title is necessarily a feminist article.

Coverage of feminist periodicals is sparse, at best, in print indexes and abstracts. *Women's Studies Abstracts* provides the most comprehensive coverage of feminist periodicals, but this source is not available as an online file. Much of the scholarship written by women, and presenting feminist perspectives, is not published in journals exclusively covering women's issues. There are rich resources available across the disciplines for researching feminist perspectives in a variety of indexes and their online equivalents. *MLA Bibliography, Sociological Abstracts, Psychological Abstracts*, and many others provide essential sources for women's studies.

One of the major problems with conducting research on feminist perspectives is the lack of appropriate terminology. The terms used in the various databases to cover feminist issues vary widely and often are not precise enough to access the literature adequately. Suzanne Hildenbrand has compared indexing terms for key feminist topics in *ERIC, Medline, PsycInfo, Sociological Abstracts, America: History and Life, Dissertation Abstracts, Mental Health Abstracts,* and *Social SciSearch*. She finds that all of these online files are somewhat inadequate in providing appropriate descriptors, and enough of them, for women's issues (Hildebrand 1986).

CITATION SEARCHING

The citation index is a special type of database which can provide excellent access to information by and about women. The Institute for Scientific Information (ISI) produces three citation indexes in both print and online versions. The online files *Arts & Humanities Search, Social SciSearch*, and *SciSearch* provide multidisciplinary access to the universe of scholarship. The print *Science Citation Index*, first published in 1963, was the first of the three citation indexes to be developed. Since citing previous work when publishing the results of research is a long tradition in the sciences, *Science Citation Index* proved to be an invaluable tool for scholars to discover who was citing whom quickly and efficiently. Subsequently, ISI introduced *Social Science Citation Index*, and *Arts and Humanities Citation Index*. Some people were skeptical when the *Arts and Humanities Citation Index* was first announced because humanities scholarship is very different in character from scientific research. Eugene Garfield, founder of ISI, noted that in scholarship of the humanities recency is not important as in the sciences. Books are more important than journals, the citation tradition is not as great, and there is less formal citing in the published literature. There is, however, considerable implicit citing in the text and illustrations in humanities literature. By implicit citing, Garfield means that papers and books in the humanities often mention earlier works in the text without providing formal citations in a bibliography or list of references (Garfield 1980).

The underlying concept of citation searching is that there is a subject relationship between a citing work and a cited work. The bibliography provided at the end of a research article presumably contains articles relevant to the topic of the source article. By searching citation indexes for known citations, researchers can uncover cited references that will greatly expand the body of literature available to them. Citation searching, therefore, can help to overcome inadequacies in indexing and lead the information seeker to a wealth of highly relevant material.

CITED REFERENCE SEARCHING

A search on a cited reference database leads users to works in the sources covered by the database that have cited a particular work. If the patrons can provide one author or, even better, a cited work relevant to their information needs, cited reference searching can open up the doors to more relevant and timely research in a way that is not as easily accomplished with subject searching. When conducting a cited reference search, we are asking the system to identify all of the works that have somehow cited a known work. In addition, citation searching provides access to cited works appearing anywhere in the document. Footnotes and references in the text or in bibliographies, letters, and brief communications, are all included. The method of online access for each of the three ISI citation indexes is basically the same, with some differences to accommodate the various types of documents included in each of the three databases. Search protocols vary from one database vendor to another, but the basic approach is the same. There are, however, differences among the citation indexes in types of material that are included. *Arts & Humanities Search* for example, provides cites to illustrations, musical scores, scripts, reviews of plays, opera, etc. *SciSearch* on DIALOG includes a Research Front field that allows the user to find all relevant source papers in a particular research area.

The key to successful cited reference searching is to start with a relevant author's name or, for a more precise result, a citation to a relevant work. With this as a starting point, a search is conducted for the work as a cited reference. The following examples, which illustrate citation searching techniques, demonstrate how potentially useful sources can be retrieved that might otherwise be missed using conventional subject and/or author searching. In the examples illustrated the DIALOG search system is used. This vendor was chosen because it also provides access to the *MLA Bibliography* database, which is used for comparative examples. It is *not* the intention of the author to compare vendors or to speak to the relative merits of one search system over another. Both BRS and DIALOG provide very clear and complete documentation on searching the citation indexes in their respective systems. This paper, furthermore, is not intended as a how-to-do-it guide. Articles by Snow (1986), Knapp (1984), Bawden (1987), Pilachowski and Everett (1985), and Janke (1980) provide helpful techniques for successful citation searching. It should be noted that the database vendors constantly improve the searching capabilities for databases, so it is essential that a searcher consult the latest documentation from the vendor. This paper discusses the usefulness of citation searching as it applies to feminist writing using sample searches as illustrations.

In the following example, the patron is interested in finding works that have cited Nancy Chodorow's book, *The Reproduction of Mothering: Psychoanalysis and the Sociology of Gender* (1978), an acclaimed scholarly discourse by a feminist sociologist. A search for the book as a cited reference in *Arts & Humanities Search* reveals that this work is heavily cited.

A cited reference search usually includes the following steps:

1. EXPAND the author or cited work
2. SELECT the relevant entries
3. TYPE (print online) the desired records

The most direct way to search for the work as a cited reference is to do an expand on the title to see how it is listed in the database as a cited work.

E CW = REPRODUCTION MOTHERING

The result is 589 matches. Bibliographic citations for the first three records (format 3 in DIALOG) are:

FEMINISM AND MODERN FRIENDSHIP – DISLOCATING THE COMMUNITY
FRIEDMAN M
BOWLING GREEN STATE UNIV, PHILOSOPHY/BOWL- ING GREEN//OH/43403; BOWLING GREEN STATE UNIV, WOMENS STUDIES /BOWLING GREEN//OH/ 43303
ETHICS, 1989, V99, N2, P275-290
Language: ENGLISH
Document Type: ARTICLE

INFANT-MOTHER FACE-TO-FACE INTERACTION – AGE AND GENDER
DIFFERENCES IN COORDINATION AND OCCURRENCE OF MISCOORDINATION
TRONICK ED; COHN JF
UNIV MASSACHUSETTS, DEPT PSYCHOLOGY/ AMHERST//MA/001003;
UNIV PITTSBURGH/PITTSBURGH//PA/15260
CHILD DEVELOPMENT, 1989, V60, N1, P85-92
Language: ENGLISH
Document Type: ARTICLE

UNCIVIL WARS – THE REPRODUCTION OF MOTHER- DAUGHTER CONFLICT AND BROWN, ROSEELLEN AUTO- BIOGRAPHY OF MY MOTHER
WOLF, M
UNIV MICHIGAN, DEPT ENGLISH/ANN ARBOR//MI/ 48109
AMERICAN IMAGO, 1988, V45, N2, P163-185
Language: ENGLISH
Document Type: ARTICLE

In order to eliminate reviews of the book from the results, the searcher adds /nrev to the search statement:

S CW = REPRODUCTION MOTHERING

This narrows the result to 552 documents.

The results can be narrowed further by limiting by language, article or non-article, publication year, etc.

In the following example, the patron is interested in any works which have cited Virginia Woolf's novel *Mrs. Dalloway*. The searcher could search the *MLA Bibliography* online by expanding Mrs. Dalloway to verify its entry form in the database and then choose the E numbers for the appropriate matches:

EXPAND MRS. DALLOWAY

Ref	Items	Index-term
E1	2	MRS. CALDWELL HABLA CON SU HIJO
E2	1	MRS. CALIBAN
E3	53	*MRS. DALLOWAY
E4	1	MRS. DANE'S DEFENSE
E5	1	MRS. DUKE'S MILLIONS
E6	2	MRS. HARRIS

Enter P or E for more

S E3

S3	53	MRS. DALLOWAY

By selecting the appropriate matches, the searcher retrieves 53 citations. The first three records, shown below, appear to be relevant to the topic:

T/3/1-3

3/3/1
8804280 88-1-211-
Women's Search for Identity in Modern Fiction
(1881-1927) Self-Definition in Crisis
Grant, Wilda Leslie
Dissertation Abstracts International, Ann Arbor, MI 1988

Sept.; 49(3): 510A.
PY: 1988

3/3/2
8801588 88-1-1415
Writing, Speech, and Silence in Mrs. Dalloway
Bishop, Edward
English Studies in Canada, Edmonton, Alberta T6G 2E5, Canada. 1986 Dec.; 12(4)397-423.
PY: 1986

3/3/3
8733390
87-1-4895
Leaden Circles Dissolving in Air: Narrative Rhythm and Meaning in Mrs. Dalloway
Walker, Ronald G.
Essays in Literature, Macomb, IL. 1986 Spring: 13(1) 57-87.
PY: 1986

For comparison, the following example utilizes the same search request, executed in *Arts & Humanities Citation Search* for cites to Woolf's *Mrs. Dalloway*.

It is always a good idea to first perform an EXPAND CW= in order to see how the work is listed in the database.

E CW=MRS DALLOWAY

Ref	Items	Index-term
E1	1	CW-MRS CULVER
E2	1	CW=MRS CUTHBERT
E3	114	*CW=MRS DALLOWAY
E4	1	CW=MRS DALLOWAY AND MRS
E5	1	CW=MRS DALLOWAY IN BOND

The search statement would then be:

? S CA=WOOLF V? (S) CW=MRS DALLOWAY

	985	CR=WOOLF V?
	114	CW=DALLOWAY
S1	112	CW=WOOLF V? (S) CW=DALLOWAY

The result is 112 documents. The first three documents retrieved are:

? T 1/3/1-3

10/3/1

01012302 Genuine Article#: R8885 Number of References 18
WHAT A LARK, WHAT A PLUNGE-FICTION AS SELF-EVA-
SION IN 'MRS DALLOWAY'
    GUTH D
       TEL AVIV UNIV/IL-69978 TEL AVIV//ISRAEL/
       MODERN LANGUAGE REVIEW, 1989, V84, JAN P18-25
       Language: ENGLISH
       Document Type: ARTICLE

    10/3/2

       0100893 Genuine Article#: R4955 Number of References:
       51
       THE WORD-SPLIT-ITS-HUSK WOOLF DOUBLE VI-
       SION OF MODERNIST LANGUAGE (WOOLF,VIRGI-
       NIA)
    SCOTT BK
       MODERN FICTION STUDIES, 1988, V34, N3, P371-385
       Language: ENGLISH
       Document Type: ARTICLE

    10/3/3

       00989932 Genuine Article#: Q9271 Number of Refer-
       ences: 7
       IMAGES OF AUTHORITY AND THE AUTHORITY OF
       IMAGES – WOOLF, BOLL AND STRAUB HUILLET
    BYG B
       UNIV MASSACHUSETTS/AMHERST//MA/01003
       MODERN LANGUAGE STUDIES, 1988, V18, N3, P38-45
       Language: ENGLISH
       Document Type: ARTICLE

This search strategy, utilizing the "s" as a connector, instructs the system to perform a subfield search, retrieving from the cited reference field, references to cited author, Virginia Woolf and cited work, *Mrs Dalloway*.

This example illustrates another advantage of citation index searching, its timeliness. There is a significant difference in recency of retrieved documents from the searches for *Mrs. Dalloway* in the *MLA Bibliography* and *Arts & Humanities Search*. These sample searches were performed in early 1989. The first three records retrieved from the citation search are for documents published in 1989 and 1988. Note, however, that in the search of the MLA Bibliography the first document retrieved was a 1988 dissertation but the following two records had 1986 publication dates. The timeliness of the ISI citation databases is at least partly due to the fact that the editors do not supply subject descriptors, but instead, simply rely on permuted titles for subject access. The records are added to the database rapidly, resulting in a very current database file. A particularly attractive feature of the *Arts & Humanities Search* database is its inclusion of "implicit" citations that are provided for works that may be the subject of articles, but are not given formal cites in a footnote or bibliography. Types of works provided with "implicit" cites include paintings, literary works, dance performances, musical scores, and theatrical performances, a significant benefit for the scholar looking for references to a particular work of art. Before the advent of citation searching for the arts, it was virtually impossible to find such information in an efficient way.

In the following example, the patron is seeking sources that have cited a work by the sculptor Louise Nevelson entitled *Mirror Shadow XXIV*. A search is performed in *Arts & Humanities Search*:

E CA = NEVELSON L

The result is:

E3   36 CA = NEVELSON L

A search is then performed on Nevelson as a cited author and her sculpture, *Mirror Shadow XXIV*, as a cited work.

SS CA = NEVELSON L (S) CW = (MIRROR(W)SHADOW)

The result is:

S1	36	CA = NEVELSON
S2	2776	CW = MIRROR
S3	1339	CW = SHADOW
S4	3	CA = NEVELSON L (S) CW = (MIRROR(W)SHADOW)

If the patron was only interested in works that include an illustration of Nevelson's sculpture, the search strategy would then look like this:

SS CA = NEVELSON L (S) CW = (MIRROW(W)SHADOW(2W)ILLUSTRATION)

The result of this search is 2 documents that have cited references with illustrations of Nevelson's work. In this example, as in the Woolf example, the strategy takes advantage of subfield searching in DIALOG, that is, the system searches for the cited author, Nevelson, and the cited work, *Mirror Shadow XXIV*, both of which are drawn from the cited reference field.

Perhaps the strongest argument for citation searching is the degree of relevance of retrieved documents. Studies (Pao, He, and Worthen 1988 and Snow 1986) have shown that while traditional database searches may have higher recall rates, citation searches yield greater precision.

Attempts to find information on women scientists and the problems faced by women choosing science as a career can be particularly frustrating. Indexing terms for this topic are very difficult to get around. SciSearch offers a fresh approach to this research dilemma. If the patron has the name of a woman who has written on the topic of women in the sciences, the searcher need only do a cited reference search on that author to find additional research on that topic.

The Women's Annual 1984-85, for example, includes a review article by Betty M. Vetter on women in science and engineering. At the end of her article, the author includes a bibliography with some useful references for further research. Among the women she cites are Elizabeth Fennema, Violet B. Haas, and Margaret W. Rossiter

(Vetter 1985). One way to find more citations on the subject of women in the sciences would be to do cited reference searches for these three authors' works. The seacher expands the authors' names as cited references to verify the entries. To look for cites to Fennema's article in the *Journal of Research in Mathematics Education*, for example, the strategy would be:

EXPAND CR = FENNEMA E

There are many cites to her publications, only a few of which are shown below:

E12	1	CR = FENNEMA E, 1978, V9, P189, J RES MATH ED
E13	2	CR = FENNEMA E, 1981, V12, P3, J RES MATH ED
E14	1	CR = FENNEMA E, 1981, V12, P380, J RES MATH ED
E15	1	CR = FENNEMA E, 1982, ANN AM ASS ADV SCI

E13 and E14 are cites to the requested article so they are selected:

?S E13:E14

The retrieved result will be 3 cites to Fennema's 1981 article in the *Journal of Research in Mathematics Education*.

In this example, the searcher has limited the search to file 34 in DIALOG which covers the last six months in *Science Citation Index*. Because *SciSearch* is a such an enormous database, DIALOG has chosen to break it down into several files covering different time periods. A word of caution is in order here. One drawback of cited reference searching is that the records are entered swiftly and data may not always be exact. In the case above, a request for the cited references to Fennema's article using an exact cite, that is "S CR = FENNEMA E, 1981, V12, P380" would have missed the paper which cited her work as FENNEMA E, 1981 ,12, P33. It is always wise to expand on a cited reference to determine the various ways in which it could be entered in the database.

The following papers cite Fennema's 1981 paper:

Cooney, MP A Seminar on Women and Mathematics
Number of References: 30

Howard, GS; Smith RD Computer Anxiety in Management — Myth
  or Reality
Number of References: 20

Malcom SM Women in Science and Engineering
Number of References: 21

Beckwith, J; Woodruff M Achievement in Mathematics
Number of References: 12

If the searcher prints one of these records with all of its cited
references, the retrieved records greatly expand the body of literature that the patron has to work with on the topic of women in
mathematics. Cooney's article in *Historia Mathematica* has 30 references, most of which appear to be relevant.

09223629 Genuine Article#: R4553 Number of References: 30
A SEMINAR ON WOMEN AND MATHEMATICS
COONEY MP
ST MARY'S COLL, DEPT MATH/NTRE DAME//IN/46556
HISTORIA MATHEMATICA, 1988, V15, N4, P380-383
Language: ENGLISH
Document Type: ARTICLE
Geographic Location: USA
Subfile: SCISearch
Cited References:
 ARMSTRONG, JM, 1981, V12, P356, J RES MATH ED
 BENBOW CP, 1983, ACADEMIC PRECOCITY A
 BENBOW CP, 1980, V210, P1262, SCIENCE
 BEWER JW, 1981, EMMY NOETHER TRIBUTE
 BRUSH LR, 1980, ENCOURAGING GIRLS MA
  *
  *
 FENNEMA E, 1981, V12, P380, J RES MATH ED
  *

*
*

TOBIAS S, 1978, OVERCOMING MATH ANXI

COCITATION SEARCHING

Cocitation searching is a particularly powerful use of cited reference searching. Knapp defines cocitation searching as "searching for any document citing at least two other specified documents, usually on the same topic" (Knapp 1984). The rationale for this approach is that any work that cites two works on the same topic is probably relevant to the topic. The simplest search strategy for use in cocitation searching is:

S CR = ROSSITER MW? AND CR = VETTER B?

This search yields all of the documents that have cited both of these authors. If the authors are prolific or the names are very common, it is better to add more to the cited reference query, for example:

S CR = ROSSITER MW;1982? AND CR = VETTER B; 1976?

Knapp's article on cocitation searching provides detailed coverage of the use of this strategy for precise retrieval.

CONCLUSION

Cited reference searching offers the scholar a very rich resource for finding the often elusive literature that is feminist scholarship. In fact, the three ISI databases meet six of the seven criteria for judging databases in women's studies suggested by Josephine and Blouin. Their criteria are:

1. It should encompass the whole of women's studies — art, literature, religion, philosophy, education, psychology, sociology, history, political science, criminology.
2. It should cover both concepts and people.
3. It should cover feminist theories and issues.

4. It should represent the experience, interests, and concerns of all women — lesbians, poor, working-class, women of color, physically or mentally handicapped.
5. It should be international in coverage.
6. It should be current and retrospective.
7. It should be priced so that searches can be afforded by everyone. (Josephine and Blount 1986)

The one criterion in the above list that the citation indexes do not meet is affordability. Citation searching online is quite expensive and it is therefore imperative that online searchers make certain, before going online, that the patron knows exactly what he or she is looking for. Citation databases do not lend themselves to idle browsing due to their cost.

In conjunction with searching by subject or free text in other databases, cited reference searching yields an enormous body of literature for the feminist scholar in nearly all disciplines. Cited reference searching is particularly recommended for research topics for which the vocabulary is poorly defined, or for which descriptors provided in traditional indexes are inadequate. Cited reference searching is also recommended where recency is of utmost importance. Online cited reference searching is an important resource for feminist scholars. The recent advent of a CD-ROM version of *Social SciSearch* and a soon to be released CD for *SciSearch* offer exciting possibilities for increased access to these databases for a wider array of scholars.

REFERENCES

Bawden, David. 1987. Citation indexing. In Armstrong, C.J. and J. A. Large. *Manual of Online Search Strategies*. Aldershot: Gower.

Detlfesen, Ellen Gay. 1986. Issues of access to information about women. *Special Collections* 3:163-171.

Garfield, Eugene. 1980. Is information retrieval in the arts and humanities different from that in science: the effect that ISI's citation index for the arts and humanities is expected to have on future scholarship. *Library Quarterly* 50:40-57.

Hildenbrand, Suzanne. 1986. Women's studies online: promoting visibility. *RQ* 26:63-74.

Janke, Richard V. 1980. Searching the social sciences citation index on BRS. *Database* 3:19-45.

Josephine, Helen B. and Deborah K. Blouin. 1986. New reference sources on women: an analysis and proposal. *The Reference Librarian* 15:109-122.

Knapp, Sara D. 1984. Cocitation searching: some useful strategies. *Online* 8:43-48.

Pao, Miranda Lee, and Chunpei He, and Dennis B. Worthen. 1986. Relevance judgment. *Proc. of the American Society for Information Science* 23:261-264.

Pilachowski, David M. and David Everett. 1985. What's in a name: looking for people online — social sciences -. *Database* 8:47-64.

Snow, Bonnie. 1986. Tapping into the "invisible college" . . . online cited reference scarching. *Online* 10:83-88.

Stineman, Esther. 1987. Introduction in Loeb, Catherine et al. *Women's Studies: A Recommended Core Bibliography*. Littleton, CO.: Libraries Unlimited.

Vetter, Betty M. 1985. Science. In *The Women'a Annual, The Year in Review, 1984-85*. Boston: G.K. Hall.

Women in the National Online Bibliographic Database

Judith Hudson
Victoria A. Mills

SUMMARY. The content, coverage and availability of material about women in the national online bibliographic database (LC, OCLC and RLIN) are discussed. The common subject vocabulary, LCSH, is analyzed, and search protocols for OCLC, RLIN, LC-MARC and REMARC on DIALOG and OCLC EASI Reference on BRS are compared for their utility for research on women. Limitations in LCSH and the content of LC MARC records are identified. The national online bibliographic database is especially useful when users wish to search comprehensively for materials by a single author, in a series or about a topic, or when users wish to verify bibliographic information or locate an item which is not readily available.

The national bibliography of a country is "a bibliography which lists all the books and other publications published, or distributed in significant quantity, in a particular country."[1] In the United States, the *National Union Catalog* is the current national bibliography, providing cataloging records and locations for the majority of the books, journals and other published materials held by the Library of Congress (LC) and many other libraries in the United States.

The advent of computerized cataloging makes a national online bibliographic database possible. Presently, this national online bibliographic database does not exist as a single entity. It is, rather, the combination of several overlapping but not identical systems. For

Judith Hudson is Head, Cataloging Department, University Libraries, University at Albany, State University of New York, Albany, NY 12222, and Victoria A. Mills is Head Catalog Librarian, University of Arizona Library, Tucson, AZ 85721.

the purposes of this paper, the national database is defined as the aggregate of the cataloging records available online through LC's machine readable cataloging (MARC) tapes and through the bibliographic utilities available in the United States. This paper discusses the three major contributors to the national online bibliographic database: LC, the OCLC Online Computer Library Center (OCLC) and the Research Libraries Information Network (RLIN).

LC, which produces the *National Union Catalog*, is the major national library of the United States. One of its many services is to make cataloging records available in print and machine-readable form. The cataloging records are prepared by catalogers at LC and at certain other libraries in the United States and at the national libraries of a number of other countries. The print records are available for purchase on cards and in the *National Union Catalog*, and the machine readable records are available on LC MARC tapes.

The records included in the MARC tapes are currently divided into eight formats: books, serials, scores, audio-visual materials, maps, manuscripts and archival materials, sound recordings and computer files. At present, approximately 3,000,000 records cataloged since 1968 are available on LC MARC tapes. In addition, Carrollton Press has converted the records for over 4,000,000 titles cataloged by the Library of Congress before 1968 into machine readable form. Carrollton markets these records in the form of its REMARC tapes.

OCLC provides bibliographic services to over 6,000 member libraries, including academic and public libraries of all sizes, special libraries and school libraries in the United States, Canada, Great Britain, Europe and Australia. The OCLC bibliographic database contains records for 18,523,765 items as of January 1989.[2] These cataloging records are created by the Library of Congress via the LC MARC tapes and by the OCLC member libraries. Utilizing these bibliographic records, OCLC provides cataloging services, interlibrary loan, and serials union listing.

RLIN, a bibliographic utility provided by the Research Libraries Group (RLG), is owned and governed by its 35 member libraries. In addition to the members, approximately 200 libraries participate in RLIN through associate memberships or other arrangements with the utility. RLIN provides acquisitions, cataloging and interlibrary loan services to its users, and one of its main objectives is to facilitate resource-sharing among the participating libraries. Its bibliographic database, which includes the LC MARC tapes, contains cataloging records for millions of items, although an actual title count is not available from RLIN.[3]

The national online bibliographic database (LC/OCLC/RLIN) differs in a number of ways from the other online bibliographic data services (BRS, DIALOG, etc.) discussed elsewhere in this book. The national online bibliographic database is a compilation of cataloging records in eight different formats. The primary goal of the database is to facilitate the sharing of cataloging records and the resources they represent among U.S. libraries. The database provides bibliographic and ownership information about monographic and serial titles, including periodicals, but it normally does not provide bibliographic information about the contents of individual periodical issues or book chapters. On the other hand, the online bibliographic services provided by BRS, DIALOG, etc., offer bibliographic information about articles appearing within periodicals, chapters within monographs, technical reports and other kinds of materials that are not normally included in LC/OCLC/RLIN. These online services analyze issues of a journal, such as *Signs: Journal of Women in Culture and Society*, and often provide an abstract of each article, but they do not include information about which libraries subscribe to or own selected volumes of the journal. The form of citation, contents of records, indexing vocabulary and retrieval techniques differ greatly from one service to another. The standardization of record entry and vocabulary found in LC/OCLC/RLIN does not exist in the various online database services. While there is some overlap between materials cataloged in LC/OCLC/RLIN and those indexed in the online bibliographic services (in fact, subsets of LC and OCLC cataloging records are available in DIALOG and BRS), the two are essentially different kinds of databases, designed for different purposes and offering different, but equally valuable, kinds of information.

When, then, is it appropriate to use the national online bibliographic database? It can be consulted when a user needs complete bibliographic information for a citation, or when the user cannot remember the exact author or title of an item. It is the only source that links bibliographic information with ownership information on a national level, so it can provide information on which libraries in a state, region or the entire country own a particular title, and it can assist the user in obtaining these titles through interlibrary loan. It brings together all works (except periodical articles) by an author, so an individual author's work can be identified and located. It also brings together the titles of a series, information that can be valuable to scholars and librarians alike. It can be searched by subject, so all items on a particular subject can be brought together (although subject searching is not currently possible in all parts of the national online bibliographic database).

The national online bibliographic database is foremost an internal resource tool for libraries. Its bibliographic records are used to create local cataloging records that provide access to the collections of individual libraries and to create requests and track materials that are being borrowed from, and loaned to, other libraries. Many academic libraries, however, also make a part of this national database (either OCLC, RLIN, or one of the other, smaller bibliographic utilities) available to their public for bibliographic searching. These systems have proven to be excellent reference sources because of the size and comprehensiveness of their databases, and because they are offered free to the public and are relatively easy to search.

What would a women's studies student, scholar or librarian find in the national online bibliographic database? This national database is an excellent source for materials by, about and concerning women. It includes the holdings of many general and specialized women's collections across the country. As Sarah Pritchard points out, the collections of the Library of Congress are rich in books, printed documents, special collections, archival and nonprint resources for the study of women.[4] In addition to the Library of Congress, many university libraries have been building women's collections to support their women's studies curricula and, with few exceptions, these collections are represented in OCLC or RLIN. Some specialized women's collections are also represented in the national online bibliographic database. A selective survey of women's collections, many of which are independent of academic libraries,[5] found that 17 of the collections are currently adding their holdings to OCLC or RLIN. In addition, 18 have converted all or part of their cataloging records to machine-readable form and added them to one of the bibliographic utilities.[6]

The national online bibliographic database includes bibliographic information about women's materials in books, pamphlets, microforms, serials, audio-visual media, sound recordings, scores, maps, manuscripts, archives and computer files. It includes historical as well as current titles published in all countries and languages. The national online bibliographic database is the place to search titles mentioned in standard bibliographies or research guides for women's studies. For example, many titles mentioned in Susan Searing's *Introduction to Library Research in Women's Studies* have been cataloged by LC and all the titles can be found in OCLC or RLIN. It is also the place to search for information about large microfilm sets, early periodical titles, pamphlet and other ephemeral collections, and specialized archives and manuscripts. It contains citations to the standard, mainstream materials of importance to women's studies as well as to rare and esoteric materials in this field of study. Undoubtedly, it is the richest source of bibliographic information about women's materials that exists.

The accessibility and retrievability of the treasure trove of information in the national bibliographic database will be examined next.

AVAILABILITY

Access to the national bibliographic database is available in a variety of forms. Library of Congress MARC tapes may be purchased from the LC Catalog Distribution Service and may be mounted on a local mainframe computer or on some of the local online systems (e.g., NOTIS). In addition, DIALOG has mounted the LCMARC and REMARC tapes for searching through its dial-up system. Access to OCLC and RLIN is available by joining the utilities as a member or by purchasing "search-only" privileges.[7] As mentioned previously, many academic libraries offer their users access to OCLC or RLIN. Document delivery is available to libraries using OCLC and RLG through their interlibrary loan systems. Many of the users of RLG participate in the RLIN interlibrary loan system. Approximately 3,500 OCLC members participate in its in-

terlibrary loan system. Those parts of the national online bibliographic database that are available on BRS and DIALOG do not
have a document delivery component.

DATABASE COVERAGE

The database includes materials covering all the subject areas and
types of materials that libraries collect. Such broad coverage is important for an interdisciplinary field like women's studies because
materials covering all subject aspects of the field will be found together in this database.

Both OCLC and RLIN contain records for materials from incu-
nabula up to the present. Records are added to these databases daily
by the member libraries and weekly by the loading of MARC tapes.

Through LC's cataloging-in-publication program (CIP), records
are often prepared by LC catalogers, added to the MARC tapes and
subsequently entered into the OCLC and RLIN databases before the
item is issued by the publisher. The early availability of cataloging
information insures that there is no time lag between publication
and the entry of these items in the database. Materials issued by
small presses or by foreign publishers, which produce a considerable amount of literature of interest to scholars working in women's
studies, however, are not usually cataloged as quickly by LC and
many are not included in LC's collections. Having purchased these
types of publications, many libraries wait for a period of three to
nine months before cataloging an item in the hope that a record may
be provided by LC or another library. As a result, the entry of these
records into the database may be less timely. The time lag between
the publication of this material and the inclusion in the database
may be much longer than with other titles that are more in the mainstream of American publishing.

CONTENT OF INDIVIDUAL RECORDS

The MARC format used by the Library of Congress and OCLC
or RLIN libraries requires that data be placed in fixed and variable
fields. The records contain a variety of coded information in fixed

fields providing details about the type of material contained in the item described (e.g., the language of the text, inclusion of a bibliography, etc.), publication information (e.g., place and date of publication), and some information about the record itself (e.g., date of entry into the database). Variable fields contain information such as bibliographic description (e.g., imprint, notes), subject analysis (i.e., classification number, subject headings) and additional access points (personal and corporate authors, titles).

Most of the records cataloged by OCLC or RLIN participants are cataloged using the standards established by the Library of Congress and adhere to LC's interpretation of the *Anglo-American Cataloguing Rules*, 2nd edition. Records that do not meet LC standards are designated as such in a coded segment of the fixed fields.

Records for OCLC and RLIN are prepared by catalogers at the contributing member libraries or by the catalogers of the Library of Congress (in the case of records from LC MARC tapes). If a cataloging record for the item in hand is already available in OCLC or RLIN, a library may use that record as the basis for its own record. If no record is available, original catalogers at the library will prepare a cataloging record to be added to the database.

Two of the online bibliographic database services have mounted parts of the national online bibliographic database. BRS has made the latest four years of the OCLC database available to users. DIALOG has loaded the LC MARC tapes into a file called *LCMARC* and pre-1968 LC records into another called *REMARC*. Since these files are, respectively, a subset of the OCLC database and the LC database, they contain the same data as described above.

VOCABULARY

The records in the national online bibliographic database share a controlled subject vocabulary, the Library of Congress Subject Headings (LCSH). This subject thesaurus was created and is continually updated by the Library of Congress. LCSH is the vocabulary used to provide subject access to titles cataloged by the Library of Congress and to the cataloging records on OCLC and RLIN. LCSH, begun in 1898 and currently in its 11th printed edition, is a massive list of subject terms and their references—162,750 terms and 296,000 references as of September 30, 1987.[8] LCSH is also available on computer tape; as the LC subject authority database, it can be loaded into local online systems and is available on both OCLC and RLIN. Although the subject coverage of LCSH is very broad, it cannot be considered to be a comprehensive subject heading list covering all branches of knowledge equally. It has grown as the collection of the Library of Congress has grown and the failures in logic and consistency found in LCSH are "due to the fact that headings were adopted as needed, and that many minds participated in their choice and establishment."[9] In an effort to keep current with the expanding, changing world of knowledge, LCSH headings are created and changed on a continuous basis. Approximately 8,000 new headings are added each year by catalogers at LC and cooperating libraries.

Thousands of subject headings for women and women's issues are interspersed throughout LCSH and are connected to each other and to other relevant terms by the use of references and scope notes. While cross-references are used extensively in LCSH (130,000 in the 11th edition), many important cross-references to headings about women or women's issues are missing. For example, **Patriarchy** has a reference to it from Family, Patriarchal; but the corresponding female term **Matriarchy** has no similar reference from Family, Matriarchal. Also missing are many, but not all, cross-references from occupational terms to LC's chosen form for women in occupations. For example, **Women physicians** has a cross-reference from Physicians, Women but **Women lawyers** or **Women legislators** have no similar cross-references, an unfortunate oversight because the occupational term is a logical place for many catalog users to begin to search for materials about women in occupations.

The printed version of LCSH does not include names of people or organizations although these names will be found in the LC subject authority database and as subject headings on the cataloged records in LC/OCLC/RLIN.

Topical subject headings appear in several forms: single word (**Women,** or **Abortion**); inverted headings (**Women, Deaf** or **Infertility, Female**); qualified headings (**Women (Philosophy)**, or **Trials (Divorce)**); and multiple word headings (**Joint custody of**

children, or **Women-owned business enterprises**). LCSH makes liberal use of subject subdivisions to make headings more specific (e.g., **Women — United States — Biography**); however most of these subdivisions are not printed in the thesaurus.

LCSH reflects a white male bias in its representation of the world: men are the norm, women, the exception. The fact that LCSH contains sexist and biased terminology has troubled many librarians for years. In 1974 the Committee on Sexism in Subject Headings, sponsored by the American Library Association, presented a report documenting sexism in LCSH.[10] One of the members of the committee, Joan K. Marshall, published in 1977 a thesaurus of non-sexist, non-biased subject terminology, *On Equal Terms*, the most important work to date on women's subject headings.[11] Sanford Berman, outspoken critic of LCSH and long-time advocate of non-biased subject headings, has made numerous suggestions for changes or additions to LCSH's terms relating to women.[12] Although the Library of Congress has improved its subject terminology for women over the years, the majority of changes or additions advocated by Marshall, Berman and others have not been made to LCSH.[13]

Because the Library of Congress is often slow to add or change subject headings relating to women, the terminology used to provide subject analysis of women's materials is often neither current nor specific. Materials about family planning are given the subject heading **Birth control** although the two concepts are not the same. Materials about women fire fighters, carpenters, or college presidents will be found under the general headings **Fire fighters, Carpenters** or **College presidents** because no more specific headings exist. There are no subject headings for feminist art, drama, spiritualism or for either the presence or absence of sexism in children's literature, advertising or television. While there are headings for the effect of a husband's employment or retirement on his wife, there are no headings for a wife's effect on her husband's employment or the effect of a wife's employment on her husband. Almost any topic can affect or be affected by the female portion of the population, but the headings or subdivisions necessary to express this are not available in LCSH.

In addition, LCSH has no subdivisions that would relate general headings to a feminist perspective. Marshall suggests the subdivision "Feminist perspective" which could be used with any subject heading to relate that heading to a women's or feminist viewpoint.[14] No such subdivision has been added to LCSH.

Another problem with the subject terminology used in records in LC/OCLC/RLIN is that obsolete headings exist on the records. When a new heading is created by LC for a topic previously subsumed under another heading or when an old heading is changed, the existing cataloging records in LC/OCLC/RLIN with the old headings are not changed to reflect the new terminology. For example, the term **Single mothers** was established in 1988. Materials about single mothers were previously cataloged under the more general term **Single parents**. While currently cataloged records will be listed under **Single mothers**, older records in LC/OCLC/RLIN about single mothers will be found under the heading **Single parents**. The terms for women and feminism in LCSH in LCSH provide another telling example. Palmer notes that:

> In LCSH8, "FEMINISM" was not a legitimate heading.
> The searcher was advised to "See Woman" and "See Woman — Social and Moral Questions". On the other hand, "Women's Liberation Movement" and "Woman — Rights of Women" were legitimate headings. In the LCSH9, "FEMINISM" became a legitimate heading. To complicate matters, "Woman" was canceled as a heading and replaced by "WOMEN", and "Woman — Social and Moral Questions" was replaced by "WOMEN — SOCIAL AND MORAL QUESTIONS". Furthermore, "Women's Liberation Movement" was canceled and replaced by a reference which directs the searcher to "See FEMINISM". "Woman — Rights of Women" was canceled and replaced by "WOMEN'S RIGHTS".[15]

All of the above headings, both current and obsolete, can be found on records in LC/OCLC/RLIN. These examples demonstrate why a thorough understanding of LCSH and its history is needed for a searcher to locate all the materials on a topic.

The comprehensiveness of subject indexing creates problems for the user on LC/OCLC/RLIN. While there is no hard and fast rule about how many subject headings LC and most other American libraries which follow LC's lead will assign to a title, "economy has been a general guide."[16] American subject cataloging can not be considered indexing; it has tended to assign only those subject headings that cover the overall subject content of a title rather than providing subject headings for the specific concepts that are brought out in the various chapters or parts of a given title. As Chan explains in Library of Congress Subject Headings, LC has opted for the summarization approach to indexing.[17] The number of subject headings has increased with the advent of online catalogs and the decline of catalog cards, but improvement is still needed in the subject treatment of records in the LC/OCLC/RLIN databases.

DATABASE STRUCTURE AND INDEXING

The structure and the searching capabilities of OCLC and RLIN differ greatly. The OCLC database consists of one master record per bibliographic item with a holdings record attached which lists the libraries that own the item. The RLIN database contains separate records for each item cataloged by the libraries using the database. In most cases the records are clustered together according to a complicated algorithm designed to bring together records for the same item.

In RLIN the cataloging records for each MARC format (monographs, serials, maps, etc.) are stored in separate files, and each file has its own index. Users must specify which format or formats they wish to search. OCLC stores all cataloging records in a single file, regardless of format. Users can then choose to search all the records or to limit their searches by format.

Both OCLC and RLIN index personal and corporate names; titles, including uniform and series titles; and numeric fields such as Library of Congress control number, International Standard Book Number or Serial Number (ISBN or ISSN), Coden (for serial titles) and Superintendent of Documents number. In addition, RLIN indexes subject headings. OCLC is in the process of redesigning its search capabilities to include subject searching.

SEARCHING ON OCLC

The methods of searching the two utilities differ in many ways. OCLC uses a search key format. Each different kind of search (author, title, combined author and title, or number) requires a unique combination of characters and punctuation marks that makes up its search key. For example, a title search consists of the first three letters of the first significant word of the title, followed by the first two letters of the second and third word and the first letter of the fourth word, each separated by a comma (i.e., 3,2,2,1). OCLC searches may be qualified by publication date or range of dates, by format (books, serials, maps, etc.) or by whether the record is for a microform reproduction or not. The search key format requires that word searches (author, title) be truncated, but that searches by number fields, such as ISBN, not be truncated. At this time, neither free text searching nor Boolean searching are available, but greatly enhanced searching techniques are a part of OCLC's New Online System, planned for implementation in 1990. In addition, OCLC inaugurated a new public access system called EPIC available early in 1990. EPIC includes such enhanced searching capabilities as free text and Boolean searching.

Searchers cannot browse through OCLC indexes. If a search key retrieves multiple records, brief descriptions of each record are displayed in alphabetized order by main entry and in chronological order when the main entry is the same. This brief display contains author, title, imprint information and source of cataloging, if that source is a national library. The only other level of display on OCLC is the full MARC format. Consequently, users must have a certain amount of knowledge about the MARC format to be able to interpret what they see. Variety and choice of display are enhancements that will come with the OCLC's New Online System.

SEARCHING ON RLIN

RLIN relies on full word searching rather than search keys. Name entries, both personal and corporate, may be searched. Personal names may be searched in inverted or natural order (i.e., Bella Abzug or Abzug, Bella). Automatic truncation is provided for searching personal names, unless the searcher specifically requests an exact search for the name. Corporate names (the names of companies or other groups) are searched in natural order and truncation, although not automatic, may be specified. A corporate word search may also be requested, using a word from the name of the company or other group. Title entries may be searched in natural order, with or without truncation, and title keywords may be searched. Subject headings may be searched, and the search string may be truncated, if desired. A subject word search is also available, and subject subdivisions are searchable in all but the RLIN monographs format. The subject word search can be useful in retrieving records on topics when comprehensiveness is desirable. For example, a search on the truncated subject word "mother#" will retrieve records containing subject headings such as **"Working mothers"** and **"Surrogate mothers,"** as well as headings which begin with the word "mother."

Number searches may also be truncated. The capability of truncating an ISBN may be of particular use in searching women's materials from small presses. Because the first 5 or 6 numbers in an ISBN identify the publisher or distributor, a truncated ISBN search on those first numbers (e.g., ISBN 091327) can retrieve all publications from a certain press as long as ISBNs have been included in the cataloging records.

Other features of RLIN searching include Boolean searching within and between indexes and a method of qualifying searches called the ALSO command. When a search has retrieved fewer than 2,500 hits, the searcher can add a qualification to the search. The system will sort through the array and pull out all records that meet the specified qualification. Qualifications include: language of the text, place or date of publication, NUC code or RLIN library identifier (which indicates which library cataloged the item), microform generation, and character strings in many fixed and all variable fields. Character string searches within the ALSO command are the closest to free-text searching that RLIN provides.

Like OCLC, RLIN does not allow users to browse the indexes. When a search of the database results in multiple hits, brief records for the clusters are displayed in reverse chronological order according to the date that the first item in the cluster was added to the database. The latest imprints are not necessarily displayed first, however, because retrospective cataloging is continually occurring in RLIN libraries and older, as well as current, titles are being added to the database. As a result, clusters are not displayed chronologically by publication date, but in a seemingly random order.

RLIN provides four types of display. A one-or-two line display which contains brief author, title and imprint information is provided when a search statement brings up a multiple result (i.e., more than 1 hit). The three other displays are: a partial display containing main author, title, imprint, series, call number and brief holdings information; a long display providing all the information that normally is printed on a catalog card; and a full display in MARC format providing most of the information in the record. The user can request the preferred display. The default display format can also be specified.

DATABASE SEARCHING:
A COMPARISON BETWEEN RLIN AND OCLC

Because RLIN allows for keyword or phrase searching and for truncation of ISBNs, it is much more efficient than OCLC in retrieving materials for the study of women. Table 1 contains the search statements used in OCLC and RLIN for a personal and a corporate name, a title and a truncated ISBN search with the number and precision of results retrieved by each search.

The personal name, corporate name and title searches on RLIN yielded only records containing desired headings (100% relevancy). The corresponding personal name search on OCLC yielded 8 records which matched the desired, and one that matched the search key (Searcy, Susan E.), but not the full name. The corporate name search on OCLC yielded a low number of relevant hits because OCLC requires the the use of stopwords in corporate searches. The first three words of the corporate name searched (national, council, for) are stopwords and, as a result, were dropped from the search. The search resulted in 29 records containing 7 different corporate name headings (e.g., Institute for Research on Women (New Brunswick, N.J.), Symposium Research on Wave Action (1969: Delft Hydraulics Laboratory). The title search on OCLC resulted in

TABLE 1

Comparison of Searching OCLC and RLIN

DATABASE	SEARCH STATEMENT	RECORDS RETRIEVED	RELEVANT RECORDS	% RELEVANT RECORDS
Personal Name				
RLIN	searing, susan e	4	4	100
OCLC	sear,sus,e	9	8	89
Corporate Name				
RLIN	national council for research on women	4	4	100
OCLC	=rese,on,w	29	8	28
Title				
RLIN	introduction to library research in women's studies	1	1	100
OCLC	int,to,li,r	24	2	8
ISBN				
RLIN	093321#	72	48	66
OCLC	093321	na	na	na

24 records which contained 10 different titles (e.g., Introduction to Library Research in French Literature, Introduction to Lip Reading). Half of the hits are titles which begin with the phrase "introduction to library research."

The truncated ISBN search yielded many hits on RLIN. Two-thirds are records for titles published by Spinsters Ink/Aunt Lute, a small women's press. The other records are for titles from 4 other small presses, which are probably distributed by the same group as Spinsters Ink/Aunt Lute. The OCLC search on the truncated ISBN resulted in the message "Request Impossible." ISBN searches on OCLC cannot be truncated.

In the first three searches compared above, RLIN's full word or phrase search capability resulted in 100% relevance, while the search key approach of OCLC yielded records that did not match the desired heading. The ability to truncate ISBNs allowed for the retrieval of records from a small women's press in RLIN, while this type of search was impossible on OCLC.

SEARCHING LCMARC AND REMARC ON DIALOG

DIALOG's *LCMARC* and *REMARC* also rely on word or phrase searching. Personal and corporate authors are indexed, as are titles and subject headings. In addition, classification number, series title, named person (i.e., a personal name subject heading), conference location, conference title or year of conference, document type (e.g., book, article), edition, geographic location, intellectual level, language, LC control number (LCCN), publisher, and year of publication are indexed in both files. *LCMARC* also indexes contents notes, ISBN, government document numbers and the language of a summary, if one is included in the catalog record. Words can be truncated and adjacency can be specified. Searches can be qualified by language (i.e., English/nonEnglish) and by fiction/nonfiction. They can also be qualified by combining searches of the many indexes using Boolean operators (such as ANDing a language search with an author search to retrieve only those titles by the author which are published in the desired language).

The indexing of contents notes in the LCMARC file is noteworthy because it enhances subject searching by allowing the user to search for terms in these rich fields. Another valuable capability of LCMARC and REMARC is searching by publisher's name, which allows searchers to find materials published by small presses without knowing the ISBN. As with ISBN searches, this capability has particular relevance to research in women's studies because many women's titles are published by small presses. Truncated ISBN searches can also be conducted on the LCMARC file.

Users may browse the LCMARC and REMARC indexes. The "EXPAND" command allows the searcher to enter the index at the desired place and page forward through the index.

Records may be displayed in a number of formats, including a variety of abbreviated records, full records in card catalog format, MARC format and in a labelled format. Each time the user requests a display of records, the format must be specified; there is no default format.

SEARCHING OCLC EASI REFERENCE ON BRS

OCLC EASI Reference on BRS is a separate database containing bibliographic records from the OCLC Online Union Catalog with imprint dates falling within the most recent four years. It relies on word or phrase searching. It provides 28 different indexes, including author, title, series, subject headings, subject descriptors, various numeric fields (including LC, DDC, NLM, ISBN, ISSN, and LCCN), various note fields (such as contents notes), publisher, place or date of publication, physical description, and language of the publication. Users can search on any field or combination of fields that are indexed and can qualify searches by language, publication date or type of publication. Words can be truncated and adjacency can be specified.

The OCLC EASI Reference file also makes available features described above for LCMARC and REMARC as especially valuable for searching material on women. The features include searchability of contents notes, access to publishers' names and truncated ISBNs.

By using the ROOT command, a searcher may browse forward through the Dictionary File, which contains terms from all but the limit indexes (e.g., publication date, language). Use of this command is somewhat clumsy because the system displays only the first 100 entries beginning with the specified root in the dictionary file.

The OCLC records are displayed in a labeled format that contains most of the data contained in an OCLC MARC record. No alternative displays are available.

LOCAL SYSTEMS

Many American libraries today have implemented local online public access catalogs (OPACs) using local databases containing records for those items held by the libraries served by the OPAC. Other regional or national holding data are available only through the utilities. These local databases contain MARC records supplied by LC, the various bibliographic utilities and MARC-formatted records prepared by the libraries themselves. The great majority of records in online catalogs across the country can also be found in LC/OCLC/RLIN, but an important aspect of the records in local online catalogs is their accessibility. Increased indexing and searching capabilities may be offered in online catalogs and, in some cases, information about circulation status is provided.

GENERAL ASSESSMENT

The national online bibliographic database is a rich source of bibliographic information about women's materials. The different parts of this database, however, vary in their usefulness and each has its limitations. OCLC's current searching protocols (search keys rather than word or phrase searching) and its lack of subject and keyword access limits its usefulness in all but searches for known items. Because it has the largest number of unique records, however, OCLC remains the best source for known item searching. OCLC's New Online System for cataloging and its EPIC system for public access will greatly enhance OCLC's searching capabilities and make it a more useful part of the national online bibliographic database in the future. RLIN, BRS's *OCLC EASI Reference, LC-MARC,* and *REMARC* have much more powerful searching capabilities because they provide subject access and use more flexible searching protocols than OCLC. RLIN's limitation of free-text searching to title, corporate names and subject heading fields, however, somewhat restricts its usefulness. The *LCMARC, REMARC,* and *OCLC EASI Reference* databases provide access to much smaller databases than either OCLC or RLIN, and the cost of accessing those databases through BRS or DIALOG is passed on to the users at most libraries. These databases also do not offer the ownership information that make OCLC and RLIN so valuable.

Records in online catalogs across the country are easily accessible through a variety of flexible search protocols, but these databases usually represent only the collection of a single library. They are the logical place to search when the user wishes to know what is available in the local library.

Many of the databases that make up the national online bibliographic database (LC, OCLC, RLIN) share a common subject vocabulary. The Library of Congress subject headings are powerful tools for accessing cataloging records because they form a controlled vocabulary used in a standardized way by thousands of libraries. The very mechanism that keeps this enormous subject thesaurus controlled and that insures its standard use, however, also makes it slow to react to change and to overcome a traditionally male bias in terminology. In addition, even the best system cannot index terms that are not on the records. Subject access is limited by the small number of subject headings (an average of 1.7 per record)[18] that are usually assigned to a record. As long as the economy model of subject indexing is practiced in American libraries, comprehensive subject access through LCSH alone will not exist.

Another drawback of subject analysis using LC subject headings is that they provide no information about the perspective of the items analyzed. Researchers wishing a feminist perspective on a particular subject will find little or no assistance in identifying such materials in the content of the records.

The content of the MARC record is a problem for all machine-readable databases. Information about the intellectual content of an item is usually restricted to the title statement, the subject headings, the series title, if any, and, when available, the contents notes. Summaries of the contents of an item are restricted to certain formats: visual and instructional materials, juvenile material, archival records, etc. It has been suggested that the use of online systems will allow the library world to augment cataloging records by adding data from the table of contents to the record.[19] Such augmentation, combined with free-text searching, would provide for more detailed subject access, although the large number of records in the national online bibliographic database will always make precision or relevance a problem.

Overall, the national online bibliographic database is a useful tool for the identification and verification of women's materials in a variety of formats. Searching this bibliographic database is most productive when the user wishes to do a comprehensive search for all materials by an author, in a series, or about a topic, or when the user wishes to verify bibliographic information and/or obtain a specific item that is not available locally. The abundance of bibliographic information about women's materials in the national online bibliographic database makes it a strong component in the variety of databases that offer coverage of bibliographic information on women's studies.

REFERENCES

1. *Harrod's Librarian's Glossary.* 5th ed. Aldershot. Hants. : Gower, 1984. p. 518.

2. Rich Green. Personal communication, March 14, 1989.

3. As of May 1, 1989, the RLIN database included 34,522,264 cataloging records. This number represents the total number of records cataloged by all libraries using RLIN. It does not represent the number of unique titles included in the RLIN database.

4. Sarah Pritchard. "Library of Congress Resources for the Study of Women." *Special Collections* 3, no. 3/4:13-36 (Spring/Summer 1986). Also issued as *Women's Collections.* (New York: The Haworth Press, 1986)

5. Suzanne Hildenbrand. "Representative Women's Collections." *Special Collections* 3, no. 3/4:191-194 (Spring/Summer 1986). Also issued as *Women's Collections.* (New York: The Haworth Press, 1986)

6. The survey was conducted in November 1988. A questionnaire was sent to a 33 women's collections affiliated with a library that participates in OCLC or RLIN. Twenty-two responded (a 66.6% return rate).

7. "Search only" privileges allow libraries access to the utilities to search the databases but not to add or change the records.

8. *Library of Congress Subject Headings.* 11th ed. (Washington, D.C.: Library of Congress, 1988) p. vii.

9. *Subject Headings Used in the Dictionary Catalogs of the Library of Congress.* 5th ed. (Washington, D.C.: Library of Congress, 1948) p. iii.

10. Joan K. Marshall. *On Equal Terms: A Thesaurus for Non-Sexist Indexing and Cataloging.* (New York: Neal-Schuman Publishers, 1977), p. vii-viii.

11. J. K. Marshall. *On Equal Terms.*

12. Sanford Berman. *Prejudices and Antipathies: A Tract on the LC Subject Heads Concerning People.* (Metuchen, N.J.: Scarecrow, 1971. *The Joy of Cataloging: Essays, Letters and Other Explosions.* (Phoenix, Ariz.: Oryx Press, 1981) "Out of the Kitchen — But Not into the Catalog," *Technical Services Quarterly* 2, no. 1/2 :167-171 (Fall/Winter 1984). Also issued in *Subject Cataloging: Critiques and Innovations.* (New York: The Haworth Press, 1984)

13. A. C. Foskett. "Better Dead Than Read: Further Studies in Critical Classification," *Library Resources & Technical Services* (28, no.4: 346-359 (October/December 1984). Elizabeth M. Dickinson. *Report of the Racism and Sexism in Subject Analysis Subcommittee to the RTSD/CCS Subject Analysis Committee, Midwinter 1980.* (Chicago: American Library Association, 1980)

14. J. K. Marshall. *On Equal Terms.* p. 13.

15. Joseph W. Palmer. "Subject Authority Control and Syndetic Structure — Myth and Realities," *Cataloging & Classification Quarterly* 7, no. 2:71-93 (Winter 1986) p. 78.

16. Lois Mai Chan. *Library of Congress Subject Headings: Principles and Application.* (Littleton, Colo.: Libraries Unlimited, 1978) p. 162.

17. ibid., p. 159.

18. H. Mary Micco. An Exploratory Study of Three Subject Access Systems in Medicine: LCSH, MeSH, PRECIS. (Ph.D. diss., University of Pittsburgh, 1980)

19. Alex Byrne. "Life Wasn't Meant to Be Whimsical: Painless Subject Augmentation." *Australasian College Libraries* 4:87 (June 1986). Mark T. Kinnucan. "Tables of Contents in Online Public Access Catalogs." In *Annual Review of OCLC Research, June 1986-June 1987.* (Dublin, Ohio: OCLC, 1987) p. 27-28. Edwin D. Posey and Charlotte A. Erdman. "An Online UNIX-based Engineering Library Catalog: Purdue University Engineering Library." *Science & Technology Libraries* 6:31-43 (Summer 1986)

Women in Nonbibliographic Databases

Eleanor A. Gossen

SUMMARY. Nonbibliographic databases are a rich source of numeric and full-text information about women. The characteristics of these databases are discussed, along with strategies for identifying and accessing datasets in data archives and online bibliographic databases. Primary and secondary analysis of machine-readable numeric data promises both to supplement and complement the more traditional approaches to women's studies.

BACKGROUND

Nonbibliographic or numeric databases are different from bibliographic databases in at least three ways: in the kind of information they contain, in the tools that provide access to them, and in the ways in which they are distributed. This paper introduces the reader to machine-readable numeric data, discusses the problems involved in locating information on women in this format, and suggests strategies for accessing this material.

What exactly are nonbibliographic data? McGee and Trees define machine-readable numeric data as follows:[1]

> Data are considered machine-readable data when represented and stored in a form which can be processed by computers. Numeric data are information represented as numerical values. Such data cannot be understood without knowing what definitions are associated with quantities of attributes and are therefore amenable to statistical manipulation. The notion of

Eleanor A. Gossen is Senior Assistant Librarian, The University at Albany, State University of New York, Albany, NY 12222.

"numeric" excludes textual and therefore bibliographic databases. (p. 108)

Social scientists have used numeric data for a long time, but the
problems involved with the storage and manual manipulation of
large quantities of social science data have limited the possibilities
for analysis.[2] The development of computer systems with large storage capacities and sophisticated statistical software has enabled social scientists to conduct quantitative research on a scale only
dreamed of thirty years ago. In most social science research a good
deal of the cost and effort expended in a project goes to the collection of empirical data. If appropriate data have been collected and
made available by previous researchers, they can often be reana-
lyzed to examine different questions or to test new hypotheses. It is
sometimes possible to combine data from several studies, to add
new variables to existing data sets, or to expand the time range of a
set of data without having to recollect and reenter all the data,
thereby saving a great deal of time, effort and money. It is only
within the last two or three decades that the potential of this methodology has been widely recognized by social scientists and that
serious efforts have been made to archive machine-readable social
science data and train graduate students in computer use and the
statistical techniques they will need to deal with this kind of data.[3]
Machine-readable social science data have much to offer. In the
first place, some information is only available in machine-readable
format, particularly survey data and some census materials. Secondly, some types of information are often more easily retrieved
and manipulated in machine-readable form than they are in print
format, and sometimes more data is available in machine-readable
format than in print. Thirdly, the use of specialized statistical and
graphics software permits sophisticated analysis of data and presentation of results. For example, Robert Pierce, in an article on abortions in Manhattan, has combined and analyzed data from the New
York City Health Department and the United States Census to examine the high rate of abortions during the 1970s in an effort to
determine whether or not there was a correlation between abortions
and socioeconomic status. This analysis would have been extremely
difficult to do in pre-computer days, if only because of the volume
of data with which he was dealing.[4]

A number of books and articles discussing machine-readable databases and distribution systems in the social sciences, business and natural sciences have appeared over the last decade or so. Notable examples include a special issue of *Library Trends* edited by Kathleen Heim[5] and *Numeric Databases*, edited by Ching-Chih Chen and Peter Hernon.[6] The Heim volume discusses distribution systems for machine-readable data and the role of libraries in providing access to nonbibliographic data, while Chen and Hernon focus more specifically on discussions of the data itself. Both provide useful overviews of the field.

To introduce the reader to machine-readable data, I would like to present an example of the use one investigator made of such data in preparing for her doctoral research. Lynnette Leidy, a graduate student in the Department of Anthropology at The University at Albany, State University of New York at Albany, is investigating the sociocultural influences that affect the timing of menopause. Her hypothesis is that menopause is not just a biological event that happens to women outside of any cultural context, but that both the event itself and a woman's interpretation of it (i.e., did it happen early or late, was it "normal" or not?) are profoundly affected by sociocultural factors.

Before Ms. Leidy could begin her fieldwork to test this hypothesis, she had to investigate the biological "facts" about menopause: within what age range did menopause occur in various populations? Were there any correlations with diet and health? What was the effect of drinking and smoking on age of menopause? After consulting with faculty in her department and with the library, she identified datasets that contain information about menopause: the National Center for Health Statistics Health Interview Surveys, which provide detailed medical information on women in the United States, and data from the World Fertility Surveys, available from the International Statistical Institute in the Netherlands, which are useful for cross-cultural comparisons. Using these and other data she was able to determine the age range of menopause in large sample groups of women and to show that there was a correlation with smoking and height. Armed with this information, she was able to draw up a plan for a field project that would enable her to test the data she collected against these large-scale data collections. If data on large populations had not been available for secondary analysis and if computers with powerful statistical programs had not been available, Ms. Leidy would have had neither national nor cross-cultural data with which to compare her data, thus limiting the generalizations she would be able to draw from the data.[7]

The availability of these large data sets gave her an opportunity to become familiar with the use of data and to learn and practice the statistical techniques to be utilized with her own data. It also gave her a sense of the requirements of both the hardware and software she would be using, enabling her to design her study more efficiently and, hopefully, to avoid problems with coding and organization.

CHARACTERISTICS
OF NONBIBLIOGRAPHIC DATABASES

While bibliographic databases lead users to information in the form of citations to books, articles, and proceedings, nonbibliographic databases contain the actual data in question, which can be searched and manipulated by the user once he or she has access to it. These data range from information relayed from space satellites or the financial records of banks to the results of telephone surveys or statistics collected by an academic researcher while writing a book. Typical examples of social science numeric databases contain census data or data collected by longitudinal surveys, which follow a group of respondents over a period of years.

The methods used to generate and distribute numeric databases differ from those used to produce bibliographic databases. Most of the widely-available commercial bibliographic databases are produced by companies, government agencies or societies which have set up special units to collect and index bibliographic data. These databases are usually distributed for a fee through one of the major online networks such as BRS or DIALOG or made available on compact disc. While some nonbibliographic databases are produced commercially (the legal databases LEXIS and WESTLAW, and the Predicasts business databases, for example), most are produced by nonprofit or government agencies or scholarly researchers and are often given only limited distribution. In fact, the vast majority of nonbibliographic social science databases are not traditionally available "online" at all, but are kept in data archives that distribute them to the public.

Numeric databases have generally been housed outside traditional information centers (i.e., libraries), since only those institutions which had large main-frame computers have been able to read and analyze the data.[8] As a result, few people knew that the data were available, and even fewer knew how to use them. This situation is changing as more data become available in formats suitable for microcomputers and as more institutions start teaching courses in quantitative social science methodology. Many numeric databases are now available for purchase in the form of tapes, diskettes, or CD-ROMs; they can be mounted on a local mainframe or a microcomputer. Most of these datasets are distributed in formats that can be used on a variety of computers and manipulated through a variety of software packages. Individuals active in research on women or women's studies should know that these data are available.

EVALUATION OF NONBIBLIOGRAPHIC DATABASES

In a 1984 article,[9] Pritchard formulates a list of guidelines to be used in the evaluation of bibliographic databases in Women's Studies, including such criteria as (1) database coverage: subject, scope, completeness, timeliness; (2) content of individual records; (3) vocabulary and indexing; (4) database structure; (5) availability issues; and (6) general subjective assessment. Many of these same criteria can be used when evaluating numeric databases, but there are some additional criteria which also need to be considered. For numeric databases, it is important to know about the population being studied, the research methodology used, the questions asked, and so forth. These criteria will be specific to each dataset. The quality of documentation available for each dataset is of crucial importance because there is little or no relationship between data sets. If a data set does not have adequate documentation, it may be essentially useless to someone who has not used it before, whatever the quality of the data. Accuracy and quality of data are major concerns, for however sophisticated and innovative the analysis may be, it cannot be better than the data that are being studied. Availability is also important to consider, for many data sets have restrictions on their use, and some are only available at the institution where they are housed.

Consistency from one dataset to the next is not significant unless one plans to integrate data from two or more datasets or to use longitudinal studies such as the Census or the General Social Surveys. In this case it becomes critical to know the differences in data from one year to the next.

ACCESS

One of the most difficult issues confronting researchers who want to use machine-readable data is that of finding out what data exist on a topic and whether or not they are available for public use. It has been estimated that there are now at least 500 numeric databases available online and over 50,000 that are available for batch processing.[10] Given that there is no comprehensive listing of datasets, the process of identifying and gaining access to machine-readable data files becomes something of an art.

There are several directories of machine-readable information sources and systems that can be used to identify available data, such as the *Information Industry Market Place*,[11] the *Encyclopedia of Information Systems and Services*,[12] and the *North American Online Directory*.[13] Most of these directories, however, are of limited use in identifying nonbibliographic data on women other than demographic and marketing data that are available online through the various distributors of business data, such as Predicasts or Donnelly Demographics.[14] The bulk of numeric data listed in these directories is financial, economic, and scientific data that may not be of particular interest to researchers on women.[15] Some information on women can also be found in the standard legal online systems such as LEXIS or WESTLAW, which provide the full text of federal case law, statutes, regulations, and other legal information.

The major sources of information about datasets are the catalogs and directories produced by data archives or repositories, most of which group data by source rather than by subject. In addition, cataloging records for datasets are becoming increasingly available in the national bibliographic utilities such as the Research Libraries

Information Network (RLIN). Although articles such as McGee and Tree's "Major Available Social Science Machine-readable Databases,"[16] and Gerhan and Walker's "A Subject Approach to Social Science Data Archives"[17] do provide some general subject access, there is still a need for a comprehensive subject-based directory of machine-readable social science data files to make these data truly accessible to the research community.

DATA ARCHIVES

Data archives are compiled by organizations that collect data from the original researchers and disseminate these data to their members or the public. These organizations usually prepare catalogs or lists of their holdings and make an effort to review or clean up data if necessary before they are distributed. They act as central repositories, enabling researchers to deal with one organization that can provide access to many datafiles on various subjects, thus facilitating the sharing of data by the original researchers. The following section describes some of the major data archives in the United States that have materials of particular interest to those doing research on women or women's issues.

Inter-University Consortium for Political and Social Research
P.O. Box 1238, Ann Arbor, MI 48106
Telephone: 313-764-2570

The Inter-University Consortium for Political and Social Research (ICPSR) is one of the oldest and largest social science data archives in the world. Many universities and colleges belong to the Consortium and can obtain data through their ICPSR representative. The ICPSR collects, archives, and distributes data from government sources and from private research institutions, universities, and researchers. The ICPSR was started by a group of political scientists and retains a strong interest in political science data, although it is now collecting data from all areas of the social sciences. The bulk of the data deals with the United States, although some cross-national data and data from other countries are included.

Access to ICPSR holdings is provided through a printed *Guide to*

Resources, which lists and provides abstracts of all the data sets owned by the Consortium. The *Guide Online,* which can be accessed by members through the Consortium Data Network (CDNet), allows searching of titles and abstracts of datasets. A search of the *Guide Online* for "woman or women" in titles and abstracts yielded 89 collections of data. Some of these were longitudinal surveys such as the "Surveys of Consumer Attitudes and Behavior," or the "Retirement History Longitudinal Survey Series." These datasets have been coded for sex so that data for women can be extracted or can be compared with data for men. Other datasets, such as the "National Survey of Adolescent Female Sexual Behavior, 1976" or the series on "Women and Development" deal specifically with women. ICPSR also offers an online *Variables Database,* which permits searching by subject for specific questions asked by public opinion polls and surveys.

One particularly valuable feature of the ICPSR *Guide,* both in print format and online, is that it makes an effort to list publications derived from each dataset, whether written by the original researchers or by those who used the data for secondary analysis.

Data from ICPSR are provided on magnetic tape and are accompanied by a codebook that describes the scope of each study, the research methodology used, and the organization of the data on the tape. Users must have some knowledge of statistics and the manipulation of numeric data; some datasets are very large and require considerable expertise. ICPSR provides limited consulting services; help is also usually available through local computing centers, academic departments or libraries. In addition, ICPSR runs a summer school specifically designed to teach people how to use numeric data.

ICPSR data collections that deal with women include:

Economic Incentives, Values, and Subjective Well-Being, 1971-1974
Surveys of Consumer Attitudes and Behavior
American National Election Study Series
Convention Delegate Study of 1972: Women in Politics
Detroit Area Studies
Harris 1972 American Women's Opinion Poll

General Social Surveys
Euro-Barometer Survey Series:
  European Men and Women, May 1975
  Men, Women and Work Roles in Europe, November 1977
  Gender Roles in the European Community, April 1983
Explorations in Equality of Opportunity, 1955-1970
Project Talent Public Use File, 1960-1976
National Supported Work Evaluation Study, 1975-1979
CBS News/The New York Times National Surveys
Current Population Surveys
National Survey of Adolescent Female Sexual Behavior
Women in Development, 1979-80, 1983
Social Composition of Detroit, 1880-1900
Women in Prison, 1800-1935: Tennessee, New York, and Ohio
Women Correctional Officers in California, 1979

Henry A. Murray Research Center of Radcliffe College
10 Garden Street, Cambridge, MA 02138
Telephone: 617-495-8140

The multidisciplinary Murray Research Center focuses on the "study of lives over time," human development and social change. Its holdings include over 190 datasets that can be used for secondary analysis, replication or longitudinal follow-up. The Murray Center is unique among data archives in that it concentrates on data that illuminate women's lives and deal with issues of concern to women, including various aspects of women's work and careers, mental health, political participation, family life, widowhood and aging. The datasets held by the Center come from many different academic disciplines and, whenever possible, include the questionnaires used to collect the data, interview transcripts, and coded data sheets in addition to the data itself. The center also maintains lists of publications based on each dataset.

In addition to archiving data collected by others, the center sponsors research and workshops on such topics as methods for conducting longitudinal life course research and approaches to the secondary analysis of longitudinal data. It hosts three to five visiting scholars every year who study different aspects of women's lives or social change.

Access to the data holdings of the center is provided by the *Guide to the Data Resources of the Henry A. Murray Research Center*[18] and a separate index to methods of data collection and the content of the datasets. The Center publishes the *Murray Research Center News*,[19] which lists new acquisitions and research projects of the Center.

Recent data acquisitions include the following:

Pregnancy and Parenthood Project, 1975-1981
Longitudinal Study of Transitions in Four Stages of Life, 1970-1980
The Harlem Longitudinal Study of Urban Black Youth, 1968-1984
Adolescent and Family Development Study: 1978-1982
The Effect of the Welfare Woman's Working on Her Family, 1969-1972
Abortion Study, 1969-1984
Study of Gay Fathers, 1978
Choosing the Future: College Students' Projections of Their Personal Life Patterns, 1984
Development of Conceptions of Masculinity and Femininity, 1976

The Roper Center
University of Connecticut, U-164R, Storrs, CT 06268
Telephone: 203-486-4440

The Roper Center holds an impressive collection of survey data, most of which is coded for gender of respondent. Through the cooperation of the major survey research organizations in the United States, more than 9,000 separate studies have been made available. The center now maintains an online database that permits searching of survey questions by subject.[20]

Holdings of the Roper Center of particular interest to researchers on women include:

The American Gallup Poll Collection
The CBS/New York Times Surveys
The NORC General Social Surveys
The General Mills Family Studies
The Canadian Institute of Public Opinion Studies

For information on other sources of public opinion polls, see Sue Dodd's article in Numeric Databases, in which she gives a list of survey organizations.[21]

The Kinsey Institute for Research in Sex, Gender and Reproduction
313 Morrison Hall, Bloomington, IN 47405
Telephone: 812-335-7686

The Kinsey Institute, a non-profit corporation affiliated with the University of Indiana, also provides data on women. The Institute's data archives contain the databases generated by a number of scientific studies, including the 18,000 case histories recorded by Alfred Kinsey and his associates between 1938 and 1963. Access to this data is available to qualified researchers for a fee through the Institute's Information Service. A codebook may be purchased by potential users of this data.[22]

Human Relations Area Files
75 Prospect St., P.O. Box 2054, Yale Station, New Haven, CT 06529
Telephone: 203-777-2334

The Human Relations Area Files (HRAF) have been pioneers in cross-cultural studies of human societies. Over the years their materials have been published in hard copy and in microfiche. Recently they entered into an agreement with Silver Platter Information, Inc., to publish a series of cross-cultural compact disks which will contain full-text extracts from more than 1,000 anthropological, sociological and psychological articles on life in some 60 societies from around the world. These texts will be coded to allow for cross-cultural comparisons of cultural phenomena. They will be released in a series of topical databases covering marriage, family life, old age, death and dying, childhood and adolescence, crime and social problems, socialization and education, religious beliefs and religious practice. Each of these datasets will serve as a "natural laboratory" for the investigation of the diversity of cultures and behavior around the world. The first compact disk in this series will be released in the spring of 1989.

The HRAF have already released several ethnographic datasets on diskette. These include the Research Series in Quantitative Cross-Cultural Data, which has a dataset on general cultural and religious data and one on "Death and Dying in the Life Cycle." A "Cultural Diversity Database" contains data on 177 variables for 156 cultures.

GOVERNMENT-PRODUCED STATISTICAL DATA

Another major source of numeric data is the U.S. Government. Data are gathered by a wide variety of government agencies for their own purposes but can be used in many ways by both the private and public sectors. Much of the data is scientific or economic in nature; there are also data available from this source that can be used to investigate women's issues. The scope and means of access to this data have been well described elsewhere.[23]

ONLINE SOURCES OF INFORMATION
ABOUT NONBIBLIOGRAPHIC DATA

In addition to the catalogs of the data archives mentioned above, information about numeric data can be found in online bibliographic databases. Bibliographic databases sometimes include records for datafiles themselves. They also often list articles that describe data collections or report on research that used machine-readable numeric data. These articles can be used to locate files that are available for public use or to identify researchers who might be willing to share their data.

Research Libraries Information Network (RLIN)

Access to information about nonbibliographic datasets on women is available through the Research Libraries Information Network (RLIN), the bibligraphic processing utility of the Research Libraries Group (RLG), a consortium of research libraries committed to inter-institutional cooperation in providing access to information. RLIN includes a database of machine-readable data containing detailed records of data files held by member libraries. This database can be searched by author, title or subject. Although the database is still relatively small, its size is increasing rapidly due to a cooperative agreement between the Inter-university Consortium for Political and Social Research (ICPSR), RLG, and the University Library at the University of Michigan to enter cataloging for datasets held by ICPSR into RLIN. RLG has also made grants to various research libraries to study the use of machine-readable data files in academic settings in order to improve access.

A search of the RLIN machine-readable data file database for subject phrases **"woman# or women# or female#"** turned up 56 records. Fifty of them were records for datasets held by ICPSR. The non-ICPSR records were for datasets held by the Roper Center in Connecticut and the Social Sciences Data Archives at the University of Iowa.

RLIN provides relatively easy access to the records for data files that have been entered into the database. Records are in MARC format and contain all essential information, although in somewhat abbreviated format. As more records are entered into the system, it will become an increasingly valuable tool for identifying machine-readable data.

Online Bibliographic Databases

In an effort to determine how much information about machine-readable datafiles can be found in online bibliographic databases, the Social Sciences/Humanities section of the CROS database on BRS was searched to find articles that contained the terms **"woman or women"** and **"database$."** Nine of the 26 databases searched contained at least one match; several contained many. Of the articles located, at least six identified and described data collections. The remaining articles either could not be located easily or discussed the use or management of data rather than reporting the results of studies based on data. Among the datasets mentioned by these articles were:

National Database on Breastfeeding among Indian and Inuit Women[24]
NE-113 Regional Research Project Database[25]
People in Society Survey[26]

Online bibliographic databases can also be used to identify researchers who are working on a topic and have gathered data for analysis. For example, a paper located in *Sociological Abstracts* on BRS describes efforts "to begin to establish an empirical database to assess the health and social conditions of the contemporary urban homeless" in Los Angeles.[27]

The ERIC database proved to be a useful tool for identifying machine-readable data files related to women's role in education. ERIC uses the term "machine readable data files" as an identifier for articles *about* machine-readable data files, but *not* for the data files themselves. If this identifier is used, one ends up in much the same situation as in the search of the CROS database, i.e., one has to go to the articles themselves to see if enough information is given to locate the needed data. When the database was searched on "**(machine adj readable adj data adj file$) and (women or woman or female$ or sex$3)**" 18 documents were found, including such titles as "Microcomputer-based Access to Machine-readable Numeric Databases," "Computer Information products at NTIS," and "The National Archives and Electronic data." All of these articles consider problems relevant to the management and use of datafiles. However, when ERIC was searched using "**machine adj readable adj data adj file.TI.**", it produced 34 citations to actual datafiles. The database supplements the title with this phrase to identify datafiles. Thus, one finds titles such as "High School and Beyond: Friends (machine-readable data file)," and "Teaching Faculty in Academe, 1972-1973 (machine-readable data file)." This strategy also retrieves titles such as "Human Sciences

Activity Characteristics and Reviewer Evaluation File, HSACRE. User's guide for the machine-readable data file.'' In this case the datafile is not itself listed in ERIC, but the user's guide provides enough information to locate the data.

None of the machine-readable data files identified on ERIC are available from the Eric Document Retrieval System, although source is indicated, complete with address, telephone number and price (if known). The ERIC records are quite complete, containing abstracts which define the scope and size of the study and describing the methodology used in collecting the data. They also include the date or dates of collection and a note field for pertinent information about format and documentation.

ERIC promises to become a rich source of information about machine-readable data files. It should be particularly useful to researchers interested in women and education, for, while not all educational studies deal specifically with women, many of them are coded for gender, so information about women can be extracted. ERIC is the only bibliographic database searched other than RLIN in which citations to data files themselves were found.

Most online bibliographic services are in business to index journal articles and, since datasets are not usually published as journal articles, they are not picked up by these services. However, there is now at least one journal, *World Cultures*,[28] that is published only in machine-readable format. This journal is not yet listed in *Ulrich's* and is not indexed by any of the standard sources. As more journals appear exclusively in machine-readable formats, it seems likely that they will be picked up by the standard indexing and abstracting services.

Other Approaches to Online Bibliographic Databases

An indirect way to identify relevant machine-readable datasets is to use online bibliographic databases to identify articles based on data about women. These articles can then be consulted to find information about the data the authors used and its availability. ERIC, the Silver Platter version of PsycINFO, and Sociological Abstracts were searched using terms such as ''surveys,'' ''longitudinal surveys,'' and ''data collection'' combined with subject terms

such as "women" or "female or females." This technique identified a number of articles of potential interest, although it also pulled
up articles on the theory and practice of carrying out surveys or data
collection that did not provide useful leads to datasets. Neverthe-
less, the amount of information identified was considerable. For
example, a search of the PsycINFO CD-ROM using the terms
"longitudinal-surveys" and "women or female" produced 418
citations, many of which clearly identified the data used in the research. An article entitled "A Comparative Analysis of Two Community Stressors, Long-term Mental Health Effects,"[29] compares
the long-term mental health effects on men and women of the Three
Mile Island nuclear accident with the effects of widespread unemployment due to layoff. The article gives information on the subjects studied, sampling technique, procedure and the psychological
instruments used. While the article says nothing explicit about the
availability of the data used, the authors could be contacted for
more information. If authors were encouraged to include in their
publications specific information about the availability and scope of
data used in their research, and if data were consistently cited in
bibliographies and lists of references, online bibliographic databases could become truly valuable tools for locating data of this
kind.

OTHER SOURCES OF INFORMATION

In addition to the catalogs and online sources mentioned above,
several groups or associations are interested in machine-readable
social science data. These organizations often publish newsletters
that are useful in keeping informed about developments in the use
of machine-readable numeric data. Some examples follow.

*The International Association for Social Science Information Ser-
vices and Technology.* (IASSIST).
c/o Jackie McGee, Treasurer
The Rand Corporation
1700 Main St.
Santa Monica, CA 90406

IASSIST is an association of people interested in the acquisition, processing, maintenance and distribution of machine-readable textual and/or numeric social science data. Although this organization does not itself archive or distribute data, the *IASSIST Quarterly*[30] is a good source of information about current topics of interest. Some of the offerings are very technical computer articles, while others describe data sets or means of accessing data.

A particularly valuable feature of the *IASSIST Quarterly* is a "Contents of Current Journals" section, which reproduces the tables of contents of the latest issues of major journals such as the *European Political Data Newsletter, Historical Social Research/Historische Sozialforschung*, and *Data Users News* from the Bureau of the Census. Skimming this section every issue is a good way to find articles which deal with data on women or women's issues.

Economic and Social Research Council (ESRC)
University of Essex
Colchester C04 3SQ, U.K.

The Economic and Social Research Council of Great Britain, located at the University of Essex, publishes the *ESRC Data Archive Bulletin*,[31] which reports news about data collection and data availability in Great Britain. Each issue contains a "News" section, a list of new acquisitions, news from other data institutions and foreign archives, a "software bulletin" which discusses new developments in software, and reviews of important books.

Association of Public Data Users (APDU)
Princeton University Computing Center
87 Prospect Ave.
Princeton, NJ 08544

The Association of Public Data Users is a group of academic institutions, private corporations, planning agencies, research institutes, governmental agencies and individuals who work together to facilitate the use of public data by sharing information about datafiles and software and to increase the awareness of federal agencies about the needs of data users. It publishes a newsletter ten times per year which is a good source of current information about newly-released government datasets.

The journal *Women & Politics* (Haworth Press) has for several years published an occasional series of articles edited by Robert Darcey entitled "Women & Politics Databases." These articles review databases of particular interest to those studying women's participation in the political arena. Typical articles are: "Women and Public Policy,"[32] "Women in Organizations,"[33] and "Women and Development."[34]

CONCLUSION

This paper provides an overview of the access tools and strategies needed to ferret out information about machine-readable numeric data. It is tempting to contemplate the future and to predict what will happen. There is no doubt that machine-readable numeric data will be used more and more, especially as computer storage capacities increase and more sophisticated software becomes available for microcomputers. Newby[35] notes the sustained growth in the use of data archives in recent years. Most of this growth has been concentrated in the use of large-scale databases, especially in longitudinal surveys. He also speculates that several factors have contributed to this increased interest: increasing availability of data, growing computer literacy, a shortage of funds for the collection of primary data, and an increased interest in empirical social science research. Heavily-used databases such as the General Social Survey are already available in forms that are not dependent upon main-frame computers, as, for example, the version available from ShowCase Presentational Software of Cognitive Development, Inc. in Seattle, Washington. Accessibility will also no doubt be improved, especially as more libraries catalog local datasets and contribute records to RLIN. Several institutions have conducted surveys of datafiles available on particular campuses or in university systems, and the Research Libraries Group (RLG) has recently awarded a number of grants to explore ways to improve access to machine-readable data.

The impact of advances in telecommunications technology is unclear. High-speed computer networks such as the new National Science Foundation Network (NSFNET) may revolutionize the way in which research is conducted and allow collaborators to share electronic information via linked networks. ICPSR, for example, anticipates sending out some portion of its data orders over NSFNET in the future, using it to supplement other means of data distribution.[36] While one can probably assume that it will become easier and cheaper to send large quantities of data electronically rather than on computer tape, data archives will most likely continue to be a major force on the data scene. In the first place, they play an important role in bringing together datasets and describing them in their catalogs and guides so that the public knows what is available. Secondly, archives tend to exert quality control over the data which they accept, and often review and clean up datasets before they distribute them. They also ensure that documentation is adequate. Thirdly, they serve as a kind of buffer between the original researcher and the public, so that the collector of the data is not inundated with requests which would be both expensive and time-consuming to fill. Archives also often play an educational and consulting role and are prepared to answer questions about the use of data which might otherwise be directed to researchers who make their data available. Thus, while changes in telecommunications may well make a difference in how data are transmitted, archives will probably continue collecting and distributing data, since they are more efficient and reliable than contacts between individuals.

The amount of data on women available to the public will probably increase dramatically. New collections of data are being assembled and will be made available for use, sometimes at the institution which collected the data, sometimes through data archives, sometimes online, and sometimes on computer tape or diskette. An example of a collection currently under development is a combined textual and numeric database entitled Women and Development in the Caribbean, which is being assembled by the Institute of Social and Economic Research at the University of the West Indies. The availability of increasing amounts of numeric machine-readable data on women will make possible new approaches to the investigation of women's issues and will both complement and supplement more traditional approaches to women's studies.

REFERENCE NOTES

1. Jacqueline M. McGee and Donald P. Trees, "Major Available Social Science Machine-readable Databases," *Drexel Library Quarterly* 18 (Summer/Fall 1982), 107-134.

2. See, for example, Frank W. Moore, *Readings in Cross-Cultural Methodology*, (New Haven, CT: HRAF Press, 1966).

3. See Kathleen M. Heim, "Social Science Information Needs for Numeric Data: the Evolution of the International Data Archive Infrastructure," *Collection Management* 9 (Spring 1987), 1-53, for a discussion of the evolution of data archives.

4. Robert M. Pierce, "An Ecological Analysis of the Socioeconomic Status of Women Having Abortions in Manhattan," *Social Science and Medicine* 15 D (No. 2 1981), 277-286.

5. *Data Libraries for the Social Sciences*, ed. Kathleen Heim, *Library Trends* 30 (Winter 1982), 321-509.

6. *Numeric Databases*, eds. Ching-Chih Chen and Peter Hernon, (Norwood, N.J.: Ablex Publishing Company, 1984).

7. Ms. Leidy presented a paper, based on her research, entitled "Variation in age at menarchy and menopause with regard to measures of weight, fatness and height" at the meetings of the American Association of Physical Anthropologists in San Diego on April 6, 1989.

8. See JoAnn Dionne, "Numeric Social Science Databases and the Library," *Choice* (January 1985), 646-652, for a discussion of the place of numeric datafiles in libraries.

9. Sarah M. Pritchard, "Developing Criteria for Database Evaluation: the Example of Women's Studies," in *Evaluation of Reference Services*, ed. Bill Katz and Ruth Fraley. (New York, NY: The Haworth Press, 1984), pp. 247-261.

10. JoAnn Dionne. "Why Librarians Need to Know about Numeric Databases," in Chen and Hernon, pp. 237-246.

11. *Information Industry Market Place*, (New York: R.R. Bowker, 1981-1984).

12. *Encyclopedia of Information Systems and Services*. 6th ed. (Detroit: Gale Research, 1985/86).

13. *North American Online Directory*. (New York: R.R. Bowker, 1985).

14. For a description of several online numeric business databases, see Mick O'Leary, "Surveying the Numeric Databanks." *Database* (October 1987), 65-68.

15. See Judith Wagner and Ruth N. Landau, "Nonbibliographic Online Data Base Services," *Journal of the American Society for Information Science* 21 (May 1980), 171-180.

16. McGee and Trees, op. cit.

17. David Gerhan and Loretta Walker, "A Subject Approach to Social Sci-

ence Data Archives," in *Reader in Machine Readable Social Data*, ed. Howard D. White (Englewood, CO: Information Handline Services 1977), pp. 25-50.

18. *A Guide to the Data Resources of the Henry A. Murray Research Center of Radcliffe College: A Center for the Study of Lives*. (Cambridge, MA: Henry A. Murray Research Center of Radcliffe College, 1988).

19. *Murray Research Center News* (Cambridge, MA: Henry A. Murray Research Center of Radcliffe College).

20. Linda Langschied, "The POLL Database: Roper Center's online source for public opinion research," *IASSIST Quarterly* 11 (Spring 1987), 11-17.

21. Sue A. Dodd, "Characteristics and Sources of Public Opinion Polls in the United States," in Chen and Hernon, pp. 153-187.

22. See Gwendolyn L. Pershing, "Sex and Scholarship: the Collections and Services of the Kinsey Institute for Research in Sex, Gender and Reproduction," *Behavioral and Social Sciences Librarian* 6 (No. 3/4 1988), 129-138.

23. See Kathleen M. Heim. "Government-produced Statistical Data for Social Science Inquiry: Scope, Problems, and Strategies for Access," in Chen and Hernon, pp. 105-124; Arthur G. Dukakis and Judith W. Cohen, "Data Available from the U.S. Bureau of the Census," in Chen and Hernon, pp. 125-152; and Joseph W. Duncan, "Accessing social statistics," *Library Trends* 30 (Winter 1982), 363-373.

24. Paula J. Steward and Jean Steckle, "Breastfeeding Among Canadian Indians On-reserve and Women in the Yukon and N.W.T.," *Canadian Journal of Public Health* 78 (No. 4 1987), 255-261.

25. Jane E. Meiners and Geraldine I. Olson, "Household, Paid, and Unpaid Work of Farm Women," *Family Relations* 36 (No. 4 1987), 407-411.

26. Pamela Abbott and Roger Sapsford, "Class Identification of Married Women: a Critical Replication of Ritter and Hargens," *British Journal of Sociology* 37 (No. 4 1986), 535-549.

27. Richard H. Ropers and Richard Boyer, "Perceived Health Status Among the New Urban Homeless," *Social Science & Medicine* 37 (No. 4 1986), 535-549.

28. *World Cultures* (Irvine, CA: School of Social Sciences, University of California at Irvine).

29. Mary A. Dew, Evelyn J. Bromet and Herbert C. Schulberg, "A Comparative Analysis of Two Community Stressors' Long-term Mental Effects," *American Journal of Community Psychology* 15 (April 1987), 167-184.

30. *IASSIST Quarterly* (Princeton, NJ: Princton University Computer Center, c/o Judith Rowe, U.S. Secretariate).

31. *ESRC Data Archive Bulletin* (Colchester, UK: Economic and Social Research Council Data Archive, University of Essex).

32. Mark R. Daniels, "Women and Public Policy," *Women & Politics* 3 (Winter 1983), 67-70.

33. Barrie E. Blunt, "Women in Organizations," *Women & Politics* 6 (Spring 1986), 69-72.

34. Jane S. Jaquette, "Women in Development," *Women & Politics* 3 (Summer 1983), 125-128.

35. Howard Newby, "Looking Forward," *ESRC Data Archive Bulletin* No. 40 (May 1988), 102.

36. "Computer Networking and NSFNET: Applications for Social Science Research, *ICPSR Bulletin* 9 (February 1989): 1-3 + .

Lesbians Online

Connie Miller

SUMMARY. This paper uses the concepts of access and definition as defined by Marilyn Frye to examine and draw interpretations concerning the information by and about lesbians that can be located in online databases. The number of online citations including the term lesbian is increasing steadily and deviance-oriented literature is being replaced by acceptance-oriented literature. The acceptance-oriented literature, however, continues to appropriate lesbians' power of self-definition. Only when information by and for lesbians is searchable in online form will lesbians have unconditional access to information about themselves.

Access and definition, according to Marilyn Frye,[1] are two "faces" of power. Differences in access signify differences in power. Bosses determine both their employees' access to them and their own access to their employees. Masters have unconditional access to slaves. Unconditional access indicates total power.

The power of definition is the power to determine "what is said and sayable." The slave who excludes the master from her hut defines away her slavery. When patterns of access change, says Frye, realities change. Taking control of access results in new boundaries, new roles, and new relationships, all of which involve new definitions.

Access and definition as faces of power apply to information just as they apply to relationships between people. Those who have unconditional access to information about themselves, information that includes and reflects their own definitions of what is said and sayable, have total power. This paper uses access and definition in

Connie Miller is Head, Information and Document Delivery Services, Indiana University Libraries, Bloomington, IN 47405.

Frye's sense as faces of power to examine systematically and draw interpretations from the information about and by lesbians that can be located in online databases.

ACCESS

As documented in Jonathan Katz's *Gay American History*,[2] lesbians have long shared self-affirming information among themselves, and some have openly resisted oppression in print since at least the late nineteenth century. During the last twenty years, however, social changes have occurred that have catapulted lesbianism into the mainstream. The Stonewall Inn riots in New York in June, 1969 marked the beginning of the gay rights movement, which brought homosexual oppression into the public consciousness. In 1973 the American Psychiatric Association voted to remove homosexuality from the *Diagnostic and Statistical Manual of Mental Disorders* (DSM), a step, which, at least officially, began to shift professional attitudes to lesbians away from cure and toward support. The feminist movement, extending from the late 1960s to the present, has increased the number of women writers and researchers and, consequently, has increased the attention given to women and their choices, including lesbianism.

During this same twenty year period, online databases exploded onto the information scene. As of 1979, 59 online services offered 400 databases developed by 221 database producers. By 1988, each of these numbers had multiplied by almost ten times, and 61 gateways had sprung up.[3] But it is not the number of online sources in existence nor the fact that some sources are being published only in online form that makes the computerization of information valuable for research on lesbianism. The value of computerization lies with the increased access it provides.

When searching for feminist material, Ishbel Lochhead[4] found that "databases offer the greatest potential for access . . . because of the variety of search strategies available." Free text searching, while it can retrieve a high percentage of irrelevant citations (or, as Lochhead says, "create a lot of noise"[5]), avoids the significant problems associated with indexing[6] by allowing the information seeker to identify relevant terms not only from assigned subject fields but also from titles, abstracts, and sometimes the full text itself.

Free text searching in online databases for all forms of the word lesbian is rewarding in terms of quantity of citations. Tables A and B list the number of citations retrieved in six DIALOG *DIALINDEX* categories[7] (covering the content areas of books, book reviews, public affairs, medicine, humanities, and the social sciences) and in 13 Wilsonline databases when the truncated term "lesbian" was searched.

In the DIALOG databases, which cover time periods of 25 years or more, and in the Wilsonline databases, which cover time periods of less than six years, a significant amount of information on lesbians appears to be available, particularly in the social sciences, even when duplication of citations among categories or databases is taken into account. Books and book reviews account for a significant proportion of the citations. The average number of citations including some form of the term lesbian per database in the *DIALINDEX* category REVIEWS (five databases covering book reviews) is 190; the average numbers per database in the categories PUBAFF (15 databases covering public affairs) and SOCSCI (15 databases covering the social sciences) are 136 and 134 respectively. Forty-two percent of all the citations from the 13 Wilsonline databases come from the two book and book review databases. Book reviews also make up 17% of the 23 citations including some

TABLE A. Number of Citations Including "lesbian?" in Six DIALINDEX Categories

DIALOG Category	Number of Databases	Number of Citations	Years of Coverage
BOOKS	8	714	Pre 1900 – 1988
REVIEWS	5	950	1959 – 1988
PUBAFF	15	2046	1959 – 1988
MEDICINE	15	551	1963 – 1988
HUMANIT	13	996	1861 – 1988
SOCSCI	15	2013	1949 – 1988

TABLE B. Number of Citations Including "lesbian:" in 13 Wilsonline Databases

WILSON Database	Number of Citations	Years of Coverage
Art Index	6	Oct., 1984 - 1988
Bibliographic Index	19	Nov., 1984 - 1988
Biol. and Ag. Index	0	July, 1983 - 1988
Biography Index	6	July, 1984 - 1988
Business Periodicals Index	3	June, 1982 - 1988
Book Review Digest	111	April, 1983 - 1988
Cumulative Book Index	97	Jan., 1982 - 1988
Education Index	23	Sept., 1983 - 1988
General Science Index	5	May, 1984 - 1988
Humanities Index	25	Feb., 1984 - 1988
Index to Legal Periodicals	10	August, 1981 - 1988
Reader's Guide	64	Jan., 1983 - 1988
Social Sciences Index	127	Feb., 1984 - 1988

form of the term lesbian in *Education Index*, 40% of the 25 citations in *Humanities Index*, 34% of the 64 citations in *Reader's Guide*, and 25% of the 127 citations in *Social Sciences Index*.

Table C demonstrates that most of the online information on lesbianism has become available since 1980. Seventy percent of the 2841 citations including some form of the term lesbian have appeared online since 1980. Over half (53%) of these citations come from four databases: *Psychological Abstracts*, *Social Scisearch*, *Family Resources*, and *Sociological Abstracts*. *Psychological Abstracts* accounts for almost 20% of the total number (549 out of 2841). As a cultural and social phenomenon, lesbianism can be expected to crop up most frequently in databases designed to collect the literature about such phenomena. Lesbianism, that is, is not necessarily overrepresented in psychological and sociological databases; it does, however, appear to be underrepresented in databases

TABLE C. Number of Citations Including "lesbian?" in Selected Databases Over Time

DATABASE	1965-70	1971-75	1976-80	1981-85	1986-88	TOTALS
Social Scisearch	0	14	81	149	133	377(14%)
Disserta tion Abs- tracts	1	4	40	103	61	209(8%)
America: History and Life	0	0	24	26	4	54(2%)
Historic al Ab- stracts	0	0	8	11	2	21(.7%)
Art Modern	0	0	9	4	0	13(.5%)
Philosop her's Index	0	0	1	5	2	8(.3%)
MLA Bibliogr aphy	0	1	15	49	10	75(3%)
Religion Index	0	2	8	33	37	80(3%)
Arts & Humaniti es	0	0	0	34	52	86(3%)
ERIC	0	5	42	44	24	115(4%)
PsychInfo	16	46	124	222	141	549(19%)
Sociolog ical Ab- stracts	5	13	80	106	60	264(9%)
Magazine Index	3	11	52	98	73	237(8%)
Book Review Index	0	31	52	60	76	239(9%)
Medline	5	4	55	62	69	195(7%)

TABLE C (continued)

DATABASE	1965-70	1971-75	1976-80	1981-85	1986-88	TOTALS
Family Resources	1	14	47	150	107	319(11%)
TOTALS	31	165	638	1156	851	2841
Percent	1%	6%	22%	41%	30%	100%

related to history and literature in which lesbians could be expected to appear as contributors to social developments rather than as subjects of social scrutiny. Between the two of them, the databases *America: History and Life* and *Historical Abstracts* provide only 2.6% of the citations that include some form of the term lesbian (75 out of 2841); the same is true of *MLA Bibliography*.

To get an accurate picture of access to lesbian information online, the number of citations retrieved by a search on the truncated term lesbian must be compared with the number of citations retrieved for searches on other terms. Tables D and E provide comparative numbers of citations retrieved from the six DIALOG *DIALINDEX* categories and from selected DIALOG and Wilsonline databases when five different terms or combinations of terms were searched. In terms of numbers of citations, online access to information about and by lesbians has been improving, especially over the last eight years (see Table C). By itself, this improvement in access is gratifying. When the total number of citations for the term lesbian is compared with the total number for other terms, however, even improvement seems disappointing. Marriage and lesbianism both are experiences women choose. Even when the fact that marriage as a choice is more prevalent than lesbianism as a choice is taken into account, online databases offer much greater access to information on marriage than they do to information on lesbianism (20 times as many citations include some form of the term marriage as include some form of the term lesbian). Such differences in access, as Frye defines it in relation to power, convey the impression that some choices are more important or better than others.

Five and a half to seven and a half times more online citations include some form of the term homosexuality than include some

TABLE D. Number of Citations for Several Terms in Six DIALINDEX Categories

DIALOG Category	Homosexual	Marriage	Homophobia	Lesbian	Lesbian and Feminism
BOOKS	1768	16,239	14	714	66
REVIEWS	6811	11,623	42	950	22
PUBAFF	14,429	22,653	148	2046	166
MEDICINE	18,192	15,006	117	551	20
HUMANIT	4497	22,000	149	996	146
SOCSCI	9004	48,003	385	2013	279
TOTALS	54,701	135,524	855	7270	699

form of the term lesbianism. While, in some cases, homosexuality undoubtedly applied to both gay men and lesbians, the wide discrepancy in numbers of online citations suggests that gay males have received more attention than lesbians and that information on gay males is more accessible than information on lesbians. Morin[8] and Walters'[9] examinations of the articles listed in Psychological Abstracts under the subject headings homosexuality, lesbianism, or male homosexuality for the time periods 1967-1974 and 1979-1983 respectively support this suggestion. Morin found four times as many studies of homosexual males as of lesbians and Walters found at least two to three studies of males for every one study of lesbians.

Judging from the number of citations located through searches of online databases, information on homophobia or antihomosexual attitudes is considerably less accessible than information on homosexuality (between 37 and 64 times less accessible) or on lesbianism (seven to nine times less accessible). Morin[10] describes studies of heterosexual attitudes toward homosexuality as "the clearest example of research that is on the offense rather than the defense with regard to gay civil liberties." Such "research on the offense" accounted for only 9% of the 139 articles indexed under homosexuality, lesbianism, or male homosexuality in *Psychological Abstract* for the eight year period between 1967 and 1974. From an examina-

TABLE E. Number of Citations for Several Terms in Selected Databases

Database	Homosexual	Marriage	Homophobia	Lesbian	Lesbian and Feminism
Social Scisearch	1941	3764	41	377	13
Dissertation Abstracts	431	3844	65	209	44
America:History and Life	109	1221	1	54	20
Historical Abstracts	119	1992	2	21	7
Art Modern	43	341	0	13	11
Philosopher's Index	79	244	0	8	5
MLA Bibliography	308	1189	6	75	19
Religion Index	571	2584	15	80	11
Arts and Humanities Citation Index	335	1256	16	86	7
ERIC	439	3291	37	115	30
Psych Info	2339	14,094	112	549	54
Sociological Abstracts	934	6717	50	252	84
Magazine Index	1367	4593	11	237	9
Book Review Index	493	1883	0	239	11
Medline	5661	8640	39	195	8

TABLE E (continued)

Database	Homosexual	Marriage	Homophobia	Lesbian	Lesbian and Feminism
Family Resources	1122	8164	45	319	31
Art Index	31	87	1	6	0
Bibliographic Index	45	158	1	19	2
Business Period. Index	42	293	2	3	0
Book Review Digest	227	960	16	111	38
Cumulative Book Index	172	898	5	97	9
Education Index	83	122	7	23	0
General Science Index	111	86	0	5	0
Humanities Index	153	457	2	25	3
Index to Legal Periodicals	153	344	5	10	0
Reader's Guide	354	791	6	64	2
Social Sciences Index	238	764	8	127	23
TOTALS	17,900	67,833	588	3246	441

tion of numbers of citations alone, lesbians appear to have more access to information about themselves than to information about attitudes toward themselves.

Writing about access to material about women, Ellen Gay Detlefsen[11] points out that "information simply about women or females can be, and often is, totally reflective of male bias and traditional sex role socialization and not at all feminist, regardless of the gender of the author." Since, as Suzanne Hildenbrand[12] says, "ideology or perspective, such as feminism, is not indexed . . . ," activist literature can be extremely difficult to isolate. While the number of citations including some form of the term lesbianism available online offers some measure of the degree to which information about and by lesbians is accessible, numbers alone provide no indication of philosophy, ideology, or approach. It could be argued that access only or primarily to inaccurate or negative information is worse than no access to information at all. No reliable strategy exists that would allow a lesbian seeking self-affirming information to distinguish the useful online sources from the useless. Combining the terms lesbianism and feminism narrows the retrieval (approximately one-tenth of the citations including some form of the term lesbian also include some form of the term feminism), but inevitably eliminates some — perhaps even the most — valuable citations.

DEFINITION

The existence of information (e.g., 2841 citations including some form of the term lesbian in 16 selected databases) and the ability to find that information (e.g., free text searching of computerized databases) constitute access, one of Frye's faces of power. The other face of power, definition, adds depth and substance to access. Lesbians who have access to information about themselves know, at least, how they are being defined. Lesbians who define the information to which they (and others) have access have the power to define themselves.

Three different categories of lesbians' power to define emerged from the citations including some form of the term lesbian that are available online. While the categories themselves are arbitrary and their assignment to particular citations interpretive, the three categories fit the existing information and offer a useful tool for its analysis.

The first category applies to citations in which no trace of a lesbian power of definition is evident, sources in which "the yawning chasm between . . . critical discourse and the traditions [it] discourses [up]on"[13] is particularly apparent, sources in which researchers objectify lesbians as other. These sources frequently discuss the causes of lesbianism or suggest ways in which lesbians can be diagnosed or detected. Morin[14] believes that the "clearest example of heterosexual bias in . . . research on homosexuality" can be found in assessment diagnosis studies. Authors of first category sources are often, although not exclusively, male. An example of a first category source is the dissertation "A Sociological Approach to the Etiology of Female Homosexuality and the Lesbian Social Scene" by Kenneth A. Poole.

At the other end of the spectrum is the third category which applies to citations that center around a lesbian definition of lesbianism and/or a lesbian-based examination of heterosexual attitudes toward lesbianism. Lesbians in these sources are not objectified; on the contrary, subjective lesbian experience shapes the content. While, in actuality, only lesbians can write third category sources, identifying an author as a lesbian is impossible unless she identifies herself (some of the citations were classified as third category because the authors are self-proclaimed lesbians). Therefore, for the purposes of this classification scheme, all authors of third category sources are women, except in the case of certain book reviews. Reviews of books written by lesbians about themselves, regardless of the review author's sex, are considered third category sources. Examples of third category sources are an article called "Scratching the Surface: Some Notes on Barriers to Women and Loving" by Audre Lorde and a review by Jo Paolin of the book *A Faith of One's Own: Explorations By Catholic Lesbians*.

The second, and least concrete, category applies to citations that treat lesbianism as an acceptable rather than as a deviant choice but still objectify lesbians through language and approach. Researchers or authors of second category sources can be either male or female. Sources that focus on a disciplinary area (e.g., history or literary criticism) and include lesbianism as a valid topic for investigation fall into the second category as do reviews of books that begin with the premise that lesbianism is an acceptable lifestyle choice. Examples of second category sources are an article called "Gay and Lesbian Domestic Partnerships: Expanding the Definition of Family" by Linda Poverny and others, and the dissertation, "Themes and Portraiture in the Fiction of Ann Allen Schockley" by S. Diane Bogus.

To evaluate a sample of the information about and by lesbians accessible online, all of the citations retrieved by a search for some form of the term lesbian for the time periods 1966-1968, 1976-1978, and 1986-1988 from the databases *Sociological Abstracts* and *Magazine Index* were printed. After eliminating citations which included the term lesbian but dealt only marginally with lesbianism (e.g., the article "Domestic Labour and the Feminist Movement in Italy Since the 1970s") or citations that were too ambiguous to categorize (the article "Amazon Fantasy Trouble"), each citation was assigned to one of the three categories defined above. Category assignments were made, in most instances, from bibliographic citations and subject descriptors, rather than from sources themselves or even abstracts. When titles were ambiguous, abstracts were printed (if they were available).

For comparison, all of the citations for sources indexed under some form of the term lesbian in three different issues of the printed reference, *Alternative Press Index*,[15] were also examined and assigned to one of the three categories. Each issue covers approximately three months from one of the years 1969 (the year the *Alternative Press Index* began), 1976, or 1986. Tables F, G, and H list the number of citations from *Sociological Abstracts* and *Magazine*

TABLE F. Sociological Abstracts — Categories and Years

Years/Category	1966-1968	1976-1978	1986-1988	Totals
First	3	4	0	7
Second	2	25	53	80
Third	0	2	2	4
Uncategorized	0	3	5	8
Totals	5	34	60	99

TABLE G. Magazine Index — Categories and Years

Years/Category	1966–1968	1976–1978	1986–1988	Totals
First	1	4	0	5
Second	0	12	60	72
Third	0	8	10	18
Uncategorized	0	4	3	7
Totals	1	28	73	102

TABLE H. Alternative Press Index — Categories and Years

Year/Category	1969	1976	1986	Totals
First	0	0	0	0
Second	0	19	30	49
Third	2	39	35	76
Totals	2	58	65	125

Index online and for *Alternative Press Index* in print form that fall into the three different categories.

Before 1970, access to any category of information about and by lesbians was limited. In *Sociological Abstracts* and *Magazine Index* online, only six citations including some form of the term lesbian appeared from 1966 to 1968. Four of these six are first category citations which include no evidence of a lesbian power of definition. "Deviant Stereotypes: Call Girls, Male Homosexuals, and Lesbians" is the title from one of the citations from this time period. The five citations from *Sociological Abstracts* are all to journal articles, which appear in four different journals; the citation from Magazine Index is to an article called, "Feminist Attractions: Questions and Answers," which appears in *Seventeen*. As Table C indicates, the low number of citations including some form of the term lesbian found in *Sociological Abstracts* and *Magazine Index* during the late 1960s in representative of online retrieval in general: only 31 citations from 16 different databases covering the six year period from 1965 to 1970 include some form of the term lesbian. An examination of these 31 citations, reveals that all but three fall into the first category. Two fall into the second category, and one, the book *The New Woman* by Joanne Cooke, Charlotte Bunch Weeks, and Robin Morgan, retrieved from the *Family Resources* database, is a third category citation (classified on the basis of the notoriety of the authors).

The small number of first category citations in *Sociological Abstracts*, *Magazine Index*, and other databases reflects the small amount, in general, of information about and by lesbians available online before 1970. Limited numbers of first category citations, however, should not mask the fact that first category information about lesbians was virtually the only information available online prior to 1970. A search of the DIALOG databases, *Dissertation Abstracts* (1861 to the present) and *REMARC* (pre-1900 to 1980), for years prior to 1965 retrieved a total of 28 citations that include some form of the term lesbian. The only two citations available from *Dissertation Abstracts* both fall into the first category. Of the 26 citations available from *REMARC*, 12 are citations for sources in some language other than English, 12 are first category citations, and two are third category citations. These third category citations include a bibliographic record for *The Ladder*, the first lesbian newsletter published in the United States by the Daughters of Bilitis, and a book called *We Walk Alone* by Marijane Meaker. A database like *REMARC* — which is the Retrospective Machine Readable Cataloging database containing bibliographic records of the works cataloged by the Library of Congress (LC) that are not included in the *LC MARC* database — demonstrates that two levels of information, third category among lesbians and first category among straight people, have long been in distribution. It is the second category sources that have appeared in print relatively recently and been picked up by the mainstream online indexing services.

The first issue of *Alternative Press Index* was published in late 1969. No separate heading existed in that issue for the term lesbian. The broader term homosexuality covered sources relating to lesbians as well as gay males. Even so, *Alternative Press Index*, from the first, provided access to third category sources centered around a lesbian definition of lesbian. It was more than a decade after the first issue before the *Index* expanded its list of titles indexed to include academic journals such as the *Journal of Homosexuality* in which second category sources frequently appear.

By the late 1970s, the quantity of information about and by lesbians online was increasing and the quality of the information was changing. Second category citations were beginning to dominate in databases such as *Sociological Abstracts* and *Magazine Index* and even third category citations were beginning to appear. Only four out of the 34 citations (12%) from *Sociological Abstracts* between the years 1976 and 1978 are first category while 25 (75%) are second category. The citations in *Sociological Abstracts* include 32 journal articles from 17 different journals, although nine of the articles (28%) come from the same title, the *Journal of Homosexuality*; the remaining two citations are to conference papers. First category citations are the least common (14%) kind of citations among the 28 which appeared in *Magazine Index* between 1976 and 1978. Almost 50% (12 out of 28) of the citations are second category and almost 30% (8 out of 28) are third category. The 28 citations include 26 articles, eight of which appear in the *Journal of Homosexuality* and six in *MS.* (known for its feminist perspective), and two book reviews.

In one quarterly issue of *Alternative Press Index* published during 1976, 58 entries appear under some form of the term lesbian, approximately twice as many entries as appear in either *Sociological Abstracts* or *Magazine Index* over the three year period between 1976 and 1978. Thirty-nine of the citations in the issue are third category, and 19 are second category. The second category citations include descriptions of conferences, portraits of activists, reports on films or books, and second hand accounts of lesbian mother custody battles.

By the late 1980s, first category citations had disappeared altogether from both *Sociological Abstracts* and *Magazine Index* and the percentage of third category citations had not increased. An increase in the number of second category citations, therefore, accounted for the overall increase in the number of citations including some form of the term lesbian. Eighty-eight percent of the 60 citations in *Sociological Abstracts* between 1986 and 1988 are to second category citations, as are 84% of the 73 citations in *Magazine*

Index. Forty-one of the 60 citations in *Sociological Abstracts* are to journal articles published in 26 different journal titles. A third of the articles appear in the same publication, the *Journal of Homosexuality.* The remaining 19 citations include seven book reviews, seven conference papers, three dissertations, and two books. One of the two third category citations is a book review of a book called *Did You Realize There Were So Many Of Us? Lesbian Women in the Church,* and the other is an article from the *Journal of Homosexuality* by Judy Grahn, a lesbian poet.

Almost half (44%) of the 73 citations including some form of the term lesbian which appear in *Magazine Index* between 1986 and 1988 are to book reviews, and the 32 reviews cover only 19 unique publications. Thirty-seven citations are to journal articles and the remaining four items are to editorials, columns, or letters. The nine third category citations are made up entirely of reviews of books authored by lesbians and of articles from *MS.* magazine.

Sixty-five entries appear under some form of the term lesbian in just one quarterly issue of *Alternative Press Index* for the year 1986 — approximately the same number of citations that appear in *Sociological Abstracts* or *Magazine Index* for the entire three year period from 1986 to 1988. Thirty of the 65 entries in *Alternative Press Index* are second category citations and 14 of these are to articles in the *Journal of Homosexuality,* a publication that, by 1986, was being indexed by all three indexing services under discussion.

If access to more information is assumed to be better than access to less, and if being defined as an acceptable other is assumed to be better than being defined as a deviant other, an examination of the information about and by lesbians available in online databases reveals a trend toward improved access. The number of citations including some form of the term lesbian which appear in *Sociological Abstracts* or *Magazine Index* over the course of a year today is thirty times greater than it was in 1966 and three times greater than it was in 1976. Whereas, in 1966 virtually all the information online defined lesbians as deviant, by 1986 most of the available information defined lesbians as acceptable, and a small percentage of citations online (3% in *Sociological Abstracts* and 13% in *Magazine Index*) even offered a lesbian definition of lesbianism.

A problem that the passage of time has not solved is the problem of limiting a search only to third category sources. No assigned descriptors distinguish lesbian-defined from other-defined. While combining the term lesbian with the term feminist limits retrieval to a subset of sources likely to convey a sympathetic approach, such a subset will not necessarily include third category sources. When some form of the term feminist is combined with the set of 60 citations including some form of the term lesbian in *Sociological Abstracts* for the years 1986-1988, 13 citations are retrieved; the two third category sources which appear in *Sociological Abstracts* during that same time period are not among the 13.

The most significant and easily identifiable trend in online information about and by lesbians is the replacement of a small number of first category citations with a much larger number of second category citations. The relationship between the increase in numbers of citations and their evolution from first to second category is not one of cause and effect. These two trends, rather, are two effects resulting from the same cause. The social movements of the 1960s gave homosexuality legitimacy, not only as a lifestyle choice but also as a subject for research. The small numbers of deviance- or pathology-oriented studies gave way to larger numbers of "lifestyle and so-called gay affirmative [studies] which [have been] widely applauded by the gay and parts of the feminist movement."[16]

The move away from first category and toward second category citations combined with small increases in the number of third category citations appearing in mainstream online indexing sources seems to signal an increase in lesbian power in terms of Frye's two faces of access and definition. Greater numbers of retrievable citations implies that more information is accessible. The replacement of first category deviance-oriented information with second category acceptance-oriented information implies that lesbians' views of their own worlds are being taken into account.

In *The Social Construction of Lesbianism*, however, Kitzinger[17] argues that "gay affirmative research, far from being a liberating force, represents a new development in the oppression of lesbians." Second category sources oppress, she claims, through "their energetic attempts to shape the subjectivities of both lesbians and non-lesbians" in order to "control and contain the political challenge" that lesbianism poses.

If Kitzinger is right, the proliferation of second category citations online does provide lesbians with more access to information about themselves but, simultaneously, appropriates lesbians' power of self-definition. Access to information that shapes lesbians' conceptions of what they ought to be and that determines, for lesbians, "what is said and sayable" is conditional access. It is through specialized print sources, such as the *Alternative Press Index* and the *Lesbian Periodicals Index*,[18] rather than through online databases, that lesbians are able to locate significant amounts of lesbian-defined information. The computerization of information, however, improves access by increasing the number of access points to any one citation. Unconditional access to information about and by lesbians will be available, therefore, when print sources to lesbian-defined information become conveniently and inexpensively available online.

REFERENCES

1. Frye, Marilyn. "Separatism and Power." In *The Politics of Reality: Essays in Feminist Theory*, 95-109. Trumansburg, NY: Crossing Press, 1983.

2. Katz, Jonathan. *Gay American History: Lesbians and Gay Men in the U.S.A.* New York: Thomas Y. Cromwell, 1976.

3. *Directory of Online Databases* 9 (July, 1988): Preface, p. v. New York: Cuadra/Elsevier.

4. Lochhead, Ishbel. "Bibliographic Control of Feminist Literature." *Catalogue & Index* (Spring/Summer, 1985): 10-15.

5. Lochhead. "Bibliographic Control of Feminist Literature."

6. Hildenbrand, Suzanne. "Women's Studies Online: Promoting Visibility." *RQ* 34 (Fall, 1986): 63-74. Hildenbrand lists four different types of indexing problems encountered when searching for online information about women: (1) the failure to differentiate a topic sufficiently; (2) the failure to offer inclusive labels for records on one example of a whole class; (3) the failure to assign terms consistently or comprehensively, and (4) the failure of controlled vocabulary to express the concepts involved.

7. The six DIALINDEX categories the databases each includes are:
(1) BOOKS (Books in Print, #470; British Books in Print, #430; LC MARC, #426-27; REMARC, #421-425.)
(2) REVIEWS (Book Review Index, #137; Magazine Index, #47; Na-

tional Newspaper Index, #111; Newsearch, #211; Newspaper Abstracts; #603.)

(3) PUBAFF (PAIS International, #49; Magazine Index, #47; U.S. Political Science Documents, #93; National Newspaper Index, #111; Federal Register, #136; Washington Presstext, #145; Newsearch, #211; AP News, #258-59; UPI News, #260-61; Newspaper Abstracts, #603; USA Today Decisionline, #644; Current Digest of the Soviet Press, #645.)

(4) MEDICINE (Biosis Previews, #5; Scisearch, #34,432-34; Sport Database, #48; Embase, #72, 172; International Pharmaceutical Abstracts, #74; Medline, #155; Cancerlit, #159; Smoking and Health, #160; Nursing and Allied Health, #218; Clinical Abstracts, #219.)

(5) HUMANIT (Social Scisearch, #7; Dissertation Abstracts, #35; America: History and Life, #38; Historical Abstracts, #39; Art Modern, #56; Philosopher's Index, #57; MLA Bibliography, #71; RILM, #97; Architecture Database, #179; Religion Index, #190; Art Literature International, #191; Magill's Survey of Cinema, #299; Arts & Humanities Search, #439.)

(6) SOCSCI (Sociological Abstracts, #37; Psychological Abstracts, #11; ERIC, #1; Social Scisearch, #7; NCJRS, #21; Dissertation Abstracts, #35; PAIS International, #49; ECER/Exceptional Child, #54; Population Bibliography, #91; U.S. Political Science Documents, #93; British Education Index, #121; Criminal Justice Periodical Index, #171; Religion Index, #190; Family Resources, #291.)

8. Morin, Stephen. "Heterosexual Bias in Psychological Research on Lesbianism and Male Homosexuality." *American Psychologist* 32 (August 1977): 629-637.

9. Watters, Alan T. "Heterosexual Bias in Psychological Research on Lesbianism and Male Homosexuality (1979-1983), Utilizing the Bibliographic and Taxonomic System of Morin (1977). *Journal of Homosexuality* 13 (Fall 1986): 35-58.

10. Morin. "Heterosexual Bias in Psychological Research on Lesbianism and Male Homosexuality."

11. Detlefsen, Ellen Gay. "Issues of Access to Information About Women." *Special Collections* 3 (1986): 163-171.

12. Hildenbrand. "Women's Studies Online: Promoting Visibility."

13. Gates, Henry Louis, Jr. "Whose Canon Is It, Anyway?" *New York Times Book Review*; February 26, 1989, 41-45.

14. Morin, "Heterosexual Bias in Psychological Research on Lesbianism and Male Homosexuality."

15. Alternative Press Index. (Baltimore, MD: Alternative Press Center, Inc.). 1969-.

16. Kitzinger, Celia. *The Social Construction of Lesbianism*. Beverly Hills, CA: Sage Publications. 1987.

17. Kitzinger. *The Social Construction of Lesbianism*.

18. Potter, Clare, ed. *The Lesbian Periodicals Index*. Naiad Press, 1986.

Women of Color
in Online Databases

Janet Sims-Wood
Frances C. Ziegler

SUMMARY. The major obstacle confronting scholars researching the history of Black women in America is the lack of readily identifiable and accessible sources. Many of the Black books, journals and related materials about Blacks are not included in general indexes, printed or online. This chapter examines resources on women of color in online databases. Researchers searching databases for Black women's studies face the same problems as those encountered in general women's studies searching. A few of the general problems, how they affect research in Black women's studies, general guidelines for effective searching, current computer projects, the value of a network system in women's studies and future needs in Black women's studies are discussed.

The pioneering work, *All The Women Are White, All The Blacks Are Men, But Some Of Us Are Brave* addresses the emergence of Black women's studies. The editors assert that

Janet Sims-Wood is Assistant Chief Librarian, Reference/Reader Services Department, Moorland-Spingarn Research Center, Howard University, Washington, DC. She holds an MLS degree from the University of Maryland. She has published widely in the area of bibliographic sources on Black women and is Associate Editor of *SAGE: A Scholarly Journal On Black Women*.

Frances C. Ziegler is Reference Librarian and Coordinator of Computer Searching at the Founders Library of Howard University in Washington, DC. She holds an MSLS from Atlanta University and an MEd in educational technology from Howard University. She coordinates and conducts workshops on online and CD-ROM searching for the staff, faculty, and students. She has produced numerous reference guides to reference sources and to searching techniques. Currently, she and the media librarian, Eric White, are producing a video, ''Introduction to CD-ROM Searching.''

if one looks for "hard data" concerning curriculum relating to Black women in the existing studies of academic institutions, we are seemingly nonexistent. And yet impressionistically and experientially it is obvious that more and more study is being done about Black women and, even more importantly, it is being done with an increasing consciousness of the impact of sexual-racial politics on Black women's lives. One thinks, for instance, of Alice Walker's groundbreaking course on Black women writers at Wellesley College in 1972, and how work of all sorts by and about Black women writers has since blossomed into a visible Black female literary "renaissance." The core of courses on Black women at colleges and universities has grown slowly but steadily during the 1970s. And increasing interest in Black feminism and recognition of Black women's experiences point to the '80s as the time when Black women's studies will come into its own. Perhaps this may be seen less in teaching than in the plethora of other activity in Black women's scholarship.[1]

Dr. Bettye Collier-Thomas notes that

women have been the victims of scholarly neglect. Black women, possessing a double minority status, have received less scholarly consideration. As a result of the civil rights and feminist movements, women's history has become a legitimate area of scholarly endeavor. The national conventions of major historical associations, university and college curricula, private and public foundation grants lists, newspaper articles, media programs, scholarly and popular journals and magazines are all beginning to reflect the growing concern for the preservation, identification, research and writing of women's history. Archives and libraries now are inundated by requests for primary and secondary sources pertaining to women. Unfortunately, the demand for these resources has preceded the development of adequate research materials and tools. Many repositories are just beginning to include in their card catalogues specific categories identifying holdings related to women's history. Finding aids and bibliographies gradually are coming into existence for researchers interested in women's history. The major obstacle confronting scholars researching the history of Black women in America is the lack of identifiable, readily accessible sources.[2]

Mary Ellen Capek acknowledges that "much of that information is housed in centers, organization files, or resource collections that are underfunded and not available to students, teachers, and public users, mainstream journalists and policy makers. Much important work was and is unpublished, in working papers or conference reports, or if published, has been in alternative feminist presses or small journals, community newspapers, directories, or organization newsletters that are seldom microfilmed or indexed."[3]

This article examines the resources on women of color available in online databases. Researchers searching in databases for Black women's studies face the same problems as those encountered in general women's studies searching. A few of the general problems are cited and related to research in Black women's studies. The article also gives some general guidelines for effective searching, discusses some current computer projects, cites the value of a network system in women's studies and concludes with future research needs in Black women's studies.

RETROSPECTIVE COVERAGE

Suzanne Hildenbrand has noted that "publishers only began employing computer technology in the late sixties and it has evidently not been economically feasible for many of them to go back and load earlier years into their databases. There is, for example, no modern access to the historical literature of the 1930s, a period of great importance to women's history."[4] This has been a particular problem for early black journals and books that were not included in earlier print indexes. Missing are journals such as *The Aframerican Woman's Journal*, publishing arm of the National Council of Negro Women published during the 1940s. One of their issues concentrated on "The Negro Woman In National Defense" (Summer/Fall, 1941). *The Crisis*, the publishing arm of the NAACP, published a special issue on "Woman's Suffrage" (September, 1912). Books such as Susie King Taylor's *My Life With The 33rd United States Colored Troops* (1902) and Mary Church Terrell's *A Colored Woman In A White World* (1940) are also missing from these early book and journal indexes and certainly are not included in online databases that lack retrospective coverage.

INDEXING

Suzanne Hildenbrand notes in another article that "failure to recognize and label the women's aspect of a topic perpetuates the tradition of invisibility against which women's studies scholars struggle."[5] Some of the major indexing problems Hildenbrand cites are: (1) failure to differentiate a topic sufficiently, (2) failure to offer inclusive labels for records on one example of a whole class, and (3) omission of an important term in a controlled vocabulary.

To address some of these problems the National Council For Research On Women formed a Thesaurus Task Force And Database Steering Committee. The thesaurus was published in 1987 by Harper & Row. Mary Ellen Capek stressed that the thesaurus could be used to

> support a variety of applications. It can aid indexers and others who create as well as those who search manual and computerized filing systems; indexes for books, reports, government documents, magazines, scholarly journals, newspapers, and newsletters; multi-source indexes and reference guides, bibliographies, and abstracts of books and research articles. Another primary application will be to suggest cross references and narrower terms that can sharpen existing classification and cataloging systems. The ready availability of terms contained in the thesaurus will enable catalogers working with manual or online card catalogs to add detailed descriptors that will describe their collections more accurately and provide some imaginative correctives for biases embedded in existing classification systems. Still another use of the thesaurus will be to serve as a reference guide for nonsexist use of the language.[6]

In 1982, the American Library Association's Women's Studies Database Task Force study concluded that the existing databases covering various collections and disciplines for materials on women did not index many of the smaller presses, journals, conference reports, works in progress, etc. Moreover, many of the materials that were included in the databases were listed under inaccurate or inadequate index terms or contained abstracts that did not reflect the content of the materials. The ALA task force found that the existing classifications often overlooked emerging topics of special concern to women. The findings sparked the thesaurus project of the National Council For Research On Women. The first objective of the thesaurus project was to construct a comprehensive, machine-based index that defined, standardized and cross referenced terms that accurately described materials in the database. The ultimate goal was to produce a revised list of language — formal and informal, vernacular and scholarly — used to define women's lives and research. It was felt that development of a woman's indexing language would help other information resources improve their access to women's materials and make it easier for commercial and academic database producers to index more accurately.[7]

ETHNIC DESCRIPTORS/SUBJECT HEADINGS

Hildenbrand cites another problem in the area of ethnic descriptors. In searching for Black women, one must use multiple terms (Negro, Afro American, Black, African-American) unless the database thesaurus specifies a preferred term to use. She notes that the lack of inclusive labels for records on a specific ethnic group, especially when individual names are not known, results in missed citations. *The MLA International Bibliography* was cited as one database which yields fewer citations when searching under general descriptors than when searching by individual names.[8] This problem is particularly troubling since one of the most popular areas of research in Black women's studies is in the field of literature. For example, the pioneering work done by Gloria Hull, *Color, Sex And Poetry: Three Women Writers Of The Harlem Renaissance*, appears under the *MLA* descriptor — Black women poets, but by using the names of the writers Georgia Douglas Johnson, Alice Dunbar-Nelson or Angelina Grimke, one may find this work and other references to Black women poets.

Often students do not know individual names or the ethnic backgrounds when researching a topic. The lack of specific fields for identifying a particular population or topic results in the retrieval of those irrelevant records researchers so often cite as reasons for not using databases.

GUIDELINES FOR EFFECTIVE SEARCHING

The absence of one general basic database in women's studies necessitates the need for multiple database searching in order to collect relevant material scattered among the various commercial databases. As new concepts or terminology descriptors emerge in women's studies, descriptors should be coined and added by the database producers. Searchers must take care to use the descriptors appropriate for each database and be aware of the date that each descriptor was introduced as an index term since some women's issues have only recently received recognition (e.g., date rape, Black mother-daughter relationships, and non-sexist/non-racist materials).

Duplication is also a problem since many journals in women's studies are indexed in several databases. For example, *SAGE: A Scholarly Journal On Black Women* is indexed in *PsycInfo*, *Women's Studies Abstracts*, *Sociological Abstracts*, *Feminist Periodical Collections* and *The MLA International Bibliography*. Three of these indexes are available online as databases.

The cost of database searching has often led to low utilization of this technology by researchers, especially in women's studies. At the April, 1989 meeting of the Association of College and Research Libraries, Susan Searing discussed her study of the importance of online databases in women's studies. She reported that although most of the researchers surveyed used computers for word processing, others said they were not familiar with databases and cited the high cost of searching.[9]

CURRENT COMPUTER PROJECTS

Many databases developed by institutions and individuals, especially in women's history, are not available commercially. As a result of inadequate funding, institutions and individuals lack the time or staff available to develop and maintain files on commercial systems. Some database vendors require at least 10,000 citations to start, with regular updates due several times a year. Although most projects are initially funded by grants, they must find other sources of income to continue after the grants expire.

Databases dealing with Black and women's history materials are now being developed across the country. One such database project is The Research Clearinghouse On Women Of Color And Southern Women developed at Memphis State University. This database includes information on Afro-American, Asian American, Latino, Native American and Pacific Island women. Funded by FIPSE (Fund For The Improvement Of Post Secondary Education), the database includes over 3,000 up-to-date citations on books, chapters in books, journal articles, unpublished works and non-print media beginning in 1975. The database can be searched by author, subject, year, and type of publication and includes references on target population's health and education. The database is indexed using the *Women's Thesaurus* mentioned earlier. In 1988 the center published the file in book form. Researchers can consult the database in hard copy or arrange with the clearinghouse to have a database search prepared. The Memphis State database will be made available on floppy disk in the near future.[10]

The Afro-American Novel Project is currently under development at the University of Mississippi. Funded by a grant from the Ford Foundation, with NEH funding pending, it is the first centralized database of information on the Afro-American novel. This project is a computer based retrieval system which presently includes bibliographic citations and descriptive information on 1,063 novels and their authors. Information is collected from a number of sources, including dictionary catalogs of Black collections, bibliographies, magazines aimed at Black audiences, Black periodicals and newspapers, oral histories, book notices, Black college archives, Black publishers, yearbooks, business directories, WPA records, institutional histories, interviews, school records, photographs, personal papers, organizational papers and audio and videotapes.

Project Director Maryemma Graham has discovered what may be the second oldest novel by a Black writer—*Treading The Winepress; Or A Mountain Of Misfortune*, by Clarissa M. Thompson, published in 1885 and 1886 in the *Boston Advocate*. The oldest is *Our Nig*, by Harriet Wilson, published in 1859. Graham has found that a large number of the new novels discovered were written by women and that a surprising number were published in the South. In addition, she has found that some of the novels were self-published or subsidized by churches or other organizations and are not listed in standard references. Many are known only on the local level.[11]

VALUE OF NETWORK SYSTEMS

Susan Searing noted that "early on, women's studies librarians pointed out the need for a scholarly apparatus that included bibliographies, databases and indexes to make it easier for readers to use the written record. It was librarians who created the first book-length general women's studies bibliographies."[12]

Sarah Pritchard further states that

> to keep abreast requires an active attempt to monitor a variety of publications, organizations, conferences, and research centers, and a critical and creative use of materials in all subjects and formats. The librarian needs to reach out to various user groups and become a knowledgeable synthesizer within the subject field. This leads to a proactive approach which combines subject specialization with general reference. Maintaining files, attending meetings, providing research consultations and group orientations, developing the collections with standard and nontraditional sources, learning about the field through reading and attending conferences, combine to make the individual librarian a source of information on print and human resources, cutting across the academic/political/

grassroots boundaries by breadth of reading and local participation.[13]

Other sources vital to a researcher's network are colleagues in the
field. Bettye Collier-Thomas, Director of the Bethune Museum &
Archives; Beverly Guy-Sheftall, Director of the Women's Center at
Spelman College; Patricia Bell-Scott, editor of *SAGE: A Scholarly
Journal On Black Women*, Darlene Clark Hine, Director of the
Women In The Midwest Project, and Sharon Harley and Ruby
Sales, professors in women's studies at the University of Maryland,
are among the many resource people in Black women's history
whose expertise and advice the authors have often sought.

FUTURE NEEDS

Sarah Prichard contends that "the distribution of entire databases
on compact discs (CD-ROM) will greatly increase access in many
libraries and research centers. Large-scale general databases in all
subjects will continue to be standard for academic literature searching, with useful results for women's studies if searches are carefully
constructed and the scope of the database clearly understood."[14]
There seems to be a general consensus among the Black studies
librarians that there is now a great need for a Black studies database
online and on CD-ROM. A possible start could be the *Index To
Periodicals By And About Blacks*.
One of the major problems in researching Black women's studies
is that many of the Black books, journals and related materials are
just not included in general indexes, printed or online. Their exclusion complicates the research process since the majority of writings
in Black women's studies are published in the Black literature, although more sources are now being found in general and feminist
literature.
In addition some Black materials are not listed in Black related
indexes. For example, most of the journals of the Black sororities
are not indexed. An article on "AKA's In The Arts" which appeared in the Spring, 1987 issue of the *Ivy Leaf*, the publication of
the Alpha Kappa Alpha Sorority, might be missed by the Black
women's studies researcher because it is not indexed. Likewise,

The Spelman Messenger, which is published at one of the two Black women's colleges in the U.S., has a special issue (Winter, 1989) on the inauguration of their first woman president.

Newsletters of the Black women's organizations are rarely indexed. A scholar researching Black women workers would miss an article in the January, 1984 issue of *Truth: The Newsletter Of The Association Of Black Women Historians* on "Race, Sex and Class: Black Female Tobacco Workers In Durham, N.C., 1920-1940 And The Development Of A Feminine Consciousness."

Black newspapers are also a valuable resource. An article on researching Black women's history at the Moorland-Spingarn Research Center states that "even though there have been some attempts to index a few Black newspapers (e.g., Jacob's *Antebellum Black Newspapers*, Blassingame's *Anti-Slavery Newspapers and Periodicals*, and most recently, Bell and Howell's *Black Newspaper Index*), the majority of Black newspapers have not been indexed. As far as Afro-American women are concerned, newspapers have proved invaluable in giving biographical sketches and obituaries, and most have a women's section which discusses local and national activities, plus gives other helpful articles on health, nutrition, etc."[15]

Access to information made available about other types of materials (e.g., information on photo exhibits, the state by state women's history month kits, conference reviews, plus curriculum and educational materials for children) is also needed. Periodicals such as *Feminist Collections* review some of the items mentioned above, but this periodical is not indexed in print or online.

CONCLUSION

For women's studies, one must access print indexes, databases and human resources to extract the hard-to-find materials needed to conduct a scholarly research project. This is especially true for research on Black women since there is no specific database in Black women's studies. As this article and other articles in this book have noted, much has been done, yet there is still much to be done to get information about women to the researchers who need this information. These needs include:

1. Need for pressure from professional organizations to encourage indexing and abstracting services to cover Black women's studies.
2. Need for database producers to deal with vocabulary problems with the ultimate goal of eliminating sexist and racist terms.
3. Need for informal networks for research.
4. Need for affordable prices.
5. Need for funding for research institutes to create or maintain databases which cover Black women's studies.

Hopefully, as more research institutes develop databases, more funding will become available to make these databases easily accessible to all.

REFERENCES

1. Gloria T. Hull, Patricia Bell Scott, and Barbara Smith, eds. *All The Women Are White, All The Blacks Are Men, But Some Of Us Are Brave: Black Women's Studies.* (Old Westbury, New York: The Feminist Press, 1982), pp. xxvi-xvii.
2. Betty Collier Thomas. "Foreword," in Janet L. Sims, *The Progress of Afro American Women: A Selected Bibliography And Resource Guide.* (Westport, Connecticut: Greenwood Press, 1980), p. ix.
3. Mary Ellen Capek. "Wired Words: Developing An On-Line Thesaurus And Database For Improving Access To Women's Information Sources." *NWSA Perspectives* 5 (Winter, 1987): p. 1.
4. Suzanne Hildenbrand. "Researching Women's History On Bibliographic Data Bases," in Robert F. Allen, ed. *The International Conference On Data Bases In The Humanities And Social Sciences, 1983.* (Osprey, Florida: Paradigm Press, 1985), p. 22.
5. Suzanne Hildenbrand. "Women's Studies On-line: Promoting Visibility." *RQ* 26 (Fall, 1986): p. 66.
6. Capek. "Wired Words," pp. 41-42.
7. Capek. "Wired Words," p. 41.
8. Suzanne Hildenbrand. "Women's Studies On-line," p. 68.
9. Susan Searing. "Library Services For Nontraditional Students." (Paper delivered at Women's Studies In Academic Libraries: Current Research And Im-

plications For Service Workshop, Association Of College And Research Libraries, Cincinnati, Ohio, 7 April, 1989).

10. Brochure. Research Clearinghouse On Women Of Color And Southern Women. College Of Arts And Sciences, (Memphis, Tennessee: Memphis State University), n.d.

11. "Scholars To Study Novels." *The Oxford (Ms) Eagle*. 12 May, 1988.

12. Susan Searing. "A Quiet Revolution." *The Women's Review Of Books* 6 (February, 1989), p. 19.

13. Sarah M. Pritchard. "Linking Research Policy, And Activism: Library Services In Women's Studies." *The Reference Librarian* (no. 20, 1987): pp. 91-92.

14. Sarah M. Pritchard. "Trends In Computer-Based Resources For Women's Studies." *Feminist Teacher* 3 (Fall-Winter, 1988): p. 8.

15. Janet Sims-Wood. "Researching Black Women's History Resources And Archives At Moorland-Springarn Research Center." *Ethnic Forum* 7 (no. 1, 1987): p. 44.

BIBLIOGRAPHY

Brochure. Research Clearinghouse On Women Of Color And Southern Women. College Of Arts And Sciences. Memphis, Tennessee: Memphis State University.

Capek, Mary Ellen. "Wired Words: Developing An On-Line Thesaurus And Database For Improving Access To Women's Information Sources." *NWSA Perspectives* 5 (Winter, 1987): 1, 41-43.

Hildenbrand, Suzanne. "Researching Women's History On Bibliographic Data Bases," in *The International Conference On Data Bases In The Humanities And Social Sciences, 1983*, edited by Robert F. Allen. Osprey, Florida: Paradigm Press, 1985.

Hildenbrand, Suzanne. "Women's Studies On-line: Promoting Visibility." *RQ* 26 (Fall, 1986): 63-74.

Hull, Gloria T.; Scott, Patricia Bell; and Smith, Barbara. *All The Women Are White, All The Blacks Are Men, But Some Of Us Are Brave: Black Women's Studies*. Old Westbury, New York: The Feminist Press, 1982.

Pritchard, Sarah M. "Linking Research Policy, And Activism: Library Services In Women's Studies." *The Reference Librarian* (no. 20, 1987): 89-103.

Pritchard, Sarah M. "Trends In Computer-Based Resources For Women's Studies." *Feminist Teacher* 3 (Fall-Winter, 1988): 8-13.

"Scholars To Study Novels." *The Oxford (Ms) Eagle*. 12 May, 1988.

Searing, Susan. "A Quiet Revolution." *The Women's Review Of Books* 6 (February, 1989), 19-21.

Searing, Susan. "Library Services For Nontraditional Students." Paper delivered at Women's Studies In Academic Libraries: Current Research And Implications For Service Workshop, Association Of College And Research Libraries, Cincinnati, Ohio, 7 April, 1989.

Sims-Wood, Janet. "Researching Black Women's History Resources And Archives At Moorland-Springarn Research Center." *Ethnic Forum* 7 (no. 1, 1987): 38-47.

Thomas, Betty Collier. "Foreword," in *The Progress of Afro-American Women: A Selected Bibliography And Resource Guide*, by Janet L. Sims. Westport, Connecticut: Greenwood Press, 1980.

Women in
Developing Countries Online

Beth Stafford
Yvette Scheven

SUMMARY. Results of selected online searches for participants in a workshop on women in international development (WID) are analyzed for the three most prolific years of publication. Results are compared to similar searches of two print indexes applicable to women's studies. Findings indicate that there is almost no overlap of publication coverage between the online databases and the print indexes while it appears that "women" and considerations of gender are not prominent in the literatures of disciplines included in the databases. The databases and the print indexes also omit important materials from producers in WID. For more appropriate indexing terminology and coverage of publications, dialogue should be initiated between the producers of the print indexes as well as the online databases and the development community.

Experts in the field estimate that seventy five percent of all literature about women in the Third World emphasizes economic and social matters or circumstances and is therefore about women in international development (WID). It has also been said that the distinction between women's studies and WID is that WID has an applied focus. For example, in many areas of the world a major concern to women is the availability of a sanitary water supply literally within a few miles of one's housing site, or the supply of fuel for cooking, such as wood. The purpose of this paper is to evaluate

Beth Stafford is Women's Studies/Women in International Development Librarian, and Yvette Scheven is Bibliographer for African Studies, University of Illinois Library, 1408 W. Gregory Dr., Urbana, IL 61801.

The authors thank their colleagues who are online searchers for all their advice, cooperation, and support.

online bibliographic databases for their coverage of three topics relevant to women in developing countries. The authors have taken the role of non-searcher specialists in determining the effectiveness of database searching for actual patron requests in the coverage of issues related to women in the Third World. All online searching was performed by veteran searchers through essentially discipline-oriented databases.

WOMEN IN INTERNATIONAL DEVELOPMENT

The concept of women in international development as a field materialized from the convergence of concerns in the feminist community and in the development community, beginning in the early 1970s. Publication of *Women's Role in Economic Development* by Esther Boserup (London, 1970); passage of the Percy amendment at the initiative of women working in the United Nations (U.N.) and U.S. feminist groups and individuals (1973); and the convening of the United Nations Conference for International Women's Year on "Equality, Development and Peace" (1975) combined to articulate and legitimize concerns that an equitable share of benefits from development and social change was not being accorded to women. Women active in the U.N. and in the U.S. women's movement and people in the development community followed different routes but combined forces to establish the field of women in international development.

The U.N. Commission on the Status of Women, established in 1946, had been focussing mainly on the de jure and de facto barriers to women's equality, emphasizing their rights under the law and opportunities made available to them to exercise those rights. Although the Commission had for years studied the status of women in public and private law and also women's access to all kinds of education and employment, documentation from those studies was not widely available.

As rising numbers of developing countries joined the U.N., emphasis began to shift toward development issues throughout the organization. As a consequence, an enlarged Commission on the Status of Women worked more and more with other U.N. entities and specialized agencies in order to consider what was happening to/in women's lives as a result of national plans for social and economic development. In spite of additional documentation produced by U.N. agencies concerned with women's issues, many governments still assumed that national social and economic development by itself would bring about any desired changes for women.

In 1973 Senator Charles Percy, then on the U.S. Senate Foreign Relations Committee, introduced into pending foreign aid legislation a provision that was prompted by various efforts of many women working in the U.N. and its agencies. The amendment stated that all provisions in the foreign assistance bill that have to do with food, health, population, education, etc. shall be administered in such a way as to integrate women into all aspects of development. Academics and those affiliated with mainstream women's organizations and with religious groups involved in international development lobbied and initiated a torrent of mail and phone calls in support of the Percy amendment. These efforts convinced the responsible conference committee to pass the amendment.

The impact of the Percy Amendment has been quite dramatic. Those in the development community have expanded their conceptualizations of WID from focussing on economic and social development to include equity, employment, and empowerment. That is, a field originally seen as simply adding a concern for women to standard development theory has broadened its parameters to include other goals of the women's movement such as heightened demand for legal equity, more power for women's organizations, and concern for more jobs for professional women.

Passage of the Percy Amendment in the U.S. provided women both inside and outside governmental and multilateral agency hierarchies with a symbol of their own strength and some access to power. This strength and power within traditional and newly created power structures are the crucial components in the impact of WID on public policy.

Those from more established women's organizations incorporated development issues into their own objectives, and newer feminist groups (activist and academic) added an international dimension to their goals.

Senator Percy, as a U.S. delegate to the U.N., introduced a resolution regarding women in development into the General Assembly's Economic Committee (1974). That Committee's eventual acceptance of the resolution acknowledged Percy's assertion that the issue of WID is primarily economic instead of social.

The Percy Amendment and subsequent resolutions became symbols of women's power to women both inside and outside of development power structures. In the fall of 1974 a version of the Percy Amendment engineered and drafted by women was submitted and passed by UNESCO's governing body. Soon most U.N. agencies adopted similar resolutions.

The most profound impact of the U.N. resolution has been the shift of women's concerns from the narrow confines of the U.N. Commission on the Status of Women into the entire U.N. system.

The issue of WID has had a critical effect on scholars around the world, initially by identifying how totally inadequate available data on women were. Numerous scholarly meetings confirmed a growing interest in WID. Two new U.N. institutions were created: the Voluntary Fund for the Decade for Women and the International Research and Training Institution for the Advancement of Women (INSTRAW). The U.N. declared a Decade for Women (1976-85) as a follow-up to International Women's Year (1975). There have been three World Conferences for the U.N. Decade for Women: in Mexico City (1975), in Copenhagen (1980), and in Nairobi (1985). International disciplinary meetings began to hold panels on women. A series of International Interdisciplinary Congresses dealing with scholarly issues has been held. In the United States the Association for Women in Development (AWID) was founded in 1982.[1]

Only slightly later than the American initiatives came the U.N. initiatives, including the Decade, the World Plan of Action, and the Convention on the Elimination of All Forms of Discrimination Against Women.

Research and action about women's concerns are finally being addressed at the national level all over the world. The growth of European, Indian, African, Indonesian and Latin American women's groups and women's studies programs attests to this. Concomitant to that is the fact that many private and government grants now demand policy-relevant research to support women's attempts to integrate attention to females into national economic development plans.[2]

WORKSHOP

One response to the urgent need for data on women on the parts of researchers and practitioners deciding or implementing policy is a co-operative project between scholars at Maharaja Sayajirao (M.S.) University in Baroda, India, and the University of Illinois in Urbana-Champaign, initiated in 1985. One part of the project was an international workshop, "Women, Households, and Development: Building a Database," held in Urbana, Illinois, in July, 1988. More than sixty participants from twenty-three countries convened for intensive sessions spanning twelve days. Among the participants were scholars and professional people working in government ministries, development agencies, international organizations, universities, and private organizations.

An overall goal of the workshop was to provide a forum to synthesize and share new research methodologies and techniques or adapt old ones for obtaining data on and studying households and women. The workshop presented a systematic overview of important areas and issues in household research; facilitated work groups organized around common interests; and furnished a wide variety of resources for use during and after the workshop. Building in part on ideas from sessions on subject matter, methodology, and case studies, six self-selected work groups designed their own priorities and work plans. In addition to using resources (modules) developed by workshop staff, the interest groups needed online searching by library faculty. This paper is based on results of searches done on three of the topics determined by the interest groups: quantification of women's contributions to development, women's education and training, and women's income-generation activities.

As anticipated, workshop participants ranged from those with no previous exposure to database searching (or computers of any kind) to those who were accustomed to the concept and capabilities of database searching. That fact, combined with the mixture of subject orientation and professional interests and functions of participants,[3] and the fact that all were on campus for only a short time, presented challenges to the librarian on the workshop planning team. All of these factors had to be considered along with the fact that WID concepts are not always readily apparent to all.

In preparation for the workshop, the WS/WID Librarian consulted with online searchers in the most relevant library units. These included the Reference Department, Government Documents, and the Health Sciences, Labor and Industrial Relations, Agriculture, Home Economics, and Commerce departmental libraries. Samples of the types of questions participants would ask were distributed to each of these units. A library orientation session and tour tailored to the needs of participants were held midway through the first week of the workshop.

For online searching, major thesauri of relevant databases were examined in order to establish a list of terms most parallel to the main issues and concepts of interest to the participants. Thesauri used were for: *LABORDOC, NTIS, AGRICOLA, AGRIS INTERNATIONAL, MEDLINE*, and *CAB ABSTRACTS*. Participants determined their interests through discussion and brainstorming for the first two days of the workshop. One hundred twenty-four terms were gleaned from the various thesauri as most closely reflecting participants' priorities. They ranged from Credit Control to Deforestation to Food Policy to Legal Systems to Urbanization, and Subsistence Farming. A complete list of terms is appended.

THE SEARCHES

Database Searches

The team concept used in the workshop carried through into the searches, with the result that the subjects requested were either an amalgam of individual team members' interests, or represented a compromise that would satisfy the entire team. A typical search for an individual would undoubtedly be much more specific, if not initially, then after the searcher's interview with that individual.

Print Searches

For the sake of comparison, the two main print indexes to women's studies — *Women Studies Abstracts (WSA)* and *Studies on Women Abstracts (SWA)* — were searched. These searches were performed about ten months after the initial online searches, and proceeded as they would for an actual patron. They duplicated, as much as possible, the original search terms and time periods covered.

All Searches

The results of the database searches were analyzed by type of publication, dates covered by the searches, and country of origin of publication. The publications of international agencies were also noted. Because most searchers specifically requested English-only references, language of publication was not noted. The tables relating to the searches indicate the total number of citations on women in developing countries. Of course, far fewer citations were relevant to specific subjects.

Categories of Publications

The usual range occurred: monographs, articles, theses/dissertations, special issues of journals, bibliographies. Working papers, conference papers and reports (usually under 50 pages) were placed in one category, while monographs were identified as book-length publications, usually over 100 pages.

"Relevant" and "Less Relevant"

An item was considered "relevant" if the title and/or abstract indicated that the entire work dealt with the subject being searched. An example is the article entitled "The Value of Work-at-Home and Contributions of Wives' Household Service in Polygymous Families" for the search dealing with quantification of women's contributions.

An item was considered "less relevant" if the abstract indicated that some discussion of the subject was included *inter alia*. The abstract for the monograph, *Aspects of Adult Education* (Madras, 1982), shows that it contains, among other contents notes, "suggestions for creating and implementing programs for rural women." This was categorized as less relevant.

Time Period

For purposes of this paper, only those three years with the highest numbers of publications cited, 1984-1986, were analyzed.

Observation

Parenthetically, a number of citations retrieved on these searches referred to women in more economically developed countries. Although those citations were not counted, it became apparent that some of them dealt with the underclass in "developed" countries and except for geographic location would have had as much relevance to this study as citations referring to developing countries. Some references discussed the upper socio-economic stratum in developing countries, demonstrating additional cross-cultural similarities. Plainly stated, poor women everywhere have basically the same problems.

OTHER SOURCES

In addition to the databases actually used, some new, or relatively unknown, sources that will prove to be of particular interest when searching women internationally are mentioned below.

TABLES

Three tables for the three separate subject searches: quantification of women's contributions, education of women, and income generation have been supplied. They include information gleaned from the original online searches, and our later paper index searches. The tables include the following information:

Relevant: the number of references judged relevant to the topic
Less Relevant: the number of references judged less relevant to the topic
Monographs: the number of references found in monographs
Articles: the number of references found in articles
WP: the number of references found in working papers, conference papers and reports
Theses: the number of theses and dissertations found
Other: other formats (such as manuals, special issues of journals)
WIDC: the number of citations related to women in developing countries, but not necessarily related to the three topics.

The countries of publication and international organizations represented are listed in the appendices.

The tables are based only on references to materials actually published in the three most prolific years of publication, 1984-1986.

QUANTIFICATION OF WOMEN'S CONTRIBUTIONS

The quantification of women's contributions is a fundamental ingredient in development literature. It is especially important in developing countries, where much of women's work remains in the informal sector, including the household, the family farm, and small-scale trading. Until about fifteen years ago, because of a combination of factors (including the status of women), there were no attempts to measure this contribution. More recent attempts at measurement encountered daunting technical difficulties. Now, however, such measurement presents somewhat fewer barriers: time allocation analysis and disaggregation of data by gender are more frequently employed for quantification. In spite of some improvement in actual measurement, quantification is not particularly easy to define, especially for searching purposes. One broad definition is any measure of a woman's contribution, whether to a specific household, or to the local or national economy. The literature goes beyond measurement, of course, and covers such matters as the influence of mechanized agriculture on women's work, and the influence of women's status on types of employment. Thus, there is a broad range of literature which can be related to this topic. When the results of the searches were perused, it was decided to analyze the searches on the basis of the narrowest definition: i.e., the actual process of measuring women's contributions, including the methodology and the results. As a result, few relevant citations were found and the authors opined that the (potential) patrons would be dissatisfied with the number retrieved.

The online searchers selected two databases for this subject: *AGRIS International* and *CAB Abstracts*. *AGRIS International* corresponds in part to *Agrindex*, the monthly from FAO (Food and Agriculture Organization of the United Nations). *CAB Abstracts*, from the Commonwealth Agricultural Bureaux in Great Britain, is particularly strong in international coverage. Both are multi-disciplinary, with *CAB Abstracts* including perhaps more rural sociology and related social science sources.

The following terms were used for both databases:

WOMEN
and FAMILY or HOUSEHOLD or CONTRIBUTION
or ECONOMY or DEVELOPMENT
or ACTIVITY
or TIME USE or ALLOCATION
or NON MARKET EXCHANGE
or UNPAID or OFF FARM EMPLOYMENT or WORK
or HUMAN CAPITAL
or SOCIALIZATION or FAMILY LABOR or LABOUR

In spite of a lack of geographical descriptors, the majority of hits were related to women in developing countries. Studies of women in Bangladesh, India, Ivory Coast, Lebanon, Nepal and the Philippines were cited with reference to time allocation, assessment of women's economic contributions, reevaluation of women's work, family labor allocation, the role of farm women in agriculture, the role of women in household production systems, and concepts and indicators of women's work in Third World agriculture.

Both databases retrieved more working papers, conference pa-

Table 1. Quantification of Women's Contributions. 1984-1986 References

SOURCE	WIDC	RELEVANT	LESS RLVT	MONOGRAPHS	ARTICLES	WP	THESES	OTHER
AGRIS	22	2	4	-	-	5	1	-
CAB	60	9	10	2	8	9	-	-
SWA	30	6	12	7	11	-	-	-
WSA	27	11	6	-	16	1	-	-

pers, and reports than monographs and articles. One conference alone accounted for nine papers.

Women Studies Abstracts is arranged by broad subjects, with a subject index in each issue as well as a cumulated index in the last number of each volume. These sections were determined to be most relevant for the search: "Employment," "Family," and "Finances." Most of the relevant and less relevant citations came from "Employment." Additional entries were found in the index under "Housework," "Labor force participation," "Third World," "Income," "Rural women," and "Farmers." "Work" was the most unproductive term, probably explained by the bias towards Western, or industrialized, countries in the items indexed by *WSA*.

The citations themselves were similar to those retrieved from the online databases: women and household labor, female labor force participation, women's contributions made visible, new approach to women's participation in the economy, women-headed households and poverty, documentation of invisible work of invisible women, women's work doesn't count, women's paid and unpaid labor, unreliable accounting of women's work. Unlike the databases, most of the citations were in the form of articles. Countries and areas covered were Hong Kong, India, Kenya, Lesotho, Nigeria, Sierra Leone, Zambia, and Southern Africa, less developed countries, and developing countries.

Double checking under forty-three geographic or ethnic terms in the cumulated indexes produced no additional citations. There was also spot-checking of subject terms. The term "comparable worth" was a dead end: this has specific significance to the U.S. situation and particularly to legislation and court cases. It may be worth noting that only about one-fourth of the citations in each issue are abstracted. As a result, consulting the subject index is often a matter of blind faith, especially when the subject is not clearly evident from the title.

Studies on Women Abstracts, arranged by articles and books, is best approached through the subject index. Every entry in each issue includes a genuine abstract, thus presenting a more realistic choice to the researcher. The following terms were searched, again in addition to the geographic and ethnic designations:

employment, family, family resources, farm labour, farmers, homemakers, household income, household work, housework, labor force participation, labour, rural family, rural society, rural women, Third World development, work.

In the 1984 volume, eight of these terms appeared in the index, and they led to eighty-nine entries. Only two were considered relevant, and five less relevant. Even though most entries were indexed both by subject and geographically, we double checked fifty-one geographical headings which contained seventy-six entries. Two additional relevant citations were found, and five less relevant. However, it must be said that the time and effort expended to retrieve these few was compensated for by the richness of the abstracts.

EDUCATION OF WOMEN

This subject is so broad that normally an online searcher—and a paper-index searcher as well!—would not proceed before narrowing it considerably. However, the team approach to these searches, alluded to earlier, undoubtedly played a major part in these general conceptions of searches, and in the willingness of the online searchers to attempt them. Actually, the participants placed geographical limits on the searches, which proved to be of considerable benefit. But because of the extraordinary breadth of the topic, no attempt was made to define it for the paper searches or for analyzing results of the online searchers. The citations retrieved presented, of course, a panorama of education in all its aspects and levels.

Online searches were conducted on *ERIC* and on *LABORDOC*. *ERIC* was chosen for its obvious emphasis on education, and *LABORDOC* for its inclusion of women, and especially because of its international emphasis as the database of the International Labour Organization. Two work groups searched this topic. One had the broadest request: "Education of women, especially in Asia." This group searched *ERIC* on CD ROM. We found five relevant and six less relevant citations out of a total of eighteen from the 1984-1986 period. There were references to literacy, non-formal or adult or lifelong education, women in higher education, impact of education on women, and statistical data.

The second group used geographic identifiers: "Education of women in Australia, Kenya, Tanzania, Sudan." *LABORDOC* was used for this, yielding only ten less relevant citations. The search was interesting for a number of reasons. First, the search strategy entailed the following terms:

1. **ACCESS TO EDUCATION**
2. **EDUCATION OF WOMEN**
3. **TRAINING OPPORTUNITY or EDUCATIONAL OP-PORTUNITY**
4. **EDUCATIONAL POLICY**
5. **VOCATIONAL EDUCATION**
6. **KENYA or TANZANIA or SUDAN or AUSTRALIA**
7. **ARAB or SWAHILI or ENGLISH**
   (1 or 2 or 3 or 4 or 5) and (6 and 7).

By an oversight, women was not used as "and" but as "or," which explains the lack of relevancy to women in so many of the citations. By the same token, the citations were helpful in some-times negative ways. For instance, EDUCATIONAL POLICY never led to gender-specific references, but included several cita-tions to national development plans—which says a lot about who and what has not been thought of at national planning levels. Be-cause one of the team members is Australian, "Australia" was in-cluded in the search terms, which led to numerous citations that cannot be construed as related to women in "developing" coun-tries. On the other hand, references to a "developed" country served to emphasize the obvious: when there is lack of educational opportunity, women everywhere are usually included or at least im-plied in the discussion. Studies of women in engineering, though, are more likely to concern women in Western countries than in Asia, Latin America, or Africa—although even in this case there are exceptions. Studies about women and employment often in-clude discussion of access to education, so that by implication a search of women and employment might well result in additional, useful citations. One of the most relevant citations dealt with the

Table 2. Education of Women. 1984-1986 References

SOURCE	WIDC	RELEVANT	LESS RLVT	MONOGRAPHS	ARTICLES	WP	THESES	OTHER
ERIC[1]	29	5	6	4	6	1	-	-
LABORDOC[2]	17	-	10	6	2	1	-	*
SWA[1]	18	8	7	4	11	-	-	-
SWA[2]	13	8	5	1	12	-	-	-
WSA[1]	18	3	12	1	14	-	-	-

Notes

[1]Searches for Education, especially in Asia

[2]Searches for Education in four specific countries

* Includes one special issue of a journal

329

design of educational programs for the social and economic promotion of rural women in India and Tanzania.

Again, the paper indexes were time- and patience-consuming. For "Education, especially in Asia," *WSA* was searched in the "Education and Socialization" section and all its cross references. Further, the index was perused for appropriate geographical terms: Bangladesh, China, India, Korea, Malaysia, Philippines, Sri Lanka, Taiwan, Thailand, and Asia, East Asia, South Asia, and South East Asia. This meant, for example, that in the 1986 volume a total of 317 entries were searched: 160 in the education section, 118 cross references, and thirty-nine geographical terms in the index. The index terms led only to seven that were not found already under "education." Actually, three were in "education," but had been overlooked because there were no abstracts. The remaining four were classified in other sections and, with no abstract, one could only guess that they were less relevant.

The mix of subjects reflected the wide range of education-related research: adult education of women in rural North India, attitude towards women's literacy in Punjab, study habits and underachievement of rural girls in India, interest patterns of highly and poorly adjusted college girls. The following were judged not relevant: studies of creativity in relation to sex, development of moral judgment in boys and girls, image of Indian women in language textbooks.

Studies on Women Abstracts was searched for both education topics. For the first, more general search ("Education of women, especially in Asia"), the geographical index terms were searched first, and thirteen items were retrieved; three more were found under education, and about four were found both ways. This search was particularly rewarding in numbers of relevant and less relevant items.

For the topic of education narrowed to four countries, the success is somewhat muted by the inclusion of Australia. This search led to: relevance of schooling to jobs; feminization of teaching; enrollment in higher education; educational attainment and status; teaching of women's studies; relationship of gender, schools and jobs; and, for Australia: selection of school principals; women's studies in social work education; development of professional women; technical and further education; university admission.

INCOME GENERATION

One of the most essential concepts of WID is the generation of income. Here too, interpretation of the term is not simple. In the most narrow sense it means discussion of specific activities or projects designed to produce income for women in developing countries. For purposes of this paper it has been interpreted to refer to any type of activity in which women participate which brings income into the home, including employment.

Online databases searched for this topic were *AGRICOLA, AGRIS,* and *CAB Abstracts.* As the table of searches shows, *CAB Abstracts* was the most useful source. Terms used for *CAB Abstracts* and *AGRIS International* were:

INCOME
FAMILY BUDGET
HOUSEHOLD?
HOME ECONOMICS
LIVING EXPENDITURES
LIVING STANDARDS
OFF-FARM INCOME
OFF-FARM EMPLOYMENT
CREDIT??
BANKING
EXTENSION
APPROPRIATE TECHNOLOGY
PROJECT APPRAISAL
PILOT PROJECT?
RURAL WOMEN
FARM
FARMING
FARMS

Records retrieved were further restricted to include the term WOMEN for more specificity.

Table 3. Income Generation. 1984-1986 References

SOURCE	WIDC	RELEVANT	LESS RLVT	MONOGRAPHS	ARTICLES	WP	THESES	OTHER
AGRICOLA	146	8	12	1	2	16	-	*
AGRIS	104	38	24	13	9	37	1	**
CAB	56	24	11	7	4	22	-	-
SWA	190	7	8	5	10	-	-	-
WSA	167	4	7	1	9	1	-	-

Notes

* Chapter of a book

** One special issue of a journal; one manual

Search terms used in *AGRICOLA* were:

RURAL DEVELOPMENT – ECONOMIC ASPECTS
HOUSEHOLD INCOME
FEMALE LABOR
WOMEN – EMPLOYMENT
EMPLOYED WOMEN
EARNED INCOME
WOMEN IN AGRICULTURE
FARM INCOME
RURAL WOMEN
ENTREPRENEURSHIP
RURAL WOMEN, EMPLOYMENT

Workshop participants seemed quite happy with the results of these searches. It is noteworthy that there was very little overlap of citations among these three databases.

For this topic, a careful search through *WSA* for 1984/85 yielded 167 citations to women in developing countries. Four were considered relevant and seven less relevant. Items relevant to income generation were found under the following index terms: economic development, income, economic planning, blue collar workers, market women, and rural women. Additional relevant citations were found under Nigeria. We note that it took searches under seven different headings to arrive at eleven references.

Other terms leading to citations relevant to income generation but not published between 1984-1986 were: developing countries, economic development, Third World, income, economic planning, and other geographic and ethnic designations.

The 1984-86 volumes for *SWA* yielded 190 citations to items on women in developing countries. Seven were relevant and eight less relevant. The most useful headings in the index included: rural development, rural women, and Third World development. Although "income generating projects" was an index term, it generated only one match for the three year period. Geographic or ethnic group designations leading to relevant items were: Africa, India, Kenya, Egypt, Nigeria, and Arabs. (These last items were accessible only through these headings.) We searched ten terms for fifteen successful matches. Other terms yielding references relevant to the topic but not published in the time period selected were: agriculture, developing countries, development programs, and property.

OTHER SOURCES

There are other specialized tools, not used in this study, which are useful for research on women in developing countries.

IDRC

The International Development Research Centre (IDRC) in Ottawa, Canada, maintains a Development Data Bases service that includes eleven separate databases on its *MINISIS* system. This includes five databases produced by IDRC, five from international organizations such as FAO, and *IDRIS* (Inter-agency Development Research Information System), containing project information from several participating donor agencies, including IDRC.

Briefly, the first group, produced by IDRC, includes: *ACRONYM* (information on organizations related to the interests of IDRC); *BIBLIOL* (primarily technical and scientific research including development aid and women in international development); *DEVSIS* (Development Sciences Information System: literature produced in Canada about economic and social aspects of Third World development), *NRG* (specializing in energy problems facing developing countries), and *SALUS* (mostly low-cost rural health care and health staff power training in developing countries).

Databases from the United States Agency for International Development (USAID); Food and Agriculture Organization of the United Nations (FAO); International Labour Organization (ILO); United Nations Educational, Scientific, and Cultural Organization (UNESCO); and the U.N. Industrial Development Organization (UNIDO) constitute the second category of databases available through IDRC.

IDRIS consists of factual information on research activities located in or concerned with developing countries and funded or coordinated by any of seven cooperating organizations. These organizations are essentially science- and technology-oriented agencies in the U.S., Canada, Japan, Sweden, and West Germany. (Sweden and Japan have two participating organizations each.)

A subject search for Income Generation through the *USAID* database yielded eight relevant citations for items published between 1984 and 1986 out of a total of twenty-nine for 1978-1987. The same search through IDRC's library database *BIBLIOL* yielded eight hits for 1984-1986 out of a total of fifty-four published from 1970 to date.

Again, there was almost no duplication of hits between these and the other databases used for this study.

IRPD

Another online database useful for WID research is the *International Rural Projects Database (IRPD)* of the Settlement Study Centre (SSC) in Rehovot, Israel. It accesses primarily "fugitive" or nonconventional literature such as reports related to rural regional development plans, programs, and projects in Africa, Asia, the Middle East, Latin America, and the Caribbean. This Centre's collection is a collaborative effort with a development research organization in West Germany.

WISTAT

The United Nations' *Women's Indicators and Statistics (WISTAT)* is a new database available on microcomputer diskettes. It consists of detailed national statistics for a total of 178 countries and areas, that are available through the U.N. Secretariat, U.N. regional commissions, and specialized agencies (ILO, FAO, UNESCO, and the World Health Organization). The data are arranged by nine subject fields. Dates of coverage are roughly 1970 to 1985.

IDB

The Center for International Research of the U.S. Bureau of the Census has a database currently available only on magnetic tape called *"International Database (IDB)."* It contains demographic, economic and social statistics on all countries of the world. The data are based on census surveys and other studies conducted by host countries from about 1950 to the present. Data are nearly all analyzed by age and sex, but clearly coverage of developing countries is spotty because of wide variations between countries on when and whether national or sub-national surveys are or were made. Access to data on women is also indirect.

Agencies that are sources for *IDB* are the Bureau itself, national statistical offices, the U.N., ILO, UNESCO, WHO, World Bank, International Monetary Fund, and the Organization of European Cooperation and Development.

WOMEN'S DATABASE

A new, excellent paper source is *Base de Datos Mujer = Women's Data Base*, compiled and published by the ISIS International office in Santiago, Chile. It accesses their computerized database of information from their global network of over 10,000, mostly grassroots, contacts. The arrangement, including the indexing, is superb. The index contained terms identical to two of our searches: "income generating projects" and "women's economic contribution." On the subject "income generating projects" alone, seven relevant citations are listed. This index is especially important because it accesses material produced by grassroots groups which both online and print sources currently exclude. At this writing, only the initial issue (no. 1/2, 1988) was available to us.

OTHER INDEXES

Indexes which focus on geographical areas which include developing countries and women have not been mentioned, but should not be ignored. Two of these are *International African Bibliography* (London) and *HAPI* (Hispanic American Periodicals Index).

CONCLUSIONS

Online databases have the ability to provide access using an almost limitless number of terms, in many permutations and combinations. Print indexes, on the other hand, can approach this depth and breadth of coverage only when every citation is well abstracted and well indexed and when the researcher is prepared to invest a great deal of time and patience.

As one might expect, the online databases seem to do a far better job at retrieving conference papers, reports, and working papers. There is still a great deal of feminist scholarship and women's publications accessible only through the women's studies print tools. Therefore, these search aids are still vital to anyone seriously researching WID.

Far less obvious but still vital to the researcher are two facts. There is very little overlap between the databases searched and the women's studies print indexes. (Of the 141 journal titles retrieved, only twenty appeared in two sources, and only three in three sources.) This finding speaks to the remarkable growth of WID literature. In addition, the online databases used in this study appear not to include at least some of the most important producers of WID information: International Women's Tribune Center (IWTC) in New York, and ISIS International, headquartered in Carouge, Switzerland.

The fact that the print indexes in some cases contain more total citations on women in developing countries but fewer relevant citations in all likelihood means only that they cover the subject "women" more thoroughly but not some of the disciplines involved in WID. Conversely, some of the disciplines covered by the databases do not at this time publish as much on "women" or on gender as a factor of analysis as they might.

Because the field of Women in International Development is still so new, the main women's studies indexes have not yet developed the vocabulary necessary to access WID references. While these indexes are invaluable at including non-trade materials such as those of the IWTC and ISIS, they would do well to adopt more terms from the *Women's Thesaurus* produced by the National Council for Research on Women and the Business and Professional Women's Foundation (New York, 1987), and to establish better contact with the WID community. Online databases might include more feminist scholarship.

Likewise, readers must be aware of the vocabulary already in use. This applies not only to subjects but to geographic (or economic) terms: LDC (less developed country), Third World, developing countries, etc. Searchers need to be aware of the broad range of kinds of groups producing WID literature and take appropriate steps.

The potential for excellent coverage of women in international development may soon be achieved. The *Women's Data Base* from ISIS signals the earnest beginning of this expansion. It also appears that the traditional databases and the women's studies print tools have already begun to improve their coverage and indexing. The combination of increased research and improved access to it should help in no small way to achieve more lasting, positive impact on public policy in developing countries, and on the state of women.

NOTES

1. Most of the background information on WID as a field is based on Irene Tinker, *The Percy Amendment Promoting Women in Development: Its Origin, Meaning, and Impact* (Washington, D.C.: Equity Policy Center, 1984).

2. Personal conversation with Kate Cloud, Director of the Office of Women in International Development, University of Illinois, Urbana-Champaign, Spring, 1989.

3. It might be of interest to note that half of the participants described themselves as producers of research on women and half as consumers.

REFERENCES

Base de Datos Mujer/Women's Data Base V. 1, no. 1/2 (1988). Santiago: ISIS Internacional, 1988.

Capek, Mary E. S., *A Women's Thesaurus: An Index of Language Used to Describe and Locate Information By and About Women.* New York: Harper & Row, 1987.

HAPI: Hispanic American Periodicals Index. Los Angeles: UCLA Latin America Center, 1974—.

International African Bibliography. London: Mansell, Vol. 1, 1971—.

APPENDIX I: DATABASE SEARCH TERMS
Prepared for workshop Women, Households and Development:
Building a Database
UIUC July, 1988

Adult Education
Africa
Aggregate Data
Aging
Agricultural Banks
Agricultural Development
Appropriate Technology
Asia
Banks
Caribbean
Central America
Child Care
Child Labor
Civil Law
Credit
Credit Control
Credit Policy
Credit Transactions
Data Collecting
Deforestation
Developing Countries
Development Agencies
Development Aid
Development Banks
Development Plans
Development Policies
Development Rights – Uses and Legal Rights
Development Theories
Economic Development
Education
Education Policy
Educational Institutions
Educational Planning

Employment
Energy
Energy Consumption
Energy Policy
Energy Resources
Extension
External Debt
Family Environment
Family Farming
Family Health
Family Income
Family Labour
Family Life
Farming Systems
Female Labour
Field Activity
Food Policy
Foreign Exchange
Foreign Investment
Heads of Households
Health
Health Services
Household Consumption, Income, Expenditure
Housing
Human Resources
Income Distribution
Inheritance (Economics)
International Development Banks
International Loans
International Migration
International Programs
Labour and Employment
Land Ownership
Land Productivity
Land Resources
Land Use
Latin America
Legal Systems

Literacy
Living Conditions
Macro Economics
Maternity Benefits
Micro Economic Analysis
Micro-Environments
Migrants
Migrant Problems
Migrant Programs
Migration (Rural to Urban)
Non-formal Education
Nutrition
Nutrition Education
Nutrition Programs
Nutrition Surveys
Oceania
Off-farm Employment
One-parent Family
Outside Capital
Pilot Projects
Population Control
Poverty and Standard of Living
Project Appraisal
Public Health Legislation
Resource Allocation
Resource Conservation
Resource Development
Rural Areas
Rural Depopulation
Rural Economy
Rural Family
Rural Women
Sanitation
Self-Sufficiency
Social Stratification
South America
Subsistance Farming
Teaching Training

Technological Aid
Technology
Tenure Systems
Training
Unemployment
Unskilled Labor
Urbanization
Vocational Training
Women
Women's Education
Women's Status
Women Workers
Work Studies
World Bank
Work

APPENDIX 2: PERIODICALS AND NEWSPAPERS CITING WOMEN IN DEVELOPING COUNTRIES AND RETRIEVED FROM ONLINE DATABASES

Adult Education and Development (India): ERIC
African Affairs (UK): LABORDOC
Afrika Spectrum (W. Germany): CAB
Agricultural Situation in India: CAB
Agricultural Systems (UK): AGRIS
Agridigest (Pakistan): AGRIS
Ahfad Journal (Sudan): LABORDOC
Anthropological Quarterly (US): CAB
Asian Journal of Dairy Research (India): CAB
ASPBAE Courier (Thailand): ERIC
Aspects of Adult Education (India): ERIC
Australian Bulletin of Labour: LABORDOC
Australian Education Review: LABORDOC
Australian Journal of Social Issues: LABORDOC
Australian Quarterly: LABORDOC
Bangladesh Journal of Agricultural Economics: CAB
Canadian Journal of African Studies: CAB
Canadian Vocational Journal: LABORDOC

CERES: FAO Review on Agriculture and Development (Italy, FAO): AGRIS
Chronicle of Higher Education (US): ERIC
Comparative Education (UK): CAB, ERIC
Convergence (Canada): ERIC
Development Dialogue (Sweden): LABORDOC
East Africa Journal (Kenya): LABORDOC
Eastern Africa Economic Review (Kenya): CAB
Economic and Political Weekly (India): CAB
Economic Development and Cultural Change (US): CAB
Economic Record (Australia): LABORDOC
Education in Asia and Oceania (Thailand, UNESCO): ERIC
Educational Documentation and Information (France, UNESCO): ERIC
Food and Nutrition Bulletin (Italy, FAO): CAB
Grassroots Development (US): AGRICOLA
Higher Education Review (UK): ERIC
Human Ecology (US): CAB
Ideas and Action (Italy, FAO): CAB
IDS Bulletin (UK, Institute for Development Studies, Univ. of Sussex): CAB, LABORDOC
IFDA Dossier (Switzerland): CAB
Impact of Science on Society (UK): ERIC
Indian Journal of Adult Education: ERIC, LABORDOC
Indian Journal of Agricultural Economics: CAB
International Journal of Educational Development (UK): CAB
International Labour Review (Switzerland, ILO): LABORDOC
Journal of African Studies (US): CAB
Journal of Agricultural Economics and Development (Nigeria): AGRIS
Journal of Developing Areas (US): AGRICOLA, LABORDOC
Journal of Eastern African Research and Development (Kenya): CAB, LABORDOC
Journal of Industrial Relations (Australia): LABORDOC
Journal of Modern African Studies (UK): LABORDOC
Journal of Research (India): AGRIS
Journal of Rural Development (India): CAB
Labour and Society (Switzerland, ILO): CAB

Literacy Discussion (Iran): ERIC, LABORDOC
New Frontiers in Education (India): ERIC
Nomadic Peoples (Canada): CAB
On Campus With Women (US): ERIC
Oxford Economic Papers (UK): LABORDOC
Philippine Sociological Review: CAB
Prospects (France, UNESCO): ERIC
Review of African Political Economy (UK): CAB
Rural Africana (US): CAB
Rural Sociology (US): CAB
Selected Bibliography of Educational Materials in Pakistan: ERIC
Social Change (US): CAB
Studies in Adult Education (Tanzania): LABORDOC
UNICEF News (US): ERIC
Vocational Aspects of Education (UK): LABORDOC
WID Forum (US): CAB

APPENDIX 3: PERIODICALS AND NEWSPAPERS CITING WOMEN IN DEVELOPING COUNTRIES AND RETRIEVED FROM PAPER INDEXES

Africa (UK): SWA, WSA
Ahfad Journal (Sudan): SWA
American Economic Review (US): WSA
American Anthropologist (US): WSA
American Journal of Clinical Nutrition (US): WSA
American Journal of Physical Anthropology (US): SWA
American Sociological Review (US): SWA
Archives of Sexual Behavior (US): WSA
Australian Journal of Education: SWA
Australian Social Work: SWA
Canadian Journal of African Studies: WSA
Capital and Class (US): SWA
Chronicle of Higher Education (US): WSA
*Commerce; A Weekly Review of Indian Financial, Commercial
    and Industrial Progress*: WSA
Community Development Journal: SWA
Comparative Education Review (US): WSA

Connexions (US): SWA
Demography (India): WSA
Discourse (Australia): SWA
Economic and Political Weekly (India): WSA
Economic Development and Cultural Change (US): WSA
Educational Review (India): WSA
Ethnology (US): WSA
Everywoman (UK): SWA
Feminist Issues (US): SWA, WSA
Frontiers (US): WSA
Harvard Women's Law Journal (US): SWA
L'Homme (France): WSA
IDS Bulletin (UK, Institute for Development Studies, Univ. of Sussex): SWA
Indian Educational Review: WSA
Indian Journal of Adult Education: SWA
Indian Journal of Industrial Relations: WSA
Indian Psychological Review: WSA
Industrial Relations (US): WSA
Insurgent Sociologist (US): SWA
International Journal of Educational Development (UK): SWA
International Journal of Women's Studies (Canada): SWA, WSA
International Migration Review (US): SWA
ISIS Women's International Journal (UK): SWA
Journal of Education and Psychology (India): WSA
Journal of Family Welfare (India): WSA
Journal of Indian Education: WSA
Journal of Marriage and the Family (US): WSA
Journal of Peasant Studies (UK): SWA
Journal of Personality and Social Psychology (US): WSA
Journal of Southern African Studies (UK): SWA
Mankind Quarterly (US): WSA
Media Report on Women (US): WSA
National Women's Studies Association Newsletter (US): WSA
New Direction for Women (US): WSA
Off Our Backs (US): SWA, WSA
Open Learning (UK): SWA
Perceptual and Motor Skills (Philippines): WSA

Population (US): WSA
Population Studies (UK): WSA
Public Administration and Development (UK): SWA
al-Raida (Lebanon): SWA
Resources for Feminist Research (Canada): WSA
Review of African Political Economy (UK): SWR
Rural Sociology (US): SWA
Sex Roles (US): WSA
Signs (US): WSA
Social Action (India): SWA, WSA
Social Biology (India): WSA
Social Science Journal (US): WSA
Social Science and Medicine (UK): SWA
Social Scientist (India): WSA
Spare Rib (UK): SWA
Studies in Family Planning (US): SWA, WSA
This Magazine (Canada): WSA
UNICEF News (US): WSA
Unicorn (Australia): SWA
USA Today: WSA
Victorian TAFE Papers (Australia): SWA
Womanspeak (Australia): SWA
Women and Environments (US): WSA
Women and Politics (US): WSA
Women's Studies International Forum (UK): SWA, WSA
Women's World (Switzerland): WSA

APPENDIX 4: OTHER SERIES RETRIEVED

AGRICOLA
Working papers. (Office of WID, Michigan State University, U.S.)

AGRIS
FAO Economic & Social Development Series (Italy)
FAO, RAPA Monograph (Italy)
FAO Regional Office for Latin America & the Caribbean. Report (Chile)
FAO World Food Project. Occasional Papers (Italy)

Swedish International Development Authority. SIDA Evaluation
  Report
Women, Work & Development (ILO, Switzerland)
Working papers. (Office of WID, Michigan State University,
  U.S.)

CAB
Estudios sociales (Venezuela)
FAO Economic & Social Development Series (Italy)
PanAfrican Institute for Development. Organization &
  Management of Development Series (Cameroon).
Working papers. (Office of WID, Michigan State University,
  U.S.)

APPENDIX 5: COUNTRIES OF PUBLICATION

Australia: LABORDOC, SWA
Austria: LABORDOC
Bangladesh: AGRIS, CAB
Barbados: CAB
Cameroon: CAB
Canada: CAB, ERIC, LABORDOC, SWA, WSA
Chile: AGRIS, CAB
China: AGRIS
Colombia: AGRICOLA, CAB
Costa Rica: AGRIS, CAB
Denmark: CAB
Egypt: CAB
Ethiopia: AGRICOLA, LABORDOC
Finland: CAB
France: ERIC, LABORDOC, WSA
Honduras: AGRIS
India: AGRICOLA, AGRIS, CAB, ERIC, LABORDOC, SWA,
  WSA
Indonesia: AGRIS
Iran: ERIC, LABORDOC
Italy: AGRIS, CAB
Japan: WSA
Kenya: AGRIS, CAB, LABORDOC

Lebanon: CAB, LABORDOC, SWA
Malaysia: AGRIS, WSA
Nepal: AGRIS
Netherlands: CAB
Nigeria: AGRIS, CAB
Pakistan: AGRIS, ERIC
Philippines: AGRIS, CAB, WSA
Senegal: CAB
South Korea: ERIC
Sri Lanka: CAB, ERIC
Sudan: LABORDOC, SWA
Sweden: AGRIS, LABORDOC
Switzerland: AGRIS, CAB, LABORDOC, SWA, WSA
Tanzania: LABORDOC
Thailand: AGRIS, CAB, ERIC, LABORDOC, SWA, WSA
Tunisia: AGRIS
Uganda: LABORDOC
United Kingdom: AGRICOLA, AGRIS, CAB, ERIC, LABORDOC, SWA
United States: AGRICOLA, CAB, ERIC, LABORDOC, SWA, WSA
Venezuela: CAB
West Germany: CAB, ERIC, LABORDOC
Zambia: CAB

APPENDIX 6: ADDRESSES FOR OTHER SOURCES

International Data Base (IDB)
Center for International Research
Bureau of the Census
Scuderi Bldg., Room 409
Washington, D.C. 20233

International Development Research Centre Library
250 Albert Street
P.O. Box 8500
Ottawa
Canada K1G 3H9

Base de Datos Mujer/Women's Data Base
Isis Internacional
Casilla 2067
Correo Central 2067
Santiago
Chile

International Rural Projects Data Base (IRPD)
Settlement Study Centre
P.O.B. 2355
Rehovot 76120
Israel

Women's Indicators and Statistics Data Base (WISTAT)
United Nations Statistical Office, Room DC2-1584
New York, N.Y. 10017

Women's Studies
Curriculum Materials Online

Lucinda Rhea Zoe

SUMMARY. This article reviews a selection of databases and fields of study in terms of the impact that "mainstreaming" and feminist scholarship have had on the disciplines, rather than a detailed analysis and evaluation of each database regarding women's studies curriculum materials. The article attempts to determine the degree to which women's studies has been integrated into the academic disciplines and whether or not this integration is reflected in online sources. It covers new approaches and reports of current developments within selected disciplines and not what is available in the traditional women's studies literature. The intention here is to look specifically at articles, reports and classroom materials that deal exclusively with women's studies and curriculum development.

This article reviews a selection of databases and fields of study in terms of the impact that "mainstreaming" and feminist scholarship have had on the disciplines, rather than a detailed anaylsis and evaluation of each database regarding women's studies curriculum materials. Mainstreaming is the effort to incorporate fully the substance of women's studies into other disciplines and essentially entails full inclusion of women's studies in all teaching, scholarship and research. Within the women's studies community, the concept of mainstreaming is regarded as a key issue to be resolved. While advocates claim it will transform the curriculum radically, others are skeptical and concerned that it will diminish the political and

Lucinda R. Zoe is Assistant Director of the Center for Business and Economic Research and Instructor in the Graduate College of Library and Information Science at the University of Kentucky, Lexington, KY 40506-0270. She teaches Research Methods and Information for Women's Studies.

351

intellectual power of women's studies as a discipline in itself. The current sentiment is that women's studies needs both its own independent structures and courses as well as extensive mainstreaming projects.[1] An attempt is made to determine the degree to which women's studies has been integrated into the academic disciplines, and whether or not this integration is reflected in online sources.

CURRENT STATUS OF WOMEN'S STUDIES CURRICULUM MATERIALS

The best sources of information on curriculum materials — bibliographies, syllabi, and guides to the literature in women's studies — are to be found in journals that discuss the discipline of women's studies. The great majority of these journals and feminist periodicals are not covered in most traditional abstracting and indexing services and therefore are not machine-accessible. Since the only abstract devoted solely to women's studies materials, *Women's Studies Abstracts* and *Studies on Women Abstracts* are not available online, it seems pointless to do a serious analysis of relevant databases searching for such materials. There are, however, at least four scholarly indexing and abstracting services online that do cover a few of the major feminist and women's studies journals: *Psychological Abstracts, Social Science Citation Index, Sociological Abstracts*, and *ERIC*.[2] In fact, since 1973 *Sociological Abstracts* has included a section of feminist studies in each issue, which is available online. Several of these databases will be reviewed, along with a number of other subject-specific databases, for information on women's studies curricula.

The concept of integrating women's studies into the curriculum and the identification of acceptable materials for this endeavor are problematic and complex. For some, it is simply a matter of locating women-related materials for use in courses in order to include the thoughts and experience of women into the specific courses. It must be noted and emphasized, however, that materials by and about women are not always feminist or considered to be appropriate women's studies material. Many of these materials reflect a male bias in the conceptualization of the questions guiding the research or in the methods of data collection and continue to omit, distort, trivialize or misrepresent women, regardless of the gender of the author.

For others, the concept of integrating women's studies into the curriculum is more pedagogical in nature and involves a radical transformation in the classroom, requiring more theoretical materials, and fewer prearranged "how-to" materials. Many scholars have come to see that true curriculum integration cannot be developed without taking a much closer look at teaching methods and the presentation of knowledge in the classroom. Others are looking for materials to guide them through institutional transformations, which might include information on strategies for developing programs of activities for faculty and implementing university-wide projects. Project directors and individual faculty who have worked in this area report that the task of integrating women's studies into their curriculum in any form is more complex and explosive than anticipated. One finds that, in addition to examining the role of gender within their discipline, they are also required to analyze the structures on which their disciplines were built.[3] Women's studies curriculum materials cover a wide range of possible sources, from subject specific bibliographies to syllabi, to theoretical articles on feminist pedagogy, to materials by and about women. To assess the current status of accessible materials online, it is necessary to focus efforts in one particular area — specifically, materials exclusively on women's studies and the curriculum.

SCOPE OF WORK

This article focuses on new approaches and reports of what is currently happening within selected disciplines, rather than what is available in the traditional women's studies literature. The intention here is to look specifically at articles, reports and classroom materials that deal exclusively with women's studies and curriculum development. The purpose is two-fold: (1) to determine to what extent women's studies has been integrated, or "mainstreamed," into the disciplines and (2) to determine what material is accessible online.

For example, if management or economics professors are looking for innovative ideas for integrating women into their curricula and search online in their subject databases, what are they likely to find?

After ten years of curriculum integration and mainstreaming projects, with close to 350 women's studies programs and some 20,000 courses across the country, not to mention an explosion of new scholarship on women, what will the professors find when they do an online search of the *Economic Literature Index*, which has indexed over 260 economic journals since 1969? Has feminist scholarship actually been integrated into the discipline and will an online search provide any articles or reports from scholars or project directors on transforming the classroom? Will there be any mention of innovative syllabi or suggested course materials? Will "women's studies" be used as a descriptor in the databases in the field of economics? Another reason for this approach to examining women's studies curriculum materials online is that basic information "by and about women" that one might seek for use in the classroom is being covered in-depth in other sections of this collection. It seems unnecessary to duplicate the efforts of other contributors in this regard. Finally, it is the intention of this article not only to assess the availablity and inclusion of curriculum materials in online sources, but also to provide a current selected bibliography of standard printed sources and references on integrating women's studies into the curriculum. In this way, this contribution can serve as a guide to the best overall sources of information for women's studies curriculum materials and function as a reference tool.

METHODOLOGY

Eleven databases were chosen to evaluate for this project. Several are subject specific, such as *Management Contents, Economic Literature Index, PsycINFO, Library and Information Science Abstracts (LISA)*, and *Historical Abstracts*, while others cover a broader range of disciplines in the social and behavorial sciences such as *ERIC, Books in Print, Social Scisearch, Sociological Abstracts* and *American History and Life (AHL)*. These databases were selected to provide insight into specific disciplines concerning the degree to which women's studies has been integrated, and to identify advances made in terminology and access in the more comprehensive social science databases in which women's studies is presumed to have had a more direct impact.

The basic free-text search strategy used was simple and direct, and it was used in all eleven databases, with a few exceptions. Searches using "girls" or "female" or even "education of" women were not performed because part of this exercise was to determine the impact of over a decade of feminist scholarship and mainstreaming projects on the language and terminology used in the online sources. "Feminist" or "feminism" were not used as part of the basic search strategy in order to keep the search simple and focused. Both "women" and "curriculum" were truncated in order to pull up any variation of the terms used in a database.

(wom?n? OR wom?n?(w)studies) AND curricu?

In some cases the strategy, [**women OR women(w)studies AND curricu?**], was used as a descriptor in some large sets to focus the search and to see which databases even used "women's studies" as a descriptor. In each case, however, it was possible to determine the number of times "women's studies" appeared at all, as well as the number of cites specifically mentioning "women" or "woman" or "women's." In some databases it is necessary to use the (1W) operator, as in "wom?n?(1W)studies," to retrieve the phrase "women's studies." In these few databases the apostrophe is viewed as a single word, therefore requiring the (1W) operator between "women's" and "studies." When results looked suspiciously low, this phrasing was employed. This has been noted in the databases where it must be used. The following analysis of each database details the results of the search and outlines its usefulness as an online source for information on women's studies curriculum. A simple rating scale was used to summarize the results of the search. Each database is rated on a scale of 1-4, with four stars being a very good source – one which uses appropriate terminology and descriptors and retrieves an adequate number of relevant citations; three stars being good – appropriate terminology and some relevant citations; two stars being adequate – a few relevant cites, even if the terminology is not up to date; and one star being inadequate – lack of current terminology and very few relevant hits. The ratings are based on use of terminology and descriptors, and on the number of relevant citations in each database.

ERIC (EDUCATIONAL RESOURCES INFORMATION CENTER)

As the complete database on educational materials from the Educational Resources Information Center, one would expect *ERIC* to yield the most citations and take the lead in providing information on women's studies curriculum materials. Online since 1966, it has approximately 700,000 records and indexes more than 700 periodicals of interest to the education profession. *ERIC* is updated monthly, has a thesaurus, and is available through both DIALOG and BRS.

ERIC is a fertile ground for information. The initial search brought up 1,817 citations, with 1,335 cites that include the phrase "women's studies." To limit the search further the "women's studies" descriptor was ANDed with "curricu?" and yielded 350 cites. When that search was combined with "develop" or "development" the results fell to 224 hits. The first 10 citations were all found to be exaclty on target. "Women's Studies" is used as a descriptor, along with "Women's Education." Since both descriptors contain "womens" with no apostrophe, truncating when searching this file is suggested. A sampling of citations include: "Moving Our Minds: Studying Women of Color and Reconstructing Sociology," "Integrating a Feminist Perspective into Family Studies Courses," and "Gender and the Rise of the Novel" with "college curriculum," "course descriptions," and "womens studies" used as descriptors.

This basic search strategy could be limited further to search by subject area, such as sociology or history or economics, and come up with a useful set of resources for curriculum development. This database gets a four star rating **** for its use of terminology and detailed descriptors.

PSYCINFO (PSYCHOLOGICAL ABSTRACTS)

Covering over 1,300 journals, technical reports, conference reports, panel discussions and research from 1967 to present, *PsycINFO* is updated monthly and has over 640,000 records. *PsycINFO* and its corresponding print form *Psychological Abstracts* have a users reference manual and a *Thesarus of Psychological Index Terms*. One would think it would be a rich source of information for integrating women's studies into the discipline of psychology—a field of study that usually has course offerings in many women's studies programs—but it did not prove to be so. The original search netted 284 citations, with 17 references to "women's studies" appearing in the records. There were 24,814 references to cites with "wom?n?" OR "wom?n?(w)studies," and 1,528 of those cites used one of the terms as a descriptor. When limiting by descriptor and ANDing with "curricul?" the result was nine citations. Only two of these nine cites dealt with women's studies and the curriculum. Although "women's studies" was not used as an identifier, "working women," "education," "curriculum programs & teaching methods" and "sex discrimination" were. The cites that came up were acceptable, although a bit disappointing. Sample titles included: "The Mentoring of Nonprofessional Nonmanagerial Women who are Pursuing Upward Career Mobility," and "Into the Mainstream: Equal Educational Opportunity for Working Women."

Has women's studies been successfully integrated into the field of psychology? A quick review of the women's studies journals that are not accessible online would have one believe that there is a lot of scholarship on women in this area. The lack of appropriate descriptors and identifiers, however, and choice of what is covered in this database raises some serious doubts about the success of mainstreaming efforts in the field of psychology. If citations cannot be found in the primary source of bibliographic information—the source that "covers the world's literature in psychology and related disciplines," as it is described in the DIALOG catalog—then one wonders just how seriously the women's studies literature is considered by this discipline. This database gets a two star rating ** for lack of coverage, terminology, and descriptors used for accessing women's studies curriculum development materials.

LIBRARY AND INFORMATION SCIENCE ABSTRACTS (LISA)

Online since 1969, *LISA* provides comprehensive coverage of international materials in the field of library and information science. It is updated monthly from over 550 journals from 60 countries. The subject coverage claims to be wide-ranging and includes library services, electronic publishing, reports, conference proceedings, theses, and related areas such as archives, publishing and bookselling and education. Since there is a Women's Studies Section of the American Library Association, as well as a Feminist Task Force, both of which make significant contributions to the field of women's studies through librarianship, one would expect to see the explosion of library research in the area of women's studies reflected in one of the primary databases of the field.

The original search strategy resulted in only 12 citations. "Wom?n?" was found in the basic index 561 times and "wom?n? (w)studies" was found only twice. However, when using the (1W) operator between "wom?n?" and "studies" 79 references were retrieved. In *LISA* it is necessary to use "wom?n?(1W)studies" when searching for women's studies materials. When ANDing these 79 references with "curricul?" it resulted in only one citation. This one cite was relevant, but the meager results are hardly acceptable considering the work that is currently going on in this field. Other semi-relevant titles from the initial search were "Indexing of Feminist Periodicals" and "A Feminist Researchers's Guide to Periodical Indexes, Abstracting Services, Citation Indexes, and Online Databases." A second search of [**wom?n? and curricu?**] yielded 12 citations, five of which were relevant. Although retrieving citations to reference works demonstrates this discipline is engaged in producing some tools for use in women's studies, there were no citations directly related to integrating women's studies into the library science curriculum.

Searching *LISA* for curricular materials on women's studies was not very productive, although "women's studies" is used as a descriptor. Any effort at mainstreaming women's studies into library education is not reflected in this source of information, leading one to believe that, in fact, it has not been a successful venture. This database gets a two star rating ** for lack of citations and depth of coverage on women's studies in library education.

MLA BIBLIOGRAPHY

The MLA database, produced annually by the Modern Language Association, provides online access to the bibliography of humanistic studies. It indexes books and journal articles published on the modern languages, literature, and linguistics. Coverage begins in 1964 and includes over 1 million records with annual updates. The *MLA Bibliography* has 9,530 references to [wom?n?] in the basic index and 39 with "women's studies." When limited by descriptor, the number of references fell to 5,891. With 217 references to "curricul?," the total number of hits from the original search was seven. All seven citations were relevant hits, including one on "Changing Curricular Assumptions: Teaching and Studying Women's Literature from a Regional Perspective," and "Curriculum and Response: A Study of the Images of Black Women in Black Fiction." Although "women's studies" was not listed as a descriptor for any of these particular cites, it is used as a descriptor in the database as evidenced by the original search. Other appropriate descriptors included, "women writers," "black women," "feminist literary theory," and "curriculum." This database gets a 3 star rating *** for use of current terms and descriptors and for having at least four useful citations on women's studies and curriculum development.

HISTORICAL ABSTRACTS

Online since 1973, *Historical Abstracts* is updated quarterly and has close to 300,000 records. It abstracts and indexes the world's periodical literature in history and the related social sciences and humanities with articles abstracted from over 2,000 journals from

90 countries in some 30 languages. The database corresponds to two companion publications, *Historical Abstracts PART A, Modern History Abstracts*, and *PART B, Twentieth-Century Abstracts*. The original search strategy retrieved a total of 20 citations. "Women" appeared 6,644 times, "women's studies" 14 times, and when limited by descriptor the result was 4,394.

Ten of the 20 references were printed, and each one was a relevant hit. Although there were no references to current articles by feminist historians about "transforming the classroom" (and we know they are out there), these cites did provide good information on the history of women and education as it relates to the curriculum. Sample cites were: "Teaching and Women's Work: A Comparative Historical and Ideological Analysis," "Placing Women in the High School European Curriculum," and "Women's History in Newly Regulated Higher Education." This database gets a three star rating *** for use of women as a descriptor and for providing reference to a reasonable number of acceptable women's studies curriculum materials.

AMERICA: HISTORY AND LIFE (AHL)

AHL is updated three times a year with coverage from 1964 to the present. With close to 250,000 records, it abstracts and indexes over 2,000 journals in the sciences and the humanities in addition to monographs and dissertations that cover U.S. and Canadian history and current affairs. This database brought up a surprising number of excellent citations, with a total of 117 hits from the original search. Both women and women's studies are used as descriptors. There were 10,217 references to "women" and 115 to "women's studies." When limited by descriptor, this set resulted in 7,380. By combining the descriptor set with curricul?/DE, the net result was 60. By limiting the search further, using "curricul?/DE" as a descriptor and combining it with "develop" or "development," six very specific and useful citations were retrieved on women's studies and curriculum development. All six cites were right on target. Sample titles included "Operating by Consensus: The Collective

Approach to Women's Studies," "The Paradox of Intention and Effect: A Women's Studies Course," and "Courses on Women and Politics." *AHL* gets a four star rating **** for use of current and accessible terms and descriptors and for being a rich source for curriculum materials.

BOOKS IN PRINT (BIP)

With over 1 million records, *BIP* covers in-print and forthcoming books and is updated monthly. This file corresponds to several print publications produced by R.R. Bowker, mainly *Books in Print, Subject Guide to Books in Print* and *Paperbound Books in Print.* The database provides the record of current, forthcoming and out-of-print scientific, scholarly, technical, medical and popular books as well as children's books. A search of "women's studies" pulled up only eight citations, but the original search resulted in 13 hits. When limiting the "women set" by descriptor and ANDing with "Curricul?," the result was 11 citations. All 11 cites were useful and included specific references to books exclusively on integrating women's studies into the curriculum. Sample references included *Feminist Resources for Schools & Colleges: A Guide to Curricular Materials, Integrating Women's Studies into the Curriculum: A Guide and Bibliography,* and *Women's Place in the Academy: Transforming the Liberal Arts Curriculum.*

"Women's studies" is used as a major subject heading, as well as "education of women" and "woman." Some odd discrepancies appear in this database. For example, when the eight original results of the search using the term "women's studies" were printed, not a one of the books on integrating women's studies into the curriculum was included, although they all had the term in the title as well as in the subject heading field. In fact, there are more than 13 books in print on women's studies and the curriculum. When searching this database, it might be necessary to use the (1W) operator to pull up all references to women's studies. This database gets a three star rating *** for using women's studies as a major subject heading and for netting a reasonable number of good hits on the subject of cur-

riculum materials. Although any search of *BIP* may leave some
large gaps, it is a good point of departure for a comprehensive
search in any discipline.

MANAGEMENT CONTENTS

Management Contents covers current information on business
and management-related topics from September of 1974 through
the present. It is updated monthly, has close to 300,000 records and
indexes articles from over 120 U.S. and international journals. In
addition to journal articles, *Management Contents* also cites proceedings, transactions, business course materials, newsletters, and
research reports. The basic search of **[women or women studies
and curriculum]** yielded nine citations. Five of them were appropriate for women's studies course material, but none dealt specifically with bringing women's studies into the business classroom.
One interesting citation entitled "A Perspective on Women in Management," from the journal *Collegiate News and Views* (Vol. 35,
No.3, Spr. 1982), states that "Curricula of business schools should
incorporate classes to make the integration of women into management fields easier for men as well as women." Another equally
intriguing citation, "Sex Differences in the Choice of a Male or
Female Career Line," reports the findings of a national longitudinal
study on similarities and differences in social background characteristics, academic ability and work values among women and men in
sex-typical and sex-atypical curriculums. By limiting the "woman
set" by descriptor and ANDing with "curricul?" the results fell to
five.
    The results of the search on *Management Contents* give the im-
pression that this database is not a useful source of information on
the impact of women's studies in the business disciplines. One sus-
pects that there probably is not much information on the subject
anywhere within the business disciplines, leading one to believe
that it has not been successfully "mainstreamed." Otherwise, more
references to specific articles and reports on transforming the business classroom would be available. "Women's studies" did appear
in reference to two cites in the database, but overall access to wom-

en's studies curriculum materials is very limited in this database merits a one star * rating.

ECONOMIC LITERATURE INDEX

This database corresponds to the printed index version of *Journal of Economic Literature* and to the annual *Index of Economic Articles*. The coverage is 1969 to the present, and it has some 165,000 records which are updated monthly. Each year an additional 200 monographs are added to the file along with articles from 260 economic journals. Like the *Management Contents* file, this database did not provide a wealth of information on women or women's studies and curriculum. In fact, the original search did not net a single hit. Whereas "wom?n?(w)studies" pulled up zero references, "wom?n?(1W)studies" retrieved three citations. When searching this database, it is suggested to try all forms of "women's studies" to insure that all bases are covered.

"Women's studies" does not appear as an index term at all, although "feminist" or "feminism" pulled up 13 citations. When combined with "curricul?," it still yielded zero references. [**Women and education**] retrieved a total of 54 hits and, when combined with [**develop or development**] it resulted in four citations, none of which were particularly useful or on target. Two of them might be used as curriculum materials: one article on "Occupational Segregation, Teachers' Wages and American Economic Growth" and another on "The Political Incorporation of Women." There are indeed articles on restructuring the discipline of economics, such as Nancy S. Barrett's "How the Study of Women has Restructured the Discipline of Economics."[4] The economics professor looking for such an article, however, will not find it online in *Economic Literature Index*. Mainstreaming entails the integrating of this literature into the journals of the field and, in the case of economics, it is not apparent. Although work by and about women is being done in economics, it is not getting published in the professional literature and indexed for online retrieval. This database gets a one star * rating for a serious lack of information on the work that is being done in the area of women's studies and curriculum development and for the lack of adequate terminology and descriptors.

SOCIAL SCISEARCH
(SOCIAL SCIENCE CITATION INDEX)

This multidisciplinary database covering every area of the social and behavioral sciences is rich with a variety of information on women's studies and curriculum materials. Coverage begins in 1972, and over 1,500 social science journals throughout the world are indexed. A first run search of **[wom?n OR wom?n(w)studies AND curricul?]** yielded 38 citations. "Women's Studies" appeared in the basic index 227 times, "curricul?" 5,097 times, and "women" 24,443 times. Twenty of the original citations were printed, and all of them relate specifically to the integration of women's studies or women into the curriculum, with such entries as "Placing Women in the Liberal Arts—Stages of Curriculum Transformation," "Mainstreaming the Psychology of Women into the Core Curriculum," "Integrating Material on Women into the Social Work Research," "Integrating Content on Women into the Social-Policy Curriculum—A Continuum Model," and even "A Course Curriculum for Women and the Environment." "Women" and "women's studies" were both used as title word terms. More citations might have been retrieved using alternative terms, such as "women and education" and "development." One might also limit the search by discipline and come up with a more focused list of citations. This database merits a four star **** rating for the number of recall and relevancy resulting from the search.

SOCIOLOGICAL ABSTRACTS

Sociological Abstracts corresponds to the printed index of the same name. This database covers the world's literature in sociology and related disciplines in the social and behavioral sciences. It covers over 1,200 journals in addition to other serial publications, conference reports, case studies, panel discussions and monographs. The coverage is 1963 to the present, and it is updated three times a year. With over 270,000 records, it is a rich source of information for women's studies. In fact, it lists women's studies as one of its major subject areas. The original search resulted in 127 citations. When limiting the "women set" by descriptor and ANDing with "curricul?" the net result dropped to 60. By further limiting "curricul?'' by descriptor, the result was six citations, all of which were excellent. Although the original search pulled up 16 references to "wom?n?(w)studies," when using the (1W) operator 169 references were retrieved. Using only this "women's studies" set and ANDing it with "curricul?" it resulted in 23 citations.

Sample titles from the limited search included "Integrating Content on Women into the Social Policy Curriculum: A Continuum Model," "Student and Faculty Perceptions of Women's Content in the Curriculum," and "Women's Studies Curriculum Development: A View from the United States." "Women's studies," "women" and "women's issues" are all major identifiers, while "women, woman, and female" were all major descriptors. Relevant section headings in the database included "feminist studies" and "feminist/gender studies." This database merits a four star **** rating for use of current and appropriate terms, broad coverage, and high recall and relevancy.

CONCLUSION

Have mainstreaming and feminist scholarship had a visible impact on the disciplines? To what degree has women's studies been fully integrated into all teaching, scholarship and research? Is this reflected in online databases? Even after a decade of rigorous curriculum integration and mainstreaming projects, the answers to these questions are not uniformly positive.

At the request of the Ford Foundation, Formative Evaluation Research Associates (FERA) undertook a study to evaluate the impact of mainstreaming projects. A comparative approach was taken, and five colleges and universities which had mainstreaming projects underway were contrasted with five schools which had not. FERA found that, by and large, new course development and revisions, shifts in research directions, and the acquisition of new resources were the most notable accomplishments of curriculum integration projects. Curricular change varied greatly according to discipline. In areas such as anthropology, English, sociology, and history, faculty noted higher rates of curriculum integration, course change and changes in research than did the faculty in political science, philosophy, business and economics, and biology. In addition, they noted as well that leadership, follow-through and discipline sanction are key characteristics that support or retard efforts for change.[5]

Discipline sanction and follow-through are critical issues with regard to the full inclusion of women and women's studies in all teaching, research and scholarship. If journal editors in the academic mainstream do not consider contributions on women's issues seriously, and thus, do not publish works in these areas, then women's studies will continue to be relegated to the margins of academia, and studies of women will not become established as a part of continuing scholarly traditions. Transformation of the traditional disciplines through full integration of women's studies values and scholarship will not happen without the cooperation of editors, publishers, indexing and abstracting services, and producers of online databases. This article has identified existing gaps in some disciplines. Feminist scholars must continue to write and publish in the women's studies literature, but must pursue vigorously publishing in their mainstream journals as well. Otherwise, the likelihood of material with a feminist perspective becoming accessible through online sources and making its way to the audience which is in most need of it are marginal. If economics professors are transforming their classrooms, their colleagues must become aware of the transformation and be able to find it in their professional literature.

Overall, there is a good deal of women's studies curriculum materials available online. The researcher still must be prepared to access a number of databases as well as search the women's studies literature in printed form to prepare themselves fully for a curriculum integration project. It is recommended that online searchers begin their searches by consulting a thesaurus, if available, and using the EXPAND command on "women" to identify the terms and descriptors in any given database. One should also use both the truncated version of women's studies — (wom?n?(w)studies) — and the version employing the use of the (1W) operator — (wom?n?(1w) studies). By using both versions to create an initial set one is likely to retrieve all forms of the phrase. The searcher should be prepared as well to try a number of variations on "girls" and "females" and "education of women." Other useful search terms for retrieving additional materials are "feminist," "bibliography," "collection" and "resources." The following list of sources represents a basic core bibliography for integrating women into the curriculum. Several of these tools include extensive bibliographies by subject area in addition to model programs, syllabi, teaching methods and recommended approaches for integrating the scholarship and perspectives of women into the curriculum.

NOTES

1. Stimpson, Catharine R. and Cobb, Nina Kressner. *Women's Studies in the United States, A Report to the Ford Foundation* (New York: Ford Foundation, 1986)
2. Detlefsen, Ellen Gay. "Issues of Access to Information About Women," *Women's Collections: Libraries, Archives and Consciousness* (New York: The Haworth Press, 1986)
3. Aiken, Susan Hardy et al. "Trying Transformations: Curriculum Integration and the Problem of Resistance," *SIGNS: Journal of Women in Culture and Society*, (1987, Vol. 12, no 2)
4. Barrett, Nancy S. "How the Study of Women has Restructured the Discipline of Economics." In Langland, Elizabeth and Walter Gove, eds. *A Feminist Perspective in the Academy: The Difference It Makes,* pp. 101-109. (Chicago, IL: The University of Chicago Press, 1981)
5. Formative Evaluation Research Associates (FERA). "Including Women in the Curriculum: A Study of Strategies That Can Make it Happen," Workshop Agenda Proceedings, September 19, 1988. Ann Arbor, MI: FERA, 1988.

SELECTED BASIC BIBLIOGRAPHY

Ballou, Patricia K. *Women: A Bibliography of Bibliographies*. Boston: G.K. Hall, 1980.
Chapman, Anne. *Feminist Resources for Schools and Colleges: A Guide to Curricular Materials* 3rd Ed. New York: Feminist Press, 1986.
Cruikshank, Margaret, ed. *Lesbian Studies, Present and Future*. Old Westbury, NY: The Feminist Press, 1982.
Culley, Margo and Catherine Portuges, eds. *Gendered Subjects: The Dynamics of Feminist Teaching*. Boston, London: Routledge & Kegan Paul, 1985.
Eichler, Margrit. *Nonsexist Research Methods: A Practical Guide*. Boston, MA: Allen and Unwin, Inc., 1988.
Feminist Periodicals: A Current Listing of Contents. Madison, Wisconsin: Office of the University of Wisconsin System Women's Studies Librarian, 1981-.
Franzosa, Susan Douglas and Karen A. Mazza. *Integrating Women's Studies into the Curriculum: An Annotated Bibliography*. Westport, CT: Greenwood Press, 1984.
Fritsche, JoAnn, M., et al. *Toward Excellence & Equity: The Scholarship on Women as a Catalyst for Change in the University* (Orono, ME: University of Maine, 1984)

Loeb, Catherine R., Susan E. Searing, and Esther F. Stineman. *Women's Studies: A Recommended Core Bibliography, 1980-1985*. Littleton, CO: Libraries Unlimited, 1987.

Searing, Susan E. *Introduction to Library Research in Women's Studies*. Boulder, CO: Westview Press, 1985.

Schmitz, Betty. *Integrating Women's Studies into the Curriculum: A Guide and Bibliography* (New York: The Feminist Press, 1985)

Spanier, Bonnie, Alexander Bloom, and Darlene Boroviak, eds. *Toward a Balanced Curriculum: A Sourcebook for Initiating Gender Integration Projects* (Cambridge, MA: Schenkman Publishing, Co., 1984)

SUMMARY OF RESULTS

Database	Recall-- # of Citations Retrieved				Limit/DE	Rating
	wom?n?	curricul?	wom?n? studies	search strategy		
ERIC	20,980	93,237	1,335	1,817	350	4 ****
PsycINFO	24,814	22,332	17	284	9	2 **
LISA	561	2,648	79*	12	--	2 **
MLA Bib	9,530	217	39	7	--	3 ***
Historical Abstracts	6,644	983	14	20	14	3 ***
AHL	10,217	1,658	115	117	60	4 ****
BIP	15,650	1,959	8	13	11	3 ***
Management Contents	5,017	598	2	9	5	1 *
Economic Literature	900	44	3*	0	--	1 *
SSCI	24,443	5,097	227	38	--	4 ****
SOC Abstracts	20,025	1,837	169*	127/23	60/6	4 ****

* In these databases, "women's studies" can be retrieved using the (1w) connector-- wom?n?(1w)studies. In certain databases, the apostrophe is seen as a next word, so one must employ the (1W).

Women in Sport Online

Cheryl Reeves

SUMMARY. The participation of women in sports has increased dramatically over the past decade. This has led to increased interest in women and sports as a topic of research. The *Sport Database* is the only database which specifically deals with sports. Depending on the subtopic involved, other databases could provide relevant citations.

The current women's movement has had a dramatic effect on women's opportunities and achievements in sports. This is evident in the increased number of girls and women participating in all sports at all levels of competition. It is also evident in the amount of money that some women have earned in professional athletics, in the number of women and girls who participate in recreational sports, and in the increased attention paid to women athletes.

Women advanced in sports because of several factors. In the United States, women began to feel that they had just as much right as men to participate in sports at all levels. Women like Billie Jean King, encouraged by women's advances in other occupations, began to insist that professional women athletes have access to prize money comparable to their male counterparts.

Probably the most important factor in increased women's participation in sports was Title IX of the Education Amendments of 1972. This Federal regulation, implemented in 1975, stated that "no person . . . shall, on the basis of sex, be excluded from participation in, be denied the benefits of, or be subjected to discrimination under any education program or activity receiving federal

Cheryl Reeves is Consultant, Deloayza Associates, Altamont, NY 12009.

financial assistance." While Title IX affected all aspects of education, its effect was most apparent in athletics. From 1970 to 1979, for example, the number of female athletes in scholastic competition increased by 570%. In 1970, there were 300,000 girls participating in interscholastic athletics while in 1978 that number was 2 million (*More Hurdles to Clear* 1980).

This increased participation has also led to increased interest in studying and conducting research on women and sports. Many schools now offer courses on the various aspects of women and sports.

Several articles have examined the coverage of sports and physical education in databases, but none has dealt specifically with the coverage of women and sports (Sharma 1982, Williams and Chiasson 1983, LeBlancq et al. 1982, Belna et al. 1984). The purpose of this article is to look at a group of databases which contain information related to women and sports. The article will: (a) provide general information about the coverage of women and sports in several databases and (b) examine the coverage of three specific topics in eight databases.

DATABASES EXAMINED

Only one database examined specifically covers sports. The other databases cover particular subtopics related to women and sports. General information about these other databases can be found elsewhere in this volume.

Sport Database

The *Sport Database* is produced by the Sport Information Resource Centre (SIRC) in Ottawa, Canada. It contains bibliographic records of serials and monographs in sports, recreation, exercise physiology, sports medicine, coaching, physical fitness, training, conditioning, and the psychology, history and sociology of sport. Many of the records contain abstracts.

Subject access is provided using terms from the *Sport and Fitness*

Thesaurus, which is available online. An unusual feature of this database is a field that indicates the audience level of the document (Advanced or Research, Intermediate, Basic).

As of 1985 the database contained 164,000 documents. A search on terms for "women/girls" yielded 16,516 documents. Most of the total documents in the database are in English, but there are also documents in French (about 7%), German (about 6%), and other languages (5%). Coverage is from 1949 to the present with selected retrospective coverage. Updates are made monthly.

Educational Resources Information Center

ERIC is a source of documents on sports in educational settings. The scope note in the *Thesaurus of ERIC Descriptors* (11th edition, 1987) describes the subject descriptor "athletics" as "Sports, games, or physical contests often engaged in competitively." There are also a number of narrower terms including "womens athletics." This database might be used to research such topics as:

— participation of girls in interscholastic basketball
— techniques for teaching soccer skills to grade school girls
— women in administrative positions in intercollegiate athletics

Dissertation Abstracts Online

Doctoral dissertations and Master's theses from United States and Canadian universities on topics about women and sports are cited in *Dissertation Abstracts Online*. Almost any topic related to women and sports might be found here. Each citation is assigned one or two subject descriptors chosen by the dissertation author from the DAI Subject Classification Scheme. A free-text search on women (woman, girls, females) and sports (athletes, athletics) yielded 548 citations.

PsycINFO

The *PsycINFO* database includes citations about the psychology of sports. The database also covers sports in relation to such disciplines as psychiatry, sociology, anthropology, and education. The *Thesaurus of Psychological Index Terms* (5th edition, 1988) lists the terms "athletes" and "athletic participation." In addition to the term "sports" there are such narrower terms as "basketball," "swimming," "tennis," and "martial arts."

Representative topics which might be searched in this database are:

- attitudes toward female body builders
- differences between male and female athletes in their competitiveness
- the use of physical activity in treating depression in females

Sociological Abstracts

This database covers sociology and affiliated disciplines. In relation to women and sports, this database might be searched for such topics as:

- the difference between males and females in their habits as sports spectators
- comparison of participation by female athletes in rural versus urban areas
- violence of female spectators at sporting events
- career patterns of female coaches
- the economic potential for female professional athletes
- media images of female athletes
- sports participation of female athletes by class

Social SciSearch

Social SciSearch provides coverage of key social science journals. The records include a listing of works cited by the author. The topics on women and sports which might be searched on this database are similar to those in *Sociological Abstracts*.

MEDLARS-On-Line (MEDLINE)

MEDLINE covers all aspects of biomedicine as well as allied health fields and other fields as they relate to medicine and health care. Related topics in this database might be sports injuries in women or the effect of participation in various sports on health and fitness. Examples of topics which might be searched on this database are:

— athletic performance during menstruation
— breast injuries in female softball players
— the effect of jogging on pregnant women

Arts and Humanities SEARCH

Arts and Humanities SEARCH contains citations for a wide range of publications in the international literature of the arts and humanities. The records include a listing of references cited by the author. Some sample topics:

— depiction of female athletes in modern novels
— television coverage of women's tennis events
— women's gymnastics in women's colleges in the 1920s

In addition to these eight, there are two other databases that specifically cover sports (Sharma 1982). Because they are not available on the three major online bibliographic utilities (DIALOG, ORBIT, or BRS), they were not examined.

"Sportdokumentation" is produced by the Bundesinstitut fuer Sportwissenschaft in Germany. The database staff will search on request and will supply photocopies of articles. Further information can be obtained from:

Bundesinstitut fuer Sportwissenschaft
Hertzstrasse 1, Postfach 400109/110
5000 KOELN 40 (LOVENICH)
Telephone: 0 2234-76011 Ext. 233

"SIRLS" (Information Retrieval system for the Sociology of Leisure and Sport) is available on the University of Waterloo's (Canada) computer. The database can be accessed through Datapac, which is available through Telenet and Tymnet. For further information on "SIRLS," contact:

SIRLS
Faculty of Human Kinetics and Leisure Studies
University of Waterloo
Waterloo (Ontario)
Canada N2L 3G1
Telephone: 519-885-1211 Ext. 2560

SELECTED TOPICS

Three questions in the field of women and sports were selected for searches to be conducted across eight databases:

1. What has been the effect of Title IX on participation of female students in intercollegiate and interscholastic athletics?
2. How does steroid use affect female athletics?
3. What attitudes prevail about female athletes in terms of sex roles and sexual orientation?

The study of women and sports cuts across a number of disciplines, including education, medicine, sociology, and psychology. These three questions were chosen to reflect this variety.

Eight databases were selected for searching, based on their general availability and relevance to the topics. These were:

— *Sport Database* [SFDB]
— *Educational Resources Information Center* [ERIC]
— *Dissertation Abstracts Online* [DISS]
— *PsycINFO* [PSYC]
— *Sociological Abstracts* [SOCA]
— *Social SciSearch* [SSCI]
— *Arts and Humanities SEARCH* [AHCI]
— MEDLARS-On-Line (MEDLARS) [MESH]

8

All the databases were searched on BRS by an experienced searcher.*

All eight databases were searched on the title field. The searches were also done on descriptor and abstract fields on all databases except SSCI and AHCI, where these fields are not available.

In all three cases, the search strategy included all possible combinations of "women" and "sports."

Concept 1	Concept 2
women$	sport$
woman$	athlet$
female$	
girl$	

The number of citations in each database for the combination of these sets of terms is shown in Table I. These figures give a sense of the coverage of women and sports in these eight databases. Of course, the *Sport Database* has many more articles on specific relevant topics. *Dissertation Abstracts* reflects the kinds of topics that

TABLE I

NUMBER OF CITATIONS ON WOMEN AND SPORTS*

Database	Number
SPDB	5236
ERIC	1039
DISS	548
PSYC	618
MESH	498
SOCA	320
SSCI	205
AHCI	13

* Through December 1988

*Abbreviations used in BRS.

have been of interest in research for advanced degrees. Any of the other databases might be a good choice for a topic in the disciplines on which they focus.

Based on a review of the title and abstract, citations were judged to be "relevant," "possibly relevant," and "not relevant." "Possibly relevant" citations are those that, while not directly related to the topic, may have information that contributes to the research.

The three searches conducted on these eight databases illustrate the kind of results that might be expected in looking for information in various subdisciplines related to women and sports.

Search 1. Effect of Title IX

"What has been the effect of Title IX on participation of female students in intercollegiate and interscholastic athletics?" This question seeks information on the ways in which the implementation of Title IX affected competitive sports for women in secondary and post-secondary educational institutions. Figure 1 gives the search strategy used in *ERIC* for this topic along with the number of citations at each step. The searches on the other seven databases used similar approaches.

Only four of the eight databases yielded results when the full search, such as that illustrated in Figure 1, was used. A search which included only "Title IX" or "Title IX" plus "woman/ female" yielded citations in three of the other four databases. Table II lists the results of these searches.

FIGURE 1

SEARCH STRATEGY IN ERIC - EFFECT OF TITLE IX

Search Syntax	Number of Citations
1 (FEMALE$1 GIRL$1 WOMEN$1 WOMAN$1)	36,079
2 (INTERCOLLEGIATE INTERSCHOLASTIC) WITH (SPORT$1 ATHLETIC$1)	326
3 TITLE ADJ '9'	14
4 TITLE ADJ 'IX'	701
5 3 4	703
6 5 AND 2 AND 1	35

The following are representative titles found through this search:

— A comparison of Canadian and U.S. women's athletics since Title IX
— Back to the starting line — Title 9 and women's intercollegiate athletics
— Title IX and the minority women in sport at historically Black institutions

The only significant area of overlap was between the *Sport Database* and *ERIC*. In these two databases, there were 11 articles in common. The other overlap is shown in Table III.

As one might expect, the *Sport Database* is useful in searching any sports-related topic. It is not surprising that *ERIC* was a good source for a topic related to education. Since Title IX was implemented in 1972, examination of its implementation and effects has became a popular subject for Doctoral dissertations and Master's theses. *Dissertation Abstracts* is, therefore, a logical choice for a search on this topic. *PsycINFO* also provided a number of citations although the majority of these were not directly relevant to the question posed.

Search 2. Steroid Use

"How does steroid use affect female athletes?" This question seeks information on the medical effects of the use of anabolic steroids by female athletes. Figure 2 gives the search strategy used in *MEDLARS-On-Line* (MEDLINE) for this topic along with the number of citations at each step. The searches on the other seven databases used similar approaches.

Only four of the eight databases yielded results when the full search, such as that illustrated in Figure 2, was used. A search broadened for "steroids" plus "woman/female" yielded citations in one of the other four databases. Table IV lists those results.

Some representative titles from that search were:

— The effect of anabolic steroids on female athletes
— Anabolic steroid use and perceived effects in ten weight-trained women athletes

 —Characteristics of anabolic-androgenic steroid-free competitive male and female bodybuilders

Four of the citations in the *Sport Database* were in a language other than English. Thirteen of the citations in MESH were non-English, including nine of the relevant articles. The only significant area of overlap was between the *Sport Database* and *MEDLINE* where there were eight articles in common. The other overlap is shown in Table V.

MEDLINE is an appropriate choice for a medical topic. However, the *Sport Database* yielded as many relevant articles as the

TABLE II
NUMBER OF CITATIONS ON TITLE IX SEARCH

| Database | Number of Citations Retrieved | | | |
	Total*	Relevant	Possibly Relevant	Not Relevant
SFDB	24	24	0	0
ERIC	35	35	0	0
DISS	18	18	0	0
PSYC	0	0	0	0
	16(a)	5	5	6
SOCA	5	5	0	0
	20(a)	4	8	8
SSCI	0	0	0	0
	6(b)	3	0	3
	8(c)	1	5	2
AHCI	0	0	0	0
MESH	0	0	0	0
	2(a)	0	0	2

* The first figures listed are for a full search of relevant terms similar to that listed in Figure 1.

(a) search on terms for Title IX only

(b) search on terms for women/female plus Title IX only

(c) search on terms for intercollegiate/interscholastic plus sports plus women/female only

TABLE III
OVERLAP OF ARTICLES - TITLE IX

Number of Articles Which Overlap

Database*	SFDB	ERIC	DISS	PSYC	SOCA	SSCI
SFDB	-	11	0	1	1	1
ERIC		-	0	0	1	1
DISS			-	0	0	0
PSYC				-	0	0
SOCA					-	0
SSCI						-

* AHCI and MESH are not included because they contained no relevant citations.

medical database. The other consideration is the technical nature of many of the medical citations which might not be appropriate for some searchers. The other databases searched in this test case would probably not be good sources for this kind of topic.

Search 3. Attitudes About Sex Roles of Female Athletes

"What attitudes prevail about female athletes in terms of sex roles and sexual orientation?" This question examines attitudes about female athletes. Specifically, it looks at whether people tend to feel that female athletes do not fit female stereotypes or to label female athletes as lesbians.

Figure 3 gives the search strategy used in *PsycINFO* for this topic along with the number of citations at each step. The searches on the other seven databases used similar approaches.

All eight of the databases yielded at least one citation. Because of the large number of citations in *ERIC*, *PsycINFO*, and the *Sport Database*, those citations actually examined were limited to items published after 1979. Table VI lists those results.

Among the representative titles retrieved through this search:

—The female athletic role as a status determinant within the social systems of high school adolescents

- Self-ascribed gender roles of female athletes and nonathletes: similarities or differences?
- Lesbians and sport: the dilemma of coming out
- Comparison of attitudes and sex roles for female athletic participants and non-participants

FIGURE 2

SEARCH STRATEGY IN MESH - STEROID USE

Search Syntax		Number of Citations
1	(FEMALE$1 GIRL$1 WOMEN$1 WOMAN$1).TI,DE.	1,780,541
2	STEROID$.TI,DE.	18,497
3	STEROIDS.TI,DE.	14,741
4	2 3	30,597
5	(ATHLETE$1 ATHLETIC$1 SPORT$1).TI,DE.	15,195
6	1 AND 4 AND 5	47

TABLE IV

NUMBER OF CITATIONS ON STEROIDS SEARCH

Database	Number of Citations Retrieved			
	Total*	Relevant	Possibly Relevant	Not Relevant
SFDB	38	38	0	0
ERIC	3	2	1	0
DISS	2	0	1	1
PSYC	0	0	0	0
SOCA	0	0	0	0
SSCI	0	0	0	0
	27(a)	0	0	27
AHCI	0	0	0	0
MESH	47	35	3	9

* The first figures listed are for a full search of relevant terms similar to that listed in Figure 2.

(a) search on terms for <u>steroids</u> plus <u>women/female</u> only

TABLE V
OVERLAP OF ARTICLES - STEROIDS

Number of Articles Which Overlap

Database*	MESH	SFDB	ERIC	DISS
MESH	-	8	0	0
SFDB		-	1	0
ERIC			-	0
DISS				-

* PSYC, SOCA, SSCI, and AHCI are not included because they contained no relevant citations.

FIGURE 3
SEARCH STRATEGY IN PSYC - SEX ROLES

Search Syntax		Number of Citations
1	(FEMALE$1 GIRL$1 WOMEN$1 WOMAN$1) SAME (SPORT$1 ATHLETIC$1)	618
2	STEREOTYP$.TI,DE,AB.	6,899
3	SEXUAL ADJ PREFERENCE$.TI,DE,AB.	165
4	SEX ADJ ROLE ADJ ATTITUDE$.TI,DE,AB.	3,479
5	SEX ADJ ROLES.TI,DE,AB.	6,072
6	GAY$1.TI,DE,AB.	391
7	LESBIAN$.TI,DE,AB.	561
8	2 3 4 5 6 7	14,345
9	1 AND 8	108

The *Sport Database* and *PsycINFO* yielded the largest number of relevant or possibly relevant citations. *ERIC* and *Dissertation Abstracts* also had several items that would provide information about the topic. Nine of the citations in the *Sport Database* were in a language other than English, as was one in *PsycINFO*. The *Sport Database* had 7 citations in common with *ERIC* and 10 items in common with *PsycINFO*. *PsycINFO* also had overlap of 6 items

TABLE VI
NUMBER OF CITATIONS ON SEX ROLES SEARCH

| | | Number of Citations Retrieved | | |
Database	Total	Relevant	Possibly Relevant	Not Relevant
SFDB	120			
	61*	37	24	0
ERIC	124			
	56*	13	28	14
DISS	23	12	0	11
PSYC	108			
	79*	34	23	22
SOCA	32	7	14	11
SSCI	1	1	0	0
AHCI	1	1	0	0
MESH	5	1	0	4

* Search limited to citations published after 1979.

with *ERIC* and 9 items with *Dissertation Abstracts*. The other over-lap is shown in Table VII.

CONCLUSIONS

Women and sports, like many areas of women's studies, requires an interdisciplinary approach. Many research topics can be success-fully searched in the *Sport Database*, although only about 10% of the total citations in that database cover sports topics related to women. There are some logical choices of databases to search for other topics: *MEDLINE* for medical topics, *ERIC* for athletic partic-ipation in educational settings, *PsycINFO* for sports psychology, *Social SciSearch* and *Sociological Abstracts* for social science top-ics. Appropriate databases for other topics depend on the nature of the topic.

TABLE VII
OVERLAP OF ARTICLES - SEX ROLES

Number of Articles Which Overlap

Database	SFDB	ERIC	DISS	PSYC	SOCA	SSCI	AHCI	MESH
SFDB	-	7	1	10	3	0	0	0
ERIC		-	0	6	0	0	0	0
DISS			-	9	0	0	0	0
PSYC				-	6	0	0	1
SOCA					-	0	0	1
SSCI						-	0	0
AHCI							-	0
MESH								-

WORKS CITED

Alison Belna, Jeanne L. Spala, Centinela Hospital, and Richard W. Stark. Olympic Information in the SPORT Database. *Database* 7(3):20-26

Commission on Civil Rights, Washington, D.C. *More hurdles to clear: women and girls in competitive athletics.* 1980.

Richard LeBlancq, Howard Godfrey, Jim Wright, and Fred LaParo. Sports, leisure and recreation information on the New York Times Database. *Database* 5(3):52-53

V.S. Sharma. Information resources for recreation, leisure and sport. *Database* 5(3):32-49

Howard M. Williams and Gilles Chiasson. Computerized information retrieval: options and issues for physical education and sport. *Journal of Physical Education, Recreation and Dance* 54(1): 21-24

Women and Government Online:
Two Case Studies

Deborah Bezanson

SUMMARY. This article addresses two case studies in the area of women and government. The first case involves identifying citations on a contemporary female political figure. The study leads to three primary observations. First, the search was more successful in news and popular databases than in political science databases. Second, searching full-text online files yields more comprehensive results than searching bibliographic databases only. Third, overlap across databases, though expected, was unpredictable. For a comprehensive search on the second case, federal aid to women-owned businesses, databases from the political, business and popular fields are examined. Few databases use a controlled vocabulary which facilitates research on women's issues. Those which do are not consistent in their application of terms. Free-text strategies yield the best results.

The difficulties of researching women's studies issues in online databases have been well documented. Detlefsen (1986) and Hildenbrand (1986), among others, detail some of the problems encountered in searching feminist issues in databases which are not specifically designed to reflect the feminist point of view, and they focus on the challenges of searching with vocabularies which subsume women's issues under broader categories. Pritchard, in her 1984 article, outlines a set of criteria for evaluating databases from a

Deborah Bezanson is Coordinator, Online Services, Gelman Library, George Washington University, Washington DC 20052.

Thanks to Pat Wathen, Women Studies Specialist at George Washington University for her assistance with the research and planning for this article. Thanks to Debbie Masters, Head of Reference at George Washington University for her editorial assistance.

women's studies point of view. Using some of her suggestions, one area within women's studies — women as they interact with the government — was examined through the use of two case studies. The results are reported below.

The first case focuses on Molly Yard, a contemporary, politically active woman, currently the outspoken president of the National Organization for Women (NOW). This study allowed examination of the coverage of women's issues within the databases without concentrating on the vocabulary issues.

The second case deals with an area where vocabulary plays a more significant role. The objective was to identify citations on the role of government assistance to women-owned businesses. This topic was chosen in order to examine the progress or lack of progress which has been made in the adequacy of indexing vocabulary as well as questions of coverage and literature availability.

In the search for information on Molly Yard, the databases were examined based on the following criteria:

1. *Treatment of personal names*: Are they in natural order or inverted? Are middle initials used? Are there special fields within the record which relate to names? Are names under authority control? Are names entered consistently?
2. *Recall*: Which databases yielded the largest numbers of citations on the topic? Which results were relevant and useful? Were relevant items missed?
3. *Overlap*: How much overlap occurred in the results? Were there ways of avoiding the overlap? What implications does this have for a researcher?

Based on preliminary search for relevant information in DIALOG, BRS, and Wilsonline, the following databases were chosen: *National Newspaper Index, Magazine Index, Academic American Encyclopedia, Magazine ASAP, Newspaper Abstracts, Washington Post Online, Biography Index, Readers Guide to Periodical Literature*, and *Readers' Guide Abstracts*. Surprisingly, the following databases, *Work and Family Life, CIS Index, Dissertation Abstracts, Ageline, Social Work Abstracts, Public Affairs Information Service, Social Sciences Citation Index, Marquis Who's Who, Soci-*

ological Abstracts, *U.S. Political Science Documents*, *Family Resources*, and *Social Sciences Index*, yielded no results on a search of Molly Yard. A search of *VU/TEXT* and the newswire files yielded many citations, so *VU/TEXT* was added to the list of datafiles searched.

How are names handled in these databases? The Information Access Company (IAC) databases, *Magazine Index*, *Magazine ASAP*, and *National Newspaper Index* have a "named person"/"biographee" field, and an article type for biography. *Biography Index*, *Reader's Guide* and *Readers' Guide Abstracts* included a document type field for biography, as well as a personal name field. *Newspaper Abstracts* and *Washington Post Online* include a "named person" field. Consistency in use of these fields was not evident in the results. Generally, the name Molly Yard would appear in either the named person field or in the biographee field but usually not in both. Relevant articles were retrieved either way. The use of the biography article type was not consistent and inclusion in the search strategy did not enhance relevancy of retrieval. A free text search of the name, with no qualification as to field or article type was found to be the best strategy.

In general, all the databases used the name Molly Yard with the exception of the *Academic American Encyclopedia* which preferred Mary Alexander (Molly) Yard. *Newspaper Abstracts* sometimes used Molly Yard and sometimes Molly C. Yard. Because of the possible occurrence of middle names or initials it is generally advisable to use proximity operators which allow for up to two intervening words. In descriptor or named person fields, the name is generally inverted. In title, abstract, or full text fields, the name was usually in natural order. Therefore the best strategy is to search using operators which do not imply order or to perform searches specifying both possibilities. In DIALOG, this would be YARD(2N) MOLLY. Some false drops were encountered in the full text files and in *Magazine Index*. A citation from Magazine Index was to a book review of *Lady Molly of Scotland Yard*, and some of the articles in *VU/TEXT* were about gardening and an unrelated individual names Molly. This is still a useful strategy, however, since the percentage of relevant articles retrieved was quite high.

The databases which yielded the highest number of citations were the newswires and *VU/TEXT* with 36 records in the *UPI Newswire*, 58 listed in the *AP Newswire*, and 224 in the latest year of newspaper files in *VU/TEXT*. *Newspaper Abstracts* yielded 47 citations for the last five years, *National Newspaper Index* yielded 10 for the 10 years of its coverage and *Washington Post Online* yielded 19 for its 4-1/2 years of coverage. The other databases yielded fewer than 10 citations each. Full text databases yielded a greater number of citations than abstract databases which yielded more than bibliographic citations alone. The principle of an inverse relationship between recall and precision was not confirmed by the results. Although there was a fair amount of repetition, relevancy remained high.

The *National Newspaper Index* covers the *Washington Post*, which is also indexed by the *Washington Post Online*. Four other newspapers, the *Wall Street Journal*, *New York Times*, *LA Times*, and *Christian Science Monitor* are included in both *Newspaper Abstracts* and *National Newspaper Index*. Therefore, these three databases were compared for overlap. Unique citations were discovered in each file. *Newspaper Abstracts* yielded 16 citations on a name search of Molly Yard for the four newspapers it has in common with *National Newspaper Index*, while *NNI* yielded only nine citations in these four. Of those six citations were in common, three citations were in *NNI*, but not indexed under Molly Yard, and seven did not appear in *NNI* at all. Three citations were found in *NNI* that did not appear in our *Newspaper Abstracts* results. A subsequent search using known words from the title found one of these three citations was listed in *Newspaper Abstracts* but did not contain the name Molly Yard in the record. Comparing the coverage of *NNI* with that of *Washington Post Online*, 18 citations were found to be unique to *Washington Post Online* and one citation unique to the *National Newspaper Index*. The higher retrieval of *Washington Post Online* can be attributed, at least in part, to the full text nature of the database. Some of the articles retrieved were somewhat less focused on the topic Molly Yard, even though her name was contained in the text. One, however, entitled "The Unsinkable Molly Yard," was not listed in *NNI* at all.

The search of *Magazine Index* retrieved three citations, two of which were relevant, with Molly Yard found in the biography field. *Magazine ASAP* retrieved seven citations, including the two found in *Magazine Index*. The five new citations did not mention Molly Yard by name in the citation or descriptors but the descriptors suggested relevance.

Three Wilsonline databases, *Biography Index*, *Readers Guide to Periodical Literature* and *Readers Guide Abstracts*, identified five individual citations, all of which were relevant. All the citations in *Biography Index* and *Readers Guide* were found in *Readers Guide Abstracts*. In addition, *RGA* yielded three unique citations.

VU/TEXT yielded some interesting results especially for local coverage. Extensive overlap can be observed as different papers reported on the same story of national interest. This was especially true if a story had been covered on the newswires. However, unique citations can be found in local papers covering Molly Yard's speaking engagements in their regions. These were not always covered nationally. In an effort to decrease the amount of overlap, the search strategy was modified. The addition of **"not @3 associated / press"** to the search request eliminated articles citing the AP wire in the source field. Those articles can be picked up directly from the AP file.

The second case focused on the topic "federal aid to women-owned business." Databases were examined for recall and overlap as well as for the usefulness of the controlled vocabulary in identifying citations on the topics relating to women. The following databases were chosen for the study:

1. Political coverage: *PAIS, CIS Index, U.S. Political Science Documents*;
2. Business coverage: *ABI/Inform, Trade and Industry Index, Business Dateline*, and *PTS Promt*; and
3. Popular coverage: *Magazine Index* and *National Newspaper Index*.

Public Affairs Information Service (PAIS) uses a controlled vocabulary published in its thesaurus *PAIS Subject Headings* (1983). The printed editions of the index also provide information about how the subject headings are applied. When using print copies of the index to check for online database vocabulary, it is advisable to be sensitive to vocabulary changes over different years of the index.

These are usually noted in a thesaurus of terms, but are often not indicated in print indexes. Using the thesaurus the term "women-owned business enterprises" was identified. A search of this term resulted in 45 citations. When combined with the coordinating terms, "government aid to business," "government loans to industry," and "federal aid," the resulting search yielded four citations relevant to the topic. An expanded strategy, searching by "wom?n" combined with **"government or federal" and "fund? or grant? or support? or assist?"**, retrieved three additional citations. One record cited a directory of "state programs and agencies aimed at assisting small business . . . with problems of women ownership." This record was index only as "small business – government aid." The other two additional citations were to different editions of "A Guide to Doing Business with the Department of State." These are not strictly about federal aid to women-owned businesses, but may be of interest to someone doing research on this topic. Curiously, while the second edition of this title is indexed under "women-owned business enterprises," the first edition is not. To retrieve the first citation using index terms, a searcher would need to use the term "*minority* business enterprises." Additional related citations may be retrieved by using terms such as "purchasing, government," to bring the total to 10 citations, or by expanding the scope of the search to include "minority business enterprises." Recall would be higher, but precision would be lower.

Information Access provides a guide to their database vocabulary entitled: *Subject Guide to the IAC Databases* (1985). The vocabulary is based on Library of Congress subject headings. Using the *Subject Guide*, the subject heading, "federal aid to women-owned business enterprises" was identified. Use of this term throughout the IAC databases achieved relevant results. In *Magazine Index*, additional citations were found by combining the broader heading "women-owned business enterprises" with free text use of the terms "government" and "federal." Since IAC database records do not contain abstracts, precision was not seriously affected. Seven additional citations relating to women-owned businesses which proved useful were found. Two examples were an articled indexed with "women in business – employment" and "Small Business Administration – federal aid," and one indexed "women in business — law and legislation" and "small business-finance." Unfortunately, the presence of a good subject heading does not guarantee that it will be applied consistently. Although IAC had an excellent heading it was not used with all relevant citations on the topic. Because there are many closely related descriptors and since the *Subject Guide* has no scope notes, all descriptors must be used to insure high recall. Since there are no abstracts, free text strategies may also be used to increase recall.

Seven relevant citations indexed under the subject heading "federal aid" were retrieved in IAC's *Trade and Industry Index*. Additional items could be retrieved linking "women-owned business enterprises" and "government" or "federal" but these were not as focused on the topic. Of the seven original *Trade and Industry* citations, four were also found in *National Newspaper Index* and one was also included in *Magazine Index*. In our expanded search, which yielded six additional citations, three overlapped with *NNI* and two with *MI*. A search of the *National Newspaper Index* using the same strategies listed above yielded no unique citations. When searching all the IAC files overlap can be eliminated using the File field to "not out" citations from files you have already searched.

The Predicasts databases provide for precise searching with their product and event codes. The following codes were identified using their *PTS User's Manual*:

pc = 921861?   for business aid programs at the state level
pc = 930861?   for business aid programs at the local level
pc = 910814?   for business aid programs at the U.S./Federal level

In deciding which of the Predicasts databases to use, *PROMT* was selected. The *F&S Indexes* cover more articles, but they rely solely on the codes and article titles. *PROMT* allows for free text searches of abstracts in addition to the codes and titles. Since there was no code specifically relating to women-owned businesses, *PROMT* was used for greater precision. The combination of free text "wom?n" with the three codes listed above resulted in four excellent articles. There was no overlap with *Trade and Industry Index*.

U.S. Political Science Documents did not have useful subject headings. In fact, the subject heading small business*man* had to be used to search for the topic! One item of some relevance, "Effectiveness of Women-Owned Business Set-Aside Contracting Goals: A Regression Analysis" was found indexed under "small businessman," "women studies," "business contract," and "government agency."

The subject heading for *ABI/Inform* and *Business Dateline* were also not suited to this topic. Few relevant articles were found in *Business Dateline*. A search of the *ABI/Inform* database for the past five years, yielded three relevant citations which were not indexed consistently. Two were coded 9521 for minority business, while the third was not. All were indexed "women," "small business" or "business ownership," and "federal" or "government."

Since many of the records found in other databases cited Congressional hearings, *CIS Index* was examined. An initial free text search using "women" or "female" in the title or descriptor fields, combined with "federal aid programs," yielded five irrelevant citations. A restructured search strategy for "women" and "small business" in titles of documents resulted in 19 citations. The 19 citations referred to only five unique hearings. The other 14 were witness records from the five hearings. Although a search may be limited to hearing records only (excluding the witness records), displays cannot be limited. Consequently, a hearing on small business enterprises with one witness addressing women's issues would be missed if the search were limited to main hearing records. However, if five witnesses at one hearing spoke to women's issues, the citation for that hearing would be listed five times in the search result if the search is not limited. The database producer is aware of the difficulty and offered the suggestion that results be typed initially in format 6 (DIALOG accession number). Then unique hearings can be identified and requested in long format. Although this method is not ideal, it does save considerable online time by avoiding printing multiple citations to the same hearing. For more comprehensive retrieval on this topic, the strategy was expanded to use "women" in the title or descriptor fields combined with "small business" in the same two fields. Entering "small(w)business" with a proximity operator improved recall since organization names and names of legislation are sometimes included in records which are not coded with the bound phrase subject heading "small business."

CONCLUSION

When searching for names of contemporary female political figures, the news and popular databases provide better coverage than political science databases. Full-text databases are most worthwhile for this type of research, especially for a graduate student, faculty member, or other advanced research. An undergraduate or researcher looking for quick background via a few good citations will probably retrieve enough material using bibliographic databases alone. Overlap is difficult to predict. For comprehensiveness, databases with overlapping coverage should be searched. Different articles will be retrieved as a result of varying indexing and selection policies.

For the case of government aid to women-owned businesses, a search of political, business, and popular databases was necessary to achieve comprehensive coverage. *CIS Index* provides excellent coverage of Congressional hearings. However, retrieving the citations effectively yet comprehensively can be challenging. *PTS PROMT* and *Business Dateline* provide some local and regional coverage but, given the number of relevant citations found in these two databases there is much that is not covered. Local legislative databases, not addressed in this research, may provide useful information on state and local government aid to women.

Because commercial databases exist in an environment where they must make money to survive, the majority of these databases are focused on large disciplines and are not as useful when searching interdisciplinary topics such as women's studies. The selection policies and indexing terms reflect the needs of the broader disciplines. In the area of women's studies, most of the useful changes in vocabulary are seen in databases which are most influenced by the Library of Congress subject headings. Even when appropriate vocabulary is available, it is not always used consistently. Searches of interdisciplinary topics such as women and government are therefore challenging for the scholar who must research many different databases, creatively using free text strategies for best results.

REFERENCES

Detlefsen, Ellen Gay. (1986) Issues of Access to Information About Women. *Special Collections* 3(3-4):163-171.
Hildenbrand, Suzanne. (1986) Women Studies Online: Promoting Visibility. *RQ* 26(1):63-74.
PAIS Subject Headings. (1984) New York: Public Affairs Information Service, Inc.
Predicasts Terminal System Users' Manual. (1986) Cleveland: Predicasts.
Pritchard, Sarah M. (1974) Developing Criteria for Database Evaluation: The Example of Women's Studies. *Reference Librarian* 11:247-261.
Subject Guide to IAC Databases. (1985) Belmont, CA: Information Access Company.

Case Study #1:   Molly Yard

Database Name	Name Related Fields	Citations Retrieved	Overlap
Washington Post Online (WPO) (4/83-11/07/88)	/na; na=	19	1/19 NNI
Newspaper Abstracts (NA) (84-10/88)	/na; na=	47	6/47 NNI
National Newspaper Index (NNI) (79-10/88)	/na; na= at=biography	10	6/10 NA 1/10 WPO
Magazine Index (MI) (59-3/70; 73-10/88)	/na; na= at=biography	3	2/3 MA
Magazine ASAP (83-10/88)	/na; na=	7	2/7 MI
Academic American Encyclopedia (Jan 1988)	/ti	1	none
Biography Index (BI) (7/84-10/88)	biography (ct) Molly Yard (ps)	1	1/1 RG 1/1 RGA
Readers' Guide to Periodical Literature (RG) (83-10/88)	biography (ct) Molly Yard (ps)	2	2/2 RGA 1/2 BI
Readers' Guide Abstracts (RGA) (9/84-10/88)	biography (ct) Molly Yard (ps)	5	1/5 BI 2/5 RG
VuText (1-10/88)	@ 8 biography	224	n/a
UPI News (4/83-11/6/88)	none	36	n/a
AP News (7/83-11/6/88)	none	58	n/a

Case Study #2:   Government Aid to Women-Owned Businesses

Database Name	Relevant Citations	Overlap
PAIS	10	3/10 CIS
CIS Index	41	3/41 PAIS
US Political Science Documents (USPD)	1	none
ABI/Inform (83-10/88)	3	1/3 T&I
Trade & Industry Index (T&I) (81-11/88)	7	1/7 ABI 4/7 NNI 1/7 MI
Business Dateline (85-12/88)	0	none
PTS PROMT (72-12/88)	4	none
Magazine Index (MI) (59-3/70; 73-11/88)	9	1/9 T&I
National Newspaper Index (NNI) (79-11/88)	4	4/4 T&I

Database Matrix

DATABASE NAME: ABI/Inform
TYPE: Bibliographic   RECORD TYPE: Abstracts
YEARS COVERED: 1971 +
VENDOR AVAILABILITY: BRS, DIALOG, Data-Star, Dialcom, Inc., ESA/IRS, Human Resource Information Network, Knowledge Index, Mead Data Central, ORBIT, VU-TEXT
SCOPE: Covers all phases of business management and administration with approximately 800 primary publications. Includes articles and journals that address many of the issues important to women.

DATABASE NAME: Abstracts of Working Papers in Economics
TYPE: Bibliographic   RECORD TYPE: Abstracts
YEARS COVERED: 1981 +
VENDOR AVAILABILITY: BRS, BRS/After Dark, BRS/Colleague
SCOPE: Citations to research reports from research centers and economics departments. Minor coverage of women and economic issues.

DATABASE NAME: Academic American Encyclopedia
TYPE:Full-text   RECORD TYPE: Articles
YEARS COVERED: Current
VENDOR AVAILABILITY: BRS, BRS/After Dark, BRS/Colleague, CompuServe, Data-Star, Delphi, DIALOG, Dow Jones News, GEnie, Quantum, Datrtext, The Source, U.S. Videotel, VU/TEXT
SCOPE: Coverage of women in general is good. Articles on contemporary as well as historic persons, events and issues can be located; however, coverage of American women and issues is better than foreign coverage. Although the publishers claim to employ gender-neutral language, male pronouns were 5.6 times as likely to appear as female pronouns.

DATABASE NAME: Ageline
TYPE: Bibliographic   RECORD TYPE: Abstracts
YEARS COVERED: 1978+
VENDOR AVAILABILITY: BRS, BRS/After Dark, BRS/Colleague
SCOPE: Monographs, chapters in books, dissertations, research in progress (funded by the U.S. Administration on Aging). Covers women in middle age and aging from a social, psychological and economic perspective.

DATABASE NAME: Agricola
TYPE: Bibliographic   RECORD TYPE: Abstracts
YEARS COVERED: 1970+
VENDOR AVAILABILITY: BRS, BRS/After Dark, BRS/Colleague, DIALOG, DIMDI, Knowledge Index
SCOPE: Journal literature, government reports, monographs, audiovisual resources. Covers home economics, child and family resources, rural sociology and family migration. Coverage of women is peripheral, relating to extension service issues of concern to women and families. Most items on women are about women in more industrialized countries.

DATABASE NAME: AGRIS
DATABASE TYPE: Bibliographic   RECORD TYPE: Citations
YEARS COVERED: 1975+
VENDOR AVAILABILITY: DIALOG, DIMDI, ESA/IRS
SCOPE: Journal literature, monographs, technical reports, patents, standards, dissertations, conference proceedings. trade catalogs, laws and regulations and unpublished documents. Covers agriculture, food, human nutrition, environment, economics, animal science, veterinary science, fisheries, forestry, natural resources, energy, and pollution. Good coverage of conferences and non-conventional literature, where most women in international development related citations are found. Wide range of journals is useful but does not seem to index WID-specific titles.

DATABASE NAME: America: History and Life
TYPE: Bibliographic

RECORD TYPE: Bibliographic citations, abstracts, book review citations
YEARS COVERED: 1964+
VENDOR AVAILABILITY: DIALOG, Knowledge Index
SCOPE: History, government, politics, society and culture of the United States and Canada, pre-history to the present, including women's studies. Women's issues are strongly represented in the literature indexed, including current affairs. Abstracts or annotates articles (including bibliographies, obituaries, review articles) selected from some 2,000 periodicals published worldwide; books and book reviews from 130 journals covering American history and dissertations from *Dissertation Abstracts International*; and selected articles from multiauthor works. 84% of entries are for English-language documents. Natural language keyword indexing and terms from a preferred subject heading list and in-house authority files.

DATABASE NAME: American Library Directory
TYPE: Bibliographic   RECORD TYPE: Directory
YEARS COVERED: Current; Updated annually
VENDOR AVAILABILITY: DIALOG
SCOPE: A directory of over 37,000 United States and Canadian libraries and related institutions. Can be used to locate libraries with collections of interest to women and women's issues. Descriptor assignment is sporadic; better results are achieved by free-text search strategies.

DATABASE NAME: Architecture Database
TYPE: Bibliographic   RECORD TYPE: Citations with notes
YEARS COVERED: periodicals, 1978+; books, 1984+
VENDOR AVAILABILITY: DIALOG
SCOPE: Covers all aspects of architecture, technical and aesthetic, all periods, worldwide; women in architecture, buildings for women. Articles in about 400 periodicals worldwide (excludes book reviews); approximately 2,000 books, pamphlets, technical literature, conference proceedings, and exhibition catalogs annually. About 50% of British origin. Descriptors from *Architectural*

Keywords thesaurus (available in print); identifiers; named person index.

DATABASE NAME: Art Index
TYPE: Bibliographic   RECORD TYPE: Citations
YEARS COVERED: Oct. 1984 +
VENDOR AVAILABILITY: Wilsonline
SCOPE: Art, in general, of all periods and places including archaeology, architecture, art history, city planning, crafts, films, folk art, industrial and interior design, landscape architecture, photography, museology, and related fields; women artists, practitioners in all the visual arts, depiction of women in art, feminist art, feminism and the arts. Covers articles, book reviews, conference reports, exhibition announcements and reviews, and reproductions of works of art in about 240 U.S. and foreign periodicals, yearbooks, and museum bulletins, mostly in English. Descriptors from a controlled vocabulary: LCSH and additional terms as needed from Wilson authority files and other indexes.

DATABASE NAME: Art Literature International
TYPE: Bibliographic   RECORD TYPE: Citations with abstracts
YEARS COVERED: 1975 +
VENDOR AVAILABILITY: DIALOG, Knowledge Index
SCOPE: Covers the visual arts in the broadest sense: fine arts, decorative arts, folk art, visual aspects of performing arts; European art since late antiquity, including Christian art in Asia Minor and Africa, colonial art, and oriental art exported to Europe; American art since the discoveries; world art since 1945 (except tribal art unrelated to the modern world); iconography of women, women artists, feminism and art. Cites articles in periodicals, collections of essays, conference proceedings; book and exhibitions reviews; books, museum bulletins, exhibition catalogs, and dissertations; published worldwide. Uses descriptors from a controlled vocabulary, *RILA Subject Headings*, plus free text additions as needed. Identifiers specifically for nationality; time period; style, medium, and form. Section headings (subject classification) and codes.

DATABASE NAME: ARTbibliographies Modern
TYPE: Bibliographic   RECORD TYPE: Citations with abstracts

YEARS COVERED: 1974+
VENDOR AVAILABILITY: DIALOG, Knowledge Index
SCOPE: Covers international 19th- and 20th-century art including artists and movements that bridge the 18th-19th centuries: fine arts, art history, folk art, design, applied arts, architecture, town planning, photography, museums, collections; women artists, iconography of women, feminism and art. Cites articles from about 500 core journals published worldwide plus selected articles from social science and humanities periodicals covered by *America: History and Life* and *Historical Abstracts*; about 1,000 books per year; exhibition catalogs; dissertations from *Dissertation Abstracts International* (1972-1983). Descriptors are the subject classification headings from the printed version, expanded and changed over time, plus personal names and names of artists' groups.

DATABASE NAME: Arts & Humanities Search
TYPE: Bibliographic
RECORD TYPE: Citations with cited references; some title enhancements
YEARS COVERED: 1980+
VENDOR AVAILABILITY: BRS, BRS/After Dark, DIALOG
SCOPE: Covers all arts and humanities from architecture to theater, including history; all women's topics addressed in any of the wide selection of journals indexed. Cites articles, letters, editorials, meeting abstracts, creative works (poems, short stories, plays, music scores), reviews of books, films, music, and theater performances published in 1,400 periodicals, plus relevant items from 4,700 journals in the sciences and social sciences; published worldwide. Citation indexing; subject access through title words and journal category.

DATABASE NAME: Avery Index to Architectural Periodicals
TYPE: Bibliographic
RECORD TYPE: Citations; MARC format for analytics
YEARS COVERED: 1979+
VENDOR AVAILABILITY: RLIN
SCOPE: Covers architecture in its broadest sense, historical and contemporary, worldwide; women in architecture, buildings of

women's institutions. Selectively indexes articles, significant book reviews and exhibition reviews in about 700 major architectural journals in English and western European languages published worldwide. Uses *LCSH*, enhanced for indexing.

DATABASE NAME: Biography Index
TYPE: Bibliographic RECORD TYPE: Citations
YEARS COVERED: July 1984+
VENDOR AVAILABILITY: Wilsonline
SCOPE: Covers biographical materials from books published in English, over 2,600 periodicals covered in other Wilson indexes, and selected additional periodicals, including the *New York Times* (obituaries). Coverage focuses on Americans.

DATABASE NAME: Biography Master Index
TYPE: Bibliographic   RECORD TYPE: Citations
YEARS COVERED: Current; updated periodically
VENDOR AVAILABILITY: DIALOG
SCOPE: Indexes over 375 biographical dictionaries and directories. Women still living have fewer references than historical figures; women of color have fewer references than other women.

DATABASE NAME: BIOSIS Previews
TYPE: Bibliographic   RECORD TYPE: Abstracts
YEARS COVERED: 1969+
VENDOR AVAILABILITY: BRS, Can-Ole, Data-Star, DIALOG, DIMDI, ESA/IRS, Mead Data Central
SCOPE: Based on the Hedge for Women, 8% of the database covers females. Life sciences including original research and reviews in biology and biomedicine. Field, laboratory, clinical, experimental and theoretical works.

DATABASE NAME: Books in Print
TYPE: Bibliographic   RECORD TYPE: Citations
YEARS COVERED: 1979+
VENDOR AVAILABILITY: BRS, BRS/After Dark, DIALOG, Knowledge Index
SCOPE: Provides publication data on books published and/or distributed in the United States. Of the 20 feminist presses searched,

75% were found. Descriptors were fairly specific when taken from *LCSH*; however, greater depth in indexing (the average number of descriptors assigned per record was 1.6) would enhance retrieval. At times descriptors not used consistently.

DATABASE NAME: CAB Abstracts
DATABASE TYPE: Bibliographic   RECORD TYPE: Abstracts
YEARS COVERED: 1972 +
VENDOR AVAILABILITY: BRS, BRS/After Dark, CAN/OLE, DIALOG, DIMDI, ESA/IRS, Japan Information Center of Science and Technology
SCOPE: Comprehensive file of agricultural information from more than fifty abstract journals covering fields of veterinary medicine, human nutrition, developing countries, leisure, recreation, and tourism. Good mix of conferences, series, monographs, articles. Indexes publications containing materials on women in developing countries.

DATABASE NAME: CIS Index
TYPE: Bibliographic   RECORD TYPE: Abstracts
YEARS COVERED: 1970 +
VENDOR AVAILABILITY: DIALOG
SCOPE: Provides current comprehensive access to the contents of the Congressional working papers published by the U.S. House, Senate and Joint committees and subcommittees each year. Relates issues to women through its abstracts of hearings, committee prints, reports, documents and other special publications of Congress.

DATABASE NAME: Comprehensive Core Medical Library
TYPE: Bibliographic   RECORD TYPE: Full-Text
YEARS COVERED: 1985 +
VENDOR AVAILABILITY: BRS, BRS/Colleague
SCOPE: Based on the Hedge for Women, 46% of the database covers females. Includes the complete text of prominent medical books and journals. A special feature is the link from selected *MEDLINE* citations to their full text in *CCML*.

DATABASE NAME: Dissertation Abstracts International
TYPE: Bibliographic   RECORD TYPE: Abstracts

YEARS COVERED: 1861 +
VENDOR AVAILABILITY: BRS, DIALOG
SCOPE: Includes citations from 1861 and abstracts since 1980 to American doctoral dissertations on all subjects. Selected masters theses were added beginning in 1962; selected British dissertations were included beginning in 1988. Dissertations written by and about women are included. Title and abstract paragraphs can be searched with free-text terms to identify work related to women's issues.

DATABASE NAME: Economic Literature Index
TYPE: Bibliographic
RECORD TYPE: Citations, abstracts for 25% of records in database
YEARS COVERED: journals, 1969 +; collected works, 1979 +
VENDOR AVAILABILITY: DIALOG, Knowledge Index
SCOPE: Indexes articles and book reviews from 260 journals and articles from approximately 200 monographs per year. Although it covers domestic and consumer economics, emphasis is on theoretical aspects of economics. Coverage of women is peripheral.

DATABASE NAME: Eighteenth-Century Short Title Catalogue
TYPE: Bibliographic
RECORD TYPE: Citations, MARC fields, library locations
YEARS COVERED: 1701-1800
VENDOR AVAILABILITY: RLIN, BLAISE-LINE (U.K.)
SCOPE: Any and all subjects on which something was printed in English anywhere in the world or in any language in the British Isles or British territories during the 18th century. Includes novels, poems, songs, arguments, harangues, and political propaganda, memoirs, letters, histories, autobiographies, etc., by women. Imprints cataloged from holdings at the British Library and about 950 libraries in Europe, North America, and Australia include books, advertisements, songs, election propaganda, society memberships, transport timetables, sessional papers of the House of Commons and more. No subject indexing.

DATABASE NAME: EMBASE – Excerpta Medica (TM)
TYPE: Bibliographic   RECORD TYPE: Abstracts

YEARS COVERED: 1974+
VENDOR AVAILABILITY: BRS, Data-Star, DIALOG, DIMDI
SCOPE: Based on the Hedge for Women, 14% of the database covers females. Biomedical journal literature with an emphasis on drugs and toxicology and coverage of human medicine, biological sciences, health economics and administration, environmental health and pollution control and forensic science.

DATABASE NAME: Encyclopedia of Associations
TYPE: Bibliographic   RECORD TYPE: Directory
YEARS COVERED: Current
VENDOR AVAILABILITY: DIALOG
SCOPE: Lists over 21,000 non-profit American associations. Can be used to locate organizations pertaining to women and women's issues. Free-text searching yielded the best results, as descriptor assignment is inconsistent and terms used are broad and non-specific.

DATABASE NAME: ERIC
TYPE: Bibliographic
RECORD TYPE: Citations for periodical articles; abstracts for *ERIC* documents
YEARS COVERED: 1966+
VENDOR AVAILABILITY: BRS, BRS/After Dark, BRS/Colleague, DIALOG, Knowledge Index, ORBIT,
SCOPE: Cites articles and *ERIC* documents, which include program descriptions, curriculum materials, bibliographies, conference proceedings, research reports. Covers women of all ages in education and human service situations. Also covers ethnic studies.

DATABASE NAME: Essay and General Literature Index
TYPE: Bibliographic
RECORD TYPE: Citations, tables of contents
YEARS COVERED: 1985+
VENDOR AVAILABILITY: Wilsonline
SCOPE: Covers humanities and social sciences; women's topics in any of those disciplines, especially literature, history, and political science. Cites articles and essays in about 300-325 collections, anthologies, festschriften and annual serials per year. Uses controlled

vocabulary based on *LCSH* plus additional terms from Wilson authority files and other indexes.

DATABASE NAME: Everyman's Encyclopedia
TYPE: Full-text   RECORD TYPE: Articles
YEARS COVERED: Current; no updates to date
VENDOR AVAILABILITY: DIALOG
SCOPE: Online version of 6th ed. of *Everyman's Encyclopedia*. An estimated 9% of the 15,000 records tagged as biographies were of women. A British slant is evident in the coverage of women biographees as well as events and issues pertaining to women. Coverage of women of color and of contemporary women is poor, perhaps due in part to the fact that the encyclopedia has not been updated in 10 years. Male pronouns were 8.3 times more prevalent than their female counterparts.

DATABASE NAME: Family Resources
TYPE: Bibliographic   RECORD TYPE: Citations, some abstracts
YEARS COVERED: 1973+
VENDOR AVAILABILITY: BRS, BRS/After Dark, BRS/Colleague, DIALOG, Human Resources Information Network
SCOPE: Contains periodical articles and includes bibliographical summaries of professionals in the field. Focuses on families, mate selection, issues relating to reproduction, dysfunctional families.

DATABASE NAME: Foreign Trade & Economic Abstracts
TYPE: Bibliographic   RECORD TYPE: Abstracts
YEARS COVERED: 1974+
VENDOR AVAILABILITY: BELINDIS, Data-Star, DIALOG
SCOPE: Covers world's literature on markets, industries, country-specific economic data and research in the fields of economics and management. Approximately 1,800 journals in addition to books, directories and reports are abstracted to provide information in all areas of economics but does not cover women's issues to any degree at all.

DATABASE NAME: GPO Monthly Catalog
TYPE: Bibliographic   RECORD TYPE: Citations
YEARS COVERED: 1976+

VENDOR AVAILABILITY: BRS, DIALOG, Wilsonline
SCOPE: Contains reports, studies, fact sheets, maps, handbooks and conference proceedings issued by all U.S. federal government agencies including the U.S. Congress. Also includes Senate and House hearings on private and public bills and laws. Covers issues related to women as they are studied by the federal government.

DATABASE NAME: Harvard Business Review Online
TYPE: Bibliographic   RECORD TYPE: Full-text
YEARS COVERED: 1971 +
VENDOR AVAILABILITY: BRS, BRS/After Dark, Data-Star, DIALOG, Human Resource Information Network, Knowledge Index, NEXIS
SCOPE: Contains the complete text of the *Harvard Business Review* from 1976 including subjects such as accounting, automation, business ethics, industry analysis, strategic planning and trade. Limited coverage of issues related to women in business.

DATABASE NAME: Historical Abstracts
TYPE: Bibliographic
RECORD TYPE: Citations, abstracts (85%)
YEARS COVERED: periodicals, 1973 + ; books and dissertations, 1980 +
VENDOR AVAILABILITY: DIALOG, Knowledge Index
SCOPE: Covers world history, 1450 to the present (excluding the U.S. and Canada), historiography, teaching history, and the historical profession; women's history and women's roles in politics, government and society. Cites articles selected from about 2,000 periodicals (and an occasional mulitauthor work) are abstracted or annotated; books and dissertations are cited. 50% are English-language documents. Uses natural language keyword indexing plus terms from a preferred subject headings list and in-house authority files.

DATABASE NAME: Humanities Index
TYPE: Bibliographic
RECORD TYPE: Citations, occasional title enhancements and notes
YEARS COVERED: 1984 +

VENDOR AVAILABILITY: Wilsonline
SCOPE: Online counterpart of the Wilson index of the same name. Covers all humanities without geographic or date limits: archaeology, art, classics, area studies, folklore, history, literature, performing arts, philosophy, religion, and related subjects; women's topics as they occur in the literature of journals in those disciplines. Lists articles, interviews, obituaries, bibliographies, book reviews; reviews of plays, operas, dance, musicals, films, TV and radio programs; works of fiction, drama and poetry in nearly 300 English-language journals (including a small number of non-English articles), cover to cover. Uses a controlled vocabulary, *LCSH*, plus additional terms from the *Humanities Index* authority file, the literature itself, reference works, and other Wilson indexes.

DATABASE NAME: Index to Legal Periodicals
TYPE: Bibliographic   RECORD TYPE: Citations
YEARS COVERED: Aug. 1981+
VENDOR AVAILABILITY: LEXIS, WESTLAW, Wilsonline
SCOPE: Includes citations to periodical articles, statutes and case notes and book reviews from approximately 500 law journals and reviews (mostly English language). Access by controlled vocabulary is possible with a limited number of descriptors relating specifically to women. All areas of law relevant to women are covered.

DATABASE NAME: LABORDOC
DATABASE TYPE: Bibliographic   RECORD TYPE: Abstracts
YEARS COVERED: 1965+
VENDOR AVAILABILITY: ARAMIS, ESA/IRS, Human Resources Information Network, ORBIT Search Service
SCOPE: Abstracts and indexes journal and monographic literature in the field of labor. Provides worldwide coverage with emphasis on industrial relations, labor law, employment, working conditions, vocational training, labor-related aspects of economics, social development, rural development, and technological change. Includes publications of a major international women in international development organization and a women's journal published in a developing country.

DATABASE NAME: LC MARC
TYPE: Bibliographic   RECORD TYPE: MARC
YEARS COVERED: 1968 +
VENDOR AVAILABILITY: DIALOG
SCOPE: Includes cataloging records for books, serials, scores, sound recordings, music, maps, audiovisual materials, manuscripts and archival materials and computer datafiles cataloged by the Library of Congress. Does not include records for periodical articles. Covers materials from all countries and in all written languages. Coverage of materials by and about women and on women's issues is good. Provides access to records for titles published by small women's presses.

DATABASE NAME: Legal Resources Index
TYPE: Bibliographic   RECORD TYPE: Citations
YEARS COVERED: 1980 +
VENDOR AVAILABILITY: BRS, BRS/After Dark, DIALOG, Knowledge Index, LEXIS, Mead Data Central, WESTLAW
SCOPE: Indexes 750 law journals and 7 law newspapers, selected books and articles in the law-related periodical literature. All major English language sources are covered. Case notes, news, letters, book reviews and commentaries are also indexed. Access by controlled vocabulary, which includes a number of descriptors relating specifically to women. Covers women's issues as related to law.

DATABASE NAME: LEXIS
TYPE: Non-bibliographic   RECORD TYPE: Full-text
YEARS COVERED: Varies
VENDOR AVAILABILITY: LEXIS
SCOPE: The LEXIS service includes full-text of all reported federal and state court cases. It also includes full-text of federal statutes and regulations and statutes from 28 states. A number of topical databases (e.g., Federal Labor, Insurance Law) are also included. No controlled vocabulary is provided, but editorial enhancements such as annotationns and syllabuses (on Supreme Court cases) provide some additional subject access. All areas of law relating to women are included.

DATABASE NAME: LISA (Library & Information Science Abstracts)
TYPE: Bibliographic   RECORD TYPE: Abstracts
YEARS COVERED: 1969+
VENDOR AVAILABILITY: DIALOG, ORBIT
SCOPE: Covers reports, conference proceedings, theses, monographs and more than 550 journals from 60 countries. Includes reference work on women's studies—directories, bibliographies, guides—but very little on the impact of women's studies on library education. Requires tricky searching to retrieve phrase "women's studies" even though it is used as a descriptor.

DATABASE NAME: Magazine ASAP
TYPE: Bibliographic   RECORD TYPE: Full-text
YEARS COVERED: 1983+
VENDOR AVAILABILITY: BRS, BRS/Colleague, DIALOG, NEXIS
SCOPE: Includes the full-text of over 100 popular magazines selected from those analyzed for *Magazine Index*. Individual women may be more easily identified through full-text coverage.

DATABASE NAME: Magazine Index
TYPE: Bibliographic   RECORD TYPE: Full-text
YEARS COVERED: 1959-1970, 1973+
VENDOR AVAILABILITY: BRS, BRS/After Dark, BRS/Colleague, DIALOG, Knowledge Index, NEXIS
SCOPE: Covers more than 435 popular magazines in subjects such as current events, performing arts, political science, public opinions, business, sports, recreation and travel, science and technology, consumer affairs, and more. Includes women in news stories as well as a wide range of issues important to women.

DATABASE NAME: Management Contents
TYPE: Bibliographic   RECORD TYPE: Abstracts
YEARS COVERED: 1974+
VENDOR AVAILABILITY: BRS, Data-Star, DIALOG, ORBIT
SCOPE: Provides information on business and management related topics to assist in decision making and forecasting. Articles from over 120 U.S. and international journals as well as proceedings,

transactions, business course materials, newsletters, and research reports are fully indexed and abstracted to provide up-to-date information in the areas of accounting, decision sciences, finance, industrial relations, managerial economics, marketing, operations research, organizational behavior and public administration. Selective coverage of women's issues and topics provided.

DATABASE NAME: Marquis Who's Who
TYPE: Bibliographic   RECORD TYPE: Directory
YEARS COVERED: 1982+
VENDOR AVAILABILITY: DIALOG
SCOPE: Provides brief biographical sketches of prominent persons residing in the United States, Canada and Mexico. Entries for women comprise approximately 6% of the database. Most women biographees included achieved prominence in either traditionally female occupations or in the arts. Women of color not well represented.

DATABASE NAME: MEDLINE
TYPE: Bibliographic   RECORD TYPE: Abstracts
YEARS COVERED: 1966+
VENDOR AVAILABILITY: BRS, BRS/After Dark, BLAISE-LINE, DIALOG, DIMDI, Mead Data Central, NLM, PaperChase
SCOPE: Based on the Hedge for Women, 33% of the database covers females. All aspects of biomedicine, including the allied health fields as well as the biological and physical sciences, humanities, and information science as they relate to medicine and health care. Search for any disease in women and for women in the health care professions. A special feature of BRS *MEDLINE* is the ability to link from selected citations to the full text of the item.

DATABASE NAME: Mental Health Abstracts
TYPE: Bibliographic   RECORD TYPE: Abstracts
YEARS COVERED: 1969+
VENDOR AVAILABILITY: DIALOG, Knowledge Index
SCOPE: Includes journal articles, books, chapters in books, dissertations, technical reports and conference proceedings. Covers women from a mental health and psychological perspective.

DATABASE NAME: MLA Bibliography
TYPE: Bibliographic
RECORD TYPE: Citations, occasional notes
YEARS COVERED: 1964+
VENDOR AVAILABILITY: DIALOG, Knowledge Index, Wilsonline
SCOPE: Covers medieval and modern languages, linguistics, folklore; depiction of women in literature and folklore, feminist theory and criticism, women as professional authors, artists, and critics. Indexes critical, scholarly articles in approximately 3,000 periodicals and series and in collections of essays, books, and dissertations. Excludes book reviews and original creative works. Approximately 50% of the source documents are in English. Must use all ethnic descriptors (Black, Afro-American & Negro). Descriptors: Black women novelists, Black female protagonists, Black heroines, etc.

DATABASE NAME: National Newspaper Index
TYPE: Bibliographic   RECORD TYPE: Citations
YEARS COVERED: 1979+, but coverage of Washington Post and Los Angeles Times begins 1982.
VENDOR AVAILABILITY: BRS, BRS/After Dark, BRS/Colleague, DIALOG, Knowledge Index
SCOPE: Contains over 1,691,069 citations. Indexes *Christian Science Monitor*, *New York Times*, *Wall Street Journal* completely. Coverage for the *Los Angeles Times* and *Washington Post* is selective, limited to items of national and international interest. Women's issues are covered very well in this popular database.

DATABASE NAME: NCJRS (National Criminal Justice Reference Service)
TYPE: Bibliographic   RECORD TYPE: Abstracts
YEARS COVERED: 1972+
VENDOR AVAILABILITY: DIALOG
SCOPE: Abstracts periodical articles and chapters in books. Covers women in relation to the criminal justice system.

DATABASE NAME: Newspaper Abstracts
TYPE: Bibliographic   RECORD TYPE: Abstracts

YEARS COVERED: 1984+
VENDOR AVAILABILITY: DIALOG
SCOPE: Indexes *American Banker, Atlanta Contsitution, Atlanta Journal, Boston Globe, Chicago Tribune, Christian Science Monitor, Denver Post, Detroit News, Guardian & Guardian Weekly, Houston Post, Los Angeles Times, New Orleans Times-Picayune, New York Times, Pravda, St. Louis Post Dispatch, San Francisco Chronicle, USA Today, Wall Street Journal, Washington Times* and the Black Newspaper Collection. Covers women and women's issues as they are presented in these newspapers.

DATABASE NAME: Newsearch
TYPE: Bibliographic   RECORD TYPE: Citations
YEARS COVERED: Current month
VENDOR AVAILABILITY: BRS, BRS/After Dark, DIALOG, Knowledge Index
SCOPE: Covers newspapers and business, legal and general interest periodicals. Includes women and women's isues in these areas.

DATABASE NAME: OCLC
TYPE: Bibliographic   RECORD TYPE: MARC
YEARS COVERED: 16th century to the present
VENDOR AVAILABILITY: OCLC Online Computer Library Center, Inc.
SCOPE: Includes cataloging records in LC MARC format for books, serials, manuscripts and archival materials, maps, scores, audio-visual materials, sound recordings, and computer datafiles, cataloged by the Library of Congress and over 3,000 libraries from many parts of the world. Excludes records for periodical articles. Covers all subjects in all written languages, with location information about the titles listed. Provides good coverage of materials by and about women and of women's issues. Although records contain *LCSH* or Sears subject headings, subject access is available only through OCLC's EPIC public access system. EPIC provides the best access to the OCLC database.

DATABASE NAME: OCLC EASI Reference
TYPE: Bibliographic   RECORD TYPE: MARC
YEARS COVERED: Current 4 years

VENDOR AVAILABILITY: BRS, BRS/After Dark
SCOPE: The latest 4 years of the OCLC database (see above) are available using BRS search protocols.

DATABASE NAME: PAIS International
TYPE: Bibliographic   RECORD TYPE: Citations
YEARS COVERED: 1972 +
VENDOR AVAILABILITY: BRS, BRS/After Dark, Data-Star, DIALOG, Knowledge Index
SCOPE: Indexes public policy and political science issues. Covers over 1,200 journals and 8,000 books, pamphlets, government publications, agency reports and other documents each year. Public policy, economic and development issues relating to women are included.

DATABASE NAME: Philosopher's Index
TYPE: Bibliographic
RECORD TYPE: Citations, approximately 60% with abstracts; title enhancements
YEARS COVERED: U.S. periodicals and books, some gaps, 1940 +; journals of the western world, 1964 +; dissertations, 1980 +
VENDOR AVAILABILITY: DIALOG
SCOPE: Covers all fields of philosophy including the philosophy of disciplines; feminist theory, philosophers' ideas on women, philosophical issues involving women (ethics, peace, abortion), but overall strength on women is not great. Includes articles in about 300 periodicals currently, U.S. and British emphasis (more than 400, including ones no longer indexed); books, proceedings; excludes book reviews. Uses descriptors from the *Philosopher's Index Thesaurus* (1979) and descriptors used earlier; format varies. Descriptor and named person fields not entirely distinct.

DATABASE NAME: Psyc/INFO
TYPE: Bibliographic   RECORD TYPE: Abstracts
YEARS COVERED: 1967 +
VENDOR AVAILABILITY: BRS, BRS/After Dark, BRS/Colleague, DIALOG, Knowledge Index, Data-Star, DIMDI
SCOPE: Abstracts articles from the world's journal literature and dissertations in psychology and fields related to psychology. Cover-

age of women is good. Based on the Hedge for Women, 19% of the database covers females. Search this database for the psychological woman: normal women or mentally impaired women — at home, at work, as mothers, etc.

DATABASE NAME: PsycALERT
TYPE: Bibliographic   RECORD TYPE: In-process file of citations
YEARS COVERED: Current 6 months
VENDOR AVAILABILITY: BRS, BRS/After Dark, DIALOG
SCOPE: Covers periodical articles. Includes information about articles in the process of being indexed for *Psychological Abstracts* from the most important journals indexed by that service.

DATABASE NAME: Readers' Guide Abstracts
TYPE: Bibliographic   RECORD TYPE: Abstracts
YEARS COVERED: 1983 +
VENDOR AVAILABILITY: Wilsonline
SCOPE: Covers approximately 200 periodicals in a wide range of subjects. Includes coverage of women and women's issues.

DATABASE NAME: Readers' Guide to Periodical Literature
TYPE: Bibliographic   RECORD TYPE: Citations
YEARS COVERED: 1983 +
VENDOR AVAILABILITY: Wilsonline
SCOPE: Indexes over 170 popular and general interest periodicals published in the U.S. including current events and popular culture as well as public opinion, political trends and consumer affairs. Women and women's issues covered from a popular perspective.

DATABASE NAME: Religion Index
TYPE: Bibliographic
RECORD TYPE: Citations, some with abstracts or tables of contents
YEARS COVERED: varies by type of document: 1960 +, collections; 1975 +, periodicals, book reviews; 1981 + theses; some earlier periodical articles.
VENDOR AVAILABILITY: BRS, BRS/After Dark, DIALOG
SCOPE: Covers world religion, ancient to contemporary; theology; scriptural studies; ministerial studies; and related social sciences

and humanities; attitudes toward women, women as participants in all areas of religion, feminist theology, women's history, psychology and sociology. Includes articles and book reviews in more than 400 journals plus additional ones more selectively screened; about 350 collections annually; and Doctor of Ministry dissertations. Descriptors rely heavily on *LCSH*; the most frequently used ones are listed in the printed *Religion indexes: Thesaurus* (2d ed., 1985).

DATABASE NAME: REMARC
TYPE: Bibliographic   RECORD TYPE: MARC
YEARS COVERED: 16th century to 1968.
VENDOR AVAILABILITY: DIALOG
SCOPE: Includes cataloging records prepared by the Library of Congress and converted into machine-readable form by Carrollton Press. Covers books, serials, maps, music, sound recordings and audiovisual materials. Provides good coverage of materials by and about women and on women's issues. Excludes records for periodical articles.

DATABASE NAME: Research in Progress Database (RIPD)
TYPE: Bibliographic
RECORD TYPE: Citations plus abstracts and names and addresses
YEARS COVERED: 1988+
VENDOR AVAILABILITY: RLIN
SCOPE: Produced by the Modern Language Association and Research Libraries Group, Inc. At present, covers mostly literature and language with strong women content; women's studies to be added in 1989. Entries represent articles accepted for publication by 52 journal editors and grants from the National Endowment for the Humanities for publications and conferences. The National Council for Research on Women will add entries for work by and about women.

DATABASE NAME: RILM Abstracts
TYPE: Bibliographic
RECORD TYPE: Citations, most with abstracts
YEARS COVERED: 1971+
VENDOR AVAILABILITY: DIALOG
SCOPE: Covers international music literature including theory, performance, history, pedagogy, instruments, and music in relation to

other disciplines; women musicians (composers, performers, teachers), music for women, women's songs. Includes articles from more than 300 journals worldwide, books, dissertations, catalogs, conference papers, commentaries, and reviews of books, dissertations, and recordings. Descriptors are controlled at the lead term only (*RILM English-Language Thesaurus*, 1st ed., pertains to volumes 1-10; 2d ed., 1983 pertains to volumes 11 +); subject section (classification) headings are controlled; special feature index for bibliography, discography, music, etc.

DATABASE NAME: RLIN (Research Libraries Information Network)
TYPE: Bibliographic   RECORD TYPE: MARC
YEARS COVERED: 16th century to the present
VENDOR AVAILABILITY: Research Libraries Group, Inc.
SCOPE: Includes cataloging records for books, serials, scores, sound recordings, maps, manuscripts and archival materials, audiovisual materials and computer datafiles in LC MARC format input by the Library of Congress and over 200 libraries, mostly academic or specialized, in the United States. Excludes records for periodical articles. International in coverage and includes materials in all written languages. Good coverage of material by and about women and on women's issues. Provides access to records for titles published by small women's presses.

DATABASE NAME: SCISEARCH
TYPE: Bibliographic RECORD TYPE: Citations
YEARS COVERED: 1974 +
VENDOR AVAILABILITY: Data-Star, DIALOG, DIMDI
SCOPE: The database of choice to determine if a female author in biomedicine has been cited. Because of the cited reference capability, also a good choice for locating controversial papers.

DATABASE NAME: Social Sciences Index
TYPE: Bibliographic   RECORD TYPE: Citations
YEARS COVERED: 1983 +
VENDOR AVAILABILITY: Wilsonline
SCOPE: Includes periodical articles and book reviews. Covers women generally in all areas of the social sciences: anthropology, community health, economics, geography, international relations,

law and criminology, political science, psychology/psychiatry, public administration, sociology and social work.

DATABASE NAME: Social SciSearch
TYPE: Bibliographic   RECORD TYPE: Citations
YEARS COVERED: 1972+
VENDOR AVAILABILITY: BRS, BRS/After Dark, BRS/Colleague, DIALOG, Knowledge Index, Data-Star, DIMDI
SCOPE: Includes citations to articles, book reviews, letters and a few collections of essays. International in coverage. Offers cited reference searching. Covers women across the social sciences. Uses keywords from titles of articles rather than a controlled vocabulary.

DATABASE NAME: Social Work Abstracts
TYPE: Bibliographic   RECORD TYPE: Abstracts
YEARS COVERED: 1977+
VENDOR AVAILABILITY: BRS, BRS/After Dark, BRS/Colleague
SCOPE: Includes articles, research reports, conference proceedings, dissertations and books. Covers family issues, child welfare, aging, mental health, crime from a social policy as well as a methodological perspective.

DATABASE NAME: Sociological Abstracts
TYPE: Bibliographic   RECORD TYPE: Abstracts
YEARS COVERED: 1963+
VENDOR AVAILABILITY: BRS, BRS/After Dark, BRS/Colleague, DIALOG, Knowledge Index, Data-Star, DIMDI
SCOPE: Includes journal articles, research reports, conference proceedings. International in perspective, indexes many foreign language materials. Covers women, poverty, feminism and family issues from a broadly defined sociological perspective. Includes many areas relating to women from the sociological, social policy, demongraphic and social welfare point of view.

DATABASE NAME: Sport Database
TYPE: Bibliographic
RECORD TYPE: Citations, many with abstracts

YEARS COVERED: 1949+
VENDOR AVAILABILITY: BRS
SCOPE: Covers periodical articles and monographs in sports, recreation, exercise physiology, sports medicine, coaching, physical fitness, training, conditioning and the psychology, history and sociology of sport. Only about 10% of the citations deal specifically with women and sports.

DATABASE NAME: Ulrich's International Periodical Directory
TYPE: Bibliographic   RECORD TYPE: Directory
YEARS COVERED: Current
VENDOR AVAILABILITY: BRS, DIALOG, ESA/IRS
SCOPE: Provides data on over 130,000 publications. Good coverage of feminist and women's studies titles, as well as "traditional" women's magazines, but the lack of consistent and detailed index terms makes it difficult to differentiate. Coverage of foreign titles is fair although periodicals published in third-world countries are not as well represented.

DATABASE NAME: U.S. Political Science Documents
TYPE: Bibliographic   RECORD TYPE: Abstracts
YEARS COVERED: 1975+
VENDOR AVAILABILITY: DIALOG
SCOPE: Indexes approximately 150 U.S. political science journals. Coverage not limited to domestic issues; includes foreign policy, international relations, public administration and political theory. Some coverage of women and politics.

DATABASE NAME: VU/TEXT
TYPE: Full-text   RECORD TYPE: Citations or full-text
YEARS COVERED: 1978+
VENDOR AVAILABILITY: VU/TEXT
SCOPE: Includes full-text of 40 U.S. newspapers and covers women and women's issues as they appear in the news.

DATABASE NAME: Work and Family Life Database
TYPE: Bibliographic   RECORD TYPE: Abstracts
YEARS COVERED: 1970+
VENDOR AVAILABILITY: BRS, BRS/After Dark

SCOPE: Indexes over 300 information sources including books and book chapters, articles from journals, magazines and newsletters, reports and pamphlets on topics relating to the connections between family life and the world of work. Covers alternative work arrangements, dual career families, child care issues, role of working wives and mothers and the impact of work on the family as well as the impact of the family on work.

DATABASE NAME: Washington Post Online
TYPE: Bibliographic   RECORD TYPE: Full-text
YEARS COVERED: April 1983+
VENDOR AVAILABILITY: CompuServe, DataTimes, DIALOG, Dow Jones News, Info Globe, LEGI-SLATE, NEXIS, PROFILE Informatiion, The Source, VU-TEXT
SCOPE: Full text of the daily and Sunday *Washington Post*, including columns and local news. Covers women and women's issues as presented in this paper.

DATABASE NAME: WESTLAW
TYPE: Non-bibliographic   RECORD TYPE: Full-text
YEARS COVERED: Varies
VENDOR AVAILABILITY: WESTLAW
SCOPE: The WESTLAW computer-assisted legal research services include full-text of all reported federal and state court cases. It also includes full-text of federal statutes and regulations and statutes from 28 states. A number of topical databases (e.g., Family Law, Insurance Law) are included. While editorial enhancements (synopsis, digest and topic fields as well as some annotations) provide some subject access, a controlled vocabulary is lacking. All areas of law relating to women are included.